The Sense of Sex

The Sense of Sex
Feminist Perspectives on Hardy

EDITED BY
Margaret R. Higonnet

UNIVERSITY OF ILLINOIS PRESS
Urbana and Chicago

This book is printed on acid-free paper.

Library of Congress Cataloging-in-Publication Data

The sense of sex : feminist perspectives on Hardy / edited by Margaret
  R. Higonnet.
        p.   cm.
    Includes bibliographical references and index.
    ISBN 0-252-01940-7 (alk. paper).—ISBN 0-252-06260-4 (pbk. :
alk. paper))
    1. Hardy, Thomas, 1840–1928—Political and social views.
2. Hardy, Thomas, 1840–1928—Characters—Women.   3. Feminism and
literature—England.   4. Women and literature—England.   5. Sex role
in literature.   I. Higonnet, Margaret R.
PR4757.F44S46   1993
823'.8—dc20   92-716
                                                        CIP

75651

If he could only get over the sense of her sex,
as she seemed to be able to do so easily of his,
what a comrade she would make.
    —Thomas Hardy, *Jude the Obscure*

Contents

Abbreviations

All references to the works of Thomas Hardy unless otherwise noted are drawn from the 1912 Wessex edition (Macmillan, 1912–   ).

Titles are abbreviated as indicated:

DR	(*Desperate Remedies*)
UGT	(*Under the Greenwood Tree*)
PBE	(*A Pair of Blue Eyes*)
HE	(*Hand of Ethelberta*)
FMC	(*Far from the Madding Crowd*)
MC	(*Mayor of Casterbridge*)
RN	(*Return of the Native*)
T	(*Tess of the d'Urbervilles*)
JO	(*Jude the Obscure*)
WB	(*The Well Beloved*)

Life refers to Thomas Hardy, *The Life of Thomas Hardy*, ed. Michael Millgate (Athens: University of Georgia Press, 1985)

Björk = Thomas Hardy, *Literary Notebooks*, ed. Lennart A. Björk, 2 vols. (New York: New York University Press, 1985).

Cox = R. G. Cox, ed., *Thomas Hardy: The Critical Heritage* (New York: Barnes, 1970).

Orel = Harold Orel, ed., *Thomas Hardy's Personal Writings: Prefaces, Literary Opinions, Reminiscences* (Lawrence: University Press of Kansas, 1966).

Introduction

Margaret R. Higonnet

In this collection, we begin from the premise that feminist criticism offers formidable tools for the study of texts by men. We argue that gender study is not exclusively a domain of or about women. Rather, it encourages us to examine historically the codes of both masculinity and femininity inscribed in Thomas Hardy's texts. Concomitantly, to examine the gender inflection of literary structures and discourse, we draw on both female and male theorists—Cixous and Freud, Teresa de Lauretis and Bakhtin, Poovey and Foucault.

What does it mean to apply feminist criticism to a male author like Hardy? Expressing doubts about the very possibility of such an enterprise, Paul Smith argues that "men still constitute a shadowy unlegislatable area for feminist theory."[1] By contrast to Smith's identification of theory with law, we stress that "legislation" itself is instead precisely the issue. Feminist criticism interrogates what George Eliot calls "the maxims of men"; it studies ways in which the grammar of gender regulates the construction of texts. Thus, to break open the social bonds between *lex* and *logos*, we deliberately multiply approaches to Hardy.

A male author who writes against patriarchy may seek not gender equality but rather access to the culturally delimited feminine.[2] Every author works with an artificial but nonetheless powerful set of half-formulated assumptions about the gender attributes of genre, style, and thematics. A man may write "from the feminine" or a woman "from the masculine," to expand the generic and linguistic repertoire available at any historical moment yet leave traditional underlying hierarchies of value more or less intact. One question we ask in this volume is how Hardy's appropriative, cross-gendered strategies affect readers.

Over the last decade or so, critics have shifted from thinking of "men" and "women" (as if these signs were conceptually separable) to gender studies. They have shifted from assuming a biological "sense of sex" to exploring the multiple meanings we attach to and construct through sex.

In the cultural construction of gender, a binary system of representation operates on two fronts, altering conceptions of masculinity and femininity in tandem. Gender, then, is always turned in two directions at once. This bipolarity masks other differences, such as the variety of physiques and sexual preferences or experiences of parenthood. In shifting toward the analysis of gender as a socially regulated system, feminist criticism has developed our understanding of the imbrication of gender with other social categories, such as class, age, race, rank, caste, and kinship. "Masculinity and femininity do not appear in cultural discourse, any more than they do in mental life, as pure binary forms at play. They are always already ordered and broken up through other social and cultural terms, other categories of difference."[3]

The gender system of any given historical moment is embedded in and ruled by language and narrative structure. Gender both figures and authorizes those structures. "Since gender roles are in part familial, political, social, and economic relationships, the terms in which femininity is publicly formulated dictate the way in which it is experienced."[4] Traditional boundaries between public and private also obscure the way language functions to construct gender socially.

We have become attuned to gender inflections in a broad array of literary structures. Thus, critics have differentiated the "female" from the "male" *Bildungsroman* by tracing the interplay of social codes in the formation of the individual subject; the different import of sexual experience for male and female protagonists is simply the most egregious instance of a gendered social norm that dictates sharply differentiated modes of characterization and narrative trajectory. To understand character not as a fixed identity but rather as a progressive construction means to interpret subject formation in the context of narrative features such as a masculine narrative voice, or a closure inscribed as female.

Since gender is a historical formation, it offers a tool for the analysis of periods as well. As Elaine Showalter points out, feminist criticism has long concentrated on the Victorian era, discovering in this period a hardening official line about sexual difference that masked other forms of difference and preference behind the lines. Resulting cleavages opened up a crisis of masculinity, controversy over the myth of the New Woman, and a dialectical tendency to gender whole explanatory systems—to see myth as feminine, for example, and history as masculine.[5] Authors like Thackeray, Tennyson, Meredith, and Hardy centered major texts on strong female characters, diagnosing in the condition of women symptoms of "larger" social issues they wished to address. Hardy especially has been admired for his strong, complex, "realistic," and challenging characterization of women. Yet, as Penny Boumelha argues, "the radicalism of Hardy's representation of women resides, not in their 'complexity', their 'realism' or their 'challenge to convention', but in their resistance to reduction to a single and uniform ideological position."[6]

While our theoretical articulation of gender as a historical construction and systemic process may be relatively recent, the practical and imaginative understanding of gender can be traced into the deep past. For well over a century, the issues on which this volume focuses have triggered the interest of Hardy's readers, reviewers, and critics. From the first, his representation of relationships between men and women—and the gendering of representation itself—have provoked controversy. As the psychologist Havelock Ellis points out, many readers were so "uncertain about the sex of the new writer," they were "doubtful whether to speak of 'him' or 'her' " (Cox 104). In the intervening decades our critical terminologies have changed, and with them the specific ways we frame Hardy. Yet certain constants remain, such as our continuing debates over proprieties and plausibilities, or the reliability and consistency of Hardy's enigmatic narrators.

In an age when political, social, and literary challenges were being mounted to traditional gender roles, Hardy tested and subverted constraining gender definitions to an unusual extent. He certainly would not have wanted to privilege women over men or men over women in the analysis of systems of social representation. If "woman" is a social construct for Hardy, then so is "man," as Elaine Showalter demonstrates in her pathbreaking essay on *The Mayor of Casterbridge*.[7]

At many points Hardy's characters and plots try to pair the man's story with the woman's. Tess wishfully prefaces her confession, " 'tis just the same" (287). Jude claims that "it is no worse for the woman than for the man, . . . the other victim . . . [and] helpless transmitter of the pressure put upon him" (5.4.346). This thematic core in Hardy's works gains resonance through his eye for stereotyped traits and his ear for social discourses. Hardy interpolates into his characters' and narrators' observations the maxims of his age; he densely inscribes and reviews the Victorian cultural heritage. His cultural collage enables us to study the medical, aesthetic, moral, religious, and social discourse that constructed Victorian concepts of male and female sexuality and identity. An architect himself, Hardy takes the measure of social constructions of the self, not only archeologically, to deepen our historical understanding, but also with an eye to reconstruction.

Hardy's anxieties about his own relationship to the social order, whose undertow flows throughout Michael Millgate's biography of the author, led him to expose contradictions within social hierarchies.[8] He shows how the binary opposites of masculinity and femininity blur when embodied in the individual. He makes us aware how we naturalize and universalize through the language of the body social institutions and differences. While we may be forced to read through classification schemes, he insists simultaneously that all labels that "ticket" a person, especially the most common ones of gender and class, are false. The plot thickens, as it were, whenever a character enters the stage who like Henry Knight can "pack" women into sentences, or like Farmer Boldwood deems "as essentials of the whole sex the accidents of the single one of their number he had ever closely beheld" (PBE 18.193, FMC 34.258). Like Austen's Anne Elliot, Hardy's Ethelberta warns us, "Don't you go believing in sayings. . . . they are all made by men, for their own advantages. Women who use public proverbs as a guide through events are those who have not ingenuity enough to make private ones as each event occurs" (20.151).

Furthermore, Hardy's anxiety about the literary culture of his times helped him to identify gender biases and barriers within literary hierarchies. A "lady" like Ethelberta, we are reminded, becomes "improper" when she gets into print. Gender markers reflect situational relationships of power. While the female author Elfride assumes that Knight's notebook jottings must have the concentrated form of an "embryo" and therefore tries to secure them as well as their writer, the reluctant Knight himself dismisses his notes as "rather like a balloon before it is inflated: flabby, shapeless, dead" (PBE 18.194–95). In Hardy's own experience, to have written pastoral, with minute observations on love, meant reviewers would identify him as a woman who represented "trifles" (Cox 104). Women are textualized, while texts acquire a gender. Just as Angel puzzles over Tess, "as one deciding on the true construction of a difficult passage," the narrator inscribes his patterns on the delicate "tissue" of his heroine (T 34.278).

Through a bricolage of competing discourses, he succeeds in "disintegrating," as he puts it, their hold on our perceptions of self and other. A structure of "reproduction within denial" permits Hardy's narrators to test the cultural texts that collide in the plot of a woman like Tess.[9] In turn, he complicates our understanding of a narrative authority that rests on unified social discourse. Thus he looks forward to the cultural fragmentation of Modernism and the deconstructive strategies of Postmodernism.

We should pause at the linguistic and epistemological dilemma traced here. To this risk of reproducing the very categories we interrogate, Hardy responds with direct narratorial commentary and also with multiple, mutually inconsistent authoritative voices. It is a dilemma we cannot escape as critics ourselves. We too bear the imprint of a complex contemporary gender ideology that leaves its traces in our interpretative practices. Different stakes in response to norms of masculinity and femininity may well produce different results when male and female critics inquire into similar problems.[10] Yet we may open up spaces for analysis both within and beyond a line of argument, through the polyphonic feminist practice of gathering several voices to explore a common topic.

Hardy's texts (like Ibsen's) have been censored for their sexual content, admired for their frankness, decried as misogynist, and described as feminist. Irving Howe's praise of Hardy as a "man who liked women," for example, was challenged by Mary Childers in "Thomas Hardy, the Man Who 'Liked' Women."[11] Such divided reactions bespeak the controversial centrality of these issues for our own culture. At first, most criticism of these issues in Hardy was primarily thematic in its reliance upon the very stereotypes that Hardy put into question. Among early critics, D. H. Lawrence represents the problematic ancestor hanging in the stairwell of feminist responses to Hardy, with his insistence on the qualities of the "male," the "female," or the "aristocrat" in Hardy's characters. While it directly addressed the key figures and conflicts that still give Hardy's works appeal among a broad readership that crosses class boundaries, such thematic analysis has also come under attack. Lawrence shows little concern for aesthetic, formal features; he generalizes from fictional representations of the social order; even though "the female" can inhabit a man, Lawrence appears to essentialize and moralize gender traits.

In reaction against such thematic study, critics have turned away from classifying Hardy's concepts and characters according to some ideal measure of truth about the sexes. Instead, they locate tensions within his fictive structures that correspond to the terms of discourse in the Victorian age. Whereas in the past, issues of ideology and social representation might be cast as mere content somehow framed in form, in this volume we draw on a multiplicity of critical tools to analyze structures that shape, carry, and deflect ideological issues. The study of gender enables us to discern an interplay among social, epistemological, and narrative structures, and to gain distance from their fictional claims to constitute systems of knowledge and records of the social order.

Louis Althusser, one of the thinkers who has been most useful to recent feminist thought on this matter, describes literature as a social form that contributes to the reproduction of a ruling ideology but that also offers us telltale gaps and occlusions corresponding to social contradictions. Penny Boumelha has used Althusser's theory of competing social representations to explore ambiguities in generic conventions, narrative perspectives, and characterization. According to Boumelha, these ambiguities reveal Hardy's resistance to adopting any uniform ideological position from among the shifting panoply offered by his times.[12]

An equally dramatic influence on feminist reassessments of narrative voice and characterization in Hardy has been the changing theory of the self. The notion of character, and therefore of a narratorial persona, has been broken apart, variously drawing on postmodern theories of frag-mentation, deconstructive views of the subject, and the notion of identity as an imaginary yet really experienced "subject-effect" that masks the multiplicity of interacting social forces marking our actions at any moment. Hardy's own reflections support this concept of character. He drew on the same metaphor that has subsequently generated much American feminist criticism: "man, even to himself is a palimpsest, having an ostensible writing, and another beneath the lines" (FMC 36.279).

Because gender by definition is always historically conditioned, feminist study attends to social formations and discourses that intersect with liter-ary form. Again, Penny Boumelha's book on Hardy broke ground by connecting the study of medical literature, legal discourse, and Darwinian sociology to the study of literature. She juxtaposed the work of a canonical male writer with the experimental "new fiction" of the period. More generally, the feminist turn toward a "new historicist" study of scientific discourse has fostered study of Victorian medical discourse on hysteria and the political discourse of representation. Hardy's radicalism emerges through the competing claims of gender and class in his texts; not only do the politics of class and sexuality interrupt each other, they also disrupt narrative form, as we see in the fragmentary romance sequences in *A Pair of Blue Eyes*. [13] For most of the essays in this volume, the dominant modes of social classification foregrounded in Hardy's works are gender and class.

The focus on structural contradictions and elisions produced by ideo-logical contradictions has cultivated close narrative analysis of Hardy's texts. A number of critics have focused attention on the (in)consistencies of his male narrators and tensions between plot and commentary. As Hillis Miller noted in his study of *Tess*, Hardy's works are "overdetermined" by their repertoire of contradictory formulations: "Hardy's novels are puzzling not because they contain no self-interpretative elements, but because they contain too many irreconcilable ones."[14] In the place of deconstructive observation like this, feminist critics have drawn on narra-tive analysis to deepen our understanding of the controlling or stereo-typed attitudes that infect narrative voices in Hardy's texts. Rosemarie Morgan, for example, identifies multiple narrative voices, defined by their claims of authority and attitudes, while Patricia Ingham stresses a subver-sive gap between the narrative voice and the plot. Both critics draw on Penny Boumelha's deconstruction of the fractured perspectives in these novels, which showed the need for a fresh assessment of the relationship between narrative structure and social values. Boumelha productively related her thesis—that Hardy fragments narrative authority—to her historical study of ideological conflicts in Hardy's writing and in related subliterature of the period.[15]

Likewise, feminists have reassessed Hardy's narrators in response to critics who underscore the erotic nature of the narrative act. It has become commonplace to trace a dynamic between "distance and desire" that affects both the narrator's angle of vision and the construction of plot.[16] Current studies of feminocentric literature have drawn our attention to the particular dynamic of a male author writing about a female subject. Does the sexual polarity between an author—or, more to the point, a male narrator—and his heroine imply a necessary opposition between subject and object? In Meredith's terms, if a heroine is "deeply a woman," must she be "dumbly a poet"? Do the controlling, framing, and distancing devices typical of realist fiction carry monovalent gender implications? Hardy himself encourages such speculation by his implicit sexualization of the narrative process.

Closely related work by Laura Mulvey and Teresa de Lauretis applies semiotics and psychoanalysis to study "the gaze" of the camera in film and of the narrator in realist fiction. The question of the narrator's control has been reconceived by critics like Judith Wittenberg, Kaja Silverman, and T. R. Wright, who have used visual theory to analyze the eroticism embedded in narrative acts.[17] Significant for both characterization and reader-response, the "gaze" serves as a relay of power between the subject and object of perception; feminist work has helped us recognize how often that dynamic engenders the subject as masculine, and the object of the gaze as feminine. Film theory likewise has heightened our understanding of such features in a text as angles of vision, shallow and deep focus, and the complex, gendered relationships between narrators and implied readers. It enables us to attend in greater detail to narrative plotting and sequence, in their functional relation to representations of narrative voice and gaze. This collection does not elide the political side of feminist criticism, but it does connect the speculation about literature's potential effects on the reader to close analysis of narrative structures.

As I indicate in this overview, we build on a broad range of critical trends today, from gender analysis and new historicism, psychoanalysis and film studies, to theories of ideology and discourse. If some past interpreters have served us as warning posts, by virtue of their unconscious tendency to sexist and classist stereotyping (about "male fantasy," "woman's power of suffering," or an ahistorical "female state"), others, such as Elaine Showalter and Mary Jacobus, have worked to invigorate our thinking. Much in the way that Dale Kramer's collections explore the diversity of recent Hardy criticism, including genre analysis, feminism, psychoanalysis, reader-response, and deconstruction, the contributors to this volume explore the diversity *within* criticism that addresses the construction of gender in Hardy. An "alternative Hardy," to borrow Lance St. John Butler's phrase, occasions multiple feminist responses.

The intersection between gender and narrative theory provides the focus of my own study, in which I examine the problem of defining a character's "voice" separate from that of the narrator. In *Tess*, Hardy addresses this issue of representation through the gender split between male narrator and female protagonist. By centering his tale on a woman who encounters difficulty in telling her own story, Hardy finds a metafictional figure for the outer margins of expressivity. He experiments with the possibility of tracing gender in a voice (or even in silence). The misfit between a hypothetical truth or story and its reception or misreading is, of course, one of Hardy's main preoccupations. *Tess* thus exemplifies the nineteenth-century flowering of the feminocentric novel as occasion for narrative experiment and for reflection upon the status of narrative.

In the second essay, Elizabeth Langland presents the shift from study of female characters to the study of gender. In an earlier essay, Langland had focused on female protagonists in *Jude the Obscure* but turns here to Jude himself. In this thwarted *Bildungsroman,* Jude struggles to define his own subjectivity but falls prey to discordant discourses of masculinity and social power. His ambivalence toward an inner voice that society encodes as feminine leads both to his desire for Sue and ultimately to her rejection and destruction. A detailed examination of Jude's self-construction within terms of masculinity and femininity enables Langland to highlight decisive turns in the plot and enhance our sense of the interconnections between the two protagonists of this novel.

Linda Shires turns the question of gender as a feature of narrative structure around entirely, challenging recent critiques of Hardy for their reductive treatments of his deliberately ambiguous representations of power. Shires draws on a poststructuralist theory of narrative to assess the gender complexity of paradigmatic events, such as Oak's wounding of a ewe in *Far from the Madding Crowd.* Hardy continually reassigns the terms of power and gender and thus disrupts their social meanings, even though these may be put schematically back into place through conventional figures of closure such as marriage or death.

In a second group of essays, contributors draw on analytic tools from other disciplines to probe Hardy's representation of female figures. Elizabeth Bronfen introduces the larger questions of semiotics and narrative structure. She applies Lévi-Strauss to explain the obsessive troping she finds in the deaths of Hardy's heroines, who become signs for power, gender, and signification itself. The themes of feminine displacement, death, and doubles connect Hardy to certain disturbing obsessions of nineteenth-century literature.

Medical history provides a complementary background for Kristin Brady's study of hysteria among Hardy's female characters. Brady starts from the narrators' admiration for women who challenge contemporary norms. At the same time, she finds, most strikingly in *Jude*, a contrary movement toward examining these women's behavior with a tone of detachment and clinical precision that mimes determinist scientific discourse of the period about "woman's nature." Drawing on this historical context, Brady traces Hardy's contradictory narrative stance to his own disavowal of the body language and biological status identified with women. Thus these oscillations in the commentary offer a pathological signifying chain, whose signified is not so much the hysterical female character as an embedded "textual hysteria."

The authors of two other essays also draw on Freudian views of sexuality to explicate Hardy. The first addresses a group of narrative poems. U. C. Knoepflmacher traces the recurrent figure of a ruined female edifice, a "dream-memory" of a maternal envelope that metaphorically yokes houses, maternity, and death. The early Hardy plays with the impossibility of constructing any woman's architecture, save a coffin. In response to his wife's death, however, Hardy obsessively reopens the grave and reconstitutes the past. Emma's death gave imaginative access to the poet's otherwise silenced relationship to his mother Jemima, whose traces are left in the themes of eviction and repossession in a number of the later poems, most powerfully in "The Meeting of the Twain."

James Kincaid calls upon us to examine the way the themes of child-beating, voyeurism, and sadomasochism are gendered when reenacted by actively participating readers. In his view, identificatory sadomasochism marks our relationship as readers to the male victim (Jude), while a more destructive, voyeuristic distance marks our pleasure in the torment of the female victim (Sue). Typical of the distance between this contribution and the kind of Freudian interpretation one might have encountered a generation ago is the stress on the reader's implication in the gendering of narrative value.

Hardy's fascination with visual art has invited application of film theory about the gaze. Dianne Sadoff draws a close comparison between angles of vision in Hardy's *Tess* and Roman Polanski's *Tess*. Like Kincaid, she finds "cultural sadomasochisms" in the representation of this heroine, but argues that Hardy's ambivalence complicates the seduction plot in the novel. One of the ways that Hardy "lives" today, of course, is via film translation; his popularity as a mass-media subject for BBC and major studios testifies to the (erotic) power of visual elements in his work, a power that feminist psychoanalysis can help to explicate. In the latter part of her analysis, Sadoff turns away from the transhistorical, universalist assumptions embedded in psychoanalysis and structuralism, in order to stress institutional hierarchies, modern technology, and the marketplace of cultural consumption. Thus she supports a move toward historically situated feminist analysis.

To explain Hardy's contradictory reputation among feminists, Judith Mitchell investigates the relationship between the angle of narrative vision and the gendering of Hardy's inscribed reader. Mitchell contrasts the voyeurism and fetishism of female and male characters observing the objects of their desire in several texts. Hardy's narrative techniques focus the reader's attention on the bodies and observations of female characters, while pulling us away from their consciousness. Mitchell raises the troubling question of reconciling readerly pleasure with feminist analysis.

The contributors of the last group of essays juxtapose Hardy's representations of class and gender. For Robert Kiely, the theme of solitude, a central metaphor for the problems of narrative representation, bears the differentiating traces of one's site on a social map of class and gender. He notes ways in which certain characters of *The Woodlanders* are excluded from the social network *and* from the bourgeois marriage plot of the novel. His study renews our understanding of Hardy's treatment of landscape, by bringing to bear Foucault's theory of discursive power and a more cinematic theory of specular, that is, alienated representation. He argues that the patterns of misreading, evacuation, and impersonation apply to male and female figures alike, undermining any access to "Nature unadorned" by narrative artifice.

The chess games in *A Pair of Blue Eyes*, according to Mary Rimmer, embed socioeconomic structures and strictures on gender relations. "Club laws" and conquest masked as a mere game govern in the wider world and determine the trajectory of Elfride's quest for fulfillment. Rimmer challenges the formalist, collaborative theories of play in descriptions of chess by Caillois, Huizinga, and Freud; she shows the deep socioeconomic biases of games in Hardy. Through these symbolic forms, the society both oppresses and expresses its interpretation of proper structures of power. In turn, as an echo of narrative play itself, the game puts into question the narrator's relationship to his protagonist.

A buried parallel between sexual desire and social desire concerns John Kucich, who traces the complexities of "honesty" as a recurrent Victorian concern in Hardy's novels. Kucich observes that Hardy links sexual roles and their inversion to order (or disorder) in the symbolic realms of class and ethics. Hardy is fascinated with transgressions of these linked sets of norms, and uses them not only to play out social anxieties about class and sexuality but also to define an "antibourgeois" creativity. Here too, then, a symbolic gendering of transgressive desire and transcendent order shadows Hardy's understanding of his own art.

The issues of gender and class definition meet head on in *The Hand of Ethelberta,* one of Hardy's most underrated novels. Penny Boumelha sees in this sophisticated comic work a fusion of the plot of ambition with the plot of marriage that subverts the common terms of both the male and the female *Bildungsroman.* Since Ethelberta's hand is to be awarded by a plot from her own hand, Hardy's narrative dissolves the ideology of passivity and graceful unconsciousness that governs the usual heroine's pursuit of marriage. Yet Ethelberta does not find untrammeled entry into a masculine plot. It is no accident that one of Ethelberta's poems is entitled "Cancelled Words." She must adopt a masculine voice; she obtrusively alludes to male predecessors in her poetic forays. These cross-gender markers suggest that "some form of linguistic self-alienation is the condition of social survival for a woman."

Thus, we explore not only the current diversity in feminist criticism but the range of materials Hardy's texts offer for feminist analysis as well. Although the contributors pursue a number of different approaches and start from several texts in Hardy's *oeuvre,* they converge on similar scenes and narrative features. Hardy's imbricated structures lead us to meet in tracing the intersections of gender and class, slippages between narrative subject and object, and underground connections of the narrator's gaze to the reader's response. We meet in our common sense of where the problems lie: While some evidence points to Hardy's resistance to reductive classification schemes, other evidence points to his entanglement in the very categories he questions. The force of the issue finds expression in the metanarrative role of gender for Hardy: all observation, including representation itself, is inflected by relationships of gender and class. We engage in a debate, which we hope the readers will join.

Most important, from a theoretical perspective, we as a group renew the analysis of gender as a feature of narrative discourse. We remind the reader that gender is only one of several classification schemes structuring and structured by the social order. By reassessing the interdependence of description, narrative logic, and characterization, we draw attention to the links between social conventions of gender and the gendering of literary conventions. From a historical perspective, we show that feminist criticism has made a significant, both probing and subtle, contribution to our understanding of a major male author.

NOTES

1. Paul Smith, "Men in Feminism: Men and Feminist Theory," in *Men in Feminism*, ed. Alice Jardine and Paul Smith (New York: Methuen, 1987), 38. Smith's polemical complaint about exclusionary feminist practices is included in a collection by multiple hands, from multiple perspectives.

2. See Elizabeth Langland and Laura Claridge, "Introduction," *Out of Bounds* (Amherst: University of Massachusetts Press, 1990), 3–4.

3. Cora Kaplan, *Sea Changes: Culture and Feminism* (London: Verso, 1986), 148.

4. Mary Poovey, *The Proper Lady and the Woman Writer: Ideology as Style in the Works of Mary Wollstonecraft, Mary Shelley, and Jane Austen* (Chicago: University of Chicago Press, 1984), x.

5. Showalter, "The Rise of Gender," in *Speaking of Gender*, ed. Elaine Showalter (New York: Routledge, 1989), 9. See Elliot L. Gilbert, "The Female King: Tennyson's Arthurian Apocalypse," in Showalter, 182.

6. Penny Boumelha, *Thomas Hardy and Women: Sexual Ideology and Narrative Form* (Totowa, N.J.: Barnes, 1982), 7

7. Showalter, "The Unmanning of the Mayor of Casterbridge," in *Critical Approaches to Thomas Hardy*, ed. Dale Kramer (London: Macmillan, 1979), 99–115. See also William Mistichelli, "Androgyny, Survival, and Fulfillment in Thomas Hardy's *Far from the Madding Crowd*," *Modern Language Studies* 18, no. 3 (1988), 53–64.

8. Millgate, *Thomas Hardy, a Biography* (Oxford: Oxford University Press, 1985).

9. Kevin Z. Moore, *The Descent of the Imagination: Postromantic Culture in the Later Novels of Thomas Hardy* (New York: New York University Press, 1990), 8.

10. See Elaine Showalter, "Critical Cross-Dressing: Male Feminists and the Woman of the Year," *Raritan* 3 (Fall 1983): 139–43; and Jardine and Smith, *Men in Feminism*.

11. Irving Howe, *Thomas Hardy* (London: Macmillan, 1967), 108; Mary Childers, "Thomas Hardy, the Man Who 'Liked' Women," *Criticism* 23 (1981): 317–34.

12. See Louis Althusser, *Lenin and Philosophy and Other Essays*, trans. Ben Brewster (New York: Monthly Review, 1970), 127–86; Boumelha, *Hardy and Women*, 4–8 and passim.

13. See John Goode, *Thomas Hardy: The Offensive Truth* (Oxford: Blackwell, 1988), vii, 9.

14. J. Hillis Miller, *Fiction and Repetition: Seven English Novels* (Cambridge: Harvard University Press, 1982), 128.

15. Boumelha, *Hardy and Women*; Rosemarie Morgan, *Women and Sexuality in the Novels of Thomas Hardy* (London: Routledge, 1988); Patricia Ingham, *Thomas Hardy* (Atlantic Highlands, N.J.: Humanities, 1990).

16. See, for example, J. Hillis Miller, *Thomas Hardy: Distance and Desire* (Cambridge, Mass.: Belknap, 1970); Joseph Boone, *Tradition Counter Tradition: Love and the Form of Fiction* (Chicago: University of Chicago Press, 1987); and T. R. Wright, *Hardy and the Erotic* (New York: St. Martin's, 1989). Structural theory

about the erotic functions of narrative may be compared to the sweeping fear of Stephen Heath "whether there is not in male feminism . . . always potentially a pornographic effect" ("Male Feminism," in Jardine and Smith, *Men in Feminism*, 4).

17. Laura Mulvey, *Visual and Other Pleasures* (Bloomington: Indiana University Press, 1989; Teresa de Lauretis, *Alice Doesn't: Feminism, Semiotics, Cinema* (Bloomington: Indiana University Press, 1984); Judith Wittenberg, "Early Hardy Novels and the Fictional Eye," *Novel* 16 (1982): 157–64; Kaja Silverman, "History, Figuration and Female Subjectivity in *Tess of the d'Urbervilles*," *Novel* 18 (1984): 5–28; Wright, *Hardy and the Erotic*.

A Woman's Story:
Tess and the Problem of Voice

Margaret R. Higonnet

What concept of voice is embedded in the telling of a woman's story? Much feminist debate has focused on the issue of whether women writers have a voice of their own. Can a male writer's narrative translate the language of women, a "muted" group, into that of his own "dominant" group?[1] What does it mean for a male narrator to represent a woman's silence? Since the silences and silencing of Tess Durbeyfield have attracted critical controversy, this essay focuses on Hardy's shaping of her voice and story. It identifies gender codes through which Hardy defines Tess's voice and its relationship to those of men. Hardy's project of truthfully representing a woman's language becomes entangled in his concern to dismantle clichés about masculinity and femininity. It also intersects with his critique of stereotypes of class. As he works through the problem of Tess's voice, he turns it into an allegory about the artist's social otherness and an occasion to find a new, more "feminine," poetic voice.

Hardy's devices can help us explore ways of defining voice, a topic subsumed by most theory under narrative voice. Narratology gauges the distance between a narrator and a character's words or thoughts in terms of technical devices, such as free indirect speech.[2] Linguistics helps us to appreciate an author's (or character's) lexical range, favored rhetorical figures, dialect, or typographically indicated intonations.[3] Such technical inquiry, however, has generally avoided the complex topic of the gendering of voice.

Fidelity to a hypothetical character's voice, whether in conversation or in letters, has long been considered a test of artistic excellence by both authors and critics. "One of the tests of quality in a novelist is the skill with which dialogue between characters is presented. In reading dialogue, we feel particularly close to the 'reality' with which the novel is linked."[4] Having been attacked in early reviews for inserting inappropriate language into his rural characters' mouths, Hardy claimed both his own fidelity and his authorial right to freedom in representing idiom. Yet readers pointed to a gap in class, or sociolect; modern readers similarly have pointed to a gap in "genderlect."

Because he pays acute attention to traits of "masculinity" or "femininity" in a voice, Hardy's mimetic strategies foreground some of the difficulties embedded in a "masculine" narrative about a female protagonist. At times his narrators assume the authoritative stance of realist fiction that implies an objective, even transparent, transcription of a character's "story" is possible. With very different effect, they also enter into a kind of dialogue with their subjects, which I describe as an "exchange" of voice.

In publishing the first edition of *Tess of the d'Urbervilles: A Pure Woman, Faithfully Presented*, Hardy paradoxically justified his "attempt to give artistic form to a true sequence of things" (T xv). In the tension between art and truth, what is at stake is the fictional suppression of Tess's voice. Silent and cold as a "marble term" while Alec imprints a kiss on her cheek, Tess resists the imprint of men's values and actions. As a woman, she becomes a physical boundary marker set at the margins of sexual maturity, of respectability, and of death. As a "term," she marks the limits of conventional understanding and points to her own unspoken experiences that lie beyond the boundary of the text.

The question of silence and censorship arose immediately upon publication. Hardy contended that his heroine (i.e., he) had been muted by what he calls the "merely vocal formulae of society" (xvii). He "got into hot water," as he put it, for his attempt to give words to Tess's story, encountering first publishers' cuts and then critical outrage.[5]

Can a man implicated in patriarchy speak for a woman constrained by it? Responding to censorship both in the fictional past and in the reception of his book, Hardy claims to present a "faithful" echo of his heroine's elusive voice. His exploration of a woman's voice in *Tess* harks back to traditional realist notions of transparency and looks forward to modern concepts of narrative experiment. The autonomous selfhood and therefore voice of a literary character are never more than useful fictions within the fiction. Narratorial language mediates our illusion of hearing a singular character's voice, as it mediates our perception of a singular narrative voice. Slipping between the two, critics tend to subordinate the theory of a character's voice to that of narrative voice, even as they take for granted some definition of a character's voice in order to talk about narrative personae. Postmodernist theory further forces us to interrogate the singularity of subjectivity: can we speak of Tess as a unitary person, or of "the" narrator? If we think of the self as a site of social production, an intersection of discourses rather than a pure origin of expression, then the goal of giving voice to a woman's story comes to seem more like a dream.

Tess of the d'Urbervilles can be read as a nineteenth-century prelude to such twentieth-century questioning. While others laugh at the marriage of a lecherous milker with a calculating widow, who catches him by concealing the terms of her inheritance, Tess flees in silence from the jocular account of their mistaken identities and story-telling. *"This question of a woman telling her story"* is to her "the heaviest of crosses" (29.232–33, my italics).

One reason it is so hard for women to tell their story may be that men won't listen; certainly this is Tess's experience. But beyond that, women's pains and feelings may be "indescribable by men's words," as Hardy wrote in *Desperate Remedies*.[6] At times of intense misery, "a woman does not faint, or weep, or scream as she will in the moment of sudden shocks. When lanced by a mental agony of such refined and special torture that it is indescribable by men's words, she moves among her acquaintance much as before, and continues so to cast her actions in the old moulds that she is only considered to be rather duller than usual" (DR 13.285). Similarly Bathsheba finds herself speechless: "I cannot tell you. It is diffi-cult for a woman to define her feelings in language which is chiefly made by men to express theirs" (FMC 51.405).[7]

Hardy addresses the "question of a woman telling her story" in part by quoting the words spoken by Tess's hypothetical voice—her dialogue, her letters—to which he gives distinctive traits that reflect her specific values, experiences, and gender. More problematic material lies in the intermedi-ate domain of free indirect discourse, the mediated summaries of Tess's thoughts and conversations. Hardy's *narrator*, moreover, swiftly outlines a set of events that constitute Tess's story, a story that she herself then tries to tell. Banal as it may seem, this narrative order produces a woman's "voice" that will always necessarily be belated.

Hardy deviates from the traditional realist writer's attempt "faithfully" to present a heroine, because he stresses the construction of Tess's story. As in *Jude the Obscure*, Hardy offers in *Tess* "a series of seemings," the illusory schemata by which Tess and those around her read her life. Among those readers we must include the narrator himself, for Hardy avails himself of the artist's last resource, the reflexively ironic presentation of his narrator, in order to shadow the possibility of misrepresentation.

Hardy goes beyond the familiar narrative pose of empathy with his heroine. The story of Tess teaches us that voice takes on full, phenomeno-logical, existence only in its reception and repetition or assimilation. By whistling, Tess gives voice to the bullfinches, before a hidden, eavesdropping audience. The birds "go back" in their singing unless Tess whistles for them. Just so, Hardy implies, Tess's fluty voice would be lost without a narrator's elicitation of it. It is in Hardy's interest, of course, to suggest a subliminal identity between his heroine and his narrator as an anchor for the authenticity and "reality" of his tale.

The first part of this study locates ways in which voices in *Tess* are gendered. More consciously than most authors, Hardy constructs a code to define the differences between the voices of men and women.[8] As we shall see, Hardy specifically encodes Tess's voice as feminine. That encoding, however, becomes entangled in the problem of individuating her voice. Like George Eliot, Hardy opposed his heroine's individual voice to the unnatural laws and maxims of men. Thus her voice as sign of femininity constitutes the "Other" of social discourse. Yet Hardy's effort to singularize his heroine also leads him to differentiate her voice from stereotypes of the feminine. This artistic dilemma echoes larger difficulties within the novel.

The topic of voice as we confront it here is neither narrowly linguistic nor simply thematic. Voice becomes an intrinsic feature of plot. Hardy traces two intersecting vocal trajectories: an elective affinity between Tess and Angel leads eventually to a convergence not only of their views but of their voices into a harmony beyond gender. "All the while they were converging, under an irresistible law, as surely as two streams in one vale" (20.165). Their developing relationship, in turn, is a model for that of the teller to his tale.[9] Through the course of the novel, the dialectic between a variable narrative voice and Tess's quoted or echoed voice becomes an explicit theme and problem. This dynamic exchange between character and narrator grounds the hermeneutic claims of understanding and fidelity.

From the outset, Hardy maps a repressive set of discourses that are inadequate to true morality and inimical to the development and expression of Tess's selfhood. Hardy shows their dehumanizing effects on men as well as women; to show how ineluctably these discourses shape our thoughts and phrases, he ironically puts quotations from the master text of the Bible into the mouths of those who challenge its application to the individual case. Notably, Hardy encodes most of the "merely vocal formulae" of the Bible or "ordinances of civilization" as masculine. The narrator opposes men who follow the Word to women who follow the truths of their heart.[10] Unlike her minister husband, for example, Mrs. Clare embraces her son without regard for "the stains of heterodoxy." "What woman, indeed, among the most faithful adherents of the truth, believes the promises and threats of the Word in the sense in which she believes in her own children, or would not throw her theology to the wind if weighed against their happiness?" (53.470). Tess's "rash" reaction to Church precepts at the death of her child Sorrow confirms this antagonism between maternal instinct and moral "formulae": she flees the "whispers" of churchgoers, defiantly pleads with the orthodox Vicar for Christian burial, and becomes assimilated to a "Nature who respects not the social law."

Nature respects instead individual difference. The inadequacy of received texts seems universally applicable, but the focus of moral formulae on chastity orients their attack against women. One voice oppressing women, for example, is the "trade voice" of the man who paints Mosaic laws on barns: "THOU, SHALT, NOT, COMMIT—." What he calls the "tex" links Tess to sex, and though unjustly applied to "dangerous young females" like herself, "the words entered Tess with accusatory horror" (12.101–12). An Augustinian at heart, for whom chastity is a matter of the will and not of the body, Hardy challenges the Clare family's Pauline cult of chastity. Tess's human complexities resist their stereotype of the "simple" or "unsullied country maid" and make it difficult "to apply the words" of Proverbs 31 to her genuine virtue.

Hardy does not allow Tess to remain a totally passive object of description by his male characters. Nonetheless he demonstrates that when she does speak up, men try to silence her. Despite his sympathy for her, the young Vicar exclaims, "Don't talk so rashly" (14.124). At other moments, men silence her by rejecting her words or interpreting them through stereotypical codes. In one of the most dramatic scenes of the novel, Alec argues that women don't mean what they say.

> "I didn't understand your meaning till it was too late."
> "That's what every woman says."
> "How can you dare to use such words!" she cried, turning impetuously upon him, her eyes flashing as the latent spirit (of which he was to see more some day) awoke in her. "My God! I could knock you out of the gig! Did it never strike your mind that what every woman says some women may feel?" (12.97)

Adrian Poole observes of this exchange, "She is taking possession of a cliche, and this is inseparable from the taking possession of her own body at this moment. In the face of men's threat to dispossess the woman of her own body, of the right to speech—to reduce her to physical and linguistic cliche—, Tess re-claims that body and that right to speech, repossessing the discarded and supposedly empty shell" ("Men's Words," 342).

Angel too embraces stereotypes of femininity. When he idealizes her as Demeter and Artemis, she responds, "Call me Tess." "Yet the slave to custom and conventionality," he translates her "no" into "yes": "his experience of women was great enough for him to be aware that the negative often meant nothing more than the preface to the affirmative" (T 28.224). He condescendingly interprets her "self-suppression," as if he were interpreting a text.

"She is a dear dear Tess," he thought to himself, as one deciding on the true construction of a difficult passage. "Do I realize solemnly enough how utterly and irretrievably this little womanly thing is the creature of my good or bad faith and fortune? I think not. I could not, unless I were a woman myself."(34.278)

Just as Angel must learn at the outset of his stay in Talbothays to differentiate the typical and unvarying country man "Hodge" into "beings of many minds, . . . men every one of whom walked in his own individual way the road to dusty death," so he must learn to "disintegrate" the falsifying projections by men onto individual women (18.152).

Social codes confine women in history. The past as masculine event ironically names the present. In a controversial instance, the narrator comments on the unspeakable violence done to Tess by Alec in the well-named woods of The Chase. In this symbolically darkened and dimmed setting, the narrator ironically suggests that historical justice somehow visits the sins of the fathers upon the daughters, whereas a closer examination even of that maxim suggests instead a historical repetition of the sins of powerful men against simple peasant girls. Here we find one of the cruxes in interpretation of the novel, for giving voice to the historian is one of the narrator's functions that splits the narrative voice asunder and severs it from the "woman's story."

Opposed to men's maxims, then, we find complex womanly experience, given expression in Tess's voice, one of Hardy's most brilliant inventions. Fluty, murmuring, quavering, stammering, panting, its breaks and stops call to mind Julia Kristeva's *semeiotike*, that theory of fluidity, contradiction, disruption, and silence in a feminine, pre-Oedipal language. Hardy's narrator assimilates three features above all to the feminine: Tess's "native phrases," her emotional fusion of body and words, and her silences.

The opening chapters link Tess's voice to her mother's through their love of song, superstitions, and use of dialect. As Ralph Elliot suggests, Hardy's "reliance upon archaic or local language seems like a deliberate attempt to free contemporary English of its more inhibiting, 'male' associations."[11] In manuscript, Hardy initially added dialectal phrasing, heightening his heroine's links to an archaic, rural society. The figure called Love or Rosemary (before she became Tess) started off in the first pages of Hardy's draft speaking standard English even at home; manuscript changes then *added dialect* for Tess, especially in states of emotion, "when excited by joy, surprise, or grief" (MS f19).[12] In yet later versions, dialect took on class and intellectual connotations: Tess, who plans to become a school teacher, speaks "ordinary English abroad and to persons of quality" (3.21).

Bilingual by training, once Tess leaves home she speaks a refined "Sixth

Standard" English, close to that spoken by the better educated characters of the novel, though less abstract and complex. Through Angel she acquires the repertoire of a more educated, disillusioned, middle-class man. Indeed, later editions stripped dialect from Tess's speech after she leaves Marlott, a process that Laird attributes to Hardy's desire to dignify Tess.[13] These changes created a problem: how to mark Tess's voice as that of a woman.

Hardy dealt with that problem, I think, by foregrounding features that he could encode as feminine. He counterbalanced the more universal and sophisticated features in Tess's acquired language, by assimilating her speech to her body and to nature. Hardy's notebooks record the semiotic truth that "there are looks, & tones, & gestures, which form a significant language of their own" (Björk 1.3). Hardy enumerates bits of her body and, as he does so, introduces the notion of body language: "her mobile peony mouth and large innocent eyes added eloquence to colour and shape." Not her words but her peony mouth, displaced from speech into a flower of speech, has "eloquence." Likewise, her "eloquent" eyes "flash" and confess. "Every seesaw of her breath, every wave of her blood, every pulse singing in her ears was a voice that joined with nature in revolt against her scrupulousness" (28.228).

Of a woman's speaking "parts," the heart is one of the most important. When Tess baptizes her dying child Sorrow, she speaks "boldly and triumphantly in the stopt-diapason note which her voice acquired when her heart was in her speech" (14.120).[14] Here, the musical term "stopt-diapason," for the muffled, higher note reached when an organ pipe is stopped, evokes harmonious sublimity. At the same time, it reminds us of the "stops" in Tess's speech, the breaks that mark the muffling of her story.

Tess's fragments and her fusion of body with language typify Hardy's representation of her voice as a vehicle of poetic truth, whose breaks fall naturally rather than according to the dictates of art and grammar. During her engagement, for example, Tess speaks in ecstatic fragments, dictated by the "leapings of her heart," the voice and laughter of a woman in love: "Some of the dairy-people, who were also out of doors on the first Sunday evening after their engagement, heard her impulsive speeches, ecstasized to fragments, though they were too far off to hear the words discoursed; noted the spasmodic catch in her remarks, broken into syllables by the leapings of her heart, as she walked leaning on his arm; her contented pauses, the occasional laugh upon which her soul seemed to ride—the laugh of a woman in company with the man she loves and has won from all other women—unlike anything else in nature" (31.249). This "articulatory physiology" (Elliot 340) links natural, spontaneous poetry to the feminine.

One of the most extraordinary passages in which Hardy uses body language to express Tess's feelings is the lunchbreak during the Marlott harvest, when she suckles the infant Sorrow who has been brought to her: "When the infant had taken its fill the young mother sat it upright in her lap, and looking into the far distance dandled it with a gloomy indifference that was almost dislike; then all of a sudden she fell to violently kissing it some dozens of times, as if she could never leave off, the child crying at the vehemence of an onset which strangely combined passionateness with contempt" (14.114). Such preverbal communication with the preverbal Sorrow links the woman's sexual and linguistic roles in a traditional way. Furthermore, Tess's violence here evokes a particular form of "maternal anger" not often recognized in literature written by men. Hers is certainly the anger of the repressed voice, but it is also the anger of the exploited body, of a maternity whose pleasures have been fatally contaminated by rape. This anger will find expression finally in violence (Ingham 74).

Essential to Hardy's presentation of Tess as a young woman who yearns to leave her body behind while stargazing is the treachery of a woman's body as voice. Holes in your stockings "don't speak," says her mother Joan, but her "developing figure" does—and it "belies" her age. Angel, when he wishes to decode Tess's rejection of marriage, "conned the characters of her face as if they had been hieroglyphics" telling him what he wants to hear (28.225). Tess finally mutilates her eyebrows to prevent men from "conning" the hieroglyphs of her face and taking it as a screen for their projections.

Beyond body language lies silence as a feminine form of speech, whose multiple moral and sexual meanings underscore its significance as a way for Tess to voice herself.[15] For Tess is "impressed" by soundlessness "as a positive entity rather than the mere negation of noise" (19.157). When she forces Alec to let her out of the gig, her "strategic silence" tells him she has lost her hat on purpose (8.66). When Angel presses her to marry him, her silence bespeaks her self-effacement on behalf of her friends and his well-being (31.246). Still later during their engagement, Tess's silence concerning her past voices her irrepressible desires as well as her mother's advice. At different moments, then, silence can voice resentment, conscience, or erotic drives.

Yet finally, her vow not to write Angel until written to bespeaks "dumb and vacant fidelity" (35.296). Imposed silence is the badge of woman's subjection and the sign of her vacancy, her chastity. The moment when Tess does speak out is catastrophic; as the title of the next "phase" reveals, if she speaks, "the woman pays." Tess knows this economy of speech: "She would pay to the uttermost farthing; she would tell, there and then" (34.284). Ironically, when she and Angel are united, she urges him to mute the past. She has become like one of the polar birds at Flintcomb-Ash: "gaunt spectral creatures with tragical eyes—eyes which had witnessed scenes of cataclysmal horror in inaccessible polar regions of a magnitude such as no human being had ever conceived, . . . but of all they had seen which humanity would never see, they had brought no account" (43.367). "Dumb impassivity" records the journey of such travelers through pain.

II

To record silence necessitates a narrator's voice. "She thought," writes Hardy, "without actually wording the thought, how strange and godlike was a composer's power, who from the grave could lead through sequences of emotion, which he alone had felt at first, a girl like her who had never heard of his name" (13.107).

To speak for Tess means to define a particular woman's voice. Herein lies a problem. For to present Tess in her womanhood, the phases of maiden, mother, wife, mistress, and murderess, means to assimilate her to conventions about different feminine voices. Conversely, to distinguish Tess in her particularity seems to entail—for Hardy at least—assimilating her to masculine discourse.

Tess "herself," as we have already seen, rejects the body language conventionally assigned to women. After her confession, she rejects the feminine hysterics and "feminine" strategy of intimacy that might have enabled her to hold Angel. Her attempts to distinguish herself from the conventions of femininity elicit D. H. Lawrence's explanation of her plight as "despising herself in the flesh, despising the deep Female she was."[16]

Part of Tess's development, as even Alec notices, consists in her adopting Angel's "speech and phrases" (32.260). She proves her "reverential fidelity" to her husband—a model for the narrator's fidelity—by repeating verbatim Angel's syllogisms in "crystallized phrases." She learns and repeats his songs. More important, she turns his words to serve her own insights, as Adrian Poole has acutely observed:

> "Our tremulous lives are so different from theirs, are they not?" he musingly observed to her, as he regarded the three figures [of her milkmaid-companions.]
> "Not so very different, I think," she said.
> "Why do you think that?"
> "There are very few women's lives that are not—tremulous," Tess replied, pausing over the new word as if it impressed her. (29.235)

For Angel's elitist reflection on the unthinking masses, she substitutes a more accurate polarity between the secure lives of men and "tremulous" lives of women. She insists that we must read through the lens not only of class but of gender.

Before she ever meets Angel, one may catch in Tess's vivid, metaphoric speech about blighted worlds as "stubbard trees" certain philosophic turns of phrase and questioning. These were not learnt "by rote," as Angel condescendingly suspects, since he judges her by her social origins. Tess knows "the ache of modernism" because "advanced ideas are really in great part but the latest fashion in definition—a more accurate expression by words in -logy & -ism, of sensations which men [& women] have vaguely grasped for centuries" (Hardy's insertion, MS f137–38, 19.160). Over time Tess does become more articulate in her pessimism. Hardy intensified the fluency and depth of her voice in his revisions "by increasing our sense of the different languages she speaks" (Poole 341, 342–43). Technically, the different linguistic repertoires she masters complicate our sense of Tess's voice. While our multiple discourses "speak" her, at the same time we hear her transfer codes to make them fit better the actualities she observes.

The last phase in her development is to pass from voice to écriture, from oral to written forms. The comparatively late location of Tess's letters to Angel, which we read first broken off, then transcribed in full, supports the illusion that Tess has developed from a meditative milkmaid into an articulate subject capable of verbalizing in writing her sense of selfhood. The late letter that follows Angel in his peregrinations is indeed passionate and eloquent, sufficiently powerful to wrench Angel out of himself and to call him back to her. Fragmentary echoes of her writing (when Hardy describes its reception by Angel) confirm the hermeneutic pattern of "antiphony" postulated in this essay. Her voice by passing from oral to written form acquires the necessary substantiality to be "heard," to be repeated and understood.

III

This leads into the second part of my argument. An exchange of voice lies at the very heart of Tess's relationship to Angel Clare. At the outset, Angel is drawn to Tess precisely because she seems to echo his own thoughts, in a different register. He recognizes his own skepticism in her remarks, which distinguish her voice for him from among those of the other dairy-folk. We may detect a certain narcissism in his very respect for her: "At such times as this, apprehending the grounds of her refusal to be her modest her modest sense of incompetence in matters social and polite, he would say that she was wonderfully well-informed and versatile—which was certainly true, her natural quickness, and her admiration for him, having led her to pick up his vocabulary, his accent, and fragments of his knowledge, to a surprising extent" (28.225). But Angel is also drawn to the "soft and silent Tess" (24.190). His embrace "stills" and deflects her attempts to confess; he interrupts with belittling assumptions and defers her speech: "No, no—we can't have faults talked of . . . you shall tell me anything . . . not now" (25.197, 33.269). She responds with "mute obedience." Their courtship, then, is marked by a conflict between his attraction to her conventionally feminine Otherness, including her muteness, and his sympathetic identification with her intimations of philosophic alienation (his own form of Otherness).

In a development inverting that of Tess, Angel acquires the body language of a farmer, more expressive eyes, and phrases like "a drop of pretty tipple." He assimilates a cottager's "tone" much to the horror of his superfine clerical brothers, who hear his "growing social ineptness." Her shift is marked by gender, his by class. This process of mutual adaptation comes to grief with the climactic double confession on the wedding night. Angel "seemed to be her double" (34.285) in telling Tess his story; as she responds she sees "tis just the same!" He, however, cannot grasp the parallel until he draws closer to the phenomena of nature, learns to recognize the "mutely Miltonic" among the countryfolk, and hears "the voices of inanimate things" (18.152–53). He must discern the new note of Tess in the babble of conventions in order to respond; symbolically he cannot receive her letters until he is psychologically ready to answer.

Once in Brazil, Angel recounts not only his own story but that of Tess to a stranger.[17] The retransmission of Tess's story catalyzes his return and the final modulation of his voice. Broken by illness and emotion, his sentences are interrupted by pauses and dashes, much as Tess's have been in the past. " 'Ah—it is my fault!' said Clare. But he could not get on. Speech was as inexpressive as silence" (45.484). At Stonehenge finally, he renounces speech altogether.

The narrative traces these two main intersecting lines, the masculinization of Tess's voice and the feminization of Angel's.[18] Their reciprocal transformation is possible, because our gendering of language is both arbitrary and ambivalent. As Hillis Miller puts it in a reading of Virginia Woolf, the great modern theorist of literary androgyny, ways of writing "like a woman" or "like a man" "tend to change places or values in the moment of being defined and enacted."[19] Hardy uses the symmetrical structure of the novel to reinforce the themes of language and silence and understanding through exchange.

Beyond Tess's exchange of voice with Angel lie parallels between her voice and that of the polyglot narrator. A number of critics have noted a "feminine principle" in the narration.[20] Hardy appears to have constructed deliberate parallels between what the narrator says and what Tess says or thinks. This convergence bears on Tess's development. Hardy, Mary Jacobus says, "starts with an unformed heroine, and shows us the emergence of a reflective consciousness close to his own" ("Tess's Purity," 324). The congruence between Tess and the narrator also bears on Hardy's basic project, his desire to create the ventriloquistic illusion that for once we can hear a woman's story. Hence the ambiguous parallel between the narrator's use of superstition and the heroine's inclination to lend it credence, or between Hardy's notorious penchant to formulae of philosophic fatalism (called "Tessimism" by one reviewer) and Tess's view of life on this "blighted" star (*Life*, 265). The poetry of her ecstatic speech and her flavorful analogies (the lords and ladies, the stubbard trees) actualize another aspect of the author's own craft.

In addition, we may point to a number of close verbal echoes that assimilate her prophetic knowledge to a narrator's control and omniscience. Tess is permitted to foresee Angel's complaint that she is not the woman he has been loving: "she you love is not my real self, but one in my image; the one I might have been!" (33.273). Tess's ability to enter into another resembles her sensitivity to the voices of nature; commenting on those crepuscular moments when she intensifies natural processes until they seem a part of her own story, the narrator declares that her pathetic projections are not a fallacy but in a sense true: "For the world is only a psychological phenomenon and what they seemed they were" (13.108). Implicitly, Tess becomes a figure for the imagination.

IV

Briefly, by way of a conclusion, I want to review three problems directly related to Tess's voice. First, the complexity—even inconsistency—of the narrative voice. Hardy's effort to wrestle with the codes of masculinity and femininity ironically traps him in their repetition. In narrating Tess's struggle against the "tex" of womanhood, Hardy attempts to break the hold of such discourses over the individual. Yet at the same time, in proposing to represent Tess "faithfully" as a "pure" woman, he inexorably falls subject to other, equally conventional discourses. Within Hardy's system of polarities, "sex and nature are assigned to the female" in an ideological tragedy that forces Tess to play the conventional passive role.[21]

Hardy's divided view of conventions about the feminine continuously complicates the narrative representation of Tess. We may admire, for example, his empathetic depiction of Tess wandering at dusk, hearing "formulae of bitter reproach" in the gusts of oncoming night. The scene vividly attests to her imagination, her internalization of social attitudes ("what they seemed they were"), and the identification of an outsider with the realm of nature. Simultaneously, however, the narrator affirms his distance from Tess's self-condemnation and his superiority to "moral hobgoblins" (13.108). The split structure, recreating the narrative hierarchy, undermines the autonomy of Tess as subject and by its inconsistency also undermines the authority of the narrator.[22] By opening a gap between masculine authority and feminine illusion, Hardy puts back into question the whole project of narrative fidelity. The only possible fidelity seems to lie in acknowledging distortion by gender.

At a second level, gender categories contaminate our criticism too. Many readers privilege the more sensually expressive, that is, the more "natural" heroine of the manuscript (Love, Cis, or Rosemary) as the true Tess. Her sensuality and attachment to her rural roots seem to them to make her a more credible woman than the Tess of the final version, held to falsify Hardy's "original intention" (Jacobus, 331). Confusion extends to discussions of Tess's language, which tend to slip between questions of sexual explicitness and linguistic repertoire. Some see in the purging of dialect from Love's voice a bowdlerization of her sensuality. More accurately, in revising Hardy both muted and heightened Tess's sensual entanglements, both blurred and intensified her gender traits. The "late" Tess speaks in a mixed voice that links her to "the field-woman" as well as to Angel and the narrator. At both ends of this spectrum we are dealing with repertoires (i.e., with the reproduction of linguistic stereotypes).

More positively, this intersection of conflicting repertoires points toward a hermeneutic exchange of voice between Tess and of the narrator. Reading the novel as a metanarrative about voice helps us see in greater detail not only problems Hardy encountered in his narrative, but his achievement. Tess's postulated voice permits a creative extension of authorial voice. In part, a nineteenth-century male writer may center his fiction on a female protagonist in order to expose the contradictions of bourgeois, particularist individualism or the inequities of existing gendered hierarchies. In part, also, his effort to represent "faithfully" a heroine's voice and experience leads him toward an unrepresented zone of experience and language.

This experiment in a "feminine" voice sheds light on Hardy's much debated narrative gaps. The unseen rape, the missing four-page note to Angel, the omitted double confession have been condemned as suppressions of Tess's voice and experience, or even censorship of moments when Hardy's male rivals possess his beloved heroine.[23] In a review for the *Fortnightly Review* (1892), Francis Adams complains, "The gaps that represent bad work are too large and too frequent." Franz Stanzel suggests that

Hardy censored his own text to prevent readers from reaching an independent (negative) opinion of his heroine.[24]

From a feminist perspective, Childers charges that Hardy "takes away from Tess all power to speak what she means" (329). Boumelha finds Tess's consciousness all but edited out, part of a larger tragic pattern, "the ideological elision of woman, sex, and nature." This elision means that Tess is "most woman" when she is "dumb" (122–23). Hillis Miller complains in *Fiction and Repetition* about the "effacement" of Tess's violation and "the similar failure to describe directly all the crucial acts of violence which echo Tess's violation before and after its occurrence" (118). Such charges are particularly ironic, given Hardy's own struggle against the gaps imposed by censorship. His "Explanatory Note" to the first edition complains of the "piecemeal mode of parturition" and his need to rejoin limbs and trunk.[25] Again in the *Life*, he describes the struggle in virtually sexual terms, as one to preserve "the novel intact," not "mutilated" by censorship to eliminate "improper explicitness" of certain passages (*Life*, 232).

Interpreted as an assimilation of Tess's "feminine" language, Hardy's pauses acquire fresh complexity. In one sense, the blank pages between "phases" constitute a silent "body language" for Hardy's text. Such breaks, of course, have no single meaning, as the interplay between the two central examples makes clear. The gap between Alec's discovery of the sleeping Tess and the beginning of the second phase symbolically renders the tearing of flesh that it literally does not describe; such a gap is a pure literary convention for the socially taboo or the unspeakable. When Hardy, however, repeats this narrative gap on the wedding night, at the moment when Tess reveals her innermost secret—that is, the secret moment that we know as the previous gap in the narrative—he ironically plays upon an (absent) hymeneal rupture, the unconsummated marriage, and points us toward another initiatory knowledge, for which Angel is not ready. The result is that Hardy brings to the foreground the sexuality of story telling. Reversing the teleological (male) sexual drive to which Peter Brooks compares narrative, these sexual breaks in Hardy mime the rupture enacted by women's storytelling. They foreshadow the broken line that Virginia Woolf would describe in *Room of One's Own*.

Hardy's silences reproduce but displace Tess's difficulty in coming to speech. We have been asked whether her story will "bear" telling, a burden it seems, that Tess alone must take on. A curious inversion takes place: the narrative becomes the margin for her silently spoken secret, raising the question of the propriety of narrative-making itself. The problem of giving voice to a woman's story ironically becomes a figure for the problem of giving voice to experience and to the Other at all.

Hardy's silences experiment with a discourse he encoded as feminine. Such experiments are typical of nineteenth-century fiction.[26] We must not forget, however, that the construction and figurative transposition of a "feminine" discourse contain the seeds of their own destruction. Repeatedly, resistance to the social code of gender is undermined by the reinscription of a gendered linguistic code. By setting these tensions up, Hardy exposes the perpetual displacement of woman as figure. The violence and other costs of both silence and speech for women are conspicuously absent from the male narrator's domain; the presence or absence of choice makes a critical difference. Ultimately, then, Hardy forces us back upon the question whether silence expresses the ineffable or more simply records the unspeakable, and the most pervasive form of violence against women.

NOTES

An earlier version of this essay appeared in *Out of Bounds: Male Writers and Gender(ed) Criticism*, ed. Laura Claridge and Elizabeth Langland (Amherst: University of Massachusetts Press, 1990).

1. See Elaine Showalter, "Feminist Criticism in the Wilderness," in *The New Feminist Criticism: Essays on Women, Literature, and Theory*, ed. Elaine Showalter (New York: Pantheon, 1985), 262.

2. Susan Sniader Lanser usefully summarizes theories of reported speech and the "chain of authority" from historical author to character in her chapter on "textual voice," in *The Narrative Act: Point of View in Prose Fiction* (Princeton: Princeton University Press, 1981), 137–48.

3. See R. W. V. Elliott, *Thomas Hardy's English* (Oxford: Blackwell, 1984) and Raymond Chapman, *The Language of Thomas Hardy* (London: Macmillan, 1990).

4. Chapman, *The Language of Thomas Hardy*, 125.

5. "I have for a long time been in favour of woman-suffrage. . . . I am in favour of it because I think the tendency of the woman's vote will be to break up the pernicious conventions in respect of women, customs, religion, illegitimacy, the stereotyped household (that it must be the unit of society), the father of a woman's child (that it is anybody's business but the woman's own) . . . and other matters which I got into hot water for touching on many years ago." Letter of 11/30/06 to Mrs. Fawcett, cited in Gail Cunningham, "Thomas Hardy: New Women for Old," *The New Woman and the Victorian Novel* (London: Macmillan, 1978), 115. A. O. J. Cockshut, however, believes that "the attempt to turn Hardy into a feminist is altogether vain"; cited by Elaine Showalter, "The Unmanning of the Mayor of Casterbridge," in *Critical Approaches to the Fiction of Thomas Hardy*, ed. Dale Kramer (Totowa, N.J.: Barnes, 1979), 101.

6. There is for any modern reader an obvious irony in giving these lines about the incapacity of men's words to a narrator who though anonymous, by his elaborately wrought, semireligious language, assimilates himself to the highly edu-

cated and confessional, masculine, roles of artist and priest. Omniscient condescension to the species "woman" here might not indicate conscious irony. In *Tess* and *Jude* such contradictions are probably deliberate, for they constantly rend the text.

7. Adrian Poole, "Men's Words and Hardy's Women," *Essays in Criticism* 31 (1981): 328–45, stresses Hardy's sensitivity to "the effort of men's words to circumscribe and describe, confine and define, women's bodies" (329). Hardy thematizes the difficulty throughout his *oeuvre*, as in *A Pair of Blue Eyes*, where Knight, who lacks "the trick of reading the truly enigmatical forces at work in women," "could pack them into sentences like a workman, but practically was nowhere" (20:226, 18:193).

8. Previous studies have focused on Tess's physical description and the sexualization of the masculine narrator's relationship to her: Mary Jacobus, "Tess's Purity," *Essays in Criticism* 26 (1976): 318–38; Penny Boumelha, *Thomas Hardy and Women: Sexual Ideology and Narrative* (Totowa, N.J.: Barnes, 1982). On masculine traits in the narrator's voice, see also Joseph A. Boone, *Tradition Counter Tradition: Love and the Form of Fiction* (Chicago: University of Chicago Press, 1987); Mary Childers, "Thomas Hardy, the Man Who 'Liked' Women," *Criticism* 23 (1981): 317–34.; Vernon Lee, "Hardy," in *The Handling of Words and Other Studies in Literary Psychology* (London: Lane 1923), 222–41; Tony Tanner, "Colour and Movement in Hardy's *Tess of the D'Urbervilles*," *Critical Quarterly* 10 (Autumn 1968): 219–39.

9. The seduction plot that molds the relationship of Tess to the narrator is the subject of Dianne Sadoff's essay in this volume. For repetition in narrative representation, see Hillis Miller's chapter on Hardy in *Fiction and Repetition: Seven English Novels* (Cambridge: Harvard University Press, 1982). Penny Boumelha refers to "narrative androgyny" in the narrator's relation to Tess: "she is not only spoken by the narrator but also spoken *for*" (*Hardy and Women*, 120).

10. Joan Durbeyfield is an obvious exception. On the "disease in language, see Charlotte Thompson, "Language and the Shape of Reality in *Tess of the d'Urbervilles*," *ELH* 50 (1983): 729–62.

11. Rather than a significant experiment by Hardy involving linguistic gender differences, Ralph W. V. Elliot finds inconsistency (*Thomas Hardy's English* [Oxford: Blackwell, 1984], 337); Adrian Poole finds "uncertainty," "Men's Words," 345n.24.

12. References to the manuscript are drawn from *Tess of the d'Urbervilles: A Facsimile of the MS*, ed. Simon Gatrell (New York: Garland, 1986). A close examination of these changes reveals that Hardy also localized the vocabulary of John Durbeyfield, as well as that of Joan and Tess (see the edition of 1892). Significantly, however, the narrator's comments stress *women's* use of dialect rather than that of John.

13. John Tudor Laird, *The Shaping of "Tess of the d'Urbervilles"* (Oxford: Clarendon, 1975), 184.

14. This passage raises the question of the narrator's shifting relationship to Tess, for it adds that the voice "will never be forgotten by those who knew her." To explain the vocal mosaic of a narrator at times close to Tess, at times distant, Rosemarie Morgan argues for splintered narrative personae, U. C. Knoepflmacher for multiple narrators.

15. Childers observes that silence may express power ("Thomas Hardy," 322).

She believes that the muting of his female characters "suggests Hardy's own submission to censureship and sensitivity to criticism" (333). Wayne P. Anderson describes silence as a means of characterization and of drawing the reader into the narrative. "The Rhetoric of Silence in Hardy's Fiction," in *Critical Essays on Thomas Hardy: The Novels,* ed. Dale Kramer (Boston: Hall, 1990), 86–100.

16. D. H. Lawrence, "Study of Thomas Hardy," in *Phoenix: The Posthumous Papers,* ed. Edward D. McDonald (1936, rpt. New York: Viking, 1972), 486.

17. Angel is both a shadow of the narrator and a projection of the reader; his poeticisms and conventionalism echo apparently deliberate misreadings of Tess by the narrator and our own problems of reception, which prevent us from hearing Tess's story. More positively the reader and the narrator, of course, strive like Angel to receive Tess's wounded name into our "bosom."

18. Showalter notes generally that for Hardy's heroes "maturity involves a kind of assimilation of female suffering, an identification with a woman which is also an effort to come to terms with their own deepest selves" ("Unmanning," 101).

19. J. Hillis Miller, "Mr. Carmichael and Lily Briscoe: The Rhythm of Creativity in *To the Lighthouse,*" in *Modernism Reconsidered,* ed. Robert Kiely (Cambridge: Harvard University Press, 1983), 188.

20. Irving Howe finds "a curious power of sexual insinuation, almost as if he were not locked into the limits of masculine perception but could shuttle between, or for moments yoke together, the responses of the two sexes" (*Thomas Hardy,* [London: Macmillan, 1967], 109). Showalter considers Hardy "one of the few Victorian male novelists who wrote in what may be called a female tradition" ("Unmanning," 99) and finds in his work "a consistent element of self-expression through women" "as screens or ghosts of himself" (101).

21. Cf. Boumelha, *Hardy and Women,* 123; Boone, *Tradition;* Patricia Ingham, *Thomas Hardy,* (Atlantic Highlands, N.J.: Humanities, 1990), 72–73, 90.

22. Boone, *Tradition,* argues that the linear seduction plot repeats through its relentless rhythms of pursuit and flight the violation it describes. Similarly, David Lodge complains that Hardy "undermines our trust in the reliability of Tess's response to Nature, which is his own chief rhetorical device for defending her character" (*Language of Fiction* [New York: Columbia University Press, 1966], 76). Boumelha comments on "Hardy's increasing interrogation of his own modes of narration": "The disjunctions in narrative voice, the contradictions of logic, the abrupt shifts of point of view . . . disintegrate the stability of character as a cohering force, they threaten the dominance of the dispassionate and omniscient narrator, and so push to its limit the androgynous narrative mode that seeks to represent and explain the woman from within and without" (*Hardy and Women,* 132). James Kincaid revalues "the large and the local gaps" as evidence of creative "tentativeness and inconsistency," i.e., of openings rather than foreclosures ("Hardy's Absences," in Kramer, *Critical Approaches,* 202).

23. John Bayley, *An Essay on Hardy* (Cambridge: Cambridge University Press, 1978), 183.

24. Adams, in *Thomas Hardy and His Readers: A Selection of Contemporary Reviews,* ed. Laurence Lerner and John Holstrum (New York: Barnes, 1968), 89.

Franz Stanzel, Hardy: *Tess of the d'Urbervilles,"* in *Der moderne englische Roman: Interpretationen,* ed. Horst Oppel (Berlin: Schmidt, 1963), 38–40.

25. See Sadoff's interpretation of this fetichistic description, in this volume.

26. Margaret R. Higonnet, "Writing from the Feminine: *Lucinde and Adolphe,"* *Annales Benjamin Constant* 15 (1986): 28.

Becoming a Man in *Jude the Obscure*

Elizabeth Langland

Because Thomas Hardy's representations of women, by and large, exceed the simple stereotypes scholars initially identified as characteristic images of women, feminist critics early turned to his novels. While those first studies opened up possibilities of a rewarding feminist approach to Hardy, recent work looks more broadly at gender, exploring the problem of masculinity as well as femininity. Poised between centuries (nineteenth and twentieth), between cultures (rural and urban), and between classes (peasantry and middling), Hardy engaged profound social dislocations in ways that disturbed the stability of gender classifications. His representation in *Jude the Obscure* of the social and material construction of masculinity and femininity reveals something that feminist and gender critics are only beginning to explore: the extent to which patriarchal constructions of masculinity become constrictions and, when inflected by class, create contradictions for individual males. To speak of "patriarchy" in this way exposes a basic truth. Patriarchy (like the resistance to it) is not only outside but also inside, structuring language, logic, our very understanding of human subjectivity. Part of the novel's brilliance derives from Hardy's ability to represent Jude's battle with the class and gender self-constructions his culture offers him. His embattlement gives the novel its richness and generates its tragic denouement.

The novel articulates Jude's dilemma of identity largely through his conflicting responses to his cousin, Sue Bridehead. This interpretation of *Jude the Obscure* turns attention away from questions of the authenticity of Sue's character—where it has often focused[1]—and queries instead Sue's place in the construction of Jude's masculinity, her role as catalyst for the text's trenchant critique of gender and class paradigms. In an earlier article, I have demonstrated that Sue as character is filtered almost entirely through Jude's perspective.[2] Thus, she is known to us through his experience and interpretations of her. I will argue here that Jude increasingly embraces relationship with his cousin as a means of self-fulfillment.[3] He seizes upon her as an answer to the difficulty of "growing up," his feeling that "He did not want to be a man" (1.2.15). Through kinship and twinship with Sue, Jude seeks an alternative to the frustrating constructions of his masculinity that his culture holds out.[4]

By linking issues of self-definition to cultural practices, discourses, and institutions, Teresa de Lauretis and Linda Alcoff provide a way of thinking about a human subject "constructed through a continuous process, an ongoing constant renewal based on an interaction with the world . . . [defined] as experience. 'And thus [subjectivity] is produced not by external ideas, values, or material causes, but by one's personal, subjective engagement in the practices, discourses, and institutions that lend significance (value, meaning, and affect) to the events of the world.'" Alcoff goes on to note that this is the process "through which one's subjectivity becomes en-gendered."[5]

We may merge this concept of subjectivity with a Bakhtinian distinction between authoritatively persuasive and internally persuasive discourses that interact in the historical and cultural construction of a subject. Often, Bakhtin explains,

> an individual's becoming, an ideological process, is characterized precisely by a sharp gap between these two categories: in one, the authoritative word (religious, political, moral; the word of a father, of adults and of teachers, etc.) that does not know internal persuasiveness, in the other internally persuasive word that is denied all privilege, backed up by no authority at all, and is frequently not even acknowledged in society (not by public opinion, not by scholarly norms, nor by criticism), not even in the legal code. The struggle and dialogic interrelationship of these categories of ideological discourse are what usually determine the history of an individual ideological consciousness.[6]

Bakhtin offers an important dialogical model of an individual's engagement with the world, the struggle between the authoritatively persuasive and the internally persuasive word. In the wide gap between the two, however, he locates idealistically the possibility of individual choice and control over one's destiny.

In contrast, I would agree with Alcoff that authoritative discourse often takes on the aspect of the internally persuasive word, if not at first then at last.[7] De Lauretis explains further: "Self and identity, in other words, are always grasped and understood within particular discursive configurations. Consciousness, therefore, is never fixed, never attained once and for all, because discursive boundaries change with historical conditions."[8] Such a theory allows us to account for Jude's initial embrace, rejection, and final recuperation of his culture's religious, political, sexual, and moral discourses: the authoritative word of a father, of adults, of teachers. Jude's longing for Sue Bridehead is culturally embedded within this dynamic: he interprets her as that which his culture forbids. As an alternative to authoritative discourses, she embodies the internally persuasive voice.

It is a striking detail of the novel that Jude longs for Sue before he sees her, before he has even seen a picture of her. Why? Sue is introduced early in the novel in Aunt Drusilla's comments to a neighbor overheard by Jude. She links her two foster children through their love of books—"His cousin Sue is just the same" (1.2.9). Yet, she also contrasts Sue, a "tomboy," to Jude, a "poor useless boy," who has the sensibility and frame of a girl. Slender and small, Jude weeps easily and feels pain keenly: "he was a boy who could not himself bear to hurt anything," a tendency the narrator terms, only half-ironically, a "weakness of character" (1.2.13). Jude feels the assaults of his life so sharply that he wishes "he could only prevent himself growing up! He did not want to be a man" (1.2.15). Jude's desire to evade the constraints of manhood leads him to posit an alternative that he reifies in the character at once like and unlike him, his cousin, Sue.

The problem of becoming a man and the prohibition of Sue Bridehead are linked in Jude's mind by the early events at Marygreen and Aunt Drusilla's comments on the tragic issue of Fawley marriages. If marriage is fatal to one Fawley, the same blood flowing through two linked individuals must culminate in tragedy. Sue is, therefore, forbidden to Jude. Hardy encodes that prohibition as a function of fate or nature. Aunt Drusilla warns: "Jude, my child, don't *you* ever marry. 'Tisn't for the Fawleys to take that step any more" (1.2.9). Hardy himself defined his concern in the novel as "the tragic issues of two bad marriages, owing in the main to a doom or curse of hereditary temperament peculiar to the family of the partners."[9] The idea of hereditary taint reproduces in the narrator's attitudes the same conflicts that doom Jude. Such fatalistic discourse disguises the extent to which actual institutions coerce and thwart individuals, a process traced throughout the novel, which contemporaneous critics rightly recognized as a trenchant attack on authoritarian social practices and institutions.

That attack begins in the early events of the novel when Jude is hired to scare away the rooks come to peck the grain in Farmer Troutham's field. "His heart grew sympathetic with the birds' thwarted desires" (1.2.11), and he lets them feed until surprised by his angry employer who beats him. That beating, which chastens desire, initiates Jude's reluctance to become a man, at least a man fashioned after the class models most readily available to him.

In the process of formulating his identity, Jude fastens on Christminster and becoming a "university graduate," "the necessary hallmark of a man who wants to do anything in teaching" (1.1.4). Both are associated with Mr. Phillotson, his early model, and both are utterly distinguished from his current life, substituting as they do a middle-class for a lower-class model of manhood. Ironically, his aunt puts the idea in his head that such an occupation might suit her "poor boy." After Troutham fires Jude, she complains: "Jude, Jude, why didstn't go off with that schoolmaster of thine to Christminster or somewhere?" (1.2.14). He reverently anticipates that "Christminster shall be my Alma Mater; and I'll be her beloved son, in whom she shall be well pleased" (1.6.41). Although the Latin makes the school his mother, in fact, by entering Christminster, Jude would embrace an established patriarchal tradition, a fact underscored in the Biblical passage that Jude's rhetoric echoes: "This is my beloved Son, in whom I am well pleased" (Matthew 3:17).

Hardy frames the larger issue of Jude's struggle with social codes by stressing his desire to learn the languages of the past. Jude will master Latin and Greek with the goal of ultimately being authorized to speak as an educated, middle-class man. Latin, in particular, holds power over him even before he knows anything about it except its ascribed value. His longing for that authority culminates in a fanciful idea of Christminster as a "new Jerusalem" (1.3.20) and as a "mistress" (1.3.22) who is beckoning him to his fulfillment. The intensity with which Jude applies himself to these dead languages reveals their power, which is not simply the authoritatively persuasive word of his "fathers" and of the past, but quickly becomes an internally persuasive word guiding Jude's first major struggle toward self-definition. His ability to use Latin and to understand Latin will determine his behavior at later moments of crisis.

Until he is nineteen, Jude's sexual impulses are held completely in abeyance by his infatuation for the scholastic life. But Jude's encounter with Arabella Donn temporarily displaces the authority of intellectual discourse with another ideology. Generally, Jude's distraction has been interpreted as a capitulation to his natural sexual instincts, what the narrator characterizes as "The unvoiced call of woman to man, which . . . held Jude to the spot against his intention—almost against his will" (1.6.44). But sexual desire is not, in fact, what traps Jude. Notably, he is never the sexual aggressor with Arabella; she sees all his advances as "rather mild!" (1.7.52), and she has to plot rather cleverly to bring him to the point.

Two cultural paradigms of masculinity motivate Jude's divided drives. The first dictates that a "natural" man will find the stimulus of a proximate woman sufficient to arouse strong sexual desire, and it cuts across classes. The second involves the rhetoric of chivalric or honorable love and courtship and belongs more properly to the middle and upper classes. According to the first essentialist discourse, men are sexually different from women.[10] Even Phillotson, a middle-aged, staid scholar, can consummate and reconsummate his marriage with a rigid and unresponsive Sue Bridehead. He, after all, is a "man." Thus, although the rhetoric of the novel presents Jude's weakness for women as a fault, it also insists on that "weakness" or susceptibility as important evidence of manliness. When Jude fails to live up to other discursive formulations of his masculinity, this one never fails him, as we shall discover in the crucial final scenes of the novel.

Surprisingly, this rhetoric of manliness is not undercut by the behavior of Arabella Donn, who is always equally ready to engage in sexual relations. We may attribute that curious gap to the presence of the second authoritative discourse we have identified. When Jude becomes sexually involved with Arabella, he simultaneously becomes entangled in another discourse of manliness whose hallmark is romance, chivalry, and honor: "It was better to love a woman than to be a graduate, or a parson; ay, or a pope!" (1.7.53). These two discourses cooperate to construct the "gentle-man," a middle-class ideal. Notably, Phillotson is as bound by the second discourse as Jude; it initially determines his decision to let Sue leave him to go to Jude. He justifies his decision to Gillingham in the following way: "I don't think you are in a position to give an opinion. I have been that man, and it makes all the difference in the world, if one has any manliness or chivalry in him" (4.4.278).

Jude's susceptibility to the chivalric code of helpless women and protective and honorable men allows Arabella to use her claim of pregnancy to trap him into marriage. In spite of the fact that Jude knows too well "that Arabella was not worth a great deal as a specimen of womankind," "he was ready to abide by what he had said, and take the consequences" and "save [her] ready or no" (1.9.65, 70). His susceptibility to this discourse—a function of his middle-class aspirations—distinguishes Jude's "finer" aspirations and sensibilities from the "peasant cynicism" of country women like Arabella and Aunt Drusilla. According to their discourse, he is a "simple fool" (1.9.65) and "poor silly fellow" (1.9.66). When Arabella's plot is revealed, Jude vaguely ponders not his own folly, but "something wrong in a social ritual" (1.9.70). In fact, Jude's construction of manliness betrays him because he applies a middle-class ethic to Arabella's classic peasant ruse.

After Jude should have learned the bankruptcy of this patriarchal code of male honor and female victims—in its inapplicability to his relationship with Arabella where he is the defenseless innocent and she the practiced seducer—it seems inexplicably naive of him to persist in it. Yet such persistence provides another example of the ways in which authoritative discourses becomes internally persuasive. Indeed, Jude clings to such constructions both because they define him as middle-class and because they define him as masculine (not simply as male). Jude learns from Arabella *not* to question the adequacy of such formulations but only to "feel dissatisfied with himself as a man at what he had done" (1.10.76).

Such class and gender constructions of his masculinity come to seem essential to Jude's identity. When Arabella and Jude separate at her instigation, Jude returns to his dream of education in Christminster, motivated by another pair of self-images. First, he reaffirms his dream of modeling his manhood and *embourgeoisement* on the schoolteacher, Phillotson. In addition, he pursues an elusive superiority and gender neutrality figured by his middle-class cousin, Sue Bridehead, whom he has seen only in a photograph. The narrator explains this new motive as "more nearly related to the emotional side of him than to the intellectual, as is often the case with young men." It really is surprising that Jude should be led to Christminster by a photograph, especially after his disastrous marriage. But we accept the motive, I believe, because we recognize that Sue offers an alternative version of his problematic self. She is like Jude, after all, also "of the inimical branch of the family" (2.1.90).

Entering Christminster at evening, Jude immediately feels himself in the presence of "those other sons of the place" (2.1.93), a kind of patrillineage that seems to promise accommodation for a humble laborer. But in the morning, "he found that the colleges had treacherously changed their sympathetic countenances. . . . The spirits of the great men had disappeared" (2.2.97). Although Jude is momentarily impressed by the dignity of manual labor, what the narrator calls a "true illumination"—that the "stone yard was a centre of effort as worthy as that dignified by the name of scholarly study within the noblest of colleges"—he soon loses this impression "under the stress of his old idea" (2.2.98). Ironically, this discourse of manual labor's dignity stems from the middle-class intellectual elite, and the very condescension implicit in the perspective undermines its validity. So the narrator reproduces in his own rhetoric the conflicts that will doom Jude. Because Jude will *be* a manual laborer denied access to scholarly pursuits, the gap opened up will lead him increasingly to Sue as an authentic alternative. Not surprisingly, then, no sooner is Jude aware of the gap between his aspirations and his pursuits than his passion for Sue intensifies. He insists his aunt send his cousin's portrait, "kissed it—he did not know why—and felt more at home. . . . It was . . . the one thing uniting him to the emotions of the living city" (2.2.99).

This extraordinary scene of alienation and "at homeness" makes Sue pivotal to the construction of Jude's identity. Jude's claim of blood and emotional kinship (she "belongs" to him) suggests that his investment in her is deeply tied to his gender identity (2.2.103). Before meeting her, Jude has already internalized Sue's being as essential to his own subjecthood, a process intensified by his aunt's prohibition that "he was not to bring disturbance into the family by going to see the girl" (2.2.99). Sue represents what is in him but also what he is not to seek in himself, which is here coded as the feminine. His desire to discover that alternative, of course, results from his frustrations with both lower-class social definitions of manhood and the conflicts introduced by middle-class codes. When he first locates Sue, he "recognized in the accents certain qualities *of his own voice.*" (2.2.103) [my emphasis]. Later Jude sees Sue, dressed in his clothes, as "a slim and fragile being masquerading as himself on a Sunday" (3.3.173). He affirms, "You are just like me at heart!" (4.1.243). Phillotson corroborates the "extraordinary sympathy, or similarity, between the pair. . . . They seem to be one person split in two!" (4.4.276). Jude appropriates Sue to ground his floundering self in her "social and spiritual possibilities" (2.3.107).

Jude alternates between reflections on Sue as an "ideality" or a "divinity"—totally divorced from the coarse Arabella—and sexual longings for her. The tension in Jude's view has often been interpreted as stemming from Sue's "inconsistency"—her waxing hot and cold, her frigidity coupled with her desire for attention. But this approach to her character as a charming neurotic tends to ignore her fictional, cultural, and tendentious construction. I propose, instead, that the tension within the narrator's depiction of Sue reflects Jude's complex investment in her, which also causes him to hide from her his marriage to Arabella.

The urgent need Jude feels for Sue stems from his increasingly precarious sense of masculine identity and social significance. Comparing Christminster's "town life" to its "gown life" (2.6.139), he characterizes the former as the "real Christminster life" (2.7.141). The text implies that, if Jude were not possessed by "the modern vice of unrest" (2.2.98), not a "paltry victim of the spirit of mental and social restlessness" (6.1.393–94), he might be able to have a more authentic existence, that is, one grounded in a secure sense of who and what he is. At such moments, the narrator seems implicated in the same ideological illusions and conflicts that condemn Jude. The idea of an authentic existence is problematic in the text. Thus, Jude flounders among social markers for masculine identity and increasingly turns to Sue as the source of his meaning, finally concluding, "with Sue as companion he could have renounced his ambitions with a smile" (2.6.137). Of course, Jude is naive to believe he can easily renounce his ambitions; they are already too important to his self-concept, as we shall see.

In the novel's first half, Jude progresses from would-be intellectual, to honorable young husband (Marygreen), to would-be intellectual again (Christminster), to would-be ecclesiastic (Melchester)—each stage dominated by a particular authoritative discourse that promises to make a man of Jude. All the while Jude keeps in reserve his dream of Sue as a means to construct a self outside unsatisfactory patriarchal models: "To keep Sue Bridehead near him was now a desire which operated without regard of consequences" (2.4.121). Only the force of his need explains why Jude cannot tell Sue of his marriage to Arabella and must instead project his failure and secretiveness onto her as *her* inconsistency. When he finally and belatedly informs her and lamely excuses himself—"It seemed cruel to tell it"—she justly rebukes him, "To yourself, Jude. So it was better to be cruel to me!" (3.6.198).

When Jude finally reveals his marriage to Arabella, he also begins to generalize about Sue as a "woman." Such generalizations characterize the two points in the narrative when Jude must defend himself against separation from Sue, first here and then at the end of the novel. Previously, Sue has been represented in a more gender-neutral way, as a "tomboy," who joins boys in their exploits, or as a "comrade" with a "curious unconsciousness of gender" (3.4.179), who mixes with men "almost as one of their own sex" (3.4.177). Impelled to defend his own sexuality, Jude now stresses Sue's need to exercise "those narrow womanly humours on impulse that were necessary to give her sex" (3.6.200). Sue both is and is not a typical woman depending on Jude's psychosocial investment in her. At those points when he fears he will lose her, he tends to brand her typical of her sex to distance himself from his need for her. He repeats this distancing act at Susanna's marriage to Phillotson: "Women were different from men in such matters. Was it that they were, instead of more sensitive, as reported, more callous and less romantic?" (3.7.209).

Sue's self-generalizations as woman have a somewhat different textual function. She says, for example, in reference to herself, "some women's love of being loved is insatiable" (4.1.245). Such comments reinforce Jude's characterizations of Sue as asexual "spirit," a "disembodied creature," a "dear, sweet, tantalizing phantom—hardly flesh at all" (4.5.294). The spiritualization preserves her as the endlessly desired object, a Shelleyan Epipsyche. The text demands, above all, "the elusiveness of her curious double nature" (4.2.251).

The last half of the novel focuses the tension between Jude's need to be the man his culture demands and his desire to locate a more fulfilling existence outside custom and convention. When Jude argues his similarity to his cousin—"for you are just like me at heart"—she demurs, "But not at head." And when he insists, "we are both alike," she corrects him, "Not in our thoughts" (4.1.243). Their disagreement arises because Sue's attractiveness disrupts but cannot displace the categories of masculinity Jude has already internalized. Jude is drawn in two directions because he can never fully abandon the categories of thought he has imbibed from his culture.

Constructed as an outsider to patriarchal culture, Sue can articulate social tensions that Jude can then increasingly recognize. She argues, "the social moulds civilization fits us into have no more relation to our actual shapes than the conventional shapes of the constellations have to the real star-patterns" (4.1.246–47). When Sue asks Jude, hypothetically, if a woman with a repugnance for her husband ought "to try to overcome her pruderies," he responds in contradictory ways, "speaking as an order-loving man . . . I should say yes. Speaking from experience and unbiased nature, I should say no" (4.2.252). Shortly thereafter, under pressure of his love for Sue, Jude announces, "my doctrines and I begin to part company" (4.2.258). After he passionately kisses Sue, Jude realizes that "he was as unfit, obviously by nature, as he had been by social position, to fill the part of a propounder of accredited dogma." Yet barred by Sue's marriage to Phillotson and his own marriage to Arabella, Jude has recourse to the category of "woman" to explain his difficulties: "Strange that his first aspiration—toward academical proficiency—had been checked by a woman, and that his second aspiration—toward apostleship—had also been checked by a woman. 'Is it,' he said, 'that women are to blame.' " (4.3.261).

The conclusion, "women are to blame," lodges Jude's reasoning within a traditional framework that takes him back to the Garden of Eden, Genesis, and Eve's temptation and fall. Although Jude should reject a discourse so inadequate to his experience, instead he reauthorizes its tenets on women. Such constructions are so essential to his subjectivity that they cannot be completely abandoned. Indeed, it is important to Jude that "he might go on *believing* as before but he *professed* nothing" (4.3.262, my italics).

The role of women as temptresses in this narrative corresponds to an ideology of masculinity that suggests sex is, for a man, a snare that leads first to entrapment, then disillusionment, and even damnation. As we have seen, a deep ideological subtext of the novel argues that a "man" is inherently disposed toward sexual relations and will find women a lure to physical intimacy. The fact that sexual familiarity may culminate in contempt does not prevent his being ready to behave sexually on the next encounter. A companion ideology stipulates that, whatever his feelings, a "gentle-man" will then behave honorably toward the "victimized" woman. The logic of these interlocking ideologies supports Jude's sexual relations with Arabella, both initially and following a chance encounter after several years' separation.

Jude's embrace of the gentlemanly ethic allows the lower-class Arabella repeatedly to exploit him. Similarly, when Arabella later appeals to Jude to follow her to her hotel to hear her story, and Sue objects, Jude argues: "I shall certainly give her something, and hear what it is she is so anxious to tell me; no man could do less!" (5.2.318). Arabella pronounces, "Never such a tender fool as Jude is if a woman seems in trouble" (5.2.324).

All of Jude's justifications of his behavior produce essentialist views of men and women. When Sue asks, "Why should you take such trouble for a woman who has served you so badly," he responds, "But, Sue, she's a woman, and I once cared for her; and one [a man] can't be a brute in such circumstances" (5.2.319). In response to Sue's accusation that his behavior is "gross," Jude replies, "You don't understand me either—women never do!" (4.5.293). By generalizing from "you"—Sue—to "women," Jude also implicitly generalizes from "me"—Jude—to "men." Women do not understand men or male sexuality.

Jude's determination to fulfill a "man's" obligations to Arabella exerts a sexual coercion on Sue, who precipitously agrees to sleep with Jude to erase Arabella's claims on him. When Sue's capitulates, Jude transfers to her his sexual allegiance and chivalric code. Arabella is no longer "a woman" but her clever self: "You haven't the least idea how Arabella is able to shift for herself" (5.2.322).

The sexual possession of Sue marks a crux in the novel and in Jude's self-construction. It permits him to define his male "nature" as one given to sensual indulgence—wine, women, and blasphemy. But he also aspires to a value outside a carnal construction of his masculinity that he locates in his relations with Sue. He tells her: "All that's best and noblest in me loves you, and your freedom from everything that's gross has elevated me, and enabled me to do what I should never have dreamt myself capable of, *or any man*, a year or two ago" (5.2.320, my italics). The kinship Jude feels for this female self allows him to move beyond the patriarchal imprimatur, defining an identity he had not believed accessible to himself or any man. In the "nomadic" phase of their life together, Jude "was mentally approaching the position which Sue had occupied when he first met her" (5.7.373).

Their kinship will be undermined by the cultural codes that define Jude's masculinity. Although Jude is represented as sharing Sue's anxiety about the constraints of marriage, his behavior is simultaneously shaped by Biblical injunctions on manhood: "For what man is he that hath betrothed a wife and hath not taken her?" (5.4.338). And although the couple is exquisitely happy in their life together—returned, in Sue's words, to "Greek joyousness" (5.5.358)—Jude reveals his continuing attraction to Christminster in the Model of Cardinal College he and Sue have made for the Wessex Agricultural Show. Despite the narrator's insistence on Jude's independence of thought, he chooses to bake "Christminster cakes" when he is pressed for employment after his illness. Arabella neatly pinpoints his continuing obsession and slavery to his former ideals: "Still harping on Christminster—even in his cakes. . . . Just like Jude. A ruling passion." Sue admits: "Of course Christminster is a sort of fixed vision with him, which I suppose he'll never be cured of believing in. He still thinks it a great centre of high and fearless thought, instead of what it is, a nest of commonplace schoolmasters whose characteristic is timid obsequiousness to tradition" (5.7.376).

Arabella's accidental meeting with Phillotson, immediately following her rencontre with Sue, sets the stage for the series of reversals or "returns" that conclude the novel. Her crude invocation of Old Testament law and learning as a model for contemporary behavior prepares us for the way in which Jude, as well as Phillotson, will be drawn back to the authority and consequence held out to them as men in a patriarchal society. Arabella states: "There's nothing like bondage and a stone-deaf taskmaster for taming us women. Besides, you've got the laws on your side Moses knew. . . . 'Then shall the man be guiltless; but the woman shall bear her iniquity' " (5.8.384). Arabella's addendum—"Damn rough on us women; but we must grin and put up wi' it!"—comfortably accepts a damaging gender bifurcation that Jude and even Phillotson have struggled to overcome in their response to Sue Bridehead. When Sue questions, "Why should you care so much for Christminster?" Jude replies: "I can't help it. I love the place. . . . it is the centre of the universe to me, because of my early dream. . . . I should like to go back to live there—perhaps to die there!" (5.8.386). Part 5 culminates with the realization of his dream to return there; Part 6 culminates with the realization of his dream to die there.

We, too, ask Sue's questions: why does Jude suddenly develop a passionate desire to return to Christminster for this Remembrance Day, and why does he return in a way so entirely forgetful of Sue and his children? Then, why does Jude persist in his resolve to seek work in Christminster after it has become the scene of his grotesque tragedy and can serve only as a reminder of that tragedy? In fact, the text occludes these questions and shifts focus to Sue Bridehead's intellectual, sexual, and emotional degradation. But there are significant ideological implications in that textual strategy. These breaks and shifts reveal their inner logic if we keep our eye on Jude's alternating evasion and pursuit of manhood.

Jude's return to Christminster spells a rejection of Sue and a reembrace of the patriarchal discourse that originally attracted him. Whereas on one level it seems absurd to say that Jude has rejected Sue since he pleads for her emotional and physical return to him, the subtext of the novel argues differently. By returning to Christminster, Jude privileges a hierarchic order in opposition to his more egalitarian relationship with Sue. Indeed, by delaying the search for housing, he shifts the burden of their relationship onto Sue, who bears the visible evidence of their three children and her pregnancy while he again becomes, in effect, the unencumbered novice who first entered the city several years earlier. When he again seeks lodging in his old quarter, Beersheba, he continues to replicate his earlier patterns. The unbearable poignancy of the novel's last section derives not only from the representation of Sue's collapse but also from the painful tension between Jude's embrace and rejection of Sue, a rejection that demands the collapse of her textual function as a significant alternative.

Jude longs for the spirit of the law, but is drawn to the letter as primary ground of his identity. Jude finally seeks an authority to define the meaning of his life, and he must do that from within the system, from a position that validates the system and its judgments of him as a failed man who has "missed everything." This final need for authority explains Jude's return to Christminster. Jude wants that intellectual milieu to frame the tragic limitation of his manhood. *If,* as Sue says, Christminster is only a "nest of commonplace schoolmasters," then Jude's life is a relative success. To give his life the tragic cast he favors, he must reauthorize Christminster. Relationship with Sue originally provided a focal point for a critique of authoritative discourse. Now that relationship, in its domestic and quotidian aspects, cuts away the ground of meaning necessary to Jude's "tragedy." The triumphant tragedy of Jude's life is only apparent when inscribed within the dominant, authoritative discourse of Christminster. It is under that authority that he can echo Shakespeare's *Romeo and Juliet* in summarizing his life: "However, it was my poverty and not my will that consented to be beaten. It takes two or three generations to do what I tried to do in one" (6.1.393).

The narrative sequence supports a reading of Jude's return to Christminster as a rejection of Sue Bridehead. First, Jude chooses to return on Remembrance Day when the city is teeming with visitors. Upon arrival he initially insists that "the first thing is lodgings," but he quickly abandons that goal in his desire to hurry to the procession, ignoring Sue's demurral: "Oughtn't we to get a house over our heads first?" Although "his soul seemed full of the anniversary," Jude announces that Remembrance Day is really "Humiliation Day for me!" a "lesson in presumption," an image of his own "failure" (6.1.390). Of course, to see his failure is also to see the possibility of success, to see that he might have become "a son of the University." The Alma Mater as pater familias. As it begins to rain and "Sue again wished not to stay," Jude grows more enthusiastic as he rediscovers old friends and reevaluates his life. He says he is "in a chaos of principles— groping in the dark—acting by instinct and not after example" (6.1.394), thereby grounding his identity in the context of Christminster and its definitions of success. Through that prism he reexamines his life, granting to Christminster authority to write his "romance," the middle-class tragic romance of the common man: "I'm an outsider to the end of my days!" (6.1.396).

Throughout the entire day, through thunderstorms and drenchings, Jude ignores his pale, reluctant wife and his several children to bask once more in the reflected glory of Christminster, "to catch a few words of the Latin," and so, in spirit, join the fraternity that has otherwise excluded him. He may tell Sue that "I'll never care any more about the infernal cursed place," but as they belatedly begin to search for lodgings, Jude is drawn to "Mildew Lane," close to the back of a college, a spot he finds "irresistible" and Sue "not so fascinating" (6.1.396). She is finally housed outside Sarcophagus and Rubric Colleges, Hardy's symbolically appropriate names, and she contemplates "the strange operation of a simple-minded man's ruling passion, that it should have led Jude, who loved her and the children so tenderly, to place them here in this depressing purlieu, because he was still haunted by his dream" (6.2.401). Jude's pursuit of his "dream" has left Sue and the children terribly exposed, and the events culminate in Father Time's suicide and murder of the other two children. Sue claims responsibility for these tragic events and neither the narrator nor Jude disputes her interpretation, yet responsibility really belongs to Jude who, in returning to Christminster, rejected Sue and his children for his old "dream."

Sue now takes on the narrative function of justifying Jude: "My poor Jude—how you've missed everything!—you more than I, for I did get you! To think you should know that [the chorus of the *Agamemnon*] by your unassisted reading, and yet be in poverty and despair!" (6.2.409). There is nothing in the narrative that contradicts Sue's assessment. Thus the text can endorse the position that Jude "missed everything" while Sue, in getting Jude, apparently "got" what she wanted. It is ironic that she, who was supposed to be what he wanted, now stands debased, as the coin he received for his labors, an emblem of what riches he has missed.

It is a further irony that the only blame Jude accepts is for "seducing" Sue, a grotesque reinterpretation of his desire for Sue. He claims, "I have seemed to myself lately . . . to belong to that vast band of men shunned by the virtuous—the men called seducers. . . . Yes, Sue—that's what I am. I seduced you. . . . You were a distinct type—a refined creature, intended by Nature to be left intact" (6.3.414). The idea of Jude as seducer presents an absurd reduction of their complex relationship with its twin fulfillments of independence and happiness. But a reconstruction of the scenario with himself as seducer serves the function of reconstructing yet another social aspect of Jude's manhood.

As Jude adopts these conventional, middle-class gender terms, he deprives Sue of any meaningful textual role outside parallel gender stereotypes, which dictate that the chaste but violated female move toward self-sacrificing, punitive, masochistic degradation. We return, once more, to the generalizations about women that were absent during the long emotional and sexual intimacy between Jude and Sue: "Is woman a thinking unit at all, or a fraction always wanting its integer?" (6.3.424). The text's positioning of comments like this one suggests that Sue's function as desirable other, a space free from the socially coded and rigid definition of manhood, has been exhausted or used up. In order for Jude to reclaim the construction of his manhood implicit first in Christminster and then in his relationship with Arabella, Sue must be reinterpreted as merely a pathetic woman whose mind has become unhinged. Hence, her "inconsistency."

This strict sexual bifurcation figures in the novel's closing rhetoric. Sue says to Jude, "Your wickedness was only the natural man's desire to possess the woman" (6.3.426). And, on Sue's return, Phillotson says ominously, "I know woman better now" (6.5.442). Sue accounts for her own role in the relationship by admitting to an "inborn craving which undermines some women's morals. . . . the craving to attract and captivate, regardless of the injury it may do the man" (6.3.426).

Jude returns to the twin evils of his life, his "two Arch Enemies . . . my weakness for womankind and my impulse to strong liquor" (6.3.427). He embraces in his Christminster dreams and the cruel reality of marriage to Arabella the same constricting construction of his manhood which figured prominently in the opening pages of the novel. Although drunk, Jude calls up the established discourse of manliness to justify remarrying Arabella: "I'd marry the W—— of Babylon rather than do anything dishonourable. . . . marry her I will, so help me God! . . . I am not a man who wants to save himself at the expense of the weaker among us!" (6.7.461–62). By sacrificing himself to the sham of this "meretricious contract with Arabella," Jude, of course, preserves a definition of manhood essential to his identity.

The honor, the rectitude, the righteousness, and the learning that Jude claims as the hallmarks of his middle-class manhood allow him to die with the words of Job on his lips: "Let the day perish wherein I was born, and the night in which it was said, There is a man child conceived" (6.11.488). Such an invocation accords well with the other discourses Jude has previously embraced.

In *Jude the Obscure*, Hardy has given us a novel in which the authoritatively persuasive word ultimately becomes the internally persuasive one in the construction of one man's subjectivity. In the process, Hardy has revealed masculinity as a cultural and social class construct, one that coerces and limits individuals even as it holds out the irresistible promise of conferring definitive meaning on their lives. In Jude's longing for Sue, Hardy has made us feel the poignant desire for a self free from such coercive definitions, the need for some more flexible way to confront the problem of "growing up ... to be a man," for some way to feel satisfied with himself as a man (1.2.15). In Sue's emotional and intellectual collapse, which proleptically justifies Jude's return to the Christminster way, he has made us feel the virtual impossibility of any individual defining himself in opposition to the dominant culture of his or her society. Jude's death and Sue's degradation, the events concluding the novel, arrest but do not resolve the text's testing of discursive formulations of gender paradigms. The anticipated unfolding of a subject proves to be an involution, a collapse inward resisted only by social practices and discourses that mock the idea of individual self-determination and locate self-fulfillment in death.

Early in her relationship with Jude, Sue Bridehead claims that, "We are a little beforehand, that's all" (5.4.345). In fact, she is only partly right; Jude and Sue are constructed by the very terms they seek to transcend. The lingering sadness of this novel lies in its apprehension of the ways destructive cultural self-constructions ultimately reach out to claim them, the ways, indeed, they are always already within, crucial to the formation and development of individual subjecthood and therefore perilous to reject. This modern understanding of the problematic subject and the material basis for subjectivity allows Hardy to give us a trenchant interrogation of the cultural construction of gender paradigms and their often contradictory inflections by class. It also allows him to generate a new form of tragic irony in the disparity between what we can understand and aspire to and what we can ultimately become—undermined, as we are, from within. Hardy's depiction of this ineluctable dilemma of identity gives him a distinctive place in the Victorian canon and suggests significant links with a modern sensibility, which has been acknowledged in his poetry but not so readily in his novels. In this regard, we may recognize Hardy as both the most modern of Victorians, and, in the poignancy of his final novel, the most Victorian of moderns.

NOTES

1. In 1895 Hardy wrote about *Jude the Obscure,* "Sue is a type of woman which has always had an attraction for me, but the difficulty of drawing the type has kept me from attempting it till now" (letter to Edmond Gosse, November 20, 1895, in F. E. Hardy, *The Life of Thomas Hardy* [London: Macmillan, 1962], 280). Albert J. Guerard, *Thomas Hardy: The Novels and Stories* (Cambridge: Harvard University

Press, 1949), 113. Irving Howe has characterized that type as the "epicene woman"—the ethereal, spiritualized, undersexed coquette who drives men to distraction. So summarized, Sue Bridehead may seem a monstrously unpleasant person, as unpleasant as most fictional neurotics. But she is, as it happens, one of Hardy's most appealing heroines" (*Thomas Hardy* [New York: Macmillan, 1967], 143, See also A. Alvarez, who asserts, "in creating [Sue] Hardy did something extraordinarily original: he created one of the few totally narcissistic women in literature, but he did so at the same time as he made her something rather wonderful." "Afterword," Thomas Hardy, *Jude the Obscure* (New York: New American Library, 1961), 410. These contradictory assessments result, in part, from a failure to account for Jude's perspective on and construction of his cousin.

2. See Langland, "A Perspective of One's Own: Thomas Hardy and the Elusive Sue Bridehead," *Studies in the Novel* 12 (Spring 1980): 12–28. Michael Millgate locates an ambivalence in Hardy himself: "the book's implied judgment of Sue's character and conduct seems finally uncertain and inconsistent" (*Thomas Hardy: A Biography* [Oxford: Oxford University Press, 1982], 353–54).

3. Hardy's novel *The Well-Beloved*, the writing of which frames *Jude the Obscure*, also deals with a man's idealization of a female figure, but, here, the idealization is so explicit that critics immediately recognize the women—Avice one, two, and three—as reflections of Jocelyn Pierson's needs. For example, J. Hillis Miller remarks, "The drama of *The Well Beloved* is throughout a more internal one [than that of *Jude*]. It is the story of the single consciousness divided against itself, striving to merge again with itself, seeing in others even of the opposite sex, only its own double" (*Fiction and Repetition* [Cambridge: Harvard University Press, 1982], 160). From the perspective of *The Well Beloved*, it is not difficult to see how Sue Bridehead, too, is a narcissistic projection of Jude's ambivalent wishes. We might also argue that Jocelyn's fitful response to the beloved and her shifting incarnations also expresses his desire for yet fear of the feminine.

4. One critic who has, surprisingly, approximated some of my insights, although within a very different theoretical framework, is D. H. Lawrence, *Phoenix: The Posthumous Papers of D. H. Lawrence*, ed. E. D. McDonald (New York: Viking, 1936), 497–510. That is, where I would not follow Lawrence's essentializing discourse of male and female, I find very insightful his apprehension of the coercive force Jude exerts on Sue to fulfill his needs. Joseph Wiesenfarth points to the Lacanian implications of Jude's and Sue's behavior, noting that "they seek the Other to validate their own sense of self. . . . [but ultimately] Jude and Sue repudiate the penis [sexual desire] for the phallus ['an approved male dominated cultural code']." I emphasize instead Hardy's focus on Jude and the social construction of character (*Gothic Manners and the Classic English Novel* [Madison: University of Wisconsin Press, 1988], 152).

5. Linda Alcoff quoting Teresa de Lauretis in "Cultural Feminism Versus Post-Structuralism: The Identity Crisis in Feminist Theory," *Signs*, 13 (Spring 1988): 423.

6. M. M. Bakhtin, *The Dialogic Imagination: Four Essays* (Austin: University of Texas Press, 1981), 342.

7. Alcoff, "Cultural Feminism," 428–33.

8. Teresa de Lauretis, "Feminist Studies/Critical Studies: Issues, Terms and Contexts," in *Feminist Studies/Critical Studies,* ed. Teresa de Lauretis (Bloomington: Indiana University Press, 1986), 8.

9. "To Edmund Gosse: Nov. 10, 1895," in *The Collected Letters of Thomas Hardy,* eds. Richard Little Purdy and Michael Millgate, vol. 2 (Oxford: Clarendon Press, 1980), 93.

10. In an illuminating article that employs the insights of Austin and speech theory, William R. Goetz makes a similar observation about the status of the "natural." Goetz notes that, "In *Jude the Obscure* the natural law initially seems to be prior to the social law, which must be interpreted as either an "enunciation" or a deformation of it. By the end of the novel, these two laws are threatening to collapse into one." Ultimately, we discover these are "false options . . . between a life in society and a life in nature. There is no authentic possibility of a life outside of the law in *Jude*" ("Felicity and Infelicity of Marriage in *Jude the Obscure,*" *Nineteenth Century Fiction,* 38 [Sept. 1983]: 212–13).

Narrative, Gender, and Power in *Far from the Madding Crowd*

Linda M. Shires

Are you a woman?
   —Thomas Hardy

The woman—for it was a woman—approached.
                        —Thomas Hardy

In chapter 44 of *Far from the Madding Crowd* Bathsheba Everdene, Mrs. Troy, runs away and hides in a fern brake. In a sudden act of revolt, born of humiliation at the hands of her husband, who has just confided his unsurpassed love for the dead Fanny Robin, Bathsheba seeks escape from a domain of male victimization. Running without direction in the darkness, she happens by chance on a thicket that seems familiar and drops down into a deep slumber. This seemingly protected spot, so like the tree-hung enclosure where Tess d'Urberville loses her virginity, appears far more congenial than it is in actuality. Bathsheba, stripped of a role and a right she thought was hers, wishes to slip back into a void of pregendered nothingness. The possibility of death, which she seriously entertains, signifies peace from gender struggle and specifically what she perceives as male domination. On a deeper level, however, Bathsheba here enacts a crisis of gender.[1]

Her disappearance into this wet hollow is fully emblematic of a return to the womb. Indeed, because it is extremely damp, she even loses her voice, the most authoritative, acculturated aspect of herself. Losing her power over language, the strong farmer is reduced to a lost infant. It is as if Hardy, who has revealed Bathsheba, in the early part of the text, to be a colorfully coy temptress and has later shown her as a willful woman in a male profession, forces her to start over again.

On the level of story, this pivotal scene not only continues to define the heroine but also functions as a rebirth. Relying on condensation as if a dream, it also operates as a triple gender scenario: it is a fantasy of gender annulment, a scene of gender mixing, and a drama of sexual choice. In this sense, chapter 44, to which I will return, incapsulates the deepest concerns of the novel.

From its publication, *Far from the Madding Crowd* generated, like other novels by Hardy, extensive commentary on gender and power. But more than others, it encouraged comment and confusion about sex and gender— both that of its author and that of its hero and heroine, Gabriel Oak and Bathsheba Everdene. When *Far from the Madding Crowd* appeared anonymously in the *Cornhill Magazine,* the *Spectator* review of January 3, 1874, insisted that Thomas Hardy's serial must have been written by a woman, none other than the George Eliot of *Adam Bede.* Such a mistake fascinates by its utter rightness and wrongness. For the reviewer accurately picks up the gender blurring of the text, but attributes it to a woman with a man's name who has written a patriarchal pastoral. In so doing, he mistakes the situation of the novel's authoring for the very topic of the narrative. Hardy, however, has taken immense pains to write a nonpatri- archal pastoral, so seduced is he by his own love for the unaggressive feminine, which he does not limit to one sex.

Hardy was reported to have been both flattered and distressed by the authorial gender confusion.[2] He must have been equally frustrated, however, by the critical reception of his heroine. To Henry James she was "inconse- quential, wilful and mettlesome," "unable to be understood or liked."[3] The reviewer of the *Observer* was even more critical, citing her lack of modesty and expressing sorrow that "Gabriel Oak was not sufficiently manly to refuse to have anything more to say to such an incorrigible hussy."[4] Aligning biology, stereotyped gender roles, and power, both reviewers fail to respond to the signifying activity of this text, which totally destabilizes gender and power.

Feminist critics have not paid sufficient attention to *Far from the Mad- ding Crowd,* but when they have written on it, they have often just reversed the male Victorian reviewers' opinions. The two most recent assessments, while allowing for female sexuality as resistance in a male- dominated world, read the text as a male discourse intent on taming the heroine.[5] These critics do not judge Oak as lacking in manliness; indeed, they read him as a patriarch who would control Bathsheba from the start, and who does so in the end. They interpret Bathsheba, in turn, as passively entangled in a sexual ideology that positions any woman in terms of her being desired but not in terms of her desiring. In their view, Bathsheba is objectified by the regard of her suitors.[6] The woman farmer, so resistant to becoming man's property, is gazed at obsessively by Oak, taken in by the sexual aggressor Troy, humiliated first by him and then by the persistence of Farmer Boldwood, broken, and married off to Oak in a final gesture of Hardyesque taming.[7]

Such feminist criticism, eloquent and important though it clearly is on the issue of woman's oppression, runs the risk of reverse sexism, while it concurrently denies female agency. As Michèle Barrett has argued: "An analysis of gender ideology in which women are always innocent, always passive victims of patriarchal power, is patently not satisfactory."[8] This is a particularly grievous error in the case of Hardy's work, not because he is a woman-worshipper, itself suspect, but because his texts award and deny power of differing kinds to both sexes unpredictably. His commitment to documenting the vagaries of existence mandates that, in spite of the sexual ideologies of his day, he does not believe in a dialectical theory of power where one sex oppresses the other, but rather in power as shifting, as attained and lost by multiple negotiations that cross gender, age, and class in a world he perceives as inconsistent, illogical, and "made up so largely of compromise" (5.42). His point of view is part of, but not a mere reflection of, a conflict over gender and power being waged at the site of late-Victorian female subjectivity.

Gender and power are not permanently aligned in *Far from the Madding Crowd*. Joining feminist theory to a theory of narrative informed by psychoanalysis and semiotics, I expose some of the ruptures and excesses that continually destabilize power and gender. I am specifically concerned with the representation of gender and how it alters in the text before sexual difference is reestablished through the fixing of closure.[9] My methodology could be adapted for an analysis of class and other marks of difference, but space does not permit an adequate working out of these complications.

While preceding feminist readings align power with the male and victimization with the female, and thus the cultural construction of gender with biology, I argue for Hardy's representations of gender as subtle, mobile, and heterogeneous. I analyze the representation of masculinity through the seemingly male-engendered events of gazing at the female and of wielding weapons. Finally, two critical events of gender crisis and choice will serve as examples for my analysis of femininity. Feminists must attend more closely not only to those social meanings kept in place by alignments of gender and power at the start and the close of a text but also to those which circulate disruptively. Such a strategy can splinter the monolith of patriarchy and make room for female power.

II

Because any narrative organizes signifying activity and places signifying units in that field, elements of narrative such as story, character, temporal order, and others function as signs in the same way that a word or image does. Thus a given narrative, like *Far from the Madding Crowd* can be broken down and segmented in order to identify the most stressful points of emphasis and strain which are organized by structure and stabilized by closure. Although the narrative system appears to determine a given text's meaning by containing the play of narrativity within a closed form, a narrative structure can never guarantee or exhaust meaning.[10]

An "ideal" narrative, according to Tzvetan Todorov, (111), begins with a stable situation: (here, for instance, steady bachelor Oak, sheep-owner, observes and hopes to marry the young Bathsheba). There follows a state of disequilibrium, which in this text has much to do with gender, sexuality, and social power: (Bathsheba refuses him; Oak loses his ability to provide for a wife; Bathsheba inherits her uncle's farm; she falls in love with and marries Troy; Boldwood falls in love with her etc.). By the action of a force directed in the opposite direction, the equilibrium is reestablished: Bathsheba recognizes that she does not want to lose Oak, now her farm manager, a landowner himself, and a friend, so she visits him, indicating her interest sufficiently enough that he proposes again and they marry.[11]

A story recounts this type of transformation in two ways. It syntagmatically places events in a sequence to organize signifying relations of addition and combination. For example, Bathsheba sends a Valentine to Boldwood, he falls in love, he gazes on her at the market. But events are also structured paradigmatically so that one event replaces another, organizing relations of substitution and selection based on location, character, or event type, as when a herd of sheep, Fanny Robin, and Sergeant Troy all die. For purposes of analysis, then, a story can be segmented into events, and events can be distinguished from each other (and so identified as signifiers) according to the way in which the story sets them in a structure of syntagmatic and paradigmatic relations.

As is obvious from the examples, the paradigmatic structure of a story stresses the importance of closure as a means of containing the movement that the syntagmatic structure produces, halting the linear unfoldings with a closure that discloses. Thus, while *Far from the Madding Crowd* propels its story forward through postponement (organizing a field of commutable and plural meanings through misunderstandings, chance connections, and so forth, which all delay closure), it also structures events paradigmatically to reach that point of closure where all story movement ceases: Gabriel and Bathsheba finally marry.

Narratology can thus aid in answering questions that earlier feminist critics have not worked out: What is the nature of Oak's masculinity and power? How have they been negotiated in the text? And how does the construction of masculinity in the text provide a context for interpretation of the closure? Finally, how are we to assess Bathsheba at the end of the text—is she really just stifled and recuperated by Oak?

Oak's story is that of the loss and regaining of power and masculinity. With his initial failure at shepherding, he loses all stakes in a better life and must start over, humbling himself, as it turns out, before Bathsheba. He becomes, in fact, a servant to the woman farmer, who acts with the "arrogance and reserve" of an Olympian (10.92). She commands and demands, treating him little better than Troy will treat her.

But, in addition, Oak's story is that of gender blurring. The text posits male gender identity in economic, emotional, linguistic, legal, and moral terms. But gender essences for men or women do not exist. Members of each sex bear traits opposite to those by which hegemonic culture would define them. Oak's traits of passivity, modesty, and trusting patience belong to the gender role that Victorians attributed to the female, a role most explicitly defined (as the opposite of Bathsheba) by the chorus of locals, and best exemplified in Fanny Robin. Oak, like Tess, falls asleep at critical moments; he does not, like Henchard, attempt to repress the feminine in himself. Rather, he attempts to repress male desire.

One can argue, in fact, that for Oak to regain power and reestablish his "proper" gender role, the masculinities of Troy and Boldwood must do each other in. Oak can become empowered only through his relation to them (his difference from them) and theirs to each other. He does not become empowered merely by sexual opposition through his relation to Bathsheba or merely by comparability to other men who traffic in women, but also by difference from other men. The central issue here is whether or not Oak regains his masculinity at the close through the defeat of Bathsheba, through her losing her pride and her independence.

The typical pattern of generic closure for the realist novel that is also domestic romance, a patriarchally controlled heterosexual marriage, does not tell the whole story, though many critics read the text through its closure, while still allowing for its problematic ending. This ending validates friendship as the only fitting rationale for marriage. It also fixes gender and power so that Bathsheba is recuperated into the domestic sphere as wife to the new master who is cheered with cannon shot for his success by a chorus of male friends and subordinates. To realign power with the male, the closure puts in jeopardy both female power outside the domestic sphere and male passivity. Yet closure must be interpreted in light of what has come before—what this closure means, then, depends on what Gabriel and Bathsheba and power have also come to mean. Textual movement around the stake of masculinity and power can be clearly seen by examining the apparently fixed gender value of certain "middle" paradigmatic events, male gazing and the wielding of weapons.

Critics have noted Hardy's persistent fascination with the play of gazes, whether narcissistic into mirrors, or scopophilic objectification and fetishization. *Far from the Madding Crowd* provides a perfect example of this fascination and many readers have commented on the repetition of gazing.[12] Gazing is most prominent in this novel when the male looks at the female, as in the inauguration of the story when Gabriel watches Bathsheba, who is preening in a mirror. This accident piques his curiosity enough to prompt subsequent spying on her. And the first event of male gazing is further reinforced in the text by the pleading looks of Boldwood, who "had never before inspected a woman with the very centre and force of his glance" (17.134). His looks take the measure of Bathsheba carefully and, at first, secretly. Furthermore, Troy's "gaze" is described as initially "too strong to be received point-blank with her own" (24.185). She does, however, fairly soon afterward, allow the glint of his sword blade to sow and reap around her body—shaping her as if she were a cutout.

Yet it is insufficient to dwell on the paradigmatic comparability of these looks, collapsing them into a monolithic patriarchal male gaze. All events of gazing might seem to signify the same thing: possession of the female as object. Yet because a paradigmatic event is part of a syntagm that necessarily changes its value, each event of male gazing signifies somewhat differently.

The alignment of gazing with male power is disrupted doubly in *Far from the Madding Crowd*, both by significant differences among the looks and by exposure of the female as gazer. Oak, to be sure, idealizes Bathsheba and even casts her as a divinity, a version of Venus, Ashtoreth, as well as a fleshly country girl. Initially, in the role of male investigator who gazes at woman as enigma, he stereotypes her and prides himself that he can win her. Yet the value of his gazing shifts significantly as the story unfolds.

Troy's gazing is more sexually aggressive than Oak's, but it is by no means one-sided. Although we think of him as the supreme tempter with his extraordinary sword-play, he confides that he would not have married Bathsheba unless she were an Aphrodite who, in fact, seduced him. His perception of Bathsheba as an active gazer herself is perhaps best substantiated by the fact that she gets entrapped by his spur and dazzled by his brilliant brass and scarlet during her nightly "looking" around the homestead, when "watching is best done invisibly" (24.182) and by her later race through the night after him.

Moreover, Troy even plays the spectacle for Bathsheba, not merely with his dazzling swordplay, but through masquerade when he assumes her identity. Donning her bee-hiver's outfit, Captain Troy flirts with being feminized, at being the object of her gaze, but he also removes cultural "armour" from her. "He looked such an extraordinary object in this guise that, flurried as she was, she could not avoid laughing outright. It was the removal of yet another stake from the palisade of cold manners which had kept him off" (27.206). In this drama of sexual likeness and reestablished difference, Troy seduces Bathsheba into intimacy with him and into a further recognition of her seductive powers. This patriarchal gaze is matched. On both sides, however, the romance of projected desire soon fades only to be replaced by negative views.

Of the three men, Boldwood, wishing to possess Bathsheba, gazes most perniciously and unrelentingly. His looks follow her wherever she goes and his looks, Hardy implies, go everywhere. Boldwood even demands that she wear a ring for six years in secret courtship as a promise that she will wed him in the end. His "ideal passion" (14.112) distorts his life as much as it distorts hers, and in a way finally more dangerous than Troy's fickle and wandering gaze. Once Boldwood looks directly at her, this "hotbed of tropic intensity" is struck for life.[13] He is a man always "hit mortally, or he was missed" (18.137). Therefore, his love must remain in the mode of idolatry, but as worship of what? For with Boldwood we see the immense cost of the sadistic quality of the male gaze when it turns into masochism and he becomes his own victim. It is not Bathsheba that Boldwood worships—she is not, finally, the object of his patriarchal male gaze. Rather, Boldwood worships his own ability to look, his own sexual urge, and his own imagined objectification. It is no accident that Boldwood places the Valentine from Bathsheba in the corner of his looking glass, and then a day later jumps out of bed and catches sight of himself there, "insubstantial in form" during a fit of "nervous excitability" (14.114). Only being seen by Bathsheba will restore his form. The natural scene of the next morning is described in terms of "flameless fire," blurred whiteness, and polished marble, with grass encased in icicles bristling through snow like "curves shapes of old Venetian glass" (14.115). Boldwood becomes the very glass of his gaze. If he cannot serve as an acknowledged sexual object, death appears welcome. Yet the discipline of imprisonment will objectify Boldwood in the end. When imprisoned and watched for the rest of his life, he is punished for more than for the murder of Troy. He is also punished for what the murder signifies; Boldwood is condemned in this text for looking too much, for desiring too much.

Oak is more persistent in his gazing than Troy, but, unlike Boldwood, Gabriel does not idealize or objectify Bathsheba when she has once rejected him. Nor is he, like Boldwood, fascinated with his own ability to possess. He modifies his gaze to accommodate to changing circumstances, resolving not to be governed by an uncontrollable male desire. Through the unfolding of the text, Oak alters his view of her quite considerably, without losing his desire for her. Like Troy, he is initially stunned by her physical attractiveness and, like Boldwood, he is captivated emotionally. Yet during the course of the novel, he criticizes her for her own exhibitionism and narcissism, at the same time he is curbing his own looking. Specifically, he confronts her with her brutal handling of Boldwood—the careless seduction, the broken promises, and her lack of self-control, all of which aid another in ruining himself. Some critics have argued that Oak retreats from desire through moralism, a point of view certainly substantiated by the hierarchy of discourses in the text and by his position as the main filter of events. Yet there is a larger point to be made. Oak criticizes Bathsheba for her own patriarchal toying with another as if he were a mere object, a criticism of her that she comes to share: "I've been a rake" (51.409). Thus, Oak is not retreating from desire into moralism, but is attempting to redefine desire, both his own and Bathsheba's.

Power relations inscribed in this realist novel by the event of gazing, then, are not as stable as the regime itself. Further discriminations can be drawn from the examples above. The conjunction of manliness and lack of power occurs through narrative event at the site of each male character discussed, but to a different degree and with a different value. The man with the most relentless gaze, Boldwood, is the least powerful as the events of the story progress. The text posits that for him lack of power and manliness are in contradiction. His very masculinity, in other words, is at stake in his power struggle over the body/image of Bathsheba. With his first loss of her to Troy, his response is self-denial: "I had better go somewhere alone and hide" (31.234); with his second loss of her to Troy, his response is to kill that more powerful male, annulling entirely the possibility of future comparisons, except those provided by remorseful memory. It is clear that Boldwood signifies a desperate, bullying, and self-consuming masculinity that the text needs to eliminate.

Lack of power and manliness are also in contradiction for Troy, although he is flexible enough to play briefly with powerlessness, even as he is divided enough to harbor sentimental and self-indulgent grief over the dead Fanny. When he dresses up in Bathsheba's clothes, becoming her object while he also resembles the female as object, he is quick to reestablish male/female difference. His flirtation with the unheroic lasts only momentarily: " 'Would you be good enough to untie me and let me out? I am nearly stifled inside this silk cage' " (27.206) and leads directly to a reassertion of male military power on the same evening with the sword exercise before a static Bathsheba. The next time Troy dresses up will not be in female garb but as a "male performer" (50.390). Although the later scenes emphasize the new conjunction of acting with masculinity (Troy is Professor of Gymnastics, Pugilism, Sword Exercise, Roughriding, etc.), the syntagm also demonstrates that when Troy is "not himself" and Bathsheba is present, he feels as stifled as if he were dressing up as a lady. Indeed, his cross-dressing and acting suggest that masculinity is a kind of garb, but a necessary prop to support the requirements of Troy's subjectivity.

Lack of power and manliness are combined without contradiction at the character site of Gabriel Oak. If annulment of identity is necessary for Boldwood and the reassertion of sexual difference is necessary for Troy, gender mixing is possible for Oak. One of the most important scenes in the text illustrates this gender mixing in light of Oak's curbing of his sexual interest in Bathsheba.

This scene forms part of another paradigmatic pattern of events: the male use of phallic weapons. Busy with sheepshearing, Oak notices Boldwood's sudden and commanding appearance on the hillside. Bathsheba blushes, rides off, and returns in her new, stylish, myrtle-green riding habit. "Oak's eyes could not forsake them; and in endeavoring to continue his shearing at the same time that he watched Boldwood's manner, he snipped the sheep in the groin" (22.170). Other feminists have interpreted this scene by connecting it to earlier and later scenes where men bear phallic weapons: Troy's sword, Boldwood's gun.[14] They interpret Oak's cut as directed against Bathsheba, whom the ewe represents (about to be branded with her sign BE). And the words of the text here do support such a reading. It is implied that Oak is getting back at his mistress. Bathsheba, Oak tells us, knew that she was the cause of the wounding, "because she had wounded the ewe's shearer in a still more vital part" (22.170).

Yet there is another paradigmatic connection that alters the meaning of this event: the earlier wounding of sheep. An early chapter called "Bathsheba's Departure—A Pastoral Tragedy" features Oak as primarily responsible through negligence for the wounding, and subsequent death, of his sheep just after Bathsheba has left the neighborhood. The narrator describes Oak's response to the dead carcasses: "Oak was an intensely humane man . . . A shadow on his life had always been that his flock ended in mutton—that a day came and found every shepherd an arrant traitor to his defenseless sheep. His first feeling now was one of pity for the untimely fate of these gentle ewes and their unborn lambs" (5.40–41). This passage describes a shepherd in the pastoral world touched by a natural tragedy. Although he has already been stung by the intensity of sexual passion, this scene shows us the Oak who has put thoughts of Bathsheba aside as he confronts his failed labor. Oak the caretaker, who winces if he hurts a ewe, tenderly identifies with the animals. The sheep are an extension of himself—his object of care, his livelihood, his companions.[15] Although he has been affected by Bathsheba's beauty enough to propose marriage, Oak mourns the loss of his sheep more than the loss of her. This concern for his labor and for the animals he tends is not erased by subsequent events. Indeed, it is reinforced by his dexterous surgery on Bathsheba's flock with an "instrument of salvation," a "trochar, with a lance" (21.161).

By the time Oak sees Boldwood approach Bathsheba, he has learned to control his sexual desire for her and has repeatedly schooled himself with "the abiding sense of his inferiority to both herself and Boldwood" (22.170). Only "manly resolve" (22.170) has enabled him to "realize he had no longer a lover's interest in her" (22.170), helping him to conceal feelings that cannot be entirely banished. Resolutions, in other words, vulnerable constructions though they may be, are being made and usually kept. On the occasion of sheepshearing, Oak slips with the knife. Sexuality and jealousy have mastered him momentarily. The "routine" (22.170) with which he stops the flow of blood, however, speaks to the routine with which he stops his own desire. Becoming phallic when he views what he perceives as a budding love relationship, he quickly returns to the role of healer. If the ewe is an emblem for Bathsheba, then, it is as much an emblem of his own femininity, his softness, which he must wound sadistically, in a symbolic act of self-castration, to avoid being more deeply wounded. Hurting the ewe distracts him from the world of love, just as mourning the loss of sheep earlier supplanted Bathsheba's departure in importance.

The scene of sheepshearing locates gender with Oak but sexual difference with the sighting of Bathsheba and Boldwood. Just as the ewe is feminine, representing Bathsheba, it is also able to signify the vulnerability of Oak. By extension, in a double cut of himself, Oak wounds not only male desire but also his female sentiment. Yet his manliness and power, though revealed to be vulnerable, are not left in doubt. Nor are they reasserted through an extreme display of masculinity.[16]

Fixed gender roles that oppress women harshly, especially when allied with class inferiority, as in the case of Fanny Robin, are important in this text. But a connection of power with the male sex and victimization with the female sex oversimplifies the struggle of gender and power. In spite of the controlling framework of sexual difference, this novel features a passive and an active sexuality, which are themselves complicated by a sadism becoming masochism and a masochism becoming sexual repression, as well as a scopophilia that can turn into exhibitionism. Such complications continue to destabilize the text even though a happy marriage ends it.

III

If Hardy deals with masculinity and power through representations of gender aligned with the events performed by three men, thus dividing up the possible varieties and shifts of male power, he locates the issue of femininity and power largely with the events of one female character, Bathsheba. It would be disingenuous for any critic to ignore the importance of Fanny Robin in a discussion such as this one, for she claims, in one sense, the most power of any woman in the text. She is worshipped, wept over, and even paid tribute to by Bathsheba herself. Yet she is most interesting for contrast.

In this section of the essay, I argue that through the representation of Bathsheba in two critical scenes that jeopardize and fix her sexual identity Hardy poses the question of "What is woman?" His answer is an unconventional organization of gender and power. These events, particularly, mark discursive struggle over the cultural construction of femininity: Bathsheba's viewing of Fanny's corpse and her flight to the fern brake.

When Fanny Robin is known to be dead, Bathsheba performs the traditional courtesies extended to a servant of the family: she sends for the body and has the coffin brought into her house. Yet, she also senses that there is something extraordinary about this servant. "Bathsheba had grounds for conjecturing a connection between her own history and the dimly suspected tragedy of Fanny's end" (43.337). When Liddy quickly repeats a rumor that Fanny has born a child who is also lying in the coffin, Bathsheba decides she must learn more. At first, she walks to Oak's cottage for help, but turns back, resolving to discover the truth by herself. It is significant that she does so because the scene becomes a startlingly powerful confrontation of a woman with femininity. Having pried open the lid of the coffin and having seen Fanny and her child, Bathsheba does not register femininity, but the trace of masculine betrayal: "conclusive proof of her husband's conduct" (43.340).

Continuing to view the corpses, Bathsheba confronts the female as Other who has come between herself and her husband. It is shocking to face her blonde-haired, white-faced rival. On the one hand, she wishes to obtain equal power by dying. Yet, on the other hand, she wishes for the power to hurl recriminations at a Fanny still alive. Recoiling almost immediately from death wishes and anger, Bathsheba prays for Fanny instead, placing flowers around her hair. In so doing, she symbolically embraces her likeness, as if intuiting here what she later acknowledges in another act of placing flowers: that she and Fanny are victims of Troy.

With the entrance of Troy himself, the private agony of Bathsheba is set into a larger sexual drama. For Troy organizes the scene in terms of kinds of womanliness by first kissing Fanny and then boldly stating: "This woman is more to me, dead as she is, than ever you were, or are, or can be" (43.345). Shutting out Bathsheba entirely, he addresses Fanny as his true wife. In other words, though both women hold the position of "wife," Troy claims Fanny is more his wife, more womanly than Bathsheba. He exposes fully the gap that exists for him between the ideal (now dead) and the real (still alive) of femininity. In addition, though the point is not made directly by Troy, Fanny is the truer wife because she has produced his child, because she is a mother, while Bathsheba is not.

If this scene, through Troy's intervention, posits womanliness as beauty, innocence, and fertility, it also posits such femaleness as dead. Throughout the text Troy's actions with Fanny are judged harshly, as is his treatment of Bathsheba here. More crucially, Hardy is not supporting the ideology of womanliness as child-producing, an important aspect of the ideology of angel in the house. He kills the mother here as he destroys her or her children elsewhere in his novels. Likewise, this scene calls into question the ideology of the woman as child-figure. During the conversation with Troy, Bathsheba cries out against severance of the union with him. She exclaims as a child might: "Kiss me too, Frank—kiss me!" (43.344) in what is described as "abnormal and startling" in its "childlike pain and simplicity . . . from a woman of Bathsheba's calibre and independence" (43.344). This representation of woman as mother or as child is not the "ideal" against which women are to be measured in this text.

Bathsheba's complicated encounter with Fanny's corpse first stages a scene of castration of the female, which marks the female as lack, both through Bathsheba's power being stolen by Fanny and then through its being negated by Troy. (In addition, Fanny's own power is awarded to her by Troy only when she is dead). Conversely, the male is awarded knowledge of "true" femininity; he is empowered by having had the body and devotion of one woman and the love and jealousy of another. And he is further marked as having the phallus by having fathered a child (though the fact that the child is dead too, and ungendered by the narrative, is a significant Hardy qualification that reinforces his prior and subsequent treatment of Troy's masculinity).

It is highly significant that Bathsheba runs away. Seeing the representation that Troy would attach to Fanny and herself, Bathsheba no longer recognizes the woman she is. The scene of the corpse, through Troy's intervention, becomes one of a misrecognition of femininity. "If she's—that, —what—am—I?" cries Bathsheba with despair and indignation (43.345). Not seeing her femaleness in his view of her femaleness, she does not know who she is. Yet she will find out.

Thus in *Far from the Madding Crowd*, Hardy questions not only conventional constructions of masculinity but also conventional constructions of femininity. In running to the fern brake, Bathsheba enters first an imaginary world and is then, just as in the last scene, reinterpellated into the symbolic order, but differently. If the first scene threatens to negate her power entirely, this scene restores it and inaugurates a different organization of gender and power. It emphasizes not what a man sees and how his view can cancel out woman's view of herself, but what she sees herself. Just as the scene of sheepshearing works to realign masculinity and power, this scene demonstrates that womanliness and power can be combined at a character site and not be in contradiction.

The scene first organizes sexuality in terms of gender blurring. Having thought of "nothing better to do with her palpitating self" (44.346) for the night, the self-divided Bathsheba wakes up, voiceless but refreshed. With the morning light, the fern brake is misty and blurred, as if gender itself were mixed in a "hazy luminousness" (44.347). The landscape is inscribed with sexual signs both masculine, such as spiky ferns and tall fungi, and feminine, such as the dawn and the pool. Bathsheba's own body is represented as a landscape of gender, but not one marked by sexual difference. Red and yellow leaves (recalling Troy's brass and scarlet uniform [24.184], but also her own "crimson" jacket and "bright" face [1.5]) entwine in her luxuriant dark hair and rest in her lap. Initially the signs are mixed together in this scene annulling difference, and nothing is awarded any particular value.

Yet, what had seemed to be a womblike haven, where she could commune with herself alone, is invaded not only by the sounds of birds, but also by the voice of a ploughboy and a team of her own horses. Masculinity intrudes, as in the corpse scene, here with the male voice and a reminder of her social position as farmer. Clearly, the boy at work with her team is a metonymy of her power and is meant to represent her masculine position in the community. In being paired with birds, however, this power is also valued as utterly natural.

As Bathsheba investigates, though, she finds the place "malignant" (44.348). Signs of sexuality begin to be sorted out; sexual difference is symbolically established by attaching values to this natural scene, which recalls earlier scenes. What she first took to be a hollow, is in actuality a swamp, a "nursery of pestilences small and great" (44.348). Up the sides of the depression leading to the swamp, rushes and blades of flag glisten like "scythes," recalling the same hollow where Troy earlier in the season had wielded his mesmerizing blade of seduction. At the bottom of the swamp ooze red and yellow fungi. Hearing sounds of another boy, Bathsheba becomes increasingly nervous. This time it is a schoolboy, one of "the dunce class apparently" (44.348), reciting the collect from a psalter. The intrusion is dismissed by the narrator as a trifle, as an amusement for Bathsheba. It does, however, seem significant that this boy is juxtaposed to the earlier one. Both go about their business. But the second is a dunce with a silly method, one of endless repetition of the words "Give us" (44.348). Unlike the first boy, this one seems quite powerless—unable to master his task at hand. We may see here some comment on Bathsheba's own failure at educating herself in another domain, love, and possibly a comment on both the technique and the content of her earlier method, Give me.

Regardless of how we interpret the contrasting boys, it is crucial that Bathsheba's recognition of her farm boy, and the descriptions of the landscape, masculinize this spot in different ways: labor, sexuality, religion, and education. For at this important moment of decision in the text—whether to return home or not—Bathsheba is envisioning what she wanted to be in her assumption of a man's role, what she has been, and what she might be. She views as malignant and death-dealing a sexual fecundity she associates with Troy and herself. From the start until now she has been too much the woman wielding power to subdue and humiliate; yet she has also been too much the powerless repeater who runs the risk of being metaphorically castrated.

But the scene does not enact just a confrontation with masculinity. Like the previous one, its major importance lies in Bathsheba's confrontation with femininity. In a critical moment, she is refeminized by encountering the one person with whom she has discussed whether or not she is too "mannish" (30.227), her maidservant Liddy. After the second boy passes by, a "form" appears "on the other side" (44.349) of the swamp, half-hidden still by the mist. This form of uncertain gender approaches Bathsheba as if it were a phantom. "The woman—for it was a woman—approached with her face askance" (44.349). Bathsheba's delayed knowledge of the gender of this figure, captured so well by the emphasized focalization, acutely pinpoints the major issue of the scene. The question in the epigraph to this essay, taken from Troy's first ensnaring of Bathsheba, becomes most resonant here: "Are you a woman?" (24.184).

Like the corpse scene, events in the swamp scene are organized around womanliness and power, but this time they are not in contradiction. Liddy does not question Bathsheba's womanliness as Troy had. In fact, she earlier had suggested that Bathsheba was too womanly (30.227). For Bathsheba to be reinterpellated into her culture, for her to go home, a woman must come to fetch her. For Bathsheba must recognize her feminin-ity and power. In finally seeing Liddy before her, and in mustering a whispered greeting, Bathsheba sees and knows her maid, and thus herself, in a drama of sexual choice. The woman whom she recognizes is female but is not a mother. Nor does she act like a child in this scene. It is also important that she is a servant. On one hand it acknowledges the cultural construction of the female in a position of servitude. On the other hand, it does not endorse such a position for Bathsheba. Rather, the presence of the servant Liddy stresses class difference and gender similarity. Bathsheba is constructed here as the female farmer who keeps a woman maidservant as well as farm boys. Thus while the first boy is a metonymy of her powerful position, Liddy is both metonymy and metaphor. She represents both a part of her mistress's power and yet shares the same gender with her mistress. This scene establishes for Bathsheba, then, sexual differentiation without loss of power.

If the corpse scene raises the question of womanliness and power, this scene answers the question in terms of the power of running a farm. With these two scenes, womanliness is redefined from innocence, motherhood, and being a "runaway wife" (44.351) to that of independence, economic wealth, and "stand[ing] your ground" (44.351).

It can be argued that after this redefinition, Bathsheba is returned to her former status. She is hardly powerful as she waits for Troy, becomes indecisive about Boldwood, and looks back at the past as if she were herself dead. Yet the effect of Troy's delay and the renewal of Boldwood's suit highlights the great difficulty of retaining female power in the realm of the patriarchal. At this point in the text the feminine is subsumed again while issues of masculinity resurface to join the hermeneutic code (what will happen next?). We no longer ask questions about Fanny (how many corpses are in the coffin?) or Bathsheba (how will she react; will she come home?) but about the men: (will Troy return? will Boldwood win her? can Oak wait?). I think that this particular redirection of the syntagm very much determines how the closure is often read, as a sign of male taming and a reassertion of male power. The return to issues of masculinity makes Bathsheba into a dependent, passive woman who waits for her husband to come home. It almost reinscribes her as a child and certainly positions her as lack. Rather than reading the closure through these reinscriptions, however, which are patriarchal, it is more productive to see the end in terms of the narrative stress points of gender struggle.

The rest of the text does not tame Bathsheba into the domestic sphere, but, rather, awards and removes, or downright denies, her access to traditional roles associated with the Victorian domestic sphere: waiting wife, widow, innocent, child bride, and mother. Hardy's criticism of female domestic entrapment is furthered by the fact that Bathsheba is not a mother—Hardy does not have her bear children. Thus *Far from the Madding Crowd* actually questions what counts as domestic, even as it redefines masculinity and femininity through the process of (re-)alignments of gender and power.

The marriage of Bathsheba and Oak, then, cannot be interpreted merely as a recuperation of Bathsheba into a patriarchal prison-house. While the closure fixes the equation of male power and female dependency, realigning cultural constructions of gender and biology, it does so only after destabilizing those alignments so forcefully that the equation itself becomes suspect. In allowing Oak the positions of both phallic male and castrated male while awarding Bathsheba the contradictory position of powerful and dependent female, Hardy is not denying power and sexuality to either sex.

Finally, Hardy's "solution" of gender mixing through power shifts does not work for one ideological end at the moment of the text's production. His writing of Bathsheba as strong and yet womanly, a farmer and wife, but not a mother, could be appropriated for different political ends in culture. Part of its own power is no doubt due to the fact that it could serve diametrically opposed interests at the same time: say, that a woman should be made more powerless by recuperation through motherhood into the domestic sphere, or that woman should be allowed more independence within it, or that woman should be liberated entirely from it. The redefinitions proposed in Far from the Madding Crowd serve no agenda in particular, except growing uncertainty at the end of the nineteenth century about: what is woman?

NOTES

A version of this essay first appeared in Novel 24, no. 2 (Winter 1991): 162–77. Reprinted with permission of the Journal.

1. For D. H. Lawrence's shrewd understanding of Hardy's treatment of gender, see his "Study of Thomas Hardy," in Phoenix: The Posthumous Papers of D. H. Lawrence, ed. Edward D. Macdonald (London: Penguin, 1961), 398–516. For important differences between Lawrence and Hardy, see Robert Langbaum, "Lawrence and Hardy," in D. H. Lawrence and Tradition, ed. Jeffrey Meyers (London: Athlone, 1985), 69–90, and Mark Kinkead-Weekes, "Lawrence on Hardy," in Thomas Hardy after Fifty Years, ed. Lance St. John Butler (London: Macmillan, 1977), 90–103. For a contemporary assessment along the same lines as that of Lawrence's but which concentrates on Far from the Madding Crowd, see William Mistichelli, "Androgyny, Survival, and Fulfillment in Thomas Hardy's Far from the Madding Crowd," Modern Language Studies 18:3 (1988), 53–64. This analysis is sensitive to the gender politics of the text, but falls into the rhetoric of fulfillment—arguing somewhat sentimentally that the "androgyny" of Oak and Bathsheba serves the "fulfillment of their humanity," not merely the "survival of their species." I am not arguing from a critical position that would rely on the terminology of androgyny or fulfillment.

2. Robert Gittings, *Young Thomas Hardy* (Harmondsworth: Penguin, 1978), 276.

3. Laurence Lerner and J. Holstrum, eds., *Thomas Hardy and His Readers* (London: 1968), 30–31. See also Michael Millgate, *Thomas Hardy* (New York: Random, 1982), 168, 173.

4. Lerner and Holstrum, *Hardy*, 35.

5. See Penny Boumelha, *Thomas Hardy and Women* (University of Wisconsin Press, 1982), 32–34, and Rosemarie Morgan, *Women and Sexuality in the Novels of Thomas Hardy* (New York: Routledge, 1988), 30–57.

6. Boumelha, *Hardy and Women*, 44; Morgan, *Women and Sexuality*, 43, 44ff.

7. For contradictions in Hardy's treatment of women and for feminist readings of his contradictions see Mary Childers, "Thomas Hardy, the Man Who 'Liked' Women," *Criticism* 23:4 (1981), 317–34.

8. Michèle Barrett, *Women's Oppression Today* (London: Verso, 1985), 110. The brevity of my remarks reduces the complexity of Boumelha's argument, however. Indeed, she is one of the first feminists to investigate Hardy's relationship to the ideologies of the period. I disagree with her method for analyzing the relations between representations and culture. And I regard *Far from the Madding Crowd* as more sophisticated an early work than she does.

9. For another and very different deconstruction of the male/female binary, see Adrian Poole, "Men's Words and Hardy's Women," *Essays in Criticism* 31:4 (1981), 328–45.

10. For a fuller discussion of the structure of story and the changing value of paradigmatic events, as well as for a working out of connections among narrative, subjectivity, and ideology, see Steven Cohan and Linda M. Shires, *Telling Stories: A Theoretical Analysis of Narrative Fiction* (London and New York: Routledge, 1988).

11. Tzvetan Todorov, *The Poetics of Prose*, trans. Richard Howard (Ithaca: Cornell University Press, 1977), 111–12.

12. Morgan, *Women and Sexuality*, 35–37, 44–46; Boumelha, *Hardy and Women*, 34–36; also Judith Bryant Wittenberg, "Angles of Vision and Questions of Gender in *Far from the Madding Crowd*," *The Centennial Review* 30:1 (1968): 25–40; and Janie Sénéchal, "Focalisation, Regard et Désire dans *Far from the Madding Crowd*," *Cahiers Victoriens et Edouardiens* 12 (1980): 73–84.

13. I thus disagree with Beegel's somewhat dismissive assessment of Boldwood, but she is right to connect him with stasis and death. See Susan Beegel, "Bathsheba's Lovers: Male Sexuality in *Far from the Madding Crowd*," in *Thomas Hardy: Modern Critical Views*, ed. Harold Bloom (New York: Chelsea, 1987), 207–26.

14. Morgan, *Women and Sexuality*, 53–57; Boumelha, *Hardy and Women*, 33.

15. See Beegel, "Bathsheba's Lovers," 216–17.

16. Gittings reports that there might have been yet another sheep-flock scene, but for Leslie Stephen's editorial control. The fourth would have contrasted even more fully the difference between Oak and Troy. This fact seems to add further weight to the argument that such care-taking scenes are not merely about labor, but also concern the construction of masculinity.

Pay As You Go:
On the Exchange of Bodies and Signs

Elisabeth Bronfen

Insigned Bodies—Embodied Signs

What happens when, in the act of exchange, a body is transformed into a sign? What does it mean that culture should depend on such a substitution, and that the body in this exchange should always and necessarily be gendered female? While speaking of woman as the privileged commodity within culture, Lévi-Strauss explains "there is no need to call upon the matrimonial vocabulary of Great Russia, where the groom was called the 'merchant' and the bride, the 'merchandise' for the likening of women to commodities, not only scarce but essential to the life of the group, to be acknowledged."[1] Exogamy, acting permanently and continually, he claims, is "the archetype of all other manifestations based upon reciprocity, and [it] provides the fundamental and immutable rule ensuring the existence of the group as a group." Because marital exchange forms the basis of all other systems of exchange, women are seen as valuables par excellence "without which life is impossible, or, at best . . . reduced to the worst forms of abjection."[2]

Lévi-Strauss describes a double exchange—both socioeconomic and semiotic. In the first place, the bartered woman is used to establish a bond between father or brother and bridegroom and in so doing ensures the existence of the community. This act of exchange is in turn symbolic, for the woman is bartered not only as a physically real body but also as a sign referring to something more and something other than her corporality. Marking a self-reflexive moment within the process of signification she becomes a signifier for exchange itself. Woman is a "valuable *par excellence*" because her double function as body and as trope points to a moment in the symbolic order where the boundary between these two functions seems to blur.

In the work of Thomas Hardy, the superlative value of woman resides precisely in the multileveled ambiguity of this kind of exchange for issues of power, gender and signification itself. For Hardy the body is not only traded, but given and received as a token or sign. As a commodity, it acts as the site of a continual slippage between any stable distinction between trope and body, between figural and literal meaning. This inability or unwillingness to secure a fundamental difference between concrete bodies and figural signs not only engenders an interchangeability between the two but also allows one level of meaning to be substituted arbitrarily and sometimes incorrectly for another. This confusion of body and sign becomes, to alter Lévi-Strauss's formulation slightly, the rule ensuring the production and dissemination of meaning. It emerges as the basis on which aesthetic and hermeneutic activities depend. At the same time, the theme of a necessary "exchange" exposes corollary violations and dangers. Consciously critical of existing power relations, though perhaps unconsciously repeating them, Hardy uses the exchange of female bodies and the forms of exchange occurring at their bodies to demonstrate how fatal it can be to confuse a body with a sign. While in Hardy's world all characters are subjected to outside forces, the female protagonist's body is most conspicuously exchanged, inscribed, gazed at, deciphered, imitated, substituted for and ultimately replaced by something else. At her body physical inscription passes into metaphorical inscription, and this troping either engenders her death or results from it.

Before analyzing why the form of payment Hardy's heroines ultimately make transpires into that of giving their lives, I want to open up another ambivalence inherent in the notion of exchange. To focus on the two male parties giving or taking the valuable—woman—obscures the fact that she, as object received, is engaged in the exchange as well. Even if she is not the instigating agent she is nevertheless implicated in the pass or substitution: she is not only parted with but parts herself (for example from her home or her virginity), and the transfer from corporality to sign inscribes itself into her body. She serves as a form of payment, but she also pays, if with nothing else than her body. When Hardy uses the phrase "the woman pays" as title for the fifth phase in *Tess of the D'Urbervilles* (1891), he refers to a figural meaning: the woman pays for transgressions in which she is involved or for trespasses committed by someone else. She is the one primarily held responsible and punished. In the eyes of the public she, rather than someone else, gets the blame, the distress, and ultimately the death sentence. In this exchange she is substituted for the other guilty person.

But need that be all? While the figural meaning points to her passive function as receiver of punishment, the literal meaning of the phrase suggests active giving, implicitly in return for or in response to something. While the figural reading suggests she is paid to secure the serenity of her community, the literal reading indicates that a purchase is made, that on some level she too gains something. And though one can read the phrase to mean she "pays" in the sense of being worth the expense or effort made for her (in which case she gratifies the person giving, receiving, or using her), the literal reading implies an act of discharging an obligation, that is, an act of self-gratification by virtue of which she releases herself from a debt. Thus, the question of payment marks a realm of transaction in which the woman is implicated not only as the pivotal, though essentially passive, point in an exchange but also as an active participant.

The notion of a remuneratory exchange includes the blurring of another set of contrasts—namely the difference between active and passive, giving and receiving, responding and inflicting, again in connection with gender designation. While a root word for paying is *pecare* (to pacify), the fact that many instances of feminine payment in Hardy involve death, suggests that pacification always also implies violence and violation. Revenge emerges as a form of payment in which exchange, violence, and appeasement most prominently intersect. Significantly in Hardy's fiction, the form revenge most often takes is to transform a woman's body into a sign. The point where violence enters into the exchange thus also forms the link between the institutionalizing action of exogamy, which turns woman into a commodity, and the cultural project of representation, which turns her into a trope.

Our cultural discourse is marked by an exchange between body and sign, by an imperative blindness toward a difference between the two. I will use a reading of Hardy's novels to tease out the implications of two central analogies between corpse and text, both involving bodies of female characters. (1) Female corpses are treated like texts in that the "disquieting strangeness" they share with art works demands and allows a reading from the onlookers.[3] They are, in short, treated like sites of inscription that must be deciphered. (2) The female body is viewed allegorically by others as though it were a figure or representation that in part always reflects and sustains the narcissism of the viewer. The feminine tissue is treated like a page onto which lovers, society's laws, or the repressed past write themselves. If in the first instance the dead feminine body functions as the necessary prerequisite for the aesthetic and hermeneutic process, the second instance implies that a process of perception that objectifies and thus depersonalizes a body in order to allow an allegorical reading, kills bodies into tropes. When the concrete dismemberment of the heroine results, does this last rhetorical turn not lose some of its innocence?

Representations in which a translation from body to sign occurs also serve a more general discussion of the relationship between the immaterial characters in a fictional story and the material characters on a page. When an allegorical reading of the heroine replaces her living body (which either leads to her concrete death or responds to it), this substitution doubles the exchange of an animate present body for an inanimate sign representing the body in its absence: an exchange characteristic of all writing.[4] As Derrida puts it, "Writing in the common sense is the dead letter, it is the carrier of death. It exhausts life. . . . All graphemes are of a testamentary essence. And the original absence of the subject of writing is also the absence of the thing or the referent."[5]

Not incidentally, it is precisely the feminine body that triggers metapoetical debates and the inability to draw distinctions between the concrete and the abstract, between the literal and the figural. For woman has also always been a privileged value in debates on the status of rhetorical language, although the position assigned to her is fraught with contradictions. On the one hand woman is often treated as an allegory, idealized or demonized, the Other,[6] while simultaneously accused of being deceptive, quintessentially duplicitous or unstable in her meaning, so that she becomes a trope for figural language itself.[7] On the other hand discussions of femininity usually locate woman closer to the real, the sensual, and argue that woman reads literally where she should read figurally.[8] Again the question of passivity subverted by activity arises, for Hardy's novels include female protagonists who are not only the victims of someone else's confusion of bodies and signs, but themselves partake in this confusion when they write literally, rather than figuratively, with their body and ultimately with their life. While the moment that subverts the opposition between difference and similarity may on one level mark the self-reflexivity of a text, I want to stress that it betrays that the inevitable turn to the rhetorical can also engender or be founded on instances of real violation. For in privileging the analogy between inanimate character (corpse) in a story and inanimate character on a page (sign or image) we may occlude the other relation, evocative rather than analogous, between the representation and the materiality of a body to which it refers.

Speaking Corpses

In *Far from the Madding Crowd* (1874) the death-scenes of the disturbing female protagonist stages an important kind of doubling: as a corpse, the female body repeats or is repeated by a figural embodiment, namely a text. Fanny Robins's passage from living body to corpse can ironically be seen as one from near-silent invisibility to speaking visibility. Her name is first mentioned in connection with her disappearance (8.77).[9]

In a gesture prophetic of the way body and story come together to form a symbolic unity only at her death, Gabriel gives money to an "unknown woman," who wishes to remove all traces of her body—"let your having seen me be a secret" (7.58)—and learns to attach a name to her only after her absence, that is, only to her image stored in his memory. Throughout the rest of her corporeal existence Robin will never again be directly addressed by her name except clandestinely by Troy. To have her name be publicly attached to her body will be the privilege of the corpse.

Instead, a series of incidents follow that confirm her process of disembodiment: in the scene at Troy's baracks she is described as a "small form" that seems human, a "little shape," a "blurred spot in the snow" (11.96–97). This is followed by her marked corporeal absence at the wedding ceremony and the equally marked absence in the text of a description of her first sexual experience.[10] After she reappears she continues to remain anonymous—a woman. Though Troy recognizes her on the road and consents to meet her, he will not openly acknowledge knowing her name. Her last living hours are spent traveling unseen and unaided by all but a dog until at the door of the poorhouse she becomes a "prostrate figure," an impersonalized traveler, a "small and supple one" (40.309). The second significant narrative ellipsis—her birth-giving and death—can be read as an ultimate confirmation of the way her corporeal presence is disavowed, negated, and exchanged for a belated acknowledgement. Only as a corpse does Fanny make her first and only public statement, can she speak the story she could not tell while alive, can she become present and visible. Put another way, Fanny, who is not skillful at using linguistic signs, can only signify through her body by turning it into a symbol, that is, by establishing a perfect correlation between signifier (body) and signified (her story), and as such effecting what Harry Berger Jr. calls a "detextualizing procedure."[11] But the price for this achieved signification is death.

The chapter in which Fanny's corpse is exposed bears the provocative title "Fanny's Revenge." This title suggests that we are to understand her death as a form of paying for the transgression committed by her as well as a form of paying Troy back for the trespass he committed against her body. Her speaking corpse embodies the past Troy has tried to keep secret and thus on a very literal level inflicts an irreparable wound upon his marriage to Bathsheba in retribution for the wound inflicted on her by Troy (the abandonment) that resulted in such a violent form of death. As a corpse, Fanny changes from a disembodied and depersonalized object of actions inflicted on her to the subject of an action—her revenge.

But can the title not also be read ambiguously to suggest that the move that lets Fanny become an active subject in the story of her life is almost immediately subverted by a countermove on the part of her survivors, which turns her again into a nondetermined, depersonalized figure, functioning as a register of the others' responses? While as a corpse she evidently poses what Margaret Higonnet has called "a hermeneutic task," the question remains whether those reading her ever really look for her story.[12] The workman Cogan's response is the first indicating that any meaning assigned to a corpse must ultimately be allegorical. By way of defending Joseph, who stopped for a drink rather than driving Fanny's corpse directly to the graveyard, he explains: "Nobody can hurt a dead woman. . . . The woman's past us—time spent upon her is throwed away: why should we hurry to do what's not required? Drink, shepherd, and be friends, for to-morrow we may be like her" (42.327). He does not see the corpse as a concrete body but as a memento mori, a sign that speaks other than itself—precisely as an allegory signifying the urgency to enjoy life.

While the responses Fanny's corpse elicits from the two characters most implicated in her death are complex, they ultimately take the same turn, and as such point to the problem inherent in the analogy between text and corpse. Blanchot has attempted to explain the fascination a corpse has in a way that will elucidate both the challenge Fanny's dead body poses to her survivors and the impossibility of looking at her with anything but an allegorizing gaze. He delineates two stages in the response to a corpse. The first, a fundamental destabilizing of established categories of reference and position: "something is there before us that is neither the living person himself nor any sort of reality, neither the same as the one who was alive, nor another, nor another thing. . . . Death suspends relations with the place. . . . place is missing, the cadaver is not in its place. Where is it? It is not here and yet it is not elsewhere; nowhere? but the fact is that then nowhere is here."[13] At the site/sight of the corpse, the real destabilizes and thus ruptures accepted cultural forms of symbolization. This strangeness promises to furnish an insight into that not yet known, into the Other outside the narcissistic gaze of self-perception and the categories of symbolization by which culture sustains itself. However, it quickly becomes a form of resemblance, and can thus be translated into representation: "The striking thing . . . is that though the remains appear in the strangeness of their solitude, as something disdainfully withdrawn from us, just when the sense of an interhuman relationship is broken, when our mourning, our care and the prerogative of our former passions, no longer able to know their object, fall back on us, come back towards us—at this moment, when the presence of the cadaver before us is the presence of the unknown, it is also now that the lamented dead person begins to *resemble himself.*"[14]

From the start Bathsheba bears "a strange complication of impulses" toward Fanny's corpse. When she finally opens the coffin she does so in an effort to find the truth of the story suggested by this death and asks "speak and tell me your secret, Fanny!" Yet the "conclusive proof of her husband's conduct" that this double-corpse offers, does not as she thinks cast light "beyond doubt" on the last chapter of Fanny's story. The moment of strangeness and insight experienced at the corpse quickly translates into one of self-recognition, as Fanny takes on the function of an allegorical figure of triumph—"in Bathsheba's wild imagining [fate had turned] her companion's failure to success, her humiliation to triumph, her lucklessness to ascendency; it had thrown over herself a garish light of mockery, and set upon all things about her an ironical smile. . . . In Bathsheba's heated fancy the innocent white countenance expressed a dim triumphant consciousness of the pain she was retaliating for her pain" (43.340–41). Thus light is only cast on Bathsheba's misconception about her marriage, so painful because it subverts her notion of being superior, unique, and original and shows her to be but a repetition, a supplement of her rival. Both the vindictive hatred she feels toward the corpse and the gesture of atonement (she lays flowers around the dead girl's head) indicate that for her the corpse functions as an empty sign onto which she can project a range of conflicting emotions.

Troy, caught in a similarly allegorizing mode of gazing, uses Fanny's corpse to demonstrate his remorse and reverence, thus exchanging the previous public disavowal with an exaggerated and eccentric acknowledgement. In his confrontation with Bathsheba he not only confesses that Fanny was a previous lover but idealizes her into the supreme and only love of his life—"This woman is more to me, dead as she is, than ever you were, or are, or can be. . . . You are nothing to me—nothing" (43.345) The bitter secret about Troy thus revealed ultimately deals less with his infidelity and deception than with his valorizing the female trope at the expense of the female body. The exchange between figural and literal is such that Bathsheba becomes "nothing" in the sight of Fanny's body decomposing into nothing, while Fanny becomes a value par excellence, the perfect lover, not although but rather because she is "dead as she is." In a perfect final act commemorating his exchange with Fanny, Troy engraves onto the tombstone marking her grave himself as subject and Fanny as reflecting object of the utterance—"Erected by Francis Troy in Beloved Memory of Fanny Robin" (46.368). This kind of clichéd public confession not only seems contingent on its object's death but ultimately serves the function of a romantic self-display.

Thus, while the detextualization occurring through Fanny's corpse ruptures the stability of Bathsheba and Troy's marriage, their allegorizing gaze immediately translates it into a representation, which in turn serves as the site for self-recognition and self-presentation and simultaneously effaces the reality of the corpse. The other secret Fanny's corpse reveals concerns the way in which the articulation of violence in representation always also contains the moment of its own failure. The corpse's ability to signify goes hand in hand with the reader's ability to mistake it for a two-fold sign—in part speaking literally, that is the story of her pregnancy and death, and in part speaking *other*, that is the version of death's meaning each viewer chooses to read into her. The fatal misdemeanor in Fanny's story, then, is that Troy can acknowledge her only as an inanimate body, as a set of characters inscribed on a tombstone, thus forcing her literally to change her body into a sign before she can be recognized.

Literature is founded on the irrevocable exchange of bodies for signs, and yet the fascination of the text, like the fascination for an *other* narrative of death, lies precisely in that corporality and violence that speech necessarily (and violently) excludes. One could say that by virtue of this effacement, narrative designation violates the lived experience of violence. As Blanchot argues: "In speech what dies is what gives life to speech; speech is the life of that death. . . . something was there and is no longer there. . . . literature is a search for this moment which precedes literature. . . . it wants . . . Lazarus in the tomb and not Lazarus brought back into the daylight, the one who already smells bad, who is Evil, Lazarus lost and not Lazarus saved and brought back to life."[15] The fascination for the female corpse, and maybe for texts in general, may lie in the fact that it opens up a space where the desire for that which ruptures the symbolic order of language and culture can be articulated while simultaneously the impossibility of fulfilling such a desire is ensured, and with it the existence of the symbolic community.

The analogy between corpse and trope exposes two allegorizing processes, structurally distinct and yet having the same kind of effacement as their goal. In the first the movement is from animate body to a deanimated corpse, which then functions as a sign and instrument of revenge. Such transformation occurred when Fanny turned herself into a speaking corpse. In the second process the movement is from the deanimated body of the corpse to a sign or narrative. When Bathsheba and Troy turn Fanny's corpse into a figure of triumph, the process of allegorization becomes part of an act of resurrection, that benefits the survivors by defusing and revising the old and affirming the new. In this act of disembodiment the figure of the corpse is refigured in a new vein (the narration). The corpse thus performs a double function: it is both an allegory and real. Moreover, the act of resurrection, when the corpse as sign is exchanged for a narrative alterior to it proves also to be a veiled instance of revenge, precisely because it robs the corpse of its initially invested sign that wreaked the first revenge. By detaching the dead woman from her self-inscribed corpse, and with it from her revenge, the second allegory works its revenge on her and her process of allegorization; it undoes both the reality of the corpse and the first allegory of the corpse, induced by the woman's self-detextualization. What we have is one exchange being exchanged for another exchange, at a moment when the implicated woman is once again passive and cannot pay back, but only be paid back. This second form of allegorization displays the survivor's privilege of having the last word, which, to reformulate Roland Barthes, liquidates and disorganizes the adversary, inflicts upon her a (narcissistically) mortal wound, covers her in silence and rapes her speech.[16] But insofar as both processes of allegorization cling to her corpse, the dead woman's body becomes a multiple trope.

On Crypts and Revenants

Tess, though never exposed as a corpse, is from the start a woman sought out by and thus forced into an exchange with the dead, who choose at her body to have their "sport" (59.508). Through the parson's discovery that Durbeyfield derives from the signature d'Urberville, the "ancient and knightly family" rise from their vault to claim kinship with their poor descendents (1.4). Thus, when Tess later says of these ancestors, "she almost hated them for the dance they had led her" (16.132), she points to another aspect of allegory informing this novel: the dance of death motif.

As Tess becomes the privileged object of an economic, erotic and tropic exchange, her story becomes an allegory of the process of dying, an interplay of wounding and retribution that occurs at her body. Her story offers both a critique of the violence engendered by the allegorizing gaze and a representation of the stages through which one must move to reach the right moment of death. Like Fanny, her body is inscribed and translated into a trope that embodies the process of death, while it simultaneously inscribes and ultimately signs life.

Tess's first introduction into the narrative prophetically marks her difference from her companions—though she is a mere "vessel of emotion untinctured by experience," a pronounced red ribbon adorns her hair. Yet the student Angel, who dances with the village girls, does not choose Tess because she remains "unobserved" until he falls "out of the dance." Only when he looks back from afar does he notice her: "a white shape stood apart by the hedge alone." Thus from the start the text presents Tess as standing apart from her companions, both because her womanly appearance is more pronounced (though this contradicts her virginal body) and because she is noticeable in her superiority only when seen from a distance, as the "pretty maiden with whom he had not danced" (2.16). At the same time her story begins with the recognition of one claim and the disavowal of another, for she is interrupted in her May Dance by her father's claim to "a-gr't-family vault-at-Kingsbere."[17] Angel's not choosing Tess, which she will later read as a metaphor for the fatal belatedness of their love, also signifies that she has already been chosen by the dead, who speak through the father's name, that she has been summoned away from the May Dance of marriage, children and old age to enter the dance macabre.

Sarah Goodwin connects Dance of Death imagery with Freud's discussion of choice in his essay "The Theme of the Three Caskets," where the correct one among three possible choices is the most attractive but also represents death.[18] Indeed, Tess also faces three choices—her ancestors, Angel and Alec—but she is as yet too innocent to choose. The plot of her story thus enacts a detour with the goal of returning to this moment of choice in such a way that Tess is no longer its object but its subject, translating, as Freud explains, necessity and destiny into choice, acknowledging death by choosing it.[19] The theme of body-sign exchange interacts with the more global representation of the death process precisely because the former is an enactment of incisions, moments where death not only underlies life but breaks through, violently ruptures and makes itself visible in its signature or trace left on living bodies. Between the ancestors' first calling of Tess and her final reciprocation (and thus completion of her exchange with them) a chiasmic arrangement marked by such moments of violent incision informs the plot of this text. Tess moves from a first bodily inscription, Alec's rape (the first moment in which the feminine body's wholeness is ruptured) through a series of self-allegorizations reciprocated by the allegorizing gaze of others. These acts whereby others or she herself kills her body into a trope repeat the first incision of death's slow process toward disintegration. Her narration to Angel becomes the first attempt to revenge her rape. After his rejection of her she returns to bodily inscription and with it the embrace of death, which leads to the completion of her rape in the murder of Alec and her subsequent disembodiment under the auspices of the law. Within this scenario the two lovers Angel and Alec embody the two aspects of the death drive as formulated by Freud.[20] Alec, the false representative of her ancestors, is an agent of duplicity and division, inscribing in an effort to fragment wholeness and taint purity, but in this destructive function he also creates tensions as a safeguard against a short-circuiting of the death process in the form of a premature stasis. Angel's inscriptions, on the other hand, are an attempt to deny division and regain the deathlike state of transparent purity before the fall.

In obeisance to the principle recommending a commodification of female bodies, her parents choose Tess to claim kin with what they think are their rich relatives. Well aware that Tess's value for this economic exchange resides in her feminine beauty, she is explicitly transformed into an object designed to arouse Alec's erotic desire. The duplicity her parents embark on, then, is that on a literal level they send her beautiful body as an ostensible sign to testify to their blood kinship, but in fact rely on transforming her into a sign of seductive womanliness. Her mother deviously dresses Tess with a pink ribbon "broader than usual," and a white frock "supplementing her enlarged coiffure" to emphasize what is already a contradiction in her appearance (7.56–57)—"a fullness of growth, which made her appear more of a woman than she really was" (5.48). As in her introductory sequence Tess serves as a valuable par excellence, stands apart from others, because her body and the meaning it signifies are forced apart. By sending Tess's body to signify *other* than what it is, thus staking a claim with a false coin, her parents are prefiguring death's fracturing of her body in rape by already forcing her to efface her natural maidenly body. The mother's strategy succeeds insofar as Tess becomes supremely attractive to Alec precisely because she signifies womanliness, not a womanly body, and the defeat of his attempts at seduction engendered by this separation also keeps his desire alive. As he will later explain, "Why I did not despise you was on account of your being unsmirched in spite of all" (46.41).

The Durbeyfield appeal ironically ricochets from hope of restored fortune, health and life to signs of death. By claiming kin with Alec on the authority of the family vault, Tess recognizes her ancestors' claim on her. By acknowledging that her body is a site where these ancestors have left their generic traces, she acknowledges that she is not only fractured by this inscription but also a metonymy of the dead. Tragically, while her significa-tion as allegory of womanliness is based on a false claim but engenders real erotic desire, her signification as metonymy of the dead is based on a legitimate claim but has in Alec a false respondent since he is himself not a genuine representative but a false copy of the D'Urbervilles. Tess recog-nizes Alec's role as a sham figure not only of her aristocratic ancestors but also of death when upon entering a church containing the tombs of her family she discovers him posing as an effigy only to wake and tempt her away from "the dynasty of the real underneath" (52.465), to which she is ever stronger drawn.

The narrator in turn uses this subverted opposition between genuine and false representation to present Tess as an allegory for the tragic belatedness of love—"the man to love rarely coincides with the hour for loving." This trope itself turns implicitly into a metaphor for the way allegories, with their slippage and deferral of full meaning, rather than symbols, are possible in the life of narrative. For the narrator continues the trope: "it is not the two halves of a perfect whole that confronted each other at the perfect moment, a missing counterpart wandered independently . . . out of which maladroit delay sprang anxieties . . . and passing-strange destinies," and one might add, the postponement of unity engendered by plot (5.49).

The description of the rape itself enacts the complex exchange of disembodiment it sets out to signify. Before her violation, Tess's body transforms into "a pale nebulousness at his feet, which represented the white muslin figure he had left upon the dead leaves. . . . she was sleeping," and the ravishment that is then inflicted on this unconscious body already perceived as a deanimated figure turns into a metaphor for inscription; "Why it was that upon this beautiful feminine tissue, sensitive as gossamer, and practically blank as snow as yet, there should have been traced such a coarse pattern as it was doomed to receive" (11.91).[21] By effacing a description of real physical violence and substituting for it a metaphorical speculation on metaphysics, the narrator repeats Alec's turning her body into a sign that must bear an other's inscription. An undoing of this alterior signature in an act of autosigning will define the ensuing trajectory of her life. But the destabilizing of any distinction between body and sign that the narrative itself enacts when concrete rape can be presented *only* as an elliptic trope points also to a disturbing duplicity fundamental to allegory in general—for in it the word precedes its incarnation and becomes flesh but simultaneously the embodiment generates meaning when the flesh becomes word.[22] For Tess, rape emerges as a form of death, in that the rupturing of the hymen irrevocably wounds the intact wholeness of her body and forces her to exchange a "previous self" for a new one (11.91), with the designation "previous self" excluding its signified even as it is uttered. Thus beyond any speculation whether this rape signifies a moment of "retribution visited" upon her body for "sins of her fathers" (placing it in the dance of death motiv), concrete death in this moment speaks through her body, becomes so to speak flesh. The multiple tropic effect we have, then, in this exchange engendered by rape is that her maidenly body dies, while simultaneously death is embodied.

Tess's ensuing melancholic desire for death transforms into various attempts at self-figuration that enhance her disembodiment by concretizing the separation between the bodily appearance and its natural meaning at the same time that she valorizes the trope over the body. At first she looks upon herself as "a figure of Guilt intruding into the haunts of Innocence," emphasizing her deathlike liminality not only by insisting on a separation between herself and nature's laws when in fact she is perfectly in accord with them (13.108). But she also kills herself into a trope along with the child she baptizes "Sorrow the Undesired" shortly before its natural death. Looking into a mirror she does not see her own physical fairness but rather reads this image of her body as a *vanitas* picture, signifying the day of her death, and with it total disembodiment, "when all these charms would have disappeared" (15.125).

The burial of her child becomes part of a recuperative act, an attempt to escape the past by annihilating "all that appertained thereto" (15.125), which culminates in a second form of self-figuration, her resurrection as "dairymaid Tess, and nothing more," that is, as insubstantial imagined figure, revealing no traces of a past. The exchange she undertakes at her person is thus the substitution of a deanimated figure for a body incised by the first traces of death. By merely changing the allegorical value of her figure from womanliness to purity, she of course structurally repeats the fateful separation between what her appearance signifies and what her body truly means. A fundamental inconsistency informs her attempt to banish "all d'Urberville air-castles in the dreams and deeds of her new life," for the dairy she choses as site of her rebirth lies near the "great family vaults of her ancestors" (15.126). She in fact constructs a crypt within herself, ambivalently hiding and securing the corpse of her maiden self. She thus disavows her ancestors in an attempt to reconstruct herself outside the dance of facticity and fracture they have led her along, while she enters her "ancestral land" as though returning to the point of her origin, in the hope of healing all previous ruptures.

In this nostalgic desire for a return to a state prior to the fall into division, impurity, and sexuality, Tess corresponds perfectly to Angel, who seeks purification from the evils of urban existence in the pastoral of dairy life. His allegorizing gaze translates the already duplicitous figure "dairymaid Tess" into a "fresh and virginal daughter of Nature" (18.155) and "actualized poetry" (26.210). In a narcissistic effort to stabilize his fractured sense of self, Tess comes to stand for all those values he lacks—purity, innocence, genuineness, newness, uncultured and unconstrained naturalness—which, if he could possess them by possessing her, would give him the sense of wholeness. In this exchange Angel seeks a deanimated figure of Nature, a phantom or corpse and not a natural feminine body, and this becomes prominent in a passage that describes Tess in the aspect when "she impressed him most deeply." In the "non-human hours" of dawn she "looked ghostly, as if she were merely a soul at large. . . . She was no longer the milkmaid, but a visionary essence of woman—a whole sex condensed into one typical form" (20.167–68).[23] This privileging of purity contains two parts. For one, his desire for her spiritualized figure suggests that the more divested she is of bodily substance and specific meaning the more entirely is she available to his libidinal investment without threatening the construction of his self-image. She must become "ghostly" to satisfy his narcissitic self-reflection to the utmost. On the other hand, purity also implies freedom of all other "imprints" (both sexual and cultural), so that once inscribed she will be a sign bearing exclusively his signature and as such testifying to its supremacy.

An obvious failure inherent in Angel's project lies in the fact that Tess, as trope for the spotlessness missing in his life, confirms this lack even as she functions to stabilize Angel's self-representation. Moreover the incrypting Tess has enacted in the course of her resurrection leaves her in a state of hesitation between two forms of living death; a mere figure or a fractured body. Her attempt at deferring the marriage expresses her desire to postpone a choice. The narrative she presents to Angel in exchange for his own confession, a narrative with which she pays for the trust and forgiveness she expects to receive and which she gives as a form of security that their marriage will, from the start, be one of honest reciprocity, marks the pivotal point in the chiasmic arrangement of her story. As I have already suggested, her narrative repeats Alec's rape in that she thus traces on the tissue of Angel's imagination a copy of the coarse pattern Alec traced on her body. If she previously tried to undo her past (including death's first incision) by killing herself into a figure, speaking for Tess becomes a way of undoing this fated transformation. She is, when she gives her narrative, a speaking corpse because at the acme of her tropic disembodiment, whose result was a total disavowal of her natural body.

Given the fact that Tess is well aware that Angel loves not her real self "but one in my image; the one I might have been" (33.273), her disclosure articulates the desire for another kind of substitution. If her rape was the result of a discrepancy between appearance (signifier) and natural body (signified), a marriage based on a similar contradiction can only become an equally fateful exchange. Since she, furthermore, conceives of their marriage as "two selves together, nothing to divide them" (32.261), its successful consummation presupposes that the division that grounds their mutual allegorization of her body must also be reversed to nothing. Giving her narrative (i.e., not denying her bodily rupture) thus also means attempting to undo the separation between her body and what it signifies, undoing the process that led to the split in herself and the split from her ideal lover. By narrating the death of her maidenhood and of her child, she reciprocates her passive reception of a wound by actively inflicting another—namely, a wound to Angel's narcissism—in the hope of thus healing her own. Her decision to reject the self-presentation that corresponds to Angel's allegorizing gaze marks the beginning of her triumph over death by acknowledging and choosing it. For the self-representation of "dairy-maid and nothing else" was based on the fundamental division of signifying "other," even though it semantically articulated a disavowal of division.

But if she gives her narrative to bring the past she has incrypted within herself into the open, Angel responds by reincryptment. Because in his eye she has become the Figure Purity, and thus the supreme safeguard to his human existence (34.286) his sense of self and of his actions in the world as meaningful are fundamentally disrupted by the revelation of her bodily impurity. Finding her tissue already with traces means in part accepting that the only possible imprint he can make is a palimpsest, which is always in danger of being subverted by previous hidden inscriptions. The uniqueness, originality and supremacy that his inscription and creation of Tess were to ensure are ambiguously threatened. His accusation "You were one person; now you are another . . . how can forgiveness meet such a grotesque—prestidigitation as that" (35.292), however, unintendedly turns into a self-accusation. For while Tess practiced deception by not telling her story earlier, the sleight of hand lay also in his allegorizing gaze, which continues to function even as it discloses itself. By insisting he loved "another woman in [Tess's] shape," by seeing her as "a guilty woman in the guise of an innocent one" he reenacts the "duplicity" he faults her with—a disaccord between appearance and body. Like Troy he valorizes the female trope over the female body; "With these natures, corporeal presence is sometimes less appealing than corporeal absence; the latter creating an ideal presence that conveniently drops the defects of the real" (36.312). Ultimately at stake, beyond any debate on the necessary *valuable* of female virginity, however, is the stability and truth of his allegorizing gaze. Because her body is the subject of Tess's revelation, its sublation becomes impossible; she thus forces Angel momentarily to acknowledge that body he has preferred to efface in his spiritualized image of her. The revelation also forces him to realize that Tess's body can incite more than one allegorization, thus putting both the validity and the uniqueness of his reading into question. Furthermore, since Tess is but a mirror image of himself, once he accepts the possibility that, while her gaze may not express any divergence she may, even as she speaks be seeing "another world behind her ostensible one, discordant and contrasting" (35.301), he opens the possibility of duplicity in his own perception of the world.

The violent incursion of the past into the present results in a feminine corpse, whose power to destabilize must be diffused. Sleepwalking, Angel enters her bedroom several nights after the nonconsummation of their marriage and murmurs "my dearest, darling Tess! So sweet, so good, so true . . . my wife—dead, dead" as he carries her outside and places her into an empty stone coffin next to the Abbey (37.316). In this state he can suspend the taboo of touching Tess imposed by his conscious mind. After kissing her the second time he breathes "as if a greatly desired end were attained" and immediately falls into a slumber of exhaustion, suggesting the completion of an orgasmic exercise. In Tess leading him home he fancies "a spirit . . . leading him to Heaven" (37.319). This corporeal enactment of a desire resides once again on a blurring of any distinction between bodies and signs. In burying a "Tess deanimated" by virtue of his designation "dead," Angel also incrypts Tess the trope of Truthfulness and Goodness. At least unconsciously, he thus secures intact as a repressed presence the figure of Tess he has created, which her bodily presence contradicts. At the same time his ambivalent attitude toward the female body as sexual object emerges. Whereas before his marriage he desired Tess as an "essence or typical form," after his marriage an erotic embrace seems possible only in a moment when he exhibits absolute possession, when the body to be embraced rests totally at his disposal—not only because it is a corpse but because it is in his power to designate it as such. In this symbolic enactment of a burial Angel exchanges Tess's living body for her corpse, doing so to preserve the figure in his mind, which will allow him, when he subsequently leaves England, to exchange her corporeal presence for an image, a "vague figure afar off," that becomes untainted in her absence; distance making "artistic virtues of . . . stains" (39.338).

Duplicitous as it may be, Angel's allegorizing gaze reciprocates and stabilizes Tess's own self-image, and with it a narcissistic desire for self-preservation. The loss of this gaze, which had momentarily barred her from choosing death, results in the return of a melancholic desire for death, as she retraces her steps back to her family vault. She realizes that by some fateful logic the price she must pay to ensure Angel's gaze is that of establishing a one-to-one correspondence between her body and the corpse he buried in effigy. Her living substantiality, irrevocably marked by rape, bars her body from being in perfect correlation with the pure figure he desires and has incrypted in his unconscious. That the realization "Bygones would never be complete bygones till she was a bygone herself" (45.391) is also a fatefully semiotic concern becomes evident in her inability to draw a distinction between body and sign the second time she repeats her rape—now paying back both Alec and Angel. For Angel's desire for purity is such that he wants her not only to signify "no trace of a division" in her self (semantic purity as chastity) but to do so in such a way that no division arises between what the body's appearance signifies and what the signified body is (structural purity as obliteration of the difference between signifier and signified). While this desired transparency was possible semantically, when Angel's gaze allegorized Tess into the figure of feminine essence, structural transparency is possible only when she moves from allegory to symbol in the detextualizing procedure that allows the body and its meaning to collapse into a perfect unity.

Paradoxically, what preserves her as a living self (though from the start already marked by death) is the allegorizing gaze that acknowledges difference and tension in its speaking *other* even as it kills the body into a trope. When she chooses to murder Alec (and thus chooses to be the death she has kept apart up to this point), she changes into a figure of death by embodying death. Through her hand death ruptures Alec's body, takes on his flesh. At the same time Tess, as instrument of death, gives up irrevocably her sense of self-preservation and changes into a disembodied figure self-reflexively signifying its own dissolution, signifying *nothing* by signifying nothing *other* than itself. Seeing her shortly before she will commit the murder, Angel has a "vague consciousness of one thing," though significantly he will recognize it only belatedly: "that his original Tess had spiritually ceased to recognize the body before him as her—allowing it to drift, like a corpse upon the current, in a direction dissociated from its living will" (45.484). Murder emerges as Tess's way of paying back Alec in the same coin—one bodily trespass reciprocates another—but it also turns into a payment Tess makes to get Angel back. Yet the price to retrieve Angel is the impossible gift of a pure body, so that Tess pays by extinguishing both the agent of her division (Alec) and the site of its inscription (her body). In so doing, she also repeats her first payment to Angel by undoing the two moments of division it contained: she substitutes for a narrative about her body the gift of her body, for the narrative about impurity one about purgation.

Hardy's narrative itself remains ambivalent as to whether a true understanding between Angel and Tess ultimately occurs when they finally consummate their marriage in the abandoned country mansion. They repeat the conditions of the pastoral setting for their first love by choosing, as then, a realm markedly outside history and culture. It remains unclear whether the move Tess makes beyond both the narcissistic realm of self-imaging and the symbolic realm of culture's moral laws is one Angel truly follows, entering with her the current of the already dead, in which she will not think "outside of now" (48.497). It also remains open whether the proximity of her death suspends for him also the economy of an allegorizing gaze and with it his demand for purity, or whether his realization of Tess's innocence and purity is yet another form of allegorizing. Finally it remains ambiguous whether he can consume the erotic embrace impossible to him before because she is what he has desired all along, a disembodied woman, so that the immanence of death has indeed purified her for him, undone the barring taint not just traced onto her body but also represented by her body.

But, regardless whether this erotic exchange is an experience of real unity or not, the fact that it depends on one partner's embrace of death casts light on the interdependence of self-preservation and allegorizing gazes. For Angel, the one who survives, must reenter both the rules of culture and the demands of his narcissistically informed libidinal economy and marry 'Liza-Lu, "a spiritualized image of Tess" (49.506). The violent rupture of the symbolic order of culture that Tess enacts through and at her body by giving and receiving death must be stabilized in the form of a reallegorization. Not only must her transgression of the law be punished by hanging, an exchange in which her dead body becomes a sign that the moral rules destabilized by her act have been reaffirmed. The text narratively reinscribes her into the language of allegory even before her hanging (significantly displaced in the text by its metonymy, the black flag of justice) is described. When the law, privileged sign of culture's symbolic order, catches up with her, she has again been transformed into an allegorical figure ambivalent in its reference, into a body sacrificed on the heathen stone altar at Stonehenge. This form, a "lesser creature than a woman" (48.505) simultaneously signifies Tess's sacrifice to nature, to culture's rules on rape and murder, to one man's inability to love a woman's body, to another's promiscuity or even to the "sport" dead knights and dames play on their descendant. But in all these readings her fulfillment is such that the series of violent incisions based always on a treatment of her body as trope is now irrevocably complete.

Allegory, of course, is grounded on a quintessential ambivalence in respect to the exchange of body with sign. For the point at which to distinguish whether this marks an instance of a word gaining body or a body objectified into a sign is not secure. Furthermore, by self-consciously admitting that it speaks *other*, allegory articulates discrepancy even as, in the act of gazing, it transforms the discrepant ambivalence of a concrete body so threatening to the self-image of the observer, into the reassuring stability of a figure. Yet what makes an allegory ultimately so pleasing it seems, is that by shifting the question of ambivalence from the literal to the rhetorical it can be signified and effaced at the same time. To take the body of a woman, deceptive to the narcissistic gaze because it will always exceed the image it is meant to reflect, and change it into a trope for deception, is a superlative prestidigitation. It means visibly acknowledging the rhetorical discrepancy (where the signifier and the signified ostensibly don't compare) in order to hide the threat of ambivalence in the realm of concrete bodies that initiated the turn to the tropic in the first place. Maybe at stake in the self-reflexive analogy of corpse and text is not only a discussion of the aesthetic as a move from the animate to the inanimate, in the course of which the author and the model are effaced. It may also give voice to the fact that the move to the rhetorical is often in response to discrepancies posed by an exchange with concrete bodies that threaten to wound our narcissism. In that the allegorizing gaze as safeguard to a stable sense of self attempts to sublate the challenge of the real, it points to another desire informing the use of tropes and thus to a moment in the analogy between corpse and text that potentially addresses questions of real violence.

NOTES

I want to express my gratitude to Eric S. Downing and Elizabeth Jane Bellamy for conversations while I was conceiving this article.

1. Claude Lévi-Strauss, *The Elementary Structures of Kinship*, revised edition (Boston: Beacon, 1969), 36.

2. Ibid., 481.

3. Sarah Kofman, *Mélancolie de l'art* (Paris: Galilée, 1985), 10–33.

4. This equation works even if the body referred to, the model for the fictional representation, is imaginary. Ong writes about the self-reflexivity of representations of death in art; "That is to say, a work about death often modulates readily, if eerily, into a work about literature. For death inhabits texts" (*Interfaces of the Word: Studies in the Evolution of Consciousness and Culture* [Ithaca: Cornell University Press, 1977], 238).

5. Jacques Derrida, *Of Grammatology*, trans. Gayatri Chakravorty Splivak (Baltimore: Johns Hopkins University Press, 1976), 17, 69.

6. Marina Warner, *Monuments and Maidens: The Allegory of the Female Form* (London: Weidenfeld and Nicolson, 1985). One of the roots for allegory is *allos*, other.

7. For a discussion of how femininity is linked with metaphor, trope, figural language, see R. Howard Bloch, "Medieval Misogyny," *Representations* 20 (Fall 1987), 1–24; Helena Michie, *The Flesh Made Word: Female Figures and Women's Bodies* (Oxford: Oxford University Press, 1987); and Jacques Derrida, *Spurs/Nietzsche's Styles*, trans. Barbara Harlow (Chicago: University Press of Chicago, 1979).

8. See Carol Gilligan, *In a Different Voice: Psychological Theory and Women's Development* (Cambridge: Harvard University Press, 1982); Ellie Ragland-Sullivan, *Jacques Lacan and the Philosophy of Psychoanalysis* (Urbana: University of Illinois Press, 1987), discusses how Lacanian topology places femininity on the side of the Real.

9. It is worth noting that the farmworkers' immediate reaction to Fanny's disappearance is to imagine her dead—burned, drowned or killed by her father's razor.

10. The counter-episode is, I would argue, the one in which Troy seduces Bathsheba with his sword exercises, and it is not only significantly present in the text but in a suggestive way casts light on the repressed "other" seduction scene. While in both seduction is linked to the threat of death, Bathsheba gets a kiss rather than death because Troy is dexterous enough with his sword not to cut into her body, while Fanny gets death as the result of a double corporeal penetration: insemination and birth-giving.

11. Harry Berger, Jr., "Bodies and Texts," *Representations* 17 (Winter 1987), 144–66.

12. Margaret Higonnet, "Speaking Silences: Women's Suicide," *The Female Body in Western Culture: Contemporary Perspectives*, ed. Susan Rubin Suleiman (Cambridge: Harvard University Press, 1986), 68–83.

13. Maurice Blanchot, *The Gaze of Orpheus*, trans. Lydia Davis (Barrytown: Station Hill, 1981), 81.

14. Ibid., 82. For a discussion of Blanchot. see also Eugenio Donato, "The Crypt of Flaubert," *Flaubert and Postmodernism*, ed. Naomi Shor and Henry F. Majewski (Lincoln: University of Nebraska Press, 1984), 30–45.

15. Blanchot, *Gaze*, 46.

16. Roland Barthes, *A Lover's Discourse: Fragments* (New York: Hill, 1978), 208.

17. Ellie Ragland-Sullivan points out that the father's name in Lacanian terminology refers to a symbolic effect of division, causing both loss of a previous wholeness, difference and individuation linking, that is, negation and naming/designating; "Lacan refers . . . to the Law of the Name-of-the-Father, a play on the identical pronunciation of French non and nom" (55).

18. Sarah Webster Goodwin, "Emma Bovary's Dance of Death," *Novel* 19 (1986), 197.

19. In the chapter entitled "I'd Have my Life Unbe" of his book *Thomas Hardy: Distance and Desire* (Cambridge: Harvard University Press, 1970), J. Hillis Miller focuses on the various configurations Tess's desire for death as a desire to erase all traces of herself, to reach a moment of complete self-erasure take on.

20. See Sigmund Freud "Beyond the Pleasure Principle" (1920), Standard Edition 18 (London: Hogarth Press, 1955).

21. J. Hillis Miller discusses the interplay between "acts of sexual conjunction, of physical violence and writing" in *Fiction and Repetition: Seven English Novels* (Cambridge: Harvard University Press, 1982), 116–46.

22. J. Hillis Miller, "The Two Allegories," in *Allegory, Myth, and Symbol*, Harvard English Studies 9, ed. Morton Bloomfield (Cambridge: Harvard University Press, 1981), 361.

23. Various other critics have discussed Angel's desire to spiritualize Tess, and thus deny her body. Penny Boumelha focuses on the way the narrator makes Tess into a transparent object or an object he wishes to penetrate *Thomas Hardy and Women: Sexual Ideology and Narrative Form* (Madison: University of Wisconsin Press, 1982), 117–34. Tony Tanner argues that what drives Tess to her death is both Angel's desire for a spiritualized Tess without a body and Alec's disregard of her spiritualized part ("Colour and Movement in Hardy's *Tess of the D'Urbervilles*,"

Critical Quarterly 10 [1968], 219–39). Helena Michie focuses on the way Tess becomes a "text to be read, interpreted, and edited by her two lovers" (*The Flesh Made Word*, 112–14).

Textual Hysteria:
Hardy's Narrator on Women

Kristin Brady

A commonplace in the longstanding controversy over Thomas Hardy's relationship to his female characters has been that from *Desperate Remedies,* the first novel, to *Jude the Obscure* and *The Well-Beloved,* the last long works of fiction, Hardy treated with increasing complexity woman's victimization by the Victorian sexual double standard. Most recently, Patricia Ingham has argued that Hardy's novels "develop a dialectical structure as the appropriating voice of patriarchy falters before the women that Hardy creates. Thus, an alternative discourse alongside the original misogyny begins to emerge even in the early novels and more fully from *The Woodlanders* onwards."[1] In Ingham's dialectic, the acts and words of Hardy's heroines come eventually to wield power over the narrator's authority. Other critics, however—particularly those who have written on *Tess of the d'Urbervilles*—locate power rather in the narrator himself, who constructs Tess and her sexuality chiefly through the exercise of a male gaze that projects its own sense of inadequacy onto her.[2]

Negotiating between these two opposing views, I argue that at the levels of characterization and of plot an enormous difference exists between the first novels, whose women generally adhere to the role of romance heroine, and the last, whose women lead lives that call those same romance roles into question; at the level of narrative discourse, however, remarkable parallels are found between the early fiction and the late, emerging chiefly from the narrator's continual engagement in the ongoing nineteenth-century discourse about "Woman's Nature." Throughout the fiction, this narratorial position remains a site of tension that exposes the contradictions in the Victorian symbolic economy and its signifying practices.[3] Here, I focus on one group of those signifying practices—the synchronic network of moral, aesthetic, and medical constructions of female sexuality—and its destabilizing function in Hardy's first and last novels.[4]

Victorian culture tended to equate woman with her potential maternal role. The traditional characterization of females as irrational and incapable of abstract reasoning was given new support by the assumption that their reproductive activity, beginning at puberty, prevented their minds from functioning as men's could: women's energies were directed below the waist, and any attempt to counter this "natural" physiological tendency could lead to serious and sometimes irreversible consequences. Consider, for example, T. S. Clouston's fantasies about the effects of educating women:

> The risks to the mental functions of the brain from the exhausting calls of menstruation, maternity, and lactation, from the nervous reflex influences of ovulation, conception, and parturition, are ruinous if there is the slightest original predisposition to derangement, and the normally profound influences on all the brain functions of the great eras of puberty and the climacteric period are too apt, in these circumstances, to upset the brain stability. Beyond all doubt, boarding-school education has not as yet been conducted on physiological principles, and is responsible for much nervous and mental derangement, as well as for difficult maternity; but if the education of civilized young women should become what some educationalists would wish to make it, all the brain energy would be used up in cramming a knowledge of the sciences, and there would be none left at all for the trophic and reproductive purposes.[5]

The notion that education created mental derangement and physical disability in women was linked to the essentialist idea of female weakness: reproductive activity was seen as distinctly pathological, an illness that could not be escaped. The tendency toward hysteria was a major symptom of this natural female disease, as were other signs of woman's instability: her vanity, her inconstancy, her tendency both to keep secrets and to speak uncontrollably. Woman's reputed virtues, such as selflessness, were also associated with her maternal function. The biological imperative of reproduction was thus used to reinforce the Victorian construction of gendered social roles, which confined women to the domestic world and enforced a cult of female chastity, while allowing men to inhabit the public as well as the private spheres. Both the celebration of virginity and the fascinated fear of the "fallen woman" suggest the Victorian need to confine female sexuality to reproduction and to keep control of that reproduction in patriarchal hands.

From the beginning of Hardy's fiction-writing career, his narrators—who consistently occupy the normative position of the male speaking to other males about women—at once undermine and support the Victorian construction of woman's nature. While challenging courtship rituals that privilege virginity and deny women's sexual responses, Hardy's narrators persist in constructing and interpreting female characters according to standard notions about woman's weakness, inconstancy, and tendency to hysteria. Hardy's women are often represented largely in visual terms, a technique that—because of what Sander L. Gilman has called "the essential iconographic nature of all visual representation"—turns them into icons and stereotypes.[6] Because cultural icons are themselves unstable, moreover, Hardy's texts construct woman in radically contradictory terms: she is both corrupt and pure, both victim and victimizer, both feminine and not feminine.

This contradictoriness in Hardy's female characters reflects an instability in the nineteenth-century's discourse of feminine sexuality, which, as Michel Foucault has argued, depended on the *"hysterization of women's bodies"* and the resulting Janus-faced idea of woman as either "Mother" or "her negative image of 'nervous woman.'" This construction reflected, in turn, a more generalized discourse that included male sexuality. Foucault notes that

> in the process of hysterization of women, "sex" was defined in three ways: as that which belongs in common to men and women; as that which belongs, *par excellence,* to men, and hence is lacking in women; but at the same time, as that which by itself constitutes woman's body, ordering it wholly in terms of the functions of reproduction and keeping it in constant agitation through the effects of that very function. Hysteria was interpreted in this strategy as the movement of sex insofar as it was the "one" and the "other," whole and part, principle and lack.[7]

In this tripartite definition of "sex," men projected onto women all that was frightening or repulsive about physical bodies, and the very construction of hysteria as a female disease was an expression of a need to keep masculinity free from corruption. As Sally Shuttleworth has pointed out, nineteenth-century culture manifested "a near-hysterical male anxiety focused on the flow of female secretions."[8] Woman's body thus became the focus of a masculine discourse that, in disavowing its own connection with the physical, was itself hysterical.[9]

In a manner that is especially intense and fraught with anxiety, the novels of Thomas Hardy participate in this hysterical discourse about the female body. Though they do indeed challenge contemporary definitions of womanhood—in fact, I would argue, precisely *because* they pursue the implications of this challenge—they can be included in what Claire Kahane has described as those "late nineteenth-century texts" that "can profitably be called premodernist and hysterical" and that, "as symptomatic narratives

. . . articulate the problematics of sexual difference, a difference challenged in great part by nineteenth-century feminism." In other words, the feminist dimension in Hardy's novels—manifest in his characterizations and in his plots—makes these works all the more hysterical by provoking in the male narrator acute anxiety and a resulting impulse for disavowal: the unconventional aspects of the women he constructs threaten his own imaginary sense of masculinity, triggering his fear of castration. Relevant here is Kahane's point that because "castration remains a trope, a figure of discourse rather than an actual physical danger the ego must avoid," men "more readily hystericize discourse" than women, for whom "rape is both a figure and a threatening possibility."[10] So Hardy's narrator hystericizes his own texts, making them say more than they mean to say by "suffering from reminiscence" of what they suppress and embodying the preoccupations and fears they cannot openly acknowledge.[11]

The characterizations of Hardy's women thus have all the contradictoriness of hysterical symptoms. The narrator, even as he constructs his women in opposition to the standard norm of woman as the weaker vessel, reverts all the more strongly to that same cultural imperative; like Sue Bridehead, his most hysterical symptom, he ultimately submits to the oppressive codes he has set out to challenge. This discordance in Hardy's narratives does not negate altogether their more direct interrogation of the position of women in Victorian society. Rather, in texts that purport to undermine the status quo, it foregrounds the contradictions in nineteenth-century systems of sexual difference—a group of signifying practices in which Hardy's texts could not help but participate.[12] I will now examine this phenomenon in Hardy's first novel, *Desperate Remedies,* and then consider its later development in *Jude the Obscure* and *The Well-Beloved.*

In *Desperate Remedies,* the narrator introduces Cytherea Graye in terms of her "many winning phases": during "pleasant doubt," during "the telling of a secret," and when "anxiously regarding one who possessed her affections" (1.8). Cytherea's character is seen immediately in terms of her changing moods, and those moods, in turn, are confined to the poses associated with courtship (Richard Taylor has called her "Hardy's first flirt").[13] It is therefore hardly surprising that at the point when Cytherea actually appears—significantly, it is as she witnesses her father's fatal fall—she is seen fainting:

In stepping, his foot slipped. An instant of doubling forward and sideways, and he reeled off into the air, immediately disappearing downwards.

His agonized daughter rose to her feet by a convulsive movement. Her lips parted, and she gasped for breath. She could utter no sound.

One by one the people about her, unconscious of what had happened, turned their heads, and inquiry and alarm became visible upon their faces at the sight of the poor child. A moment longer, and she fell to the floor. (1.8)

Though in this instance Cytherea certainly has reason to respond intensely to what she sees, the emphasis is on her swooning movements rather than on the event that occasions them, and these are focalized externally, from the narrator's point of view, as if he were one of the "people about her" witnessing her distress.[14]

It is significant that the narrator, in this first physical depiction in Hardy's novels of a woman, presents Cytherea's behavior in language that specifically suggests hysteria. Her "convulsive movement," the parting of her lips, the gasping for breath, and the inability to speak are all classic symptoms of this female malady. These details, in combination with the reference to Cytherea as a "poor child," associate the female with the infantile and move the focus of the scene from the violent physical reality of Ambrose Graye's death—the fall we witness only partially—to its physiological effect on his tremulous daughter, which completes her father's fall.

This bizarre effect is especially noteworthy when one considers the point, as Michael Millgate has suggested, that Cytherea's father "has almost wilfully precipitated her into [a helpless position] through his casualness about money and personal safety."[15] Hardy's narrator tacitly disavows the father's culpability by transferring the fall, with all its attendant connotations of physical and moral weakness, onto the hysterical symptoms of the daughter. This strategy influences Cytherea's characterization throughout the novel: at later points of crisis—when she sees Springrove just after her marriage to Manston and when Springrove rescues her from Manston—she will swoon again, revealing the inherent fragility of her female body. Cytherea's mind as well is revealed to be unstable. After her marriage to Manston, she appears, like Lucy Ashton in *The Bride of Lammermoor,* as if "her moral nature had fled," and her facial expression is "hard, wild, and unreal" (13.277). Cytherea's body and mind, like those of the hysteric in Freud's early theory, are made to bear the sins of the father.

This emphasis on female physical and mental weakness is present throughout the narrator's descriptions of Cytherea, especially in terms of her sexual responses. With Manston at the organ she feels herself, as if mesmerized, "compelled to do as she was bidden" (8.154) and "involuntarily shrinking up beside him" (8.155). When he attempts to bribe her into marriage by offering help to her brother, she appears, in terms that anticipate the imagery of hunted animals associated with Tess, like a "poor little bird" that is "terrified, driven into a corner, panting and fluttering about for some loophole of escape" (12.252).[16] When she agrees to marry Manston, she does so in a mood of "heroic self-abnegation" and thinks of her frustrated feeling for Edward Springrove by "indulging in a woman's pleasure of re-creating defunct agonies, and lacerating herself with them now and then" (12.257). Frequently, moreover, these characteristics are attributed to Cytherea not as individual to her, but as typical of her biological status as woman: Cytherea involves herself in the drama of other peoples' lives because "[y]oung women" have this "habit, not notice-able in men" (2.21); she fails to see "any but the serious side of her attachment" to Springrove because this is typical of women, while "the most devoted lover has all the time a vague and dim perception that he is losing his old dignity and frittering away his time" (3.49); she is more hopeful than her brother in times of difficulty because women have a "narrower vision" than men (3.55).

Often, the narrator's pronouncements about female nature take on an epigrammatic flavor, as if they were statements of universal wisdom. "A great statesman thinks several times, and acts," we are told after Cytherea has sent her note off to Manston, while "a young lady acts, and thinks several times" (8.159). Even the narrator's defenses of women sound like formulaic prescriptions. "Of all the ingenious and cruel satires that from the beginning till now have been stuck like knives into womankind, surely there is not one so lacerating to them, *and to us who love them,* as the trite old fact, that the most wretched of men can, in the twinkling of an eye, find a wife ready to be more wretched still for the sake of his company" (16.351, italics mine). Here, the narrator's sympathy with woman's victim-ized position has a disturbing doubleness: the satire that lacerates woman is not an external force of which she is the victim, but her own innate tendency to submit to the "most wretched of men"; and the narrator analyzes this phenomenon from his own position of chivalrous privilege, as one who *loves* women rather than as one who *is* a woman. At the basis of this narrator's construction of his female characters is his complacent sense that he and his reader stand outside the biological group he speaks of with such clinical authority. This authority is shared, moreover, with male characters in the novel. In language that echoes the gender formulas of the narrator, for example, Owen Graye tells his sister, "You know as well as I do, Cyth, that with women there's nothing between the two poles of emotion towards an interesting male acquaintance. 'Tis either love or aversion" (9.170). Cytherea is thus a specimen for narrative analysis, an object made understandable by the exclusive categories of knowledge shared among the male narrator, the male reader, and the male character. That the analysis is partially couched in terms of sympathy does not disguise the fact that the narrator speaks of her in terms of a scientific master discourse accessible to himself and to his reader but not to her.[17]

To some extent, the narrator's authoritative and essentialist vision is challenged by the presence in *Desperate Remedies* of Cytherea Aldclyffe, whose lesbian attraction to Cytherea Graye puts the older woman into a masculine position. Miss Aldclyffe is hurt that the younger woman has been kissed before, revealing that Miss Aldclyffe herself, like Springrove, wants her lover to be "a child among pleasures" (2.22). Miss Aldclyffe's logic, however, is different from that of the male who desires exclusive possession of a woman and who expects, therefore, that her lips (metonymically, her body and her sexuality) have never been touched by another man: what Miss Aldclyffe desires is a love free altogether from that corrupting taint of men that has already ruined her. A Miss Havisham in quest of her own Estella (though not for the purpose of revenge on the opposite sex), Miss Aldclyffe is disappointed that she has not found in Cytherea "an artless woman who ha[s] not practised or been practised upon by the arts which ruin all the truth and sweetness and goodness *in us*" (6.93, italics mine). For Miss Aldclyffe, an untouched Cytherea would offer the possibility of living vicariously an unruined life, of returning to an earlier state of happiness. Her disappointment in Cytherea repeats her disappointment in herself and her past: "You are as bad as I—we are all alike" (6.93).

Miss Aldclyffe does not consistently isolate herself, moreover, from patriarchal constructions of her sexuality. First, she is attracted to Cytherea partly as the daughter of her lost male lover. Second, her passion for vicarious pleasure eventually takes the form of forcing a marriage between Cytherea and her son, the living proof of her ruined state. Here the maternal impulse, seen as so central in woman by Victorian culture and by Hardy's narrator, overtakes Miss Aldclyffe's desire to find a love outside patriarchal definitions.[18] It is not surprising, therefore, that Miss Aldclyffe has a fatal stroke—the most extreme of fainting swoons—when she learns of Manston's death. Her lesbian desire never obliterates the female weakness to which she herself lays claim: "Cytherea, you know who that weak woman is" (7.442). Moreover, Cytherea's own ambivalently sexual response to Miss Aldclyffe, when set within the Gothic tradition to which Samuel Taylor Coleridge's "Christabel" belongs, can be interpreted as reinforcing the idea of an essential female corruption.[19]

In *Desperate Remedies*, the use of a scientific master discourse to analyze its female characters is generally used sympathetically. Cytherea's chief feminine inconsistency is her tendency to masochism, "her exercise of an illogical power entirely denied to men in general—the power not only kissing, but of delighting to kiss the rod by a punctilious observance of the self-immolating doctrines in the Sermon on the Mount" (12.240). Cytherea's subordinate social position is also emphasized: her vulnerability with Manston, though portrayed initially as physical, is finally associated with her desire to provide for her brother in his illness (in this she anticipates Tess, whose feeling of obligation to Alec d'Urberville for his aid to her family is an important factor in both stages of her sexual relationship with him). In these terms, the emphasis in the plot on the danger in which Cytherea finds herself—that of being the wife of a murderer, of an inconstant spouse, and of a man she does not love—constitutes an attack not on Cytherea's femaleness but on woman's powerless position in the sexual economy.

In the case of the much later and supposedly more radical *Jude the Obscure*, however, the novel's damning critique of Victorian sexual relationships is finally displaced by an appeal to woman's biological weakness, for it is Sue Bridehead's female "nature" itself, even more than social forces, that ultimately, in Jude's words, "[breaks]" her "intellect" (JO 6.10.484) and causes her to embrace exactly the oppressive conventions that she had earlier so eloquently attacked.[20] For this, Sue invites from Hardy's narrator not the sympathy he evinced for Cytherea Graye in *Desperate Remedies* but rather a measure of understanding about her social predicament combined with a cold clinical analysis of her presumed pathology and a marked antipathy toward her "nature" as a biological woman. The same disjunction does not exist in the characterization of Jude Fawley, whose victimization, like that of Tess, is presented chiefly in terms of forces outside himself. Jude is never "broken" by "*man's* nature," a term and concept that had no currency in the nineteenth century.

Hardy's choice of titles for his last novel—*Jude the Obscure* was decided upon at a late stage after he had already considered *The Simpletons, Hearts Insurgent,* and *The Recalcitrants*—reflects this assymetry in the treatment of his two lovers: Hardy's novel is not about both partners equally, but is predominantly about Jude Fawley, and his victimization is seen by both himself and the narrator as intrinsically linked to his relationships with women. The epigraph to the novel's first part, a passage from the Apocrypha about the self-destructive lengths to which men have gone for women, describes explicitly an assumption that often underlies the narrator's construction of character. This bias in the narrator's interpretive position is all the more problematic because it works against the novel's general method, which dramatizes the contradictory position within patriarchy of each of its major characters, female and male. The difficulty that Sue's characterization presents results not from her contradictory behavior—in this she is like Jude—but rather from the narrator's contradictory depiction of her, sometimes in terms of her own inborn perverseness, at other times in terms of her relationship to the Victorian ideological category of "woman's nature." This inconsistency emerges partly from the novel's portrayal of Sue in terms of the stereotypical New Woman of the 1890s, a figure who appeared to digress in such radical ways from the Victorian construction of woman but who also could be explained away in terms of this ideology.[21]

The perception of the New Woman in the nineteenth century both problematized and reinforced its ideology of gender difference. Attempting simultaneously to take control of their bodies and to use their minds, the women who assumed the role of the New Woman challenged the standard biological definitions and, in doing so, jeopardized the cultural construction not only of femininity but also of masculinity: if women could assume male prerogatives, where and how was masculinity to be constituted?[22] Thus a common anxiety about the New Woman had to do with her presumed denial or indulgence of her own sexuality—two strategies that, though radically opposed, had the common result of taking the female body out of male control. Interestingly, the consequence that was attached by the Victorians to the New Woman's independence was, once again, the nervous behavior of the female hysteric: because women were assumed to have been created to reproduce and not to think, the New Woman's mental activity could never be masculine, could never lead to rational ends. The New Woman was therefore in an especially perilous position: rejecting masculine control of her body, she fell naturally into the excessive nervousness of the hysteric. If womanhood was a pathological state, then being a "New Woman" implied an intensification of that pathology. This thinking is borne out in many late nineteenth-century medical treatises, which link an increase of hysteria with the rise of the New Woman.[23]

This essentialist view of the position of the New Woman with relation to gender ideology is actively at work in the construction of Sue Bridehead, both in the details associated with her and in the narrator's comments on her character. Even before she appears in the novel, Sue is linked up with the cantankerous "maiden" aunt whose restrictive feminine world Jude seeks to escape: Sue, we are told, was born in Drusilla Fawley's "four walls"—in the room, in fact, in which Drusilla dies—and the old woman remembers fondly that her niece had been "like a child o' my own" (JO 1.2.9). Drusilla is Sue's mother in two senses: effectively raising her in her early years, she also appears as the novel's first negative portrait of the virginal female—a witchlike exemplum of the woman whose body has not been touched by a man.[24] Drusilla thus appears as the embodiment in an earlier generation and in a rural context of the Sue type, one that the narrator continually calls "nervous" and that Hardy himself described in his 1912 preface, apparently paraphrasing a German reviewer, as "the woman of the feminist movement—the slight, pale 'bachelor' girl—the intellectualized, emancipated bundle of nerves that modern conditions were producing, mainly in cities as yet" (x).[25]

Compare this definition by Hardy to neurologist Horatio Bryan Donkin's conclusion about hysteria, written three years before *Jude* was published: "The cardinal fact in the psychopathy of hysteria is an exaggerated self-consciousness." The hysteric, according to Donkin, "is pre-eminently an individualist, an unsocial unit."[26] A similar attitude can be seen in Hugh E. M. Stutfield's 1897 review of the "neurotic school" of writing (this included *Jude the Obscure*). With self-righteous condescension, Stutfield described the early death of an "Ibsenite neuropath" who was "hopelessly vain, self-centered, neurotic, and egotistical. . . . Her self-absorption amounted to a disease," he explained, "and outraged Nature exacted the penalty remorselessly."[27] These accounts, which present moralistic judgments in the guise of scientific diagnosis, typify nineteenth-century descriptions of hysteria, summarized by Carroll Smith Rosenberg in these terms:

> Doctors commonly described hysterical women as highly impressionable, suggestible, and narcissistic. They were highly labile, their moods changing suddenly, dramatically, and for seemingly inconsequential reasons. Doctors complained that the hysterical woman was egocentric in the extreme, her involvement with others consistently superficial and tangential. Though the hysterical woman might appear to physicians and relatives as quite sexually stimulated or attractive, she was, doctors cautioned, essentially asexual and not uncommonly frigid.[28]

Smith-Rosenberg's account clearly corresponds both with Hardy's description of the New Woman in his preface and with the narrator's construction of Sue Bridehead.

The narrator's problematic relationship to Sue is obvious in his passing allusions to her as typical of the "contrite woman who always keeps back a little" (JO 6.9.479) and in his reference to her "narrow womanly humours" (3.6.200). It is also apparent, however, in what he excludes from his account. As Penny Boumelha has pointed out, Sue is much more visualized than internalized in Hardy's narration, in contrast to the constant references by the narrator to Jude's mental state.[29] In fact, the chief gap in the narrative lies not in the series of ellided lovemaking scenes but rather in the thoughts and feelings of Sue herself, which are rarely depicted or described but instead are suggested by her words and actions and guessed at by the narrator or by Jude. We are told repeatedly, moreover, that Sue's mind cannot be known and that her heart, if she has one, is a "mystery."

In his attempts to fill the gap of Sue's mind and heart with his own interpretations, Jude falls back increasingly upon stereotypical Victorian assumptions about woman's nature in general and about the pathology of the New Woman in particular. This doubling of stereotypes provides him, moreover, with an easy answer to the question—formulated at different times and in vexed tones both by him and by the narrator—of the extent to which Sue's behavior can be attributed to her own personality and the extent to which it can be linked up with her biological state as "woman." As Jude formulates the problem, "What I can't understand in you is your extraordinary blindness now to your old logic. Is it peculiar to you, or is it common to woman? Is a woman a thinking unit at all, or a fraction always wanting its integer?" (6.3.424). The answer, of course, is that both hypotheses depend on each other: Sue's pose as the New Woman and as a "thinking unit" derives from an individual "perversity" that is expressed in her independence and her sexual frigidity, but her womanhood insures that her radical ideas will lead only to inconsistency and hysteria—that she will be reduced by her female body, in other words, to "a fraction . . . wanting its integer." That Jude does himself come to this conclusion is apparent in his response to Sue's confession that she has "nearly brought [her] body into complete subjection" with Phillotson: "O you darling little fool; where is your reason? You seem to have suffered the loss of your faculties! I would argue with you if I didn't know that a woman in your state of feeling is quite beyond all appeals to her brains" (6.8.470). Never free himself from illogic, Jude had earlier challenged Sue's decision to return to Phillotson by saying, "You have never loved me as I love you—never—never! Yours is not a passionate heart—your heart does not burn in a flame! You are, upon the whole, a sort of fay, or sprite—not a woman!" (6.3.426). In other words, Jude blames Sue for her adherence to a feminine norm and for her digression from it; he sees her love as inferior to his both because she is a woman and because she is not one.

These inconsistencies in Jude's logic could be seen simply as aspects of his own characterization were it not for the fact that they are just as apparent in the narrator. It is sometimes difficult, in fact, especially when the narrator is using the convention of free indirect speech, to distinguish between Jude's thoughts and those of the narrator: the line between Jude's private interpretations and the narrator's conclusions about those thoughts is indeterminate.[30] With respect to women, moreover, the narrator and Jude—even when they speak quite separately—persistently echo each other in their interpretations. Both personify Nature as a fickle, callous female, and both speak of weakness as an essential aspect of women. When Jude says about his remarriage to Arabella, "I am not a man who wants to save himself at the expense of the weaker among us" (6.7.462), he is applying in misogynistic tones the seemingly sympathetic thinking of the narrator about the girls at Sue's Training-School in Melchester, who are described as lying in their cubicles, their tender feminine faces upturned to the flaring gas-jets which at intervals stretched down the long dormitories, every face bearing the legend The Weaker upon it, as the penalty of the sex wherein they were moulded, which by no possible exertion of their willing hearts and abilities could be made strong while the inexorable laws of nature remain what they are. They formed a pretty, suggestive, pathetic sight, of whose pathos and beauty they were themselves unconscious, and would not discover till, amid the storms and strains of after-years, with their injustice, loneliness, child-bearing, and bereavement, their minds would revert to this experience as something which had been allowed to slip past them insufficiently regarded. (3.3.168)

This polemical outburst, which sounds more characteristic of the *Tess* narrator than of the narrator in *Jude,* speaks in authoritative language against the very assumptions about breaking convention embraced by the New Woman, while also outlining in its latter parts the career of Sue's life, culminating in her grief at the loss of her children.[31] Most striking is the narrator's emphasis on "the inexorable laws of nature," which impose upon women an innate weakness that cannot be overcome by any "possible exertion of their willing hearts and abilities": long before Sue's "perversity" has been fully commented on by the narrator, the absolute futility of her attempt to overcome the limitations of her sex has been established, and the fault is not in social oppression but in the conditions of nature itself.

A similar assumption is present in the narrator's description of Sue when she is dressed in Jude's clothes. Here as elsewhere the language and tone suggest free indirect speech and hence a collapsing of the distinctions between Jude's and the narrator's responses. The narrator focalizes Jude's visual perspective and his thoughts: "Sitting in his only arm-chair he saw a slim and fragile being masquerading as himself on a Sunday, so pathetic in her defenselessness that his heart felt big with the sense of it" (3.3.173). When the woman masquerades as the man, then, she appears all the more weak and elicits from the male observer a chivalric paternalism. In these terms, it is significant that Jude—particularly in his most affectionate moments with Sue—continually addresses her as little and childlike.

Even the pattern of Sue's career as a New Woman reflects in curious ways essentialist assumptions about gender. Her early relationships with the young undergraduate, with Phillotson, and with Jude all are characterized by radical inconsistencies. In each case, she speaks eloquently in opposition to patriarchal oppression, but fails to find a satisfactory way of carrying out her ideas. Her difficulties, however, though never fully overcome, appear to diminish during the years of her adoptive and biological motherhood, at which point she shows strong maternal feelings, even for the child of Jude and Arabella.[32] Sue actually proposes marriage to Jude in response to the arrival of Father Time: "I do want to be kind to this child," she says, "and to be a mother to him; and our adding the legal form to our marriage might make it easier for him" (5.3.336). The two and a half years of nomadic wandering during which Sue's two children are born and a third is conceived is a tantalizing gap in the narration, summarized by the narrator simply as a time "not without its pleasantness" (5.7.372). In the scenes in which Sue is portrayed as a mother, her relationship with Jude seems without serious tension, and the two of them continually address each other in terms that suggest sexual closeness. Biological motherhood, it seems, has at least partially repressed the New Woman in Sue, imposing on her the conventional role of the wife whose body and desire belong to her husband. She appears to exemplify the fact that in the nineteenth century, as Mary Poovey has observed, "woman's definitive characteristic" was her "maternal instinct."[33]

Significantly, the narrator never describes Sue as manifesting nervous, contradictory, or hysterical symptoms during the time of her motherhood, and her apparent equilibrium is upset only by the gruesome death of her children, after which she abandons both her sexual relationship with Jude and her progressive ideas about woman's role. The loss of reproductive and nurturing activity destroys Sue's intellect, causing a hysterical reversal that exceeds all her earlier inconsistencies. The idea that motherhood is necessary for female mental stability is thus reinforced by the pathetic decline of Sue Bridehead—caused not by external social forces but by an irresolvable conflict between her own perverse nature and her weak female body. The deterioration of Jude Fawley is blamed on his victimization by the institutions of class and bourgeois marriage—as well as, in his view, by women themselves. Sue Bridehead, however, is finally the victim of her own sexuality, of "nature's law," rather than of arbitrary social laws. In these terms, Thomas Hardy's most powerful attack on Victorian social conventions is also his most emphatic endorsement of the biological determinism in nineteenth-century gender ideology. The narrator's construction of the New Woman leads only to his own hysterical reversal, in which the New Woman becomes an intensified version of the "Old Woman" (Drusilla?) of nineteenth-century scientific, aesthetic, and moral discourse: a perversely unstable body unable to transcend its gross physicality. The extremity of Sue Bridehead's feminism provokes in Hardy's narrator an aggressive assertion of his own sense of masculine superiority, a desperate disavowal of his own weakness.

Jude the Obscure does not necessarily represent, however, Hardy's last word in fiction. As Miller and Ingham have argued, *The Well-Beloved,* published in its final version two years after *Jude,* can be read as a critical commentary on the whole fictional corpus.[34] In this novel, the Hardyan narrator assumes an uncharacteristically ironic distance from the male protagonist, Jocelyn Pierston, who continually projects his own sense of insecurity onto a series of different women, of well-beloveds. The result of this new narrative strategy is, in Ingham's view, a judgment on "woman-focused art" and what it "does with women: the nature and extent of its attempted appropriation of them which, it demonstrates, inevitably fails." Ingham suggests, moreover, that Pierston's behavior is like "that of the narrators in Hardy's early novels who try to impose a single ideal of womanliness on all heroines through their Spencerian generalisations. Like him they fail and, presumably like him also, are now perceived as inimical to the supposed adored object."[35]

Ingham's argument is a compelling answer to a tendency in Hardy criticism to celebrate *The Well-Beloved* as both an exploration of "human nature and male psychology" and "one of a group of important nineteenth-century novels about art."[36] By rejecting the notion of Pierston as a normative or universal artist figure, Ingham draws attention to the pathology and the destructiveness of a creativity based on "the entrapment of women in the web of men's language." In making this case, however, she minimizes the continuing presence in the narrator's discourse of the nineteenth-century construction of the female body—an element that destabilizes the novel's metafictional dimension and draws the reader back to some of the preconceptions that governed the thinking of Hardy's earlier narrators. Ingham thus makes the admission—in the last paragraph of her book—that "[t]o biology, in this text Hardy, as always, gave an over-emphasis, as a reason for women being at a disadvantage," but she fails to explore the implications of this important fact.[37] Yet here again Hardy's narrator, even as he offers his most unsettling critique of the appropriating male gaze, reverts to hysterical outbursts that place on the figure of woman his own repressed fears.

The most striking instance of this hysteria in the narrator, which Ingham herself quotes only to dismiss, is his description of Mrs. Pine-Avon after her marriage to Somers:

> Mrs. Somers—once the intellectual, emancipated Mrs. Pine-Avon—had now retrograded to the petty and timid mental position of her mother and grandmother, giving sharp, strict regard to the current literature and art that reached the innocent presence of her long perspective of girls, with the view of hiding every skull and skeleton of life from their dear eyes. She was another illustration of the rule that succeeding generations of women are seldom marked by cumulative progress, their advance as girls being lost in their recession as matrons;

so that they move up and down the stream of intellectual development like flotsam in a tidal estuary. And this perhaps not by reason of their faults as individuals, but of their misfortune as child-rearers. (WB 3.4.170)

As if echoing the *Jude* narrator on "the inexorable laws of nature," this narrator insists on a "rule" dictating that women will never progress intellectually as men do because they rear children.

This judgment on Mrs. Pine-Avon, who had earlier sought to enter "the world of art" (WB 2.10.117), evades the fact, however, that her only access to that world was through her marriage to a male artist, an act that would lead to child-rearing and thus would ensure her intellectual regression. This dilemma is exacerbated by the fact that Somers himself, the artist who marries Mrs. Pine-Avon, regards both women and men in terms of stereotypically essentialist categories. In his view, women "are all alike," distinguishable only in terms of their coloring and useful only as models for his painting or as property. Upon learning that Mrs. Pine-Avon has light hair he comments, "I wanted something darker.... There are so many fair models among native English-women. Still, blondes are useful property!" (2.10.117). Established throughout *The Well-Beloved* as a sensible contrast to the idealizing Pierston, Somers is no less destructive to women. It is not surprising, therefore, that in offering advice to Pierston, Somers naturalizes and romanticizes male fickleness: "You are like other men, only rather worse. Essentially, all men are fickle, like you; but not with such perceptiveness" (1.7.37). In these initial characterizations of Mrs. Pine-Avon as aspiring to the world of art and of Somers as callous possessor of female objects, the groundwork has been established for a sexual relationship that is at least as perverse as Pierston's with the three generations of Avice Caros. In his description of the Somers marriage, the narrator's retreat to a "rule" governing the fate of all women who rear children thus constitutes another hysterical reversal, a refusal to explore the full implications of the narrative he had begun to construct. The story of Mrs. Pine-Avon's marriage to Somers is left hidden behind the narrator's defensive generalization about woman's biological status.

Another site of tension in the narrator's critique of Pierston's woman-centered artistic sensibility lies in the characterization of the second Avice as herself in pursuit of a migratory well-beloved. As Ingham suggests, this detail is one example of the fact that "the Caro women are resistant to the imposition" of Pierston's "uniform signification" and that "[t]heir individuality spills out into the corners of the text."[38] The effect of Ann-Avice's failure to fix on a single love object is not, however—as it is in the case of Pierston—to make her an artist. Rather, she merely shifts her attentions from man to man until, like Sue Bridehead and Mrs. Pine-Avon, she is changed by motherhood. After the birth of her child, she is "very much fortified by the pink little lump at her side" (2.13.140), and in her later years devotes all her energies, like Miss Aldclyffe, to acquiring for her child "what she herself had just missed securing" (3.6.190).

Significantly, Ann-Avice's pursuit of this "artistic and tender finish" (3.6.190) to her daughter's life is characterized by the symptoms of hysteria. In her sickness and excitement, she resembles the palpitating Elfride Swancourt of the early *A Pair of Blue Eyes*, whose heartbeats caused a vase of flowers to throb: "Her state was such that she could see the hangings of the bed tremble with her tremors" (WB 3.6.190). When she learns of her daughter's elopement, Ann-Avice is then "so distracted and incoherent as to be like a person in a delirium" (WB 3.6.196) and finally dies, like Miss Aldclyffe, from shock. *The Well-Beloved* thus retains the standard mind-body opposition in Victorian gender theory: the frustration of Pierston's masculine desires leads to the "strange death" of an aspect of his mind, his "artistic sense" and "sensuous side" (WB 3.8.209); the same frustration of Ann-Avice's feminine desires leads to "a long strain of anxiety" on her "feeble heart" (WB 3.6.197) and a stranger death still, that of her hysterical body. For this reason, although Hardy's narrator evades the standard closure of a romantic love plot, he does not successfully reject the "geometrical shape" (WB 3.8.216) of sexual difference as it was constructed by nineteenth-century culture. Even in this novel—which so compellingly interrogates the earlier premises of Hardy's art—the narrator's discourse is itself hystericized, revealing that hysteria is ultimately a textual rather than a physiological or psychological phenomenon, emerging from an ongoing nineteenth-century masculine discourse that seeks to evade by a process of projection and dissociation its own uneasiness about the body: woman is again the empty sign filled with a masculine fear of absence, of lack, and of corruption. Her hysteria is the projection of his.

NOTES

1. Patricia Ingham, *Thomas Hardy* (Atlantic Highlands, N.J.: Humanities, 1990), 99.

2. The best example of this argument is Kaja Silverman, "History, Figuration and Female Subjectivity in *Tess*," *Novel* 18 (1984): 5–28.

3. My approach here is influenced by Mary Poovey's adaptation of Louis Althusser (*Uneven Developments: The Ideological Work of Gender in Mid-Victorian England* [Chicago: University of Chicago Press, 1988]).

4. See Penny Boumelha on the "decisive shift of sexuality" in the Victorian period "from the area of moral discourse to that of the scientific" (*Thomas Hardy*

and Women: Sexual Ideology and Narrative Form [Sussex: Harvester, 1982], 12); Neil Hertz on the "links among erotic, political and aesthetic attitudes" ("Medusa's Head: Male Hysteria under Political Pressure," *Representations* 4 [1983]: 35); and Sander L. Gilman on the links between aesthetic and medical discourses ("Black Bodies, White Bodies: Toward an Iconography of Female Sexuality in Late Nineteenth-Century Art, Medicine, and Literature," *Critical Inquiry* 12 [1985]: 204–42).

5. T. S. Clouston, *Clinical Lectures on Mental Diseases* (Philadelphia: Henry C. Lea's son, 1884 [date of earlier English edition not given]), 371. Such ideas are prominent throughout Clouston (see 336–40, 359–64, 371–72) and the influential Henry Maudsley, whose work Hardy knew (see *Body and Mind: An Inquiry into Their Connection and Mutual Influence* [New York: Appleton, 1871], 35, 70–71, 76–79). For extended analyses of the Victorian construction of the female body, see Ellen J. Bassuk, "The Rest Cure: Repetition or Resolution of Victorian Women's Conflicts?" in *The Female Body in Western Culture: Contemporary Perspectives,* ed. Susan Rubin Suleiman (Cambridge: Harvard University Press, 1986), 139–51; Nancy Cott, "Passionlessness: An Interpretation of Victorian Sexual Ideology, 1790–1850," *Signs* 4 (1978): 219–36; Gilman, "Female Sexuality," 204–42; Thomas Laqueur, "Orgasm, Generation, and the Politics of Reproductive Biology," *Representations* 14 (1986): 1–41; Mary Poovey, "Speaking of the Body: Mid-Victorian Constructions of Female Desire," in *Body/Politics: Women and the Discourses of Science,* ed. Mary Jacobus, Evelyn Fox Keller, Sally Shuttleworth (London: Routledge, 1990), 29–46; Londa Schiebinger, *The Mind Has No Sex? Women in the Origins of Modern Science* (Cambridge: Harvard University Press, 1989); Elaine Showalter, *The Female Malady: Women, Madness, and English Culture, 1830–1980* (New York: Pantheon, 1985); Shuttleworth, "Female Circulation: Medical Discourse and Popular Advertising in the Mid-Victorian Era," in *Body/Politics,* 47–68.

6. Gilman, "Female Sexuality," 205.

7. Michel Foucault, *The History of Sexuality,* trans. Robert Hurley vol. 1 (1978; New York: Vintage, 1980), 104, 153.

8. Shuttleworth, "Female Circulation," 61. See also Gilman on "the function of the sexualized female as the sign of disease" ("Female Sexuality," 234).

9. For a fictional example of this phenomenon, see Silverman on the hysteria of Angel Clare, caused by "a disruption in the sexual economy of the look—a disturbance of that scopic regime so painstakingly put in place by the novel, within which the narrator, fully as much as the central male characters, assumes residence" ("Female Subjectivity," 14).

10. Claire Kahane, "Hysteria, Feminism, and the Case of *The Bostonians,*" in *Feminism and Psychoanalysis,* ed. Richard Feldstein and Judith Roof (Ithaca: Cornell University Press, 1989), 286.

11. For further discussion of "hysterical texts," see Mary Jacobus, *Reading Woman: Essays in Feminist Criticism* (London: Methuen, 1986), 197–274.

12. My argument here runs parallel to that of Ingham, who also examines the relationship of Hardy's narrator to the nineteenth-century construction of woman. I do not conclude, however, as Ingham does, that an alternative discourse in the

novels' plots and characterization overrides the narrator's generalizations about women. Ingham bases her conclusion on the premise that "a narrative text always implies that the narrator is subordinate to the set of events, the 'nontextual given' that he is recounting" (*Thomas Hardy*, 27). I would argue, however, that it is the narrator's desires and fears which structure the text and that, as John Goode has pointed out, the narrator "is precisely what articulates the relationship of the text to ideology itself . . . because it subjects the reader to a defined subjectivity, and thus, if it is successful, makes it visible" ("Woman and the Literary Text," *The Rights and Wrongs of Women*, ed. Juliet Mitchell and Ann Oakley [Harmondsworth: Penguin, 1976], 218–19).

13. Richard Taylor, *The Neglected Hardy: Thomas Hardy's Lesser Novels* (New York: St. Martin's, 1982), 17.

14. My reading obviously differs from that of John Bayley, who suggests that by means of the fall scene, "Cytherea herself, in her consciousness and physical being, becomes wholly realised for us" (*An Essay on Hardy* [Cambridge: Cambridge University Press, 1978], 125). For interesting discussions of the relationships of fathers to falls in Hardy's early fiction, see Judith Bryant Wittenberg, "Thomas Hardy's First Novel: Women and the Quest for Autonomy," *Colby Library Quarterly* 18 (1982): 52 and "Early Hardy Novels and the Fictional Eye," *Novel* 16 (1983): 158–59 and 162–63.

15. Michael Millgate, *Thomas Hardy: His Career as a Novelist* (London: Bodley Head, 1971), 33.

16. Lawrence Jones notes that Hardy reread *Desperate Remedies* during the period when he was writing *Tess* and suggests that there are close parallels in language and imagery between the two novels ("*Tess of the d'Urbervilles* and the 'New Edition' of *Desperate Remedies*," *Colby Library Quarterly* 15 [1979]: 195–96).

17. For an interesting discussion of voyeurism in Hardy's narrative technique, see Wittenberg, "Early Hardy Novels" 154–55. Wittenberg's emphasis, however, is on Hardy as author and artist rather than on the narrator.

18. Miss Aldclyffe is like Arabella Transome of George Eliot's *Felix Holt*, who wants Esther Lyon to marry her son, who was conceived in an adulterous liaison. As in *Desperate Remedies*, the relationship between the two women is strongly sexual. See Sally Mitchell, *The Fallen Angel: Chastity, Class and Women's Reading, 1835–1880* (Bowling Green: Bowling Green University Popular Press, 1981), 96 and T. R. Wright, *Hardy and the Erotic* (London: Macmillan, 1989), 39 on the linkage of the sexual and the maternal in Miss Aldclyffe.

19. See also Gilman, who points out that in Zola's *Nana* "part of Nana's fall into corruption comes through her seduction by a lesbian, yet a further sign of her innate, physical degeneracy" ("Female Sexuality," 237).

20. This reading is in agreement with Jacobus, who argues that "[i]t is precisely Sue's femaleness which breaks her" ("Sue the Obscure," *Essays in Criticism* 25 [1975], 321), and differs from the views of Kathleen Blake ("Pure Tess: Hardy on Knowing a Woman," *Studies in English Literature, 1500–1900* 22 [1982], 166) and Penny Boumelha (*Thomas Hardy and Women*, 153), which pin blame on social laws. Ingham sees Sue's reversal as evidence of "a new perspective, not found in

most New Woman novels" and therefore as an "innovatory narrative pattern" (*Thomas Hardy*, 95).

21. The question of whether or not Sue can be categorized as a New Woman has been controversial. Robert Gittings, for example, argues that she is a "Girl of the Period" of the 1860s rather than a New Woman of the 1890s (*Young Thomas Hardy* [Boston: Little Brown, 1975], 94–95; see also Rosemarie Morgan, *Women and Sexuality in the Novels of Thomas Hardy* [London: Routledge, 1988], 186n8). I agree with Gail Cunningham (*The New Woman and the Victorian Novel* [London: Macmillan, 1978], 80) and Wright (*Hardy* 120), who insist that Hardy was working within the tradition of New Woman fiction. It is worth noting that Hardy considered giving the titles "The New Woman" and "A Woman of Ideas" to a dramatized version of *Jude* (Millgate, *Thomas Hardy*, 312). Interestingly, a form of the novel that excludes the narrator shifts the attention of its title away from Jude to Sue.

22. See Kahane, "Hysteria," 287 on the threat posed by the New Woman.

23. See Cunningham, *New Woman*, 49 and 51; Showalter, *Female Malady*, 137; Eric Trudgill, *Madonnas and Magdalens: The Origins and Development of Victorian Sexual Attitudes* (London: Heinemann, 1976), 64. Goode comments on the Victorian equation of mannishness with too much womanliness ("Woman" 231). See also Hugh E. M. Stutfield's review of "the literature of hysteria," which included *Jude* ("The Psychology of Feminism," *Blackwood's* 161 [Jan. 1897]: 109).

24. Drusilla's small shop, with its "poor penny articles," is not unlike that of the similarly named and analogously pathetic Hepzibah in Hawthorne's *House of the Seven Gables*. Norman Page remarks on the novel's contrast between the ethereal image of Christminster and the dismal details of Drusilla's shop (*Thomas Hardy* [London: Routledge, 1977], 83). Goode suggests that the first chapter of *Jude* is a parody of the opening in *Tom Sawyer*, "where the importunity of the aunt provokes the division of labour" (*Thomas Hardy: The Offensive Truth* [Oxford: Blackwell, 1988], 146).

25. Hardy's apparent attempt to dissociate himself from the New Woman fiction may have been a response to the fact that this genre was perceived as bestial (Boumelha, *Thomas Hardy and Women*, 69).

26. Quoted in Showalter, *Female Malady*, 134.

27. Stutfield, "Feminism," 109.

28. Carroll Smith Rosenberg, *Disorderly Conduct: Visions of Gender in Victorian America* (New York: Knopf, 1985), 202.

29. Boumelha, *Thomas Hardy and Women*, 148. See also Bayley, *An Essay on Hardy*, 201. Jacobus, however, argues for the text's emphasis on Sue's consciousness ("Sue the Obscure," 307).

30. See Boumelha on the "collusion" between Jude and the narrator (*Thomas Hardy and Women*, 147).

31. On the similarities between this passage and the events of Sue's life, see Ibid., 142.

32. Boumelha points out that the New Woman novel *The Yellow Aster* also dramatizes the triumph of motherhood over feminism (Ibid., 87); in addition, she invokes George Egerton on the danger of repressing motherhood (Ibid., 89–90).

33. Poovey, *Uneven Developments*, 7.

34. Miller, *Fiction and Repetition: Seven English Novels* (Cambridge: Harvard University Press, 1982), 149 and Ingham *Thomas Hardy*, 96–99.

35. Ingham, *Thomas Hardy*, 100–101.

36. See Taylor, *The Neglected Hardy*, 157 and Miller, *Fiction and Repetition*, 148. For other readings of the novel in terms of Pierston as artist figure, see Millgate, *Thomas Hardy*, 298–99 and Page, *Thomas Hardy*, 116–19. The most romantic reader of *The Well-Beloved* is John Fowles, who accepts as natural and universal a male artist figure who is dependent on the simultaneous presence of a wifely hag and an ethereal, inaccessible muse as well-beloved ("Hardy and the Hag," *Thomas Hardy after Fifty Years*, ed. Lance St. John Butler [London: Macmillan, 1977], 28–42).

37. Ingham, *Thomas Hardy*, 103 and 109.

38. Ibid., 103.

Hardy Ruins:
Female Spaces and Male Designs

U. C. Knoepflmacher

I once inquired of her/ How looked the spot when first she settled there.
—Thomas Hardy, "Domicilium" (c. 1857–60)

. . . he found a "mine" in me, he said . . .
—Emma Hardy, *Some Recollections*
(c. 1911–12)

The houses depicted in nineteenth-century British poetry differ substantially both from earlier representations of a patriarchal seat in poems such as Marvell's "Upon Appleton House" and Pope's "Epistle to Burlington" as well as from the male mansions domesticated by female inhabitants in nineteenth-century realistic novels. In a century that separated an inner circle of female domesticity from an outer sphere of male traffic, the home became increasingly feminized, associated with childhood and hence with nurturance.[1] Yet a good many imaginative writers responded to this division by attempting to integrate gender opposites within a culturally defined feminine space. In *Jane Eyre*, for example, Ferndean replaces Thornfield Hall as a site in which an independent Jane can animate the paralyzed Rochester and enter a more equitable union. This integration, however, does not work in the same way for poets as it does for novelists; likewise, it works differently for men and women.[2] For Thomas Hardy, who preferred poetry to fiction, the recovery of the feminine was the propelling force behind his finest lyrics. Over his poetic career, Hardy wavered in his faith that the feminine, which he associated with the houses of childhood, could be recovered without the compromise of an adult masculinity. Eventually, however, in his old age, he managed to effect the "return to the native land" that Freud identified as a maternal "home" (Cixous and Clément 93).

The structures of desire devised by Hardy's nineteenth-century poetic predecessors dramatize the difficulty of finding a feminine space capable of annulling gender and rendering sexual difference immaterial. By way of contrast, the patriarchal houses that novelists enlisted as transformational space allow female occupants room enough to break down too rigidly gendered opposites. Just as Pemberley Hall crowns Elizabeth Bennet's efforts to soften Darcy's male pride (while simultaneously acting as a patriarchal corrective to her own prejudices), so are the male mansions renovated when entered by Jane Eyre, Catherine Linton, Helen Huntingdon, Esther Summerson, and even Hardy's Bathsheba Everdene.[3] In Romantic and Victorian poetry, however, such a process of renewal and restabilizing remains far more problematic. Ruins, rather than living buildings, predominate in works in which a female, rather than a male abode, becomes directly or indirectly associated with what Bachelard sees as a "dream-memory" of an original maternal envelope (Bachelard 15).

Romantic poetry all too often depicts a ruthless razing of the structures it persistently identifies with a feminine enclosure: the "purple-lined palace of sweet sin" Keats's Lamia has devised for young Lycius cannot withstand the gaze of an older male realist; the "white walls" of the shelter into which Byron's Haidee has transported her own lover crumble upon the deaths of their unborn child, herself, and her ultra-masculine father (*Lamia* 2:31; *Don Juan* 3.27.209).[4] One mode by which nineteenth-century male poets could sustain the intensity of their profound yearning for a return to a site free of strife was to link this threatened female space with death. In his influential "The Ruined Cottage" (the first book of *The Excursion* of 1814), Wordsworth lingered on the decayed structure that once housed the female figure the Wanderer had regarded as "my own child" (500). The young poet, who has been "slaking" his thirst from a nearby well, soon finds the sad account of the last "tenant of these ruined walls" far more refreshing than any classical elegy bemoaning the disappearance of woodsprites or water-nymphs (475–77).

By having male teller and male listener jointly review "that woman's suffering" (922), Wordsworth strengthens their bond as well as his own poetic identity. Margaret is cast as the alluring sleeper Cixous and Clément describe in *The Newly Born Woman*: "intact, eternal, absolutely powerless," she acts as an enabling presence for male dreamers, a second and "best mother" (66). The invigorated "old Man" who now grasps his staff with "sprightly mien," and Wordsworth's speaker, moved to bless Margaret "in the impotence of grief," can become more potent than before (965, 964). The inert female has provided male pilgrims with the starting point for their peregrinations: poet-son and Wanderer-father can now join other representative male selves, Solitary and Pastor, in public meeting places. The young speaker may profess a "brother's love" for the dead stranger the

Wanderer adopted as a daughter. Yet the speaker is also her son. As the surviving foster child of both Wanderer and Margaret, he proves more hardy than the fragile figure ravaged by wifehood, widowhood, and "maternal cares" (858). His narrative thrives on her ruin.

Whereas Wordsworth's male selves reenter a maternal house only to egress, regrouped, as a strengthened masculine unit, Thomas Hardy struggles not to repress femininity in writings that self-consciously enlist—yet also subvert—the *Heimweh,* the profound homesickness, that his Romantic and Victorian predecessors had so powerfully dramatized. Whether written at the outset or the end of his long career, a large proportion of Hardy's poems rely on an increasingly elaborate nexus of mother/feminine/house figurations to work out a gender opposition he would like to abolish. In his eagerness to annul sexual difference, Hardy eventually devises lyrics and narratives that allow him to tap something like the fluidity recent critics have noted in Freud's essay on "The Uncanny." Hardy's later poems demonstrate that femininity, as Shoshana Felman puts it, instead of acting as a "snug container of masculinity," can enter and inhabit the masculine (42). As we shall see, it was the empowering ghost of Emma Hardy that finally furnished Hardy with a means to bridge opposites. Though lost and obliterated, a *heimisch,* or "homelike," maternal place could animate a poetry in which the uncanny, or *Unheimliche,* becomes itself familiar, a "vibration of the *Heimliche*" (Cixous 545).

I

In *The Early Life of Thomas Hardy* (1928; rpt. in *The Life of Thomas Hardy,* 1962), attributed to Florence Emily Hardy yet actually composed by the subject himself, Hardy points his readers to the female place of origin of a younger Wordsworthian self by reproducing a poem he wrote sometime between the ages of seventeen and twenty. Screened from the public eye for nearly sixty years, "Domicilium" is itself a relic, much like Margaret's time-obliterated cottage. Like the Wanderer, the aged Hardy undertakes a revisitation. By returning to a setting that physically existed "nearly half a century before [his] birth," he can enlist these "Wordsworthian lines" for something more than their avowedly "naive fidelity" to a literal past (F. E. Hardy 4). For he not only restores a rural house of the 1790s but also returns to the time of Wordsworth's memorable perceptions of those maternal sister-selves placed near the ruins of Tintern Abbey or of Margaret's cot.

Still, as his reliance on the mask of Florence Hardy suggests, Hardy eschews a male guide such as the Wanderer to help him reconstruct what he calls, somewhat deceptively, a "paternal homestead." He refuses to

silence those voices whose muting was necessary for Wordsworth to solid-
ify a male poetic identity. Avoiding a male mediator such as the one who
interpreted Dorothy's eyes as "gleams" of his own "past existence" in
"Tintern Abbey" (148–49), Hardy prefers to rely on a female mediator,
"my father's mother," to help him explore his own origins (20).[5] It is the
voice of this family historian that takes over—at the exact midpoint of
"Domicilium"—the speech of the youthful male who has struggled to set
the stage in the opening three sestets.

Asked to recall the aspects of "the spot when first she settled there," the
boy's grandmother integrates the human habitat with its surrounding
wilderness:

> Our house stood quite alone, and those tall firs
> And beeches were not planted. Snakes and efts
> Swarmed in the summer days, and nightly bats
> Would fly about our bedroom. Heathcroppers
> Lived on the hills, and were our only friends;
> So wild it was when first we settled here. (31–36)

By recalling the "uncultivated slopes" of the past (27), this artless speaker
undermines the cultivation of the would-be poet who has given the name
of "domicilium" to what she, far more simply, calls "our house." Unlike
Wordsworth's Miltonic Wanderer, the grandmother is a witness who requires
no exalted correlatives. Beginning his narrative as a "man speaking to
men," the young adult soon becomes a boy again, remembering how,
awe-struck, he had deferred to the authority of an ancient who still
addressed him as "my child" (25). Aware that "hardy flowers" flourish
"best untrained" (8–9), the youngster does not want his male training to
distance him from the Hardy woman who once flowered on this site. Eager
to erase what separates them, he allows her to close the narrative he
began.

Despite his reliance on a female voice to finish his poem, the young
Hardy of "Domicilium" does not wholly reject the precedent of "The
Ruined Cottage." The grandmother's voice may receive far greater primacy than Margaret's, which, when heard at all, is smothered by her two
interpreters; but by slipping into a second childhood and blending with
plants that "lag behind the season" (721), Margaret, too, could serve as the
agent of a flickering desire to elude the adult, gendered identity Wordsworth's
male personae reluctantly accept. In contrast to Margaret, however, the
female speaker of "Domicilium" does not need to enact a death-wish to
break down the barriers between self and not self. Yet her unself-
consciousness performs a similar function for a male child conditioned to
resist boundary confusions (Chodorow 106). In addressing her son's son as

"my child," this mother figure can condense two generations into one. Although her identity remains far more social and communal than Margaret's, her memories of a continuous past have the same effect as the Wanderer's account of Margaret's dissolution into Nature. "Our house" is no more. Margaret, in the few words accorded to her, remarks how "changed" she became by her dislocation (765–67). As aware that "change has marked/ The fact of all things" (25–26), the grandmother can at least sanction the yearnings of the adolescent who wants to cling to the child self she had nurtured. She belongs to an Ur-world in which binary oppositions—outer/inner, male/female, adult/child, artifact/nature—could still dissolve.

Yet "Domicilium" also inscribes the dialectic Hardy wishes to blur. Despite his nostalgic empowerment of a female voice, the autobiographer who reproduces this youthful discourse of desire only adds to the ironies already embedded in the text. However rapt and earnest, the child listener fails to avoid his inevitable transformation into the pretentious young poet who gives the verses their Latinate title. No impersonation can reclaim the pristine "spot" glimpsed by the grandmother. She is herself but a memory-trace, having died and being "now / Blest with the blest" (20–21), as the speaker makes sure to inform us. Like Margaret, the grandmother remains a figuration of desire that must adapt itself, however reluctantly, to "change." Her utterance thus anticipates the more self-conscious appropriations of female speech Hardy undertakes in "The Ruined Maid" (1866) or in the more pathetic "Tess's Lament" (1901). In the latter poem, the dairymaid—reclaimed from Tess of the d'Urbervilles—contends that "nettle, dock, and briar" have obliterated the warm and cozy spot she once shared with a male lover (22).

In his inability to go beyond mere yearning, the Hardy of "Domicilium" cannot yet extricate himself from Wordsworth's bind. Eager to evoke the fusions he associates with a lost feminine space, the male artist nonetheless accepts his place in a circumscribed reality built on the very binaries he would gladly abolish.

II

Although Hardy would continue to covet the "spot" he had allowed the grandmother in "Domicilium" he now began to ironize the feminine and to endow the masculine with a greater authority. While writing his prize essay "The Application of Coloured Bricks and Terra Cotta to Modern Architecture" (1863), the ambitious young architect was imitating Shelley, Browning, and Tennyson, poets he regarded as more intellectual and thus more adult than Wordsworth. The ironies that "Domicilium" minimizes dominate "Heiress and Architect" (1867), the highly patterned self-dialogue in which Hardy pits a ruthless male "arch-designer" against a sentimental (and Wordsworthian) female client. Their exchange allowed Hardy to sharpen the tensions, still whimsically handled, in his first published piece of fiction, "How I Built Myself a House" (1865). There, the unwary narrator, John, who wants a home built according to specifications he and his equally naive wife, Sophia, have set down, finds himself caught between her roomy prospects and an actual structure repeatedly "lessened" by practical constraints and by the "scientific reasoning" of the designer (Orel 163).

"Heiress and Architect" relies on a "decremental structure" in order to render a prospective house dweller's lessening scope of expectations (Bailey 108). The heiress of the title clearly stands for a soul who must confront an inheritance of material diminution and death. This unnamed "she" differs as much from the buoyant Sophia as the architect who acts as her instructor differs from Mr. Penny, the droll Dickensian consulted in "How I Built Myself a House." A brutal realist, the "he" of the poem programmatically destroys his client's illusion. As her "guide," he sets out to expose her defiance of "the rule" of laws he regards as irrefutable. Her naivete about life, he insists on showing, invalidates the various shapes into which the heiress tries to wrap her desire for a space of her own. The reader is forced to share the pain of the heiress, whom Hardy subjects to an exorcism of a wishfulness he now identifies as feminine. At the same time, however, Hardy manages to induce an uncomfortably sadistic pleasure through the relentless process of reduction—and, ultimately, destruction—he carries out in the name of a realism he labels masculine.

The friction between the poem's "she" and "he" thus creates unsettling and unsettled conflicts: our emotional identification with the hopes and disappointments of the woman vies with our uneasy participation in the cruel, intellectual game by which her "cold, clear" male interlocutor systematically cuts her down. The division cannot be bridged. Despite its overschematic organization, stilted diction, and density of allusion, "Heiress and Architect" succeeds by the intensity with which Hardy turns against his own desire for fusion. Like Jude the Obscure, who is as enamored of Gothic tracery as the heiress is and as unable to find an enclosure for his idealism, the poem's "she" gradually yields to a process of disenchantment that approximates Hardy's own. Whether or not these verses specifically dramatize an actual ideological shift from "a 'Wordsworthian' to a 'Darwinian' point of view" (Bailey 108) ultimately matters less than Hardy's fashioning of an ironically handled gender dialectic that gives a new twist to the metaphoric yoking of houses, femininity, and death which he had found in Romantic and Victorian poetry.

Although the poem's "she" ostensibly takes the initiative by seeking out the advice of the "arch-designer" reputed to be of such "wise contrivance" (3), her action makes her his dependent from the very start. It is he who is given the first and last words in the ten-stanza poem. After citing the rules by which he expects the heiress to abide, the architect rejects each of the four types of building she asks him to design. Each structure proposed to house a variant form of desire is quickly exposed for its impracticability. In dismissing her requests with a brusqueness that borders on contempt, the architect not only exhibits his technical awareness but also displays his maturer grasp of "such vicissitudes as living brings" (10). He thus treats the heiress as if she were a child who must be admonished about the coming phases of life. Armed with the "facile foresight" that made Milton's archangels superior to the innocents of Eden (32), this arch-designer is overly rigid. He may be skilled in architectural proportioning ("every intervolve of high and wide" [4]), but his lesson in foreshortened expectations shows him to be too unbending.

The heiress first requests little more than the exposure to wilderness granted to the grandmother in "Domicilium." Yet she endows this building with palatial features more suited to the temperament of the "she" who had asked Tennyson to build her a pleasure home in "The Palace of Art." In "Domicilium," the wishful return to an untamed, pristine Nature had been endorsed by a poet eager to slide back into boyhood; here, however, the heiress is rebuked for a childishness branded as self-indulgence:

> "Shape me," she said, "high walls with tracery
> And open ogive-work, that scent and hue
>   Of buds, and travelling bees, may come in through,
>   The note of birds, and singing of the sea,
>   For these are much to me."
>
>   "An idle whim!"
>   Broke forth from him
> Whom nought could warm to gallantries:
> "Cede all these buds and birds, the zephyr's call,
> And scents and hues, and things that falter all,
> And choose as best the close and surly wall,
>   For winters freeze." (13–24)

The contrasting visual shape of these two stanzas (the third and fourth of the poem) are maintained in the subsequent exchanges between the two speakers. The five-line stanza given to the heiress is simpler in organization and rhyme scheme than the seven-line stanza devoted to the architect's replies. The three four-syllable lines granted to the architect vie with the single six-syllable line that acts as a distillation of the heiress's wishes. These terse, shorter lines, which begin and end the architect's rebuttals, are his most dismissive. Typographically, they do not even align with the heiress's summarizing coda, thus reinforcing his disregard for her concerns. To accentuate this disregard, the architect's appropriations of the heiress's words become cruelly parodic. Her earnest reference to the "scent and hue / Of buds" turns into a hiss of derision: "*these* buds . . . / And scents, and hues, and *things*."

But the architect's mocking transformation of the heiress's "*For* these are much to me" into his "*For* winters freeze" also suggests his prime mode of subversion. His use of "For" is strictly causal; hers betokens a denial of time's passage. The architect restructures his client's syntax by forcing sequence on what she has articulated as nonsequential. His curt "Cede" and "choose" are commands which, unlike her ambivalent "Shape me," stem from a confident knowledge of the shapes best suited to withstand the bitterness of winters. By way of contrast, the central verb in her first speech—"may come"—remains conditional, half-hidden among the nouns that come before and after. Such tentativeness captures the heiress's receptivity but also weakens her call for roomy interiors and "ogive" arches freely exposed to the outside.

The heiress's frank subjectivism allows the architect to scoff at her belief in a never-ending Spring. He gruffly insists on the primacy of a depersonalized temporal order in which one season inevitably leads into the next. The "For" he wrests from her speech and retains to close off each of their next exchanges insists on the logic of this order. Having condemned her for misperceiving external nature, the architect proceeds to steel her against internal changes he also wants her to face. With morbid glee, he predicts a future made up of successive stages of degeneration: "For you will tire" (36) and "For you will fade" (48) give way to the calculated blow he inflicts in the poem's last line: "For you will die" (60).

Relentlessly pushed into giving up her yearning to blend with some form of otherness, the heiress decides that solipsism can permit her to escape the pains of disenchantment: "Some narrow winding turret, quite mine own" (50), she "faintly" hopes, might insulate her. Yet the unsparing architect is not about to relinquish the realism Hardy sardonically exaggerates. Having repudiated every form of Romantic relation, the architect now reminds the heiress of her material connection to the outside world. Her wish for a narrowly "winding" turret defies a last set of practical considerations:

> "Such winding ways
> Fit not your days,"

Said he, the man of measuring eye;
"I must even fashion as the rule declares,
To wit: Give space (since life ends unawares)
To hale a coffined corpse adown the stairs;
For you will die." (54–60)

The coffin that is finally to house the heiress follows the "law of stable things" she has previously ignored. A stable enclosure for his client's corpse has been this arch-designer's sole design.

That the "coffined corpse" was as preeminent in the mind of the poem's own designer is borne out by the illustration Hardy drew for "Heiress and Architect" on first publishing these verses in his 1898 *Wessex Poems*. Though horizontal in its composition, the picture was printed vertically to fit the shape of the book's pages.[6] To glimpse the contents of the rectangular enclosure, one therefore has to tilt the volume. Only then can the viewer see that the arighted rectangle framed still another rectangle and recognize that the attempt to reinstate a stable horizontal axis has in effect been anticipated by four figures steadying a box that would otherwise have to be inclined or even perpendicularly held. Portrayed as silhouettes, possessing extremities but no heads, the four figures are as incomplete as the similarly cropped, cross-hatched coffin they carry. The composition accentuates a sense of mutilation: headless human beings (presumably male but curiously androgynous) carry a fragment containing the remains of a once vertical human being (made genderless by death). The drawing captures the poem's very mode, not just through its representation of a descending motion that corresponds to the "decremental structure" of the verses, but also by the cropping of the four figures who could stand for the architect's dismemberment of the heiress's four wishes.

The sketch thus reenforces the poem's increasing sense of claustrophobia. The "uneven ground" of "Domicilium," which extended as far as the "distant hills and sky" (15, 12), has been pounded into a bit of human clay packed tightly into a box within a box. The spatial subversion that "Heiress and Architect" enacts, however, goes hand in hand with Hardy's literary deconstruction of all those Romantic and Victorian poems in which pleasure domes built by male poets are associated with a distinctly feminine or feminized imagination. Undeniably attracted to the structures of Romantic idealism, Hardy still valued the workings of Romantic irony. He now refused to partake in the buildup of lush details indulged, for example, by Shelley in *Queen Mab* or Tennyson in "The Palace of Art."[7] Tennyson had been reluctant to "pull down" the overlavish structure he had built for the aesthetic "soul possessed of many gifts" ("To———. With the Following Poem ['The Palace of Art']"3). Even after he deferred to

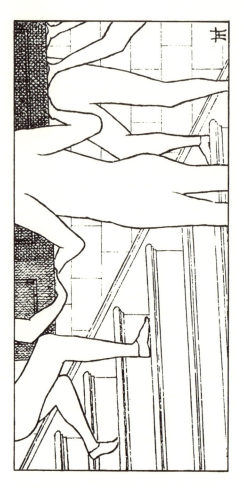

those reviewers who had deplored his imagination's insufficient "power over the feelings and thought of men" (Stevenson 136), Tennyson refused to raze an "effeminate" construct "so lightly, beautifully built" ("Palace of Art" 294). Hardy, by way of contrast, proves as intransigent as the architect who settles for the shape of a wooden coffin. Possibly remembering Tennyson's dedication to R. C. Trench, by then Bishop Trench, Hardy dedicated his own poem to A. W. Blomfield, a bishop's son and his genial employer. The dedication, as has often been noted, is deliciously ironic. For Blomfield had achieved his success as a fashionable architect by propitiating wealthy clients and by adapting himself to prevailing fashions. Hardy thus sets himself apart through the creation of Blomfield's truculent antitype—one clearly as reluctant to accommodate himself to feminine taste as Hardy remains resistant to a poetry that the mid-Victorians (including Tennyson himself) had come to regard as excessively "feminized" in its self-indulgence.

The progression in "Heiress and Architect" builds on the same "simile of human life" to which Keats had resorted in a famous letter to J. H. Reynolds when he compared "human life to a large Mansion of Many Apartments" (280–83). Keats's remarks have an obvious applicability to the poem in which the architect compels the "maid misled" (30) to confront dark passages that she, like Keats's Madeline or Lycius, would prefer to ignore. As the architect forces the heiress to wander through the "chambers" of her life, Hardy rehearses a succession of poetic genres which, he implies, have been rendered obsolete by what Keats, in his letter, calls the "advance of intellect." From her unreflecting absorption in nature (childhood), the heiress moves through socialization (adolescence), romance (sexual maturity), solipsism (old age), before confronting death; each phase is associated with a type of poetry—pastorals (such as Wordsworth's), narrative verses, love lyrics (the "little chamber" of line 37 suggesting the Romantic sonnet), elegies—and, finally, there is silence.

Such silencing fits the predisposition of the young poet, who did not publish his verses until he had exhausted his first two careers of architect and novelist. Yet Hardy's appropriation of the tropes of his favorite predecessors also suggests that, when he returned to poetry for the last three decades of his life, he was ready to see himself, like the heiress of this early poem, as the inheritor of assumptions and traditions he now needed imaginatively to relocate.[8] Hardy would overcome the binary oppositions shaping "Heiress and Architect" only after he had experienced the actual loss of a woman sharing his home. Emma Hardy's death enabled the old poet to exhume the femininity he had prematurely coffined.

III

When Emma Gifford Hardy died in November of 1912, three days after her seventy-second birthday, she left behind four completed works for the perusal of the man she had married in 1874. All these works were meant to signify the extent of her alienation from her husband. Printed by a Dorchester stationer, the volume of poems called *Alleys* (1911) and the exposition of the New Testament called *Spaces* (1912) were Mrs. Hardy's attempts to counter the unorthodoxy of the novelist who had turned poet after *Jude the Obscure* and *The Well-Beloved.* Like her unpublished fictional fragments, these rival efforts to catch the public eye had little effect on her widower. But her manuscript diary (which Hardy destroyed) entitled "What I Think of My Husband," containing "bitter denunciations, beginning about 1891 & continuing until within a day or two of her death,"9 and *Some Recollections,* her vivid account of her life before her marriage, stimulated the emotional overflow that led to the eighteen poems collected as "Poems of 1912–13" in *Satires of Circumstance* (1914), as well as to other memorializing verses both in that same volume and in its sequels, *Moments of Vision* (1917) and *Late Lyrics* (1927).

Practically all the poems Hardy wrote in response to Emma Hardy's death reverse the progression traced in "Heiress and Architect" and still observed in verses such as "Memory and I," another allegory about thwarted desire.10 The intense, child-like desire for fusion that so provoked the irascible architect now activates the passionate lyrics of a septuagenarian. In "I Found Her Out There," the mobility denied to an heiress condemned to death in life is playfully and paradoxically granted to the lively female ghost whom the speaker now reclaims. This shade bears little resemblance to the "ageing shape" that Hardy found so difficult to confront during his wife's declining years. Resurrected by her male survivor's intensity of desire, the truant ghost is exhorted to return with him to the more elemental nature "Where she once domiciled" (38).11

The male speaker of "I Found Her Out There" is the exact inverse of the architect who had forced the childlike heiress to foresee her entombment. Instead, this speaker becomes himself freed by "the heart of a child" of the uncanny sprite he urges to desert her "loamy cell" (40, 41). The subdued breezes and "singings of the sea" desired by the heiress and derided by the architect (16) have swollen into liberating storm blasts equally shared by the old man and the female "shade" who,

> maybe,
> Will creep underground
> Till it catch the sound
> Of that western sea
> As it swells and sobs
> Where she once domiciled. (33–38)

Stimulated by "the haunted heights / The Atlantic smites / And the blind gales sweep" (18–20), the wanderer finds "her" and experiences an epiphany. Hardy's speaker has traveled to the Arthurian ruins at Tintagel Head to expose himself again to the setting of the dead woman's girlhood. The visit confirms his belief that the spouse he has buried inland, so far away from these heights, can never become a quiet sleeper. Wakened by her memories, he can once more fuse with her by vicariously burrowing into her grave and sharing her presumed exultation at being released into the wild haunts of her adolescence. By relying once again on a dead female agent, like Wordsworth's Margaret or like the grandmother in

"Domicilium," Hardy, though rooted in Dorset, can imagine a "spot" devoid of binaries and antagonisms. Having liberated the man who would no longer be an architect, Emma the dream child can restore the inheritance he had progressively denied to himself as much as to the real-life Emma Gifford. The femininity he has introjected frees this male heiress from having to coffin a child heart.

That Hardy was the first to recognize the perversity of the paradoxes involved in this imaginative process of gender reconstitution seems amply evident from his other Emma poems (as well as from his fictive foreshadowings in novels like *The Well-Beloved*). He knows that the ghost he seeks out, addresses, impersonates, and causes to speak is but an aspect of himself. On reading Emma's diaries, Hardy unquestionably became aware of his own culpability. He saw himself as she had perceived him, as the jailor of the bride he had immured in Max Gate, where she had been brought under false pretenses. For his own part, Thomas also had felt betrayed. Unable to bear the older Emma's resemblance to the bride he had idealized, he punished her by allowing her the dubious status of codweller in his house. His choice of the Vergilian subtitle of "Veteris Vestigia Flammae" for the first series of Emma poems suggests his ability to reverse the roles of betrayer and betrayed. He could see himself as Aeneas and allow Emma the role of the wronged Dido. But it was the rekindling of those vestigial flames that mattered. The "woman much missed," now reborn as a trusting child, was more than a guide to Cornwall's romance. She could now once again fill the long-silent Max Gate with remembered song and sound and movement. She could bestow on him precisely what the architect had denied to the heiress.

In the Emma lyrics of *Satires of Circumstance* and *Moments of Vision,* the dramatic motions stirred up by a dead woman's "shade" help to refeminize the house in which she had been kept imprisoned. Her own powers are now respected; her airs are preeminent. Even at its most querulous, her voice is allowed a full hearing. For Hardy recognizes the importance of femininity to the continued unfolding of his imagination. He has never until now understood his bond to this "faithful phantom," who prides herself on following him so "alertly" wherever "his fancy sets him wandering" ("The Haunter" 4, 3).

Even when this ghost fussily complains about the slightest changes in the appearance of the home her architect-bridegroom had designed for her so very, very long ago, her devotion is still stressed:

> The change I notice in my once own quarters!
> A formal-fashioned border where the daisies used to be,
> The rooms new painted, and the pictures altered,

> And other cups and saucers, and no cosy nook for tea
> As with me. ("His Visitor" 6–10)

Whereas the "man of measuring eye" in "Heiress and Architect" delighted in altering his client's quarters, the man who has dared to repaint walls and relocate decorations obviously fears the reproach of one who asks him to remember "my rule here" (13). The servants hired since her death know nothing about her rule, but her widower feels compelled to carry out her wish that nothing be disturbed. Small wonder that the second Mrs. Hardy privately demurred about this ghost's stranglehold: "I may not alter the shape of the garden bed, or cut down or move the smallest bush, any more than I may alter the position of an article of furniture."[12]

Although Thomas had blamed Emma for the cooling that had marked the later years of their marriage, he could not bear to think of her as "cold, iced, forgot" as the "pretty plants" she had once tried to keep alive ("The Frozen Greenhouse" 22, 21). Her death thus led him to implant a warm domestic hearth at the center of the same "domicilium" he had periodically escaped. He had once stressed the "cold, clear view" of the manly realist "whom nought could warm to gallantries" ("Heiress" 8, 20). Now, however, he heaps gallantries on one to whom he attributed the heiress's yearning for a warm relation with a sustaining other. Comforted by the words of the voluble ghost who lives within his brain and by memories of the sound of her piano music, he dreads above all her removal into the "roomy silence" of her cemetery home. The threat of separation, which informs most of the Emma poems, is as frightening for the old man as for a small child.

Sounding very much like a mother who intimidates her child by playing on this fear, the ghost in "His Visitor" prefers the privacy of the tomb Hardy obsessively reopens in *Satires of Circumstance:*

> So I don't want to linger in this re-decked dwelling,
> I feel too uneasy at the contrasts I behold,
> And I make again for Mellstock to return here never,
> And rejoin the roomy silence, and the mute and manifold
> Souls of old. (16–20)

Unwilling to be forsaken by a ghost who prefers the "manifold" company of other dead souls, the speaker decides to partake in her reunions. In one of the finest lyrics in *Moments of Vision*, "During Wind and Rain," he places himself among the "Elders and juniors" whom Emma herself had recalled. Remembering her nostalgic account of the last house she shared with her family in Plymouth before being forced to leave the community in which she had spent her first nineteen years, Thomas appropriates Emma's moments of symbiosis and separation.

"During Wind and Rain" conflates details scattered over many pages in *Some Recollections*. Drawing on the description of Bedford Terrace, the "pleasant home" that proved to be his wife's last secure haven, Thomas relies on the hindsight by which Emma regarded this building as full of "curious omens" betokening death and dispersal for a family soon to fall from "so high" an eminence (*Some Recollections* 30–32).[13] The "They" of the poem are deliberately left unidentified. Blended through their music, the members of this domestic group lack individuality:

> They sing their dearest songs—
> He, she, all of them—yea,
> Treble and tenor and bass,
>   And one to play,
> With the candles mooning each face. . . .
>   Ah, no; the years O!
> How the sick leaves reel down in throngs! (1–7)

Who *are* "he" and "she?" The deliberate lack of specificity allows the speaker, who is so acutely aware of severance, to insert his own presence among the singers. The "nameless" singing opens an "elsewhere" for a man "capable of becoming a woman" (Cixous and Clément 93, 98). Stranded in a different era by the passage of so many "years," he nonetheless can insinuate himself into this alien, vanished household, and regard it as if he were there. Despite its insistence on separation and change, "During Wind and Rain" thus reconstitutes a "he" and a "she" among "all of them." Through a time warp, ruin and wholeness are simultaneously perceived; dispersion and integration can somehow coexist:

> They change to a high new house,
> He, she, all of them—aye,
> Clocks, and carpets and chairs
>   On the lawn all day,
> And brightest things that are theirs. . . .
>   Ah, no; the years, the years;
> Down their carved names the rain-drop ploughs. (22–28)

The scattered material objects on the lawn—with the "clocks" taking an ominous precedence in the list of a household's "brightest things"—will become permanently dissipated when a single "day" is replaced by "the years." Yet, as the last line shocks us into recognizing, the animated occupants of the building have long ago become inert objects themselves, reduced into names on tombstones. Only the single raindrop, so like the tear of a single mourner, can restore movement, stirring and ploughing up lives that have crumbled into clay.

In combining his sense of abandonment with his wife's own recorded pangs of separation from Bedford Terrace, Hardy makes the "he" and "she" of the poem stand for more than the parents whom Emma Lavinia Gifford was forced to leave behind. They also represent the aged poet and the young "she" he imaginatively joins by adding his own song to that which had once united "all of them." But his vicarious entry into another's family romance suggests that he is processing a much earlier separation. Long before Emma's death, Thomas had fashioned a powerful poem associating the domestic interior of a house with an ecstatic self-annulment through music. Though more compact than "During Wind and Rain," "The Self-Unseeing," which Hardy published in 1901 in his largely elegiac *Poems of Past and Present*, is strikingly similar.[14] In "The Self-Unseeing," just as in "During Wind and Rain," past and present are blended as well as kept apart. But the "I" who becomes a child again, dreamily at one with the smiling "She" who observes him swaying to the music of a dead "He," is a Hardy who needs no surrogate to express his profound yearning for the lost maternal shelter he wants to preserve.

In "The Self-Unseeing," the revisited Hardy home at Higher Bock-hampton is presented metonymically in the first of the poem's three quatrains. The "ancient floor" still "is"; but the "former door / Where the dead feet walked in" has been relocated (1, 3–4). The poem never identifies the owner of those feet as Hardy's father, who had died in 1892. Nor does it make clear that the ancient floor is still occupied by Hardy's octogenarian mother, Jemima Hardy, with whom he may well have shared his memory of the epiphanic moment the poem celebrates. Thus, when the second stanza opens by recalling, "She sat here in her chair, / Smiling into the fire" (5–6), it seems plausible that the speaker still has before him the same woman who, now in her old age, joins her son in remembering how she smiled while observing her child's entrancement by the music of the father-fiddler who "stood there, / Bowing it higher and higher" (7–8).

Like the change to a "high new house" in "During Wind and Rain," the upward motion of the violin presages a fall from such heights of ecstasy. Yet this family unit can no more anticipate change than the Giffords. Indeed, when the young mother smiles at her husband and at the boy who is his namesake, she helps to fuse the trio in a moment of self-forgetfulness. In "During Wind and Rain," a "he" and "she" could merge with "all of them." In "The Self-Unseeing," the "I" of the poem comes into being by recalling his oneness with the "we" presided over by the approving mother. In the last stanza, adult self-consciousness and the intoxicated self-obliviousness of the swirling boy coalesce:

Childlike, I danced in a dream;
Blessings emblazoned that day;
Everything glowed with a gleam;
Yet we were looking away! (9–12)

The poem's last line insists on a paradox. Only by refusing, like the heiress, to look at the future, can this trio avoid the foresight that might warn them that fathers die, that mothers become as "hollowed and thin" as the floors on which they tread, that boys grow into men subject to disenchantment. And yet the house of memory survives, its foot-worn floors still as visible as the sturdy peasant woman who hobbles across their surface. Dead male feet can therefore be resurrected into the living feet of poetry—a poetry that for the mature Hardy must repossess and reprocess the child's freedom of movement within a female space.

IV

After Hardy finally took his first wife to meet his mother in 1876, he kept "a complete silence" about the encounter, "and to the end of his life he never commented on the relationship between the two women" (Gittings, *Later Years* 7).[15] Yet little documentation about the actual relationship seems required. If my reading of some of the poems in the previous section is valid, the death of Emma Hardy allowed her husband to indulge in emotions that, though more suited to the loss of a mother, were kept in abeyance when Jemima Hardy died in 1904 at the age of ninety, a ruin of the once vital woman whose hold on him her son regarded with considerable ambivalence (Gittings, *Young Thomas* 24–25, 48–49).

It seems significant that the death of the matriarch who had been the "real guiding star of his early life" (Gittings, *Later Years* 118) inspired no creative outburst such as that occasioned, a decade later, by Emma's demise. "After the Last Breath (J. H. 1813–1904)," the single poem that directly memorializes Jemima Hardy in *Time's Laughingstocks* (1909), is stately and formal, a restrained tribute offered by a public "we." Even the poem that precedes it, "Night in the Old Home," avoids the I-you relation of the Emma poems. A speaker hears the voices of his family's many ghosts while visiting the now deserted house at Higher Bockhampton. Yet the mother is only one among the chorus of shades who advise the mourner to adopt their own "satisfied, placid, unfretting" mood.

The grandmother celebrated in "Domicilium," Mary Head Hardy, fares much better in *Time's Laughingstocks*. Already sixty-eight when Thomas was born, she is a maternal figure whose decay never agitated the time-conscious boy who had slept at Higher Bockhampton in the bedroom next to hers. "One We Knew (M. H. 1772–1857)," which clearly acts as a pendant to the poem memorializing Jemima Hardy, treats the grandmother as a fertile source for endless anecdotes and tales. Placed in the same position as the mother in "The Self-Unseeing," the woman who stares at a fire is directly credited as someone capable of mothering a poet-novelist's imagination:[16]

> With cap-framed face and long gaze into the embers—
> We seated around her knees—
> She would dwell on such dead themes, not as one who remembers,
> But rather as one who sees.
>
> She seemed one left behind of a band gone distant
> So far that no tongue could hail:
> Past things retold were to her as things existent,
> Things present but a tale. (27–32)

It seems noteworthy that this "she" should be hailed for possessing the very qualities of imagination that shape poems such as "During Wind and Rain" and "The Self-Unseeing," in which Hardy recalls vanished scenes not as one who remembers but as one who sees. The female shades who stimulated Hardy's imagination were, like the living women in his life, versions of the mother he could not afford directly to impersonate or appropriate. The man who confessed, in his middle seventies, that "he thought he had never grown up"[17] could present himself as the rapt listener of the grandmother who addresses him as "my child" in "Domicilium" or as the truant chided by the motherlike ghost of Emma Hardy. More important, he imposed the house of his youth, the cottage at Higher Bockhampton, where his mother continued to live, on the female structures of his poetry. Even the too narrow staircase of "Heiress and Architect" stems from a memory of the old home, "where the stairs were too narrow to save space" (Bailey 108). Had the boy once fantasized how a coffin would have to be edged down those stairs? Whether superimposed on Max Gate or on the Gifford residence of Bedford Terrace or reduced into much smaller containers—graves, coffins, the drawers and lockets containing female mementoes of the past—a Bachelardian dream-memory of a primal space, violated yet reconstituted, underlies the design of a host of Hardy's finest lyrics.

Yet if Hardy's oneiric houses helped him dramatize his sense of eviction from the primal refuge of a mother's body, his poems often try to repossess or translate a maternal abode. "Her Death and After," the early short story in verse that remained one of his favorites, depicts such a repossession. The narrator seeks a "gate" to lead him into the "tenement" where "one, by Fate, / Lay dying that I held dear" (3–6). Surveying the "piteous shine" of the rooms in which he finds a young mother on her deathbed, the speaker hears the cry of her baby daughter, soon to be orphaned (16). The dying woman admits that her visitor would have made a better father than the man she married: "Would the child were yours and mine!" (40). Eager to adopt her offspring after he hears of the degradation of "the lame lone child" (61), the speaker arranges to meet the dead woman's husband by the ruined earthworks near Dorchester's churchyard. He avoids the "hallow sod" of the woman's grave and prefers to face his rival against the backdrop of the "haggard" arena where "old Pagan echoes" still reverberate from "hollows of chalk and lime" (74, 78, 80). To reclaim the child, he concocts a fiction, professing to have fathered her. He offers the husband a choice: a duel or the gift of the little girl. Soon he is greeted by a "little voice" that comes to his "window-frame": "My father who's not my own, sends word / I'm to stay here, sir, where I belong" (119, 121–22).

What belonged to an entombed mother now belongs in the house of one who has replaced both parents. Yet the speaker who can restore a lost symbiosis is also painfully aware of the price he has had to pay, "for I'd harmed the dead, / By what I said / For the good of the living one (128–30). The irony is bitter. The desexualized love between adult and child requires the sexualization of the dead mother, defamed as an adulteress. In the drawing Hardy devised for "Her Death and After," the topography accentuates this conflict. Beyond the churchyard where a pure mother is entombed loom the pre-Roman earthworks that were converted into a "Cirque of Gladiators" (76). In Hardy's rendering, this structure, near whose walls the sexual rivals meet, resembles a giant orifice, a place of origination and exit from life.

The mother Hardy associates with his own creativity becomes a focal point for the tug-of-war between a childlike desire for sustained fusion and an adult insistence on the necessity of detachment. The conflict is evident in the curious poem "In Childbed," which Hardy placed immediately after his rather stiff memorial to Jemima Hardy in *Time's Laughingstocks*. Whereas in "Her Death and After" the male speaker replaces the young mother who died in childbirth, Hardy here animates the "spirit" of a dead mother who addresses a "me" who is her daughter and who has herself just given birth to a child. The dead mother chastens her daughter's "innocent maternal vanity" almost as sternly as the architect had checked the heiress's desire to retain some form of symbiosis. The young mother's joyful oneness with her infant, the dead woman insists, will eventually fade: "Yet as you dream, so dreamt I / When Life stretched forth its morning ray to me" (17–18). In this all-female poem, however, the younger woman does not adopt the heiress's disenchantment. Cradling her own

child (whose sex remains unspecified), she refuses to process the "strange things" uttered by this gloomy parental ghost.

In this quasi-Blakean Song of Experience, Hardy adopts the point of view of both mothers: his own offspring, his poetry, he seems to imply, originates in a symbiosis which "time unwombs" (9). This unwombing, which his poetry and fiction obsessively recreate, vies with the oneness of the "weetless child," a self-unseeing creature, cradled in its mother's arms. Although such weetlessness, or unknowing, always gives license to Hardy's characteristic irony, it also propels the desire that activates his lyrics. The "infant or thoughtless Chamber," as well as the "Chamber of Maiden Thought," can never be wholly vacated in the house of Hardy's poetry.

Despite their philosophizing and intellectualizing, Hardy's poems persistently tap the rudimentary emotions I have tried to capture in this essay. The child "who thought he had never grown up" views with the old man so fond of abstract formulations. The anger and yearnings of this child surface in unexpected places. Much has been written, for instance, about Hardy's Immanent Will and its operation in a poem like "The Convergence of the Twain," which, J. O. Bailey categorically states, "is not a personal lament; it is a philosophic statement" (266). But Hardy's treatment of the female hull of the *Titanic* allows him to find still another primal space in which an "unwombing" and the animation of new life can simultaneously occur.

Like the "maid misled" in "Heiress and Architect" and like the ruined maidens of Hardy's fiction, the ship on its maiden voyage will be undone by her unforeseen contact with an icy and "sinister mate" ("The Convergence of the Twain" 19). The violation by this growing monster floods the ship's steel chambers and opens her interior to "rhythmic tidal lyres" (6). Though ruined, however, the female wreck also becomes a habitat for new forms of life:

> Over the mirrors meant
> To glass the opulent
> The sea-worm crawls—grotesque, slimed, dumb, indifferent.
> . . . .
> Dim moon-eyed fishes near
> Gaze at the gilded gear. . . . (7–14).

As in "Heiress and Architect," so also here, Hardy evinces a sadistic delight in a grim process of denigration. The looking glasses that reflected the "vaingloriousness" of jeweled Edwardian ladies (15) now mirror dumb and elementary forms of life. The ship has become a huge coffin. The fall from high to low, the move from interiority to exteriority, noted in the poems I discussed earlier, is dramatized here as well.

Yet the invasion by crude marine creatures of the shattered interior of this Titaness also carries an affectual pleasure that goes beyond the aggressive desire to appropriate an immense womb.[18] These fetal creatures, though grotesque, facilitate our return to something primal, forgotten, "unweeting." Couching on the "stilly" floor, the ship who is a "she" has ceased to be an enclosure for civilized adults. Instead, she cradles childlike creatures at an earlier evolutionary stage. She has herself descended to an earlier state of being after her "consummation" with her mate (33). Like the ghost of a rejuvenated Emma Hardy, she can become one who stills, a nurturer. The fish who sway in the "rhythmic tidal lyres" within her are as oblivious to human "vaingloriousness" as the young boy who had swayed to music in "The Self-Unseeing." For this mother hull is herself a "domicilium," a spot for new life and for the generation of poetry.

NOTES

A version of this essay first appeared in *PMLA* 105 (1990): 1055–70. Reprinted with permission of the Journal.

1. The two most famous Victorian representations of the feminine domestic ideal are Coventry Patmore's *The Angel in the House* (1854–62) and John Ruskin's "Of Queens' Gardens" (1865). Earlier writers such as Sarah Ellis and Sarah Lewis had, however, already upheld the privatization of domestic space. The ambiguities and contradictions of sexual difference marking out separate spheres in this period have been amply analyzed by contemporary critics such as Armstrong,

Auerbach, Christ, Davidoff and Hall, Gilbert and Gubar, Houghton, Poovey, and Welsh.

2. Some feminist critics argue that a girl's relation to the unconscious, the body, and maternal rhythms is closer than a boy's (see Chodorow). While differing in their philosophical and political outlook, French feminists such as Hélène Cixous, Catherine Clément, and Julia Kristeva nonetheless posit that poets, whether male or female, are "mobile" and "open" in allowing the opposite sex "entrance" into them (Cixous and Clément 84–85). Kristeva demonstrates how male writers like Mallarmé and Baudelaire, allow the semiotic "chora," linked to the mother's body, to speak through their writing (93–98). Poetry, closer to song and pure rhythm, she argues, is less controlled than prose by the symbolic strictures of syntax.

3. Still, Gothic enclosures are far more unstable than the houses found in the traditional novel of manners. Decaying (like Wildfell Hall) or razed (like Thornfield), such buildings display a " 'ruined' architecture" that cannot be mended (Gordon 231). Thus, Hareton and the second Catherine must forsake the Heights for the Grange, while Esther Summerson must found a second Bleak House. For the transgressive qualities of the Gothic, see Jackson, Sedgwick, and Wilt, among others.

4. Quotations from the poems of Byron, Keats, Shelley, and Wordsworth are taken from Perkins.

5. Whereas James Gibson prints "Domicilium" as the first item in *Thomas Hardy, The Complete Poems*, Samuel P. Hynes places it first among the "Uncollected Poems," in volume 3 of *The Complete Poetical Works of Thomas Hardy*. Citations from Hardy's poetry are taken from Hynes and identified by line.

6. Inserted between the fourth and fifth stanzas of the poem (i.e., after the architect's "For winters freeze" and the heiress's second request), the drawing appears on page 213 of *Wessex Poems*.

7. Hardy read *Queen Mab and Other Poems* in London in 1866. For a helpful overview of his lifelong interest in Shelley, see Bartlett.

8. The idea of relocation or translocation, itself derived from Shelley, dominates Hardy's tributes to Shelley and Keats, "Shelley's Skylark" (1887) and "The Selfsame Song" (1922), poems in which he "houses" their images and words. Hardy's self-positioning in spaces once occupied by his Romantic predecessors is especially effective in "Rome: At the Pyramid of Cestius Near the Graves of Shelley and Keats" (1900) and in the powerfully evocative "At Lulworth Cove A Century Back" (1920).

9. Letter from Florence Dugdale to Edward Clodd, 16 Jan. 1913 (qtd. in Bailey 24). Ever protective of her husband, the woman Thomas wedded a year after Emma's death worries that he will wind up "believing" his first wife's accusations.

10. Placed near the end of *Poems of Past and Present* (1902), "Memory and I" also introduces a series of decremental structures and culminates with a picture of female decay.

11. Although Emma Hardy's first "domicilium" had been in Devon (which her widower also revisited), she lyrically recorded her later move from Plymouth to the "invigorating air" of North Cornwall. "I Found Her Out There" clearly records her description of the "winter waves and foam reaching hundreds of feet up the stern,"

and the "strong dark rocks with the fantastic revellings" of the marine birds (*Some Recollections* 38, 42). The same setting also acts as a backdrop for the unpublished novel *The Maid on the Shore*, which Emma wrote early in their marriage and which Thomas preserved.

"I Found Her Out There" represents a sharp departure from the four previous poems in the carefully crafted sequence of "Poems of 1912–13." In "The Going," "Your Last Drive," and "The Walk," Emma's mourner is temporally bound to her last days; in "Rain on a Grave," he is spatially anchored. Now, however, by returning to the scene of their courtship, he can wrest her (and himself) from a bondage to time and space. She is again the young woman who describes their growing attachment in their drive to Tintagel and Trebarwith Strand and other coastal places: "We grew much interested in each other and I found him a perfectly new subject of study and delight, and he found a 'mine' in me, he said" (57–58). The ghost liberated in "I Found Her Out There" is "mined" in later poems in the sequence, such as "The Haunter" and "The Voice."

12. Letter from Florence Emily Hardy to Rebekah Owen, 5 May 1916 (qtd. in Bailey 299).

13. As Evelyn Hardy and Robert Gittings were the first to recognize, Hardy not only drew on these and other details in Emma's descriptions but also chose to stress the downpour she regarded as an emblem of her final separation from her Plymouth childhood: "never did so watery an omen portend such dullnesses, and sadnesses and sorrows as this did for us" (E. Hardy 37, 68).

14. So similar, in fact, that Carl Weber mistook it for a poem about Hardy's first wife and included it in his arbitrarily constructed chronological cycle of 116 Emma lyrics (158).

15. Michael Millgate speculates that Hardy's delay in "putting himself, or his wife, squarely within his mother's orbit" stemmed from shame over his class origins. He notes that Jemima Hardy disapproved of "this deliberate avoidance of 'home'" and refused to meet the couple in any other house than her own (176–77).

16. Following Winnicott, Perry treats the mother as the other whose first domestication of space later triggers the adult mind's "energy for inner exploration" (7). In *Playing and Reality* Winnicott explains how "mental images" of the mother are reactivated in periods of transition (15, 96–97).

17. Florence Hardy to Alda, Lady Hoare, 7 April 1914. Florence Hardy was among the maternal figures in her husband's life. Writing to Lady Hoare on 9 December 1914, she claimed that her feelings for Hardy were like those of "a mother toward a child with whom things have gone wrong." (Both letters are quoted in Gittings, *Later Years* 159).

18. In discussing the so-called femininity phase or femininity complex undergone by boys in early childhood, Melanie Klein notes how the frustrated desire to appropriate the mother's "organs of conception, pregnancy, and parturition" lead the male child to "destructive tendencies whose object is the womb" (189–91). By resolving his identification with the mother, the adult male not only enhances his relation to other women but also manages to sublimate "the desire for a child and the feminine complement which play[s] so essential a part in men's work" (191).

WORKS CITED

Armstrong, Nancy. *Desire and Domestic Fiction.* New York: Oxford University Press, 1987.

Auerbach, Nina. *Woman and the Demon: The Life of a Victorian Myth.* Cambridge: Harvard University Press, 1982.

Bachelard, Gaston. *The Poetics of Space.* Boston: Beacon, 1960.

Bailey, J. O. *The Poetry of Thomas Hardy: A Handbook and Commentary.* Chapel Hill: University of North Carolina Press, 1970.

Bartlett, Phyllis. "Hardy's Shelley." *Keats-Shelley Journal* 4 (1955): 15–29.

Chodorow, Nancy. *The Reproduction of Mothering: The Psychoanalysis of Gender.* Berkeley: University of California Press, 1978.

Cixous, Hélène. "Fiction and Its Phantoms: A Reading of Freud's *Das Unheimliche* (The 'Uncanny')." *New Literary History* 7 (1976): 525–48.

Cixous, Hélène, and Catherine Clément. *The Newly Born Woman.* Trans. Betsy Wing. Minneapolis: University of Minnesota Press, 1986.

Davidoff, Leonore, and Catherine Hall. *Family Fortunes.* Chicago: University of Chicago Press, 1988.

Felman, Shoshana. "Rereading Femininity." *Yale French Studies* 62 (1981): 619–45.

Freud, Sigmund. "The Uncanny." Trans. James Strachey. *New Literary History* 7 (1976): 619–45.

Gilbert, Sandra, and Susan Gubar. *The Madwoman in the Attic.* New Haven: Yale University Press, 1979.

Gittings, Robert. *Thomas Hardy's Later Years.* Boston: Little, 1963.

———. *Young Thomas Hardy.* Boston: Little, 1975.

Gordon, Jan. "Narrative Enclosures as Textual Ruin: An Archaelogy of Gothic Consciousness." *Dickens Studies Annual* 11 (1983): 209–38.

Hardy, Emma. *Some Recollections by Emma Hardy.* Eds. Evelyn Hardy and Robert Gittings. London: Oxford University Press, 1961.

Hardy, Florence Emily. *The Life of Thomas Hardy: 1840–1928.* London: Macmillan, 1962.

Hardy, Thomas. *The Complete Poems of Thomas Hardy.* Ed. James Gibson. London: Macmillan, 1976.

———. *The Complete Poetical Works of Thomas Hardy.* Ed. Samuel P. Hynes. Vols. 1–3. New York: Oxford University Press, 1982–85.

———. *Thomas Hardy's Personal Writings.* Ed. Harold Orel. Lawrence: University of Kansas Press, 1969.

———. *Wessex Poems and Other Verses.* New York: Harper, 1898.

Houghton, Walter. *The Victorian Frame of Mind: 1830–1870.* New Haven: Yale University Press, 1957.

Jackson, Rosemary. *Fantasy: The Literature of Subversion.* New York: Methuen, 1981.

Keats, John. *The Letters of John Keats, 1814–1821.* Ed. H. E. Rollins. Vol. 1. Cambridge: Harvard University Press, 1958.

Klein, Melanie. "Early Stages of the Oedipus Complex," *Love, Guilt, and Reparation, and Other Works: 1921–1945.* New York: Dell, 1975. 186–98.

Kristeva, Julia. "Revolution and Poetic Language." Sec. 1–12. Rpt. in *The Kristeva Reader*. Ed. Toril Moi. New York: Columbia University Press, 1986. 89–136.

Millgate, Michael. *Thomas Hardy: A Biography*. New York: Oxford University Press, 1985.

Perkins, David, ed. *English Romantic Writers*. New York: Harcourt, 1967.

Perry, Ruth. Introduction. *Mothering the Mind: Twelve Studies of Writers and Their Silent Partners*. Ed. Ruth Perry and Martine Watson Brownley. New York: Holmes, 1984. 3–24.

Poovey, Mary. *Uneven Developments: The Ideological Work of Gender in Mid-Victorian England*. Chicago: University of Chicago Press, 1988.

Sedgwick, Eve Kosofsky. *The Coherence of Gothic*. London: Routledge, 1986.

Stevenson, Lionel. "The 'High Born Maiden' Symbol in Tennyson," *Critical Essays on the Poetry of Tennyson*. Ed. John Killham. New York: Barnes, 1960. 126–36.

Tennyson, Alfred, Lord. *The Poems of Tennyson*. Ed. Christopher Ricks. London: Longmans, 1969.

Weber, Carl J., ed. *Hardy's Love Poems*. By Thomas Hardy. London: Macmillan, 1963.

Welsh, Alexander. *The City of Dickens*. Oxford: Clarendon, 1971.

Wilt, Judith. *Ghosts of the Gothic: Austen, Eliot, and Lawrence*. Princeton: Princeton University Press, 1980.

Winnicott, D. W. *Playing and Reality*. London: Tavistock, 1971.

Girl-watching, Child-beating and Other Exercises for Readers of *Jude the Obscure*

James R. Kincaid

Many readers construct *Jude the Obscure* as replete with pain and sex. A few connect the pain and the sex. The ways in which pain and sex are connected doubtless vary some, all of us being different people; but I'd like to propose two broad categories that would accommodate the readerly experiences of most or all of us with this novel: homicidal voyeurism and sadism. Assuming that does not sound insulting or otherwise unpersuasive, I feel authorized to turn directly to exploring what it is readers do with *Jude.* Briefly, we readers[1] direct the voyeurism and the sadism toward children, weaving and embellishing patterns of erotic desire that take the form of an unusually violent sort of pedophilia, what today we would call physical and sexual abuse of children. Further, these pornographic projections both build on and subvert (or at least expose) the demeaning, even murderous distancing devices we use to keep desire alive, the ways in which we push people into the next county, into the role of mere objects, into childhood or some other embodiment of otherness in order to lust after them.

If, as we are repeatedly told by those who know, desire has no goal beyond its own perpetuation, no generator other than the drive to find absence, a provocative gap, it may be that *Jude* presents this "lack" in its purest figuring and allows the reader the form of erotic activity most devoted to avoiding fulfillments, endings. I suggest that the extreme or "pure" form of this empty-hence-irresistible eroticism can be located in the image of the child being beaten and that our desire and our repugnance are alerted and fed by being sometimes participant, sometimes spectator. We beat the boys ourselves and watch as the girls are being beaten. With some considerable athletic versatility, we hop from stage to audience, from sadism to voyeurism, depending on the gender of the figure we construct in the form of the child.

Explaining how this reader-as-pornographer/pervert comes into being will take some doing. To help, here are two scenes from the novel I'd like to use as keys. In the first, Jude's aunt tells a story about the twelve-year-old Sue; in the second, we are shown Jude, age 11, being beaten by Farmer Troutham:

> Many's the time I've smacked her for her impertinence. Why, one day when she was walking in the pond with her shoes and stockings off, and her petticoats pulled above her knees, afore I could cry out for shame, she said, "Move on, aunty! This is no sight for modest eyes!" (2.6.131).

> " 'Eat, dear birdies,' indeed! I'll tickle your breeches, and see if you say, 'Eat, dear birdies,' again in a hurry! . . .
> . . . Swinging his slim frame round him at arm's length, [Troutham] again struck Jude on the hind parts with the flat side of Jude's own rattle, till the field echoed with the blows, which were delivered once or twice at each revolution.
> "Don't 'ee, sir—please don't 'ee!" cried the whirling child, as helpless . . . as a hooked fish. . . . "I—I—sir—only meant that—there was a good crop in the ground—I saw 'em sow it—and the rooks could have a little bit for dinner—and you wouldn't miss it, sir—and Mr. Phillotson said I was to be kind to 'em—O, O, O!"
> This truthful explanation seemed to exasperate the farmer even more than if Jude had stoutly denied saying anything at all; and he still smacked the whirling urchin, the clacks of the instrument continuing to resound all across the field and . . . echoing from the brand-new church tower just behind the mist, toward the building of which structure the farmer had largely subscribed, to testify his love for God and man. (1.2.11–12).

These (marginal?) scenes I want to take as paradigmatic of the activity not of the novel but of readers, representing something happening not in the book but in us. As John Bayley remarks, in Hardy, "it seems to be our own activities among the constituent parts of the writing that give us our sense of what is going on";[2] and what is going on here, I claim, is erotic readerly projection into the scene. Since we are most concerned with the way gender drives these scenes apart, makes different our own participation in the beatings, we will return to some of the details in these passages, after a brief historical and theoretical excursion into Victorian child-flagellation and our own. For now, we should observe that we may read both scenes as slightly comic. Jude's whirling at the end of a man's hand has the look of common and happy adult-child play; and Sue's rebellious assault on adult power—"Move on, aunty!"—and on prudishness—she loves to offend "modest eyes"—has about it a kind of Tom Sawyer mischievousness. True, it sets us itching for the kind of punishment Tom Sawyer regularly receives, but that punishment never amounts to much, right? Fictional bad boys and girls are seldom beaten or flogged. They are "swished," which sounds downright pleasant, "licked," which sounds maternal or erotic (or both), or, as here with Sue, "smacked," which sounds like a funny noise and like kissing. Jude's breeches are "tickled." Makes us think we're doing nothing wrong, nothing very special: it's all a game, all in fun.

But even if it is all in fun (which in *Jude* it hardly can be), what we readers are doing differs sharply in these two cases. Sue's punishments are not dramatized; Jude's are. Sue's smackings are multiple; Jude's singular. Sue's offense[3] is personal, moral, sexual; Jude's is ethical and economic. The episodes with Sue are set in the past, made remote; the one with Jude is immediate and concrete. We are made aware of Jude's buttocks, not of Sue's. All these details will help us finally to understand why we position ourselves as voyeurs with Sue and as sadists with Jude, girl-watchers and boy-beaters. It will help us to understand too how it may be that the first activity is the more damaging of the two, the more insidious, the more perverse. And the moral of that is: beat me if you like, but please don't look, says the wise child; or, as Arabella (and Moses) puts it, " 'Then shall the man be guiltless; but the woman shall bear his iniquity.' Damn rough on us women" (5.8.38).

I

In the scene featuring Sue, the juxtaposition of beating with the erotic is clear. Sue is often smacked; she has exposed herself audaciously, knowingly. Causing others to blush, she must be made to blush herself, forming the connection between spanking and the enticing erotics of modesty Victorian sexologists posited. With Jude the connections are not so overt. They are, in fact, established through the slow-motion retardation of the action and the prolonged focus on the buttocks, through an emphasis on the boy's pain and soreness, and through a positioning of the language within the range of clues associated with pornography. This last is particularly important: we know we should be aroused because we are generically situated in reference to a form of literature we think ought to be erotic.

Consider the dialogue. Farmer Troutham's initial expression of anger, couched as an explanation or erotic foreplay, is familiar to us from a long pornographic tradition—"My lady must smart for this. . . . She has been very troublesome lately with these impudent drawings, but this is positively obscene. . . . Send for Susan to bring my birch rod."[4] Not incidentally, this formula from pornography has slithered over into life, as we all know from endless public displays of righteous correction and their self-justifying preludes: "You little wretch. I told you not to do that. Now you're going to get it! You've asked for it! A good, sound spanking!" The child's response in life is not usually so erotically apt as Jude's "Don't 'ee, sir—please don't 'ee . . . O, O, O!" Jude's rhythmic pleas, which exasperate Troutham further, provide an excuse for prolonging the episode and emphasizing the cadence of the blows, the beat of the beating, we might say. The fall of the hand or rod is sometimes made explicit in porn—" 'Oh-h! dear—Mama!' Swish! 'Yah-hah-ah-h!! Oh! I-will-be-good!' Swish 'Ah-h-h! Oh! I-will-never'-swish- . . . ,"[5] a form of dialogue given perhaps its highest or at least most anapestic expression in a line from Swinburne's *The Flogging-Block*: "Oh! Oh, sir! Oh, please, sir! Please, please, sir! Oh! Oh!"[6]

The image of the child being beaten, exploited relentlessly, if perhaps unconsciously, by Hollywood and Madison Avenue, is so central to our culture and so vital to our psychic structurings of desire that we may wonder why it is so seldom discussed. One answer is that, here as everywhere, desire really is connected to distance, to absence, to otherness, to silence. If we bring our collective and individual erotic attachments to child-beating up from the cellar, they cease to be erotic. But that they are dwelling down below is certain. Virtually every legislative act directed toward protecting children from abuse is compromised by its contradictory effort also to protect the abusers. We detest abuse, but not enough to abandon the palpably absurd but deeply held and deeply needed belief that such abuse has no connection in the world to "normal spanking," the presumed rights of parents, relatives, teachers, baby-sitters, or others from a wide but designated range to beat, smack, whip, fondle, caress the child's defenseless bottom. Children are thus protected only from "excessive" battering, which may sometimes mean that the law can step in to help them only with the funeral arrangements.[7]

Why is this child so erotic in the first place and why would we ever derive such satisfactions from what would seem the pointless (at least nongenital) act of hitting it on the buttocks? The most comforting position for a twentieth-century American is to claim that erotic child-beating is pretty much confined to one of the following: (a) the British, (b) the Victorians, or (c) the perverted. The notion that sexual flagellation is "a vice peculiar to the English" is often repeated, especially by English writers, as if some points of considerable national pride were at stake.[8] Patriotic Americans, and citizens of every other country, will be quick to rise to contest this claim, but tradition is nonetheless clear on the historical-cultural prominence of England. Explanations given for such prominence always include the following: the rise in prestige of the public school model and its use of flogging as a means of defining itself; the centrality of discipline and physical subjugation to various popular forms of evangelicalism; the effect of sexual repression and the forcing of people into indirect and perverse forms of sexual satisfaction; and the fact that the French were taking vigorous steps to outlaw corporal punishment everywhere, which alone might make the British eager to do just the opposite. For our purposes, it is undoubtedly important that the activity and plenty of talk about it were in the air in Hardy's time, yet we must be suspicious of all this mixing of causes with symptoms in an attempt to enclose this startling phenomenon within national boundaries and thus deny its pertinence.

If the strategy to protect ourselves by declaring all this exclusively British breaks down, perhaps we can do just as well by locating sexual child-spanking in the past, the unenlightened Victorian past, something not our own. True, we can spot some conservative Victorian speakers who will talk of the child in ways we find grotesquely alien. Some even seem to see this "child" as fairly contemptible, an inferior species altogether or, more moderately, a radically incomplete adult. Such views can happily confirm our distance and our superiority. According to these welcome speakers, one either enters into pitched battle with the child to destroy it and substitute the completed adult or, less violently, one forces the plant into blooming and, meanwhile, subdues it into being as inoffensive as possible.

Here is one of those voices, speaking of "correction": "In judicious correction, courage and perseverance are alike requisite. Crying is the defensive weapon of the child, and if this resistance is successful, by the yielding of the nurse or mother, she will often find difficulty in regaining her lost dominion."[9] One can locate similar expressions of resentment of childhood and the felt need to invade and conquer it in the sermons and correspondence of Thomas Arnold. Arnold sees his school, his tutelage, as a kind of high-speed conveyer belt, quickly manufacturing adults out of vile children through using the magic machine of flogging. Flogging, Arnold says, is justified "as fitly answering to and marking the naturally inferior state of boyhood, and therefore as conveying no particular disgrace to persons in such a state."[10] The peculiar reasoning here identifies boyhood and flogging in such a way to make an unbeaten child unnatural: being flogged defines the state of childhood. Such logic may easily be made to seem preposterous and ugly to us and may allow us to think that perhaps this whole business is another freak of those remarkably freakish Victorians.

The difficulty with this strategy for distancing the phenomenon of erotic child-beating is that it breaks down almost immediately. We find, first of all, most Victorian child-rearing manuals speaking not in alien but familiar voices, advising pretty strenuously in most cases against beating children, some even recognizing and protesting against the sexual connections established or exercised thereby.[11] More troublesome still is the persistence in our culture of the image of child-beating, particularly in genres we think of as entertaining: popular novels, movies, and comic strips. Watch the movie version of *The Bad Seed* and ask yourself what desires were being catered to in the little coda where Patty McCormack, playing not the bad-seeded Rhoda but simply herself as actress, is spanked. Why does the same practice occur so frequently in *Our Gang* and *Little Rascal* short films, in television sitcoms and feature films, and in comic strips, from the classic "Buster Brown" through "The Katzenjammer Kids" to "Lil Abner," "Winnie Winkle," and "Little Lulu."[12]

So much, then, for these strategies of denial based on historical separation. Our laws, familial practices, and forms of amusement all proclaim that this kind of eroticism is with us still. Such an announcement of survival might be titillating, but it will not make us especially uncomfortable, since we still have left to us our most powerful defense: the claim that such forms of eroticism are perverse, thus very far indeed from those normal impulses and normal modes of behavior we ourselves experience.

Even Freud, not always our friend in constructing these defensive maneuvers, distances the subject nicely for us. His famous essay, "A Child Is Being Beaten," is subtitled, "A Contribution to the Study of the Origin of Sexual Perversions."[13] It is true that he begins his essay with an unnerving observation on the surprising frequency of this child-beating fantasy among those who seek out help. He goes on, even more unnervingly, to speculate that the fantasy exists among a great many of those who do not seek out help. But he then settles down to sorting out with cool precision the kinds of "perversions" involved in different configurations of the beating scene: sadism in the beating of a rival, masochism in being beaten oneself, masochism disguised as sadism in being a spectator at the beating of others. Freud's analysis is comforting: tough, analytical, strictly empirical in its base, and modulated through distaste. He also speaks with a certainty we may find reassuring, with accents that ring with confidence: "All of the many unspecified children who are being beaten by the teacher are, after all, nothing more than substitutes for the child itself" (191). "After all . . . nothing more than . . .": these are signals of granitelike certainty, are they not? Or, perhaps, they are strained, uncertain, admissions of fear? Do they reassure, or act to give the game away, expose the carnival of question-begging and arbitrary assertiveness going on? The psyche is a strange place to go looking for reassurances; we might find anything there, including unwelcome resemblances between ourselves and the monsters we were hoping to disown.

For one thing, there are others meddling around there and explaining things differently. Havelock Ellis, for instance, sees the tie between pain and eroticism as commonplace. He has a way of saying the most outrageous things about the subject: "There is nothing necessarily cruel, repulsive, or monstrous in the idea or the reality of a whipping"; even more startling, "the general sexual association of whipping in the minds of children and frequently of their elders, is by no means rare and scarcely abnormal."[14] If this isn't abnormal, we might scream, what is? A question to be asked, perhaps, but it only points up the insecurity of any protection based on a distinction between the normal and the abnormal. We may try to externalize what we call the abnormal, but it has a way of sneaking back inside when we're not looking and taking up lodging once again.[15]

All these explications tend to support the argument that the powerful structure of desire in *Jude* that winds its way through the torturing of children emanates from the reader, from us. Such projections may, in Ellis's terms, scarcely be abnormal; but they suggest, among other things, the ways in which we tend to construct gender difference. The narrative patterns used to devise these fantasies of child-beating are, in this novel, quite different for boys and for girls. As I have said, we smack the boys ourselves, but watch the girls being beaten.

That gender is involved at all in erotic child-beating is not immediately apparent. From the standpoint of the pedophile, the child's gender is remarkably fluid: the accepted wisdom is that child love is neither heterosexual nor homosexual, but something else disconnected from gender. Even in the child-whipping pornography, there is nothing settled about the gender of anyone, disguises being used freely and one sex turning into another easily and often. Steven Marcus noted this curious "ambiguity of sexual identity," though he rushed to deny it as well, offering in the place of confusing ambiguity the assurances of bland homophobia: appearances notwithstanding, "the figure being beaten is originally, finally, and always a boy."[16]

Not so absurd as this mechanical brand of Freudianism is Jude's own humanist liberalism, his tragic sense that we are all in this together, that the purblind doomsters ripping us apart indiscriminately render distinctions based on gender (or anything else) irrelevant: "Still, Sue, it is no worse for the woman than for the man. That's what some women fail to see, and instead of protesting against the conditions, they protest against the man, the other victim, just as a woman in a crowd will abuse the man who crushes against her, when he is only the helpless transmitter of the pressure put upon him" (5.4.346). Appealing as this may be—to men—the later course of events expose it for what it is: a delusory attempt to find comfort through misogynistic comparisons. Jude argues that women, or some of them, fail to see what men, most of them, see so clearly: though women may be elbowed off the path and trodden on (by men), only fools (women) would blame the men. Men are not the villains at all, just fellow victims, even worse off (when you come to think of it) because they realize (as women do not) the absurdity of it all and have to pay double for such acuity through being taxed with brutality by the obtuse (women).

Jude's sense that he and Sue, men and women, are mutual quarry is not quite right—not right at all. Jude says here that some women "fail to see." Perhaps that's because the sightings are inaccurate and because men block all the lines of sight, hog them up, anyhow: men like Jude are endlessly busy spying on women, seeing through and for them, positioning all women as objects, blind objects. It is not a question of equal victimization—for anyone—and none of us can claim to be merely "helpless transmitters" of pressures and desires originating elsewhere.

Jude and Sue, men and women, may well be victims and deserving of pity; but they eagerly enough bully one another into torturing games and find ways to torture themselves. And we readers do not simply watch. We are playing with children here, with empty constructions; and we do with them what we will. The child, a recent social and linguistic invention, can be filled in any way we like; in *Jude,* we stuff the child with pain and with desire. We make the child represent, fill it with meaning;[17] and we do so in ways that both confirm and resent the child's distance from us. The child is Other, desired and detested, fawned over and spanked. The woman as child is distanced twice over, a double-zero and thus double-denied and double-desired. She cannot come close to us, not even close to our hand or hairbrush or whip. She is merely a creature of fantasy, an actress-victim in a flagellation drama that never ends, the object for the voyeur.

Jude as male child is closer to the pornographic reader. He is the child at the end of Farmer Troutham's hand being whacked a couple of times firmly at each revolution as he wails and pleads helplessly. He is substantial, the object of sadism. Sue is dimmer, more removed into memory, less settled in form and thus even more available to objectification. We look at Sue as she struggles to be; we watch as she is denied that substance, that subjecthood. As voyeurs, as pornographic readers of Sue, we maintain her hollowness and thus her desirability. Her tortures are more subtle or more interiorized because she is never allowed to take shape. Jude is there presenting his buttocks to be whacked. Sue, no matter how high she lifts her petticoats, can never be more than an image in the mind's eye, in our eye. Her act of defiance, her self-assertion, in fact, freezes her. We operate the controls of the freezer.

The proper place to develop this argument is by way of the novel itself, so I will close this section with a case history Ellis cites, a case history that evokes, I suggest, Aunt Drusilla's pornographic picture of Sue, an attitude that in turn suggests the pathological reader of the text—us, that is:

> When about 5 years old I was playing with a little girl friend in the park. Our governesses sat on a bench talking. For some reason—perhaps because we had wandered away too far and failed to hear a call to return—my friend aroused the anger of the governess in charge of her. That young lady, therefore, took her aside, raised her dress, and vigorously smacked her with the flat hand. I looked on fascinated, and possessed by an inexplicable feeling to which I naively gave myself up. The impression was so deep that the scene and the person concerned are still clearly present to my mind, and I can even recall the little details of my companion's underclothing.[18]

II

Jude offers us torture, both the spectacle of someone being tortured by a variety of villains and an invitation to lend a hand ourselves. The chief activity engaged in by the novel or, more exactly, the reader of the novel, seems to be the cruel flogging and slow dismemberment of its main characters, Jude and Sue. The site of the tormenting alters according to gender; but, in either case, it is a child being beaten, impaled, shredded. The reader is politely asked if he wouldn't like to direct a drama of kiddie porn, a snuff movie being played in our head, starring two cookie-bakers who act with charming innocence throughout, just "like two children" (5.5.356), as Arabella says. Even after his disastrous marriage, Jude is unspoiled by any grown-up cynicism: "he seemed to be a boy still" (1.11.85). Indeed, as the narrator insists later, it is not a matter of *seems*; Jude acts "like the child that he *was*" (3.10.233; italics mine). Sue, despite her sophistication in one or two matters, is, similarly, "such a child in others" (4.5.290) that she can be conveniently fitted into the reader's criminal pedophiliac drama. Though we don't hear any "don't 'ee, don't 'ee, oh, please sir, please sir!" from her, she does react to pain in ways wholly appropriate to this form of pornography, "her mouth shaping itself like that of a child about to give way to grief" (5.4.342).

But there are differences in the way we project these patterns of erotic abuse, differences shaped by gender. Jude is a Katzenjammer Kid carried to some homicidal limit. One of the features of pornographic child-spanking, really of child-spanking in general, is that it corrects nothing, is meant to correct nothing. If it really put an end to misbehavior, it would put an end to the erotic fun; and no one wants that. Just so, unable to learn, bouncing back fresh and ready for more at the beginning of each episode, Jude, like little Hans and Fritz, keeps asking for it and getting it—from us.

Interestingly, the novel opens with a series of rather subtle persecutions of the boy. Phillotson's leaving is presented as an exercise in half-comic cruelty: "Sorry I am going, Jude?" he asks, getting the response he (or the reader) wants—tears from the infatuated, romantic boy. In another key, Aunt Drusilla's cold detestation—she calls Jude a "poor useless boy" and says he should have died with his parents—seems grimly Dickensian, as does the contempt of the vicious neighborhood women, whose stares fall on Jude "like slaps upon his face" (1.2.9). Such an attack from "glances," from looks, is highly significant in this novel, another direct, smacking assault.

Jude is hurt, stung, sore, has to eat standing up; but there is a way in which none of this is very serious. Jude can, after all, recover; he can also, more importantly, escape these looks, these stares that are "like slaps." He can slink away: "he did not care to show himself in the village, and went homeward by a roundabout track" (1.2.13). We should remember, in our sympathy for the sobbing, beaten Jude, that for Sue there is no round-about track, no escape from the staring eyes, the eyes of the reader.

But Jude has problems of his own, of course, and no small ones. These problems are blunt, insistent, physical. He is hit, smacked, beaten. "All at once he became conscious of a smart blow upon his buttocks" (1.2.11): this odd, distanced, erotic formulation is paradigmatic for this character. He is always being bent over and whacked, "all at once," his dignity taken down along with his trousers. "On a sudden something smacked him sharply in the ear, and he became aware that a soft cold substance had been flung at him" (1.6.41). There is the same phrasing, as his bride-to-be enters by way of a pig's penis. His love for Arabella jerks him along "as a violent schoolmaster a schoolboy he has seized by the collar" (1.7.48): seized and marched off to a good, sound flogging, we may be sure.

All of Jude's punishments, in other words, amount to direct or displaced versions of the spanking of children, highly erotic and infinitely repeatable. Like those children in comic strips—Buster Brown, Perry Winkle, Hans and Fritz—he continues in his provocative behavior, his hopefulness and his idealism, and thus is regularly positioned for a trip to the woodshed. Our pornographic desire is never satiated because it is never fulfilled. The spankings do not halt the misbehavior, rather spur it on. The very same day of his theatrical spanking by Farmer Troutham, he is back in the field he has been warned out of, risking a rerun. He has been brought low by the whipping, it is true, so low that he decides he should find a way not to grow up at all, things being as shudderingly inharmonious as they clearly are in this world. Now to pederast readers, who have greatly enjoyed the spanking, this would be shocking stuff indeed, were it serious; but it is not. Instead of suicide, we get boyish resiliency, the wonderful childish eagerness to continue the erotic game, to be spanked again: "Then, like the natural boy, he forgot his despondency, and sprang up" (1.2.15). He springs up with comic and erotic elasticity, not just here, but every time he is presumably crushed: when he finds out that the acquisition of Latin and Greek will entail years of grinding work he is floored but not for long, falling under a tree and becoming "an utterly miserable boy for the space of a quarter of an hour" (1.4.31). The narrative as a whole traces one long rebound from the whipping he takes at Christminster.

Jude does not take these spankings personally. He does not resent them, feels somehow that they are deserved. After Farmer Troutham releases him, he walks away, sobbing and quivering, not, we are told, from the pain nor from any of a number of Schopenauerean reflections that might comfort him, but from "the awful sense that he had wholly disgraced himself." Like David Copperfield, another object of readerly sadism, Jude takes the sexual spankings as his due, as natural, feeling only a deep sense of shame at having behaved as he has. He harbors no anger for Troutham or for us; he isn't about to tell anyone or phone the authorities. He is the perfect target for sadism.

His life, then, follows predictably enough as a series of physical chastisements, brusque as whacks on the buttocks or flying pigs' pizzles. Arabella and her sexuality are represented as more or less one continual assault on Jude, figured most overtly in the scene where the pig-killing thrusts itself on him not as a farmer's chore, a matter-of-fact little business of life, but as a crushing series of monstrous material facts he cannot, for all his writhing, evade. His attempt to find in suicide a dignified end to it all, a rich tragic finale, is rendered farcical by the thick ice and its refusal to follow the script. Even Jude's mental torments take on a palpable and painful corporeality, as when he conjures up images of the children born to Sue and Phillotson in order to flagellate himself a little (3.8.212). His actual ending—set in vividly realized squalor, directed by the "rank passions" of Arabella, featuring Jude's drunken (childlike) helplessness—seems a kind of demonic orgy of child abuse.

But we, the abusers, do all this out of desire for Jude, out of what we might as well call love. The male child is beaten, but the beating is a lovemaking, a fondling, a stroking, the blows themselves being no more than the rhythmic beat of copulation. Thus it is that we pity Jude, extend to him our heartfelt sympathy—and feel no need to "explain" him. The situation, we will find, is very different with Sue. But Jude is directly present to us and is thus coddled in the very process of being whipped. Jude is pitied and gentled, presented as so truly victimized, his fault being only that he is too tender, too sensitive. Just like us. Farmer Troutham, who, if not a surrogate, is at least doing us all a great favor by enacting the pornographic scene, is also a knave. The management of the scene is masterful, Jude being at once a "whirling urchin," the perfect object of pedophile sadism and also a miniature St. Francis. We are allowed to enjoy the eroticism and also flatter ourselves with our superior sensibility, allowed to identify with and take the pleasure of Farmer Troutham and see him as a beast. Our identification with the beater is thus promoted and effectively screened, part of the screen being provided by the gratuitous and laboriously planted satire on the farmer's hypocrisy, the brand new church tower echoing the sounds of the spanking having been erected with the help of Troutham's subscription, "to testify his love for God and man" (1.2.12).[19]

In similar ways throughout we are enabled to keep the game going, to adore Jude by spanking him. He is, after all, a likeable sort, filled with superior qualities—a pretty fair mirror, in this regard, for us to look into. And, because he is so much like us, he is not the major pornographic prey here. We can take after him from time to time, like Pip's sister with Tickler in hand, but generally we are not much challenged by him. And desire needs the titillation of remoteness and challenge—the challenge posed, for instance, by the fiercely resistant Sue. We construct Jude, for erotic purposes, as contingent, near-at-hand (and to-hand), docile, familiar, and domestic; Sue is radically distanced, unpleasantly alien, wild, insistently other. No games could be more different than those we play with these two characters, these two genders.

These make quite strange all the signals we receive on the virtual identity of Jude and Sue. Sue's name enters the novel on the other side of an equals sign from Jude: "His cousin Sue is just the same," says Aunt Drusilla (1.2.9). The narrator calls them "almost the two parts of a single whole" (5.5.352), a perception seconded by Phillotson: "one person split in two" (4.4.276). Arabella, of all people, ends the novel by saying Sue will never find peace "till she's as he is now!" (6.11.494). All of this sounds very much like *Wuthering Heights*, like Heathcliff and Cathy, like romantic tragedy. But Sue never is, for us, anything like Jude, a fact that may mute romantic tragedy but makes it easy for us to engage in some remarkable erotic distancing. With Jude, we get close and paddle in the flesh, one might say, only so we can join him in forcing Sue into the far-away, watching her being spanked in the theatre of the mind. If Jude is the subject of uninhibited sadism, Sue is caught by the much fiercer monsters of voyeurism.

Jude provides the voyeuristic model for us. Even as a child, he is expert at finding places of concealment from which he can see without being seen. The day of his spanking he sneaks back through the fields to formulate in his gaze the erotic image of Christminster, palpitating and shimmering in the distance. He watches until the lights of the city go out "like extinguished candles": like drawn curtains, the end of lovemaking for a peeping Tom—for Jude and for us. He whispers to the breezes from the city "caressingly," and in his "romantic" attachment, holds it in his sight "like a young lover . . . his mistress" (1.3.21–22). He loves from hiding, yearns from behind bushes. He becomes so associated with concealment that even his bakery cart is fitted up with a blackened hiding place, a portable den from which he can send out "longing looks." For Jude, or at least for us voyeur readers, all this is perfect. The point is to control the erotic image by denying its physical independence, maintaining it only and always as a captive of the eye, the mind's eye. Thus Christminster is no closer for Jude when he is within the confines of its gates than when he was at the crest of the hill outside Marygreen.

Christminster, we feel, can take care of itself, can afford to be supremely indifferent to all the voyeuristic perverts using her. Not so Sue. She has had the initial misfortune to be trapped in a photograph, offering "a pretty girlish face" with a "halo" effect (2.1.90) that sets Jude off even more strongly than the "halo" (1.3.24) he had constructed around Christminster. With that photograph all his own, Jude can display it privately, even kiss it (2.2.99) to his heart's content—if it's his heart he wants to content. Not satisfied with that sort of girlie-magazine erotics, though, Jude takes to looking for Sue herself—or perhaps only a more varied image of her. Sure enough, he soon spots her, unconscious of him and nicely framed by a window in a shop he enters so he can, unseen, steal a glance (2.2.103). For some time after first fixing her in his sights, "he kept watch over her" (2.2.104) by sneaking around to places where he figures he might "gain a further view of her" (2.3.106). He takes to following her, since "to see her, and to be himself unseen and unknown, was enough for him at present" (2.2.106). Enough for him! Why it's a regular Peeping Tom's Heaven, a point that Jude (or the narrator) half-acknowledges by saying "his interest in her had shown itself to be unmistakably of a sexual kind" (2.4.114). Jude goes so far as to go skulking about "often at this hour after dusk" to "watch the shadows" on the blinds of the training school Sue is attending (3.3.171).

But Jude is no more than a starting kit, a set of hints to get the pornographic reader going in his erotic projection. And Sue is the main victim of this perverse activity, an activity so cruel it does almost make the sadism of child spanking seem like love. Sue is deeply wary of being fixed, set, photographed once and for all. She dodges brilliantly, and coura-geously creates for herself possibilities where we thought there were none.[20] Her oft-repeated "unconsciousness of gender" or, as she puts it, a total absence of any fear of men (3.4.177) is perhaps her most daring and also most pathetic defense against being set as object, as a halo-round-a-face, as game held in the sites of the voyeur's rifle.

Married or unmarried, copulating or not, Sue is not allowed to come into being, never allowed actuality. "You are often not so nice in your real presence as you are in your letters!" Jude tells her (3.6.197), providing a very mild form of the truth: Sue is not only much nicer, that is, more enticing, in letters or at a distance; she only *is* at a distance. She has no "real presence" for us, no way to break through our mechanisms of alienating in order to control and desire. Part of this pornographic distancing is exposed in the recurrent need to explain Sue, felt both by characters within the novel—from Gillingham to Jude to Arabella—to those without, from Hardy himself[21] to D. H. Lawrence,[22] to every recent critic and commentator. Explanation, we might say, is itself a form of control, of fixing and pinning the other on some distance and alluring horizon.

Among the oft-explained differences between Arabella and Sue is that Sue denies and tries to resist the inevitable objectification Arabella stoically accepts and tries hard to exploit. Sue will not live in a world that contains her in photographs and robs her of presence. Arabella practices her fake dimples, arranges her fake hair, mounts the show of fake affection because she recognizes that "poor folks must live" (1.10.75), that women can survive only by making themselves not substantial but "seen." So she arranges to be seen. It is, as she tells Phillotson, "damn rough on us women, but we must grin and put up wi' it!—Haw haw!" (5.8.384). Arabella sees no alternative, nor, for that matter, does Hardy.

But Sue will not or can not adopt Arabella's grimly comic attitude, and she is ripped apart, finally, by the most horrible form of child abuse. For a brief period she is happy with her children, present to them and they to her. When they are slashed from her, she can find no alternative to succumbing, to giving in, as she says, to the force of the Gaze, to the power of the reader's voyeurism: "We are made a spectacle unto the world, and to angels, and to men!" she repeats twice (6.3.414). She is even subject to what we gather is a form of physical punishment, as Phillotson apparently puts into practice Arabella's counsel of severity and his friend Gillingham's feeling that all would have been well had Sue been "smacked" regularly.

All this happens off-stage, more exactly, on a stage constructed not with nails and planks but with our malefic imaginations in a remote visual area. We control Sue not with our spanking hand but with our powerful eyes. "Many's the time I've smacked her" (2.6.131) and can continue to do so, in the hazy luxuriousness, the haloed luminous cloudiness of the mind's cinema. Sue is trapped in an erotic nostalgia, in a giant web of repetitious spankings that never vary and never allow escape. We can play over and over the titillating lifted skirt, the saucy come-on. In her parody of exhibitionism, her tragic assertion of independence, she tells Aunt Drusilla not to look at her exposed body, it being no fit sight for "modest eyes." But our eyes are not modest, and we can return again and again to this same scene, snuffing out her independence and brutally misreading her delightful and delicate parody.

Thus Jude is given a sonorous, moving absurdist finale: "Let the day perish wherein I was born, and the night in which it was said, There is a man child conceived." For Sue, there are no grandly expiring days or nights, just a humiliating surrender to Phillotson's punishments, which she, like the child of the comic strips and the well-conditioned child just round the corner or maybe even in the house, believes are deserved. She must writhe on and on, screaming to the readers who have projected her, constructed her beaters, and settled in as directors of this play, "Don't 'ee, sir—please don't 'ee!"

NOTES

1. "Who is this *we*, anyhow?" one might ask. The "we" in this essay is a location, a cultural positioning that is so resolutely mapped for us it cannot be unoccupied. "We" is not a person reading or even a way of reading (much less a position located within the text), but a spot from which we read, a spot that, like a restroom in a park, may be uninviting but can hardly be unvisited. It is this spot, this cultural position, that makes the sort of reading that we do inevitable.

To call this "we" perverse, pedophile, sadistic, or particularly male is a maneuver that is not so much "wrong" as a continuation of the same strategy that created the "we" in the first place. Such locating and reading as are described in this essay are made available to us by mechanisms that also allow us to deny that we are accepting them. To call this "we" a bogus "universal" concept is to mistake the armchair where one reads for the universe, to exempt oneself from the fields of power that make possible the strategies of evasion and denial being employed.

"We" in our culture is not a criminal or hidden place, a deviant or pornographic reading: it is every place, every reading. That claim is preposterous; but without it, we have no place to open our mine.

2. John Bayley, *An Essay on Hardy* (Cambridge: Cambridge University Press, 1979), 118.

3. It is interesting that Sue's offense is a blatant form of exhibitionism, given that she is later on so much the victim of voyeurs. Here, it is almost as if the subversive nature of her self-exposure wrests control away from the looker. The

exhibition, that is, so violently assaults expectations and mocks sexual desire that the exhibiting object ridicules the looker: look if you dare, but I will make fun of your looking. "Move on aunty! This is no sight for modest eyes!" seems a form of a humiliating rebuke I remember (having received) in my own youth—"When you get your eyes full, fill your pockets!", called out derisively by a female fourth-grade classmate, hanging upside-down from the playground trapeze.

4. "Lady Pokingham; Or They All Do It," *The Pearl,* 1 (July 1879); rpt. (New York: Grove, 1973), 17.

5. *"Frank" and I* (New York: Grove, 1968), 233.

6. "Algernon's Flogging," *The Flogging-Block;* from notes to Swinburne's *Lesbia Brandon,* ed. Randolph Hughes (London: Falcon, 1952), 499.

7. On the prevalence of "spanking" in America, the widespread tendency to regard the practice as normal and virtuous, and the great difficulties posed thereby for drafting or enforcing laws protecting children, see Elizabeth Pleck's excellent *Domestic Tyranny: The Making of Social Policy Against Family Violence from Colonial Times to the Present* (New York: Oxford University Press, 1987).

8. For an especially enthusiastic endorsement, see [Dr. Iwan Bloch], *Sex Life in England* (New York: Panurge, 1934). By the way, the author of this ridiculously unreliable book is apparently not Bloch at all, but one Richard Deniston. The idea is common enough and is often repeated: J. Z. Eglinton (also a pseudonym) goes so far as to say that the practice is exclusively British and that it is to be found in "*all* British erotic works" from the 1770's to the 1870's, a claim which, though untrue, does testify to the zeal some bring to the subject: *Greek Love* (London: Neville Spearman, 1971), 212.

9. *The Mother's Best Book, Or Nursery Companion; by a Committee of Experienced Ladies* (London: Kent, [1859]), 77.

10. Quoted in J. J. Findlay, *Arnold of Rugby: His School Life and Contributions to Education* (Cambridge: Cambridge University Press, 1897), 61.

11. The sexual association of flogging or spanking for both parties were clearly recognized: see John Davenport, *Aphrodisiacs and Anti-Aphrodisiacs: Three Essays on the Powers of Reproduction; with Some Account of the Judicial 'Congress' as Practised in France During the Seventeenth Century* (London: privately printed, 1869), 113. Indeed, as early as the late seventeenth century a pamphlet appeared protesting the beating of school-children's naked bottoms on the grounds of the "lechery" involved, the "appetite" and "fire" aroused in the masters: *The Children's Petition: Or, A Modest Remonstrance of That Intolerable Grievance Our Youth Lie Under, in the Accustomed Severities of the School-Discipline of This Nation. Humbly Presented to the Confederation of the Parliament* (London: Richard Chiswell, 1669), 49, 15, 11.

12. Remembering the erotic, howling please for mercy from the Victorian pornography, note the following from American comic strips: "Oh! Oh! Father! I'll Never Do It Again! Help! Yow!" ("Buster Brown"); "Oh, Oh, Oh, please don't! No! Please, father, Ow! Ow! Ow! Oh, I'll—sob—be good! Yow! Oh! Ow! How that hurts!" ("Angelic Angelina"); "I didn't mean it—I'll be good! Ouch! Ouch! YEOW! Boo-hoo! BOO-HOO!" ("The Gumps"); and the following remarkable final caption from the July 15, 1928 strip of "Winnie Winkle the Breadwinner" concerning the

little boy Perry: "So that's his idea of fun, is it! Wait'll he gets home!! I'll take his clothes offen him an tan him good and proper!!!"

13. *The Standard Edition of the Complete Psychological Works of Sigmund Freud,* trans. under gen. editorship of James Strachey, in collaboration with Anna Freud (London: Hogarth Press and the Institute of Psycho-Analysis, 1953), XVII, 175–204. Further references will be cited in the text.

14. Havelock Ellis, *Studies in the Psychology of Sex* (New York: Random, 1936), I,ii, 129, 137.

15. Far and away the most subtle and brilliant of the unsurprisingly rare treatments of this subject is Eve Kosofsky Sedgwick's "A Poem Is Being Written," *Representations,* no. 17 (1987), 110–43.

16. Steven Marcus, *The Other Victorians: A Study of Sexuality and Pornography in Mid-Victorian England* (New York: Basic, 1966), 259, 261.

17. See Sedgwick, "Poem," 126.

18. Ellis quotes this from another (unnamed) source, 141.

19. Dale Kramer wittily notes the oddity of the tone here and the apparent misdirection of the satire: "that [Jude] was caused pain would scarcely seem to justify the marshalling of the forces of humanity and religious feeling against Troutham" (*Thomas Hardy: The Forms of Tragedy* [London: Macmillan, 1975], 151–52).

20. Penny Boumelha offers what seems to me an admirably persuasive and sympathetic reading of Sue's sexual reserve as perhaps her "only rational response to a dilemma," a response that preserves her "resistance to reduction to a single and uniform ideological position" (*Thomas Hardy and Women: Sexual Ideology and Narrative Form* [Madison: University of Wisconsin Press, 1982], 142, 7).

21. See especially his letter to Edmund Gosse (20 November 1895), where he gabbles on about how Sue, though not an "invert," has but "weak and fastidious" sexual instincts (*Thomas Hardy and His Readers: A Selection of Contemporary Reviews,* ed. Laurence Lerner and John Holmstrom [London: Bodley, 1968], 123).

22. D. H. Lawrence, *Study of Thomas Hardy and Other Essays,* ed. Bruce Steele (Cambridge: Cambridge University Press, 1985). Lawrence's comments on Sue as the frightening "product" of civilization, a woman with the vital female in her atrophied, are well-known (108–9). Not so well known is his remarkable turn at the end of his essay toward a poignant sympathy for Sue and a distaste for the men who destroy her: "Why must it be assumed that Sue is an 'ordinary' woman—as if such a thing existed? Why must she feel ashamed if she is special? And why must Jude, owing to the conception he is brought up in, force her to act as if she were his 'ordinary' abstraction, a woman?" (122).

Looking at Tess:
The Female Figure in
Two Narrative Media

Dianne Fallon Sadoff

"[Thomas] Hardy was clearly in love with Tess," Donald Hall writes in an afterword to *Tess of the D'Urbervilles*, "and he leaves his male readers in the same condition" (424). In correspondence with just such a reader, Hardy wrote, "I am so truly glad that Tess the Woman has won your affections. I, too, lost my heart to her as I went on with her history" (to Sir George Douglas, 1:249). Roman Polanski, who reread *Tess* until he "knew it almost by heart," likewise adored her: "I've loved [Tess] since I first read [the novel]," he told Mitchell Glazer (41). Women readers suspect such adoration. For Kaja Silverman, Tess is *not* desirable and so seduced but mastered by the masculine gaze as figuration, split as subject, and submitted to the oscillation such instability produces; for Penny Boumelha, the narrator's fantasies of penetration and engulfment violate Tess as fully as do Alec's actions (120–22). Indeed, Hardy feels ambivalent toward the image of woman and the destiny to which he consigns her; complicit in Tess's violation, Hardy and his narrator, like Angel, participate in killing her. Yet the narrative situation of *Tess* encodes a double perspective on what critics persist in calling her "seduction." Gazed at and adored, Hardy's heroine undertakes a narrative trajectory that appropriates, complicates, and revises the seduction plot to demonstrate its duplicity for the female subject. Placing his heroine "beyond the pleasure principle," Hardy invokes figural and cultural sadomasochisms and the death drive, making his reader, whether male or female, "suffer with her," as Donald Hall says, "outrage[d] at injustice" and "more conscious than she" (424–25).

Roman Polanski, too, gazes at Tess. His camera examines the ways she seduces the spectator's attention and deploys technologies that reproduce such caring observation. Like Hardy, he feels ambivalent toward the woman he "shoots," hating her victimage and sacrifice but, himself identifying with the "seducer," believing it inevitable—and romantic. Magnifying Hardy's sadomasochisms, Polanski's visualization of *Tess* emplots perversity as the outcome and consequence of his—and Hollywood's—spectacle. For writer and filmmaker, woman's image as central to representation, her position in narrative and especially her intrication with closure, comment on the "ends" of culture and the seductive functions of narrativity. Situating itself within a film industry, Polanski's *Tess* displays Hollywood's myths of woman in positions of pain as seductive, perverse, *and* marketable. In this essay, I examine technologies of the look at the image of woman in fiction and film, at the fate of narrative and narratology in film theory, at psychoanalytic readings of woman's destiny, and at the markets for nineteenth-century narrative and twentieth-century film. Only when criticism situates its readings, I argue, in technologies of text production, can it fully account for the functions and uses of culture.

A Finely Drawn Figure

Hardy's narrative produces Tess's image through what J. Hillis Miller calls "the optical detachment of [a] spectator narrator" (*Hardy,* 50). Hardy's narrator thus superimposes perspectives of sweeping landscape and small detail, or historical event and rural moment. This "double perspective" gives Hardy's narrator the distance requisite for producing generalizations based on particular events in his story. His point of view often coincides with his characters' as they become, in turn, the fiction's focalizers: they watch one another without themselves being watched and the narrator watches them watching. This "system of looks," according to Miller, generates Hardy's ironic stance toward engagement, his dialectic of distance and desire (*Hardy,* 50, 64, 72–73, 119). In *Tess,* the narrator asks his narratee to look closely and from a distance, portraying him as a sympathetic yet "alien observer" (22.178). Viewed from the "summits of the hills that surround it," the "ungirdled and secluded" vale of Blakemore remains untrodden by London "tourist or landscape-painter"; the coastal traveler, neither despoiling by looking too closely nor appropriating by looking too distantly, may behold below him the "delicate," virginal Vale. Master of double perspective, the narrator guides this fellow traveler's gaze and "rambles" from the summits into the valley's metaphorically desirable landscape, its fertile fields "never brown" and its springs "never dry." (2.9). To guarantee the "truth" of such a spectatorial position, Hardy addresses the viewer engaged in such desiring observation: "Looking east you see High Stoy and the escarpment below it," he says to his inscribed reader of Blakemore; "On the left you see to an immense distance" (*Life,* 281).

The reader as rambler first sees Tess being looked at by others.[1] Tess "exhibits" herself at the May Day dance for a series of traveling "on-lookers" who "look long" at her country freshness, at the "spectacle of a bevy of girls dancing without male partners." Angel Clare "glance[s] over" the women, fails to choose Tess, exchanges a look with her as he departs (hers reproachful, his sorrowful), and, looking back, sees Tess's white shape—not looking back at him—standing apart from the dancing figures that seem already to have forgotten him. This scene announces the theme of the look: Tess's male spectators admire her, even if that regard, like Clare's, is "oversight." For the male gaze, solicited by the virginal ritual and the scene's promise of "consummation," structures this implicitly desiring scene. In turn, the narrator also sexualizes the narratee's gaze at Tess: "you could sometimes see," he says, making the reader picture it, "her fresh girlhood lurk in her curving womanhood." Tess's body becomes image as Hardy arouses the reader's desire to look through his narrator's visualizing maneuvers (2.10–17). Angel's gaze at Tess, then, passes to that of the inscribed reader, who, looking at Tess, falls likewise in love with her.[2]

Hardy later inscribes this relay of gazes in a figurative scene that differentiates Tess from other women in a visual field. A field-woman's body, the narrator claims, "is a portion of the field; she has somehow lost her own margin, imbibed the essence of her surrounding, and assimilated herself with it." Tess's body, on the contrary, defines its borders in defiance of fields. An unidentified eye "returns involuntarily" to her "finely drawn figure," its boundaries marked by her pink garb and "flexuous" movements. To a "person watching her," Tess "seduces casual attention" because she "never courts it, though the other women often gaze around them" (14.111–12). Already returning home to Shaston, Tess as involuntary recipient of Alec's attentions and roses had become the object of van passengers' "surprised vision" and "public scrutiny" (6.50). Thus the narrator observes Tess as a "spectacle," drawing the successive gazes of others, whether in approbation, examination, or moral inspection. Her "looks" figuratively entice him to "look." The relay of looks directed at Tess constitutes the female figure as sexually arousing, unknowingly on display and so seductive.

Hardy's narrative solicits and structures desire, Donald Hall believes, with metaphors of plenitude. Perceiving Tess's "*presence*," the "reader responds to [her] *wholeness*"—and, I would argue, exploiting Hall's pun, her "holeness." Aroused by Tess's looks, the narrator tropes her actions as sexual and inviting violation. As field-woman, she holds the corn "in an embrace like that of a lover" while the flesh on her arm, "scarified" by the stubble, "bleeds" (14.112). When Tess eats cultivated strawberries from

Alec's hand and wears his early roses, the blood thorn-pricked from her chin matches the strawberries' red juice and foreshadows the blood on her scarified wrist. These bleedings figure not only her plenitude but her permeability. As the field-woman's margin bleeds into the field's ground, Tess's blood transgresses her body's boundaries; her "brim-fulness" breathes and oozes from her body. As Angel gazes into the "red interiour" of Tess's mouth, another metaphor for her sex, he feels on his flesh an "*aura*"; the narrator spiritualizes this flush: "It was a moment when a woman's soul is more incarnate than at any other time, when the most spiritual beauty inclines to the corporeal; and sex takes the outside place in her presentation" (24.192; 27.217). Like his narrator, Hardy worries the link between woman's sex and spirit. "In a Botticelli the soul is outside the body," he wrote in his journal as he began *Tess*; it "permeat[es] its spectator with its emotions. In a Rubens the flesh is without, and the soul (possibly) within. The very odour of the flesh is distinguishable in the latter" (*Life,* 285). Failing to locate the "presence" of her sex, Hardy and his narrator imagine it fragrant, rosy, and capable of penetrating the spectator who desires to pierce, see into, and be affected by her, who watches her bleed.

The thematics of the look in *Tess* suits classical narrative cinema, which turns, as Stephen Heath theorizes, on a "series of 'looks' which join, cross through and relay one another" with a "certain reversibility." The camera looks at the scene it makes *mise en scène;* the spectator looks with the camera at the film frame; the characters look at figures within the representation (*Questions,* 119). Like Hardy's novel, Polanski's film constitutes Tess's sexuality through a relay of gazes by characters, camera, and spectator. Framed by shots of early roses, the scene in which Alec feeds Tess strawberries alternates shot-countershot to depict Tess from Alec's seductive point of view. As the camera tracks Alec's hand picking and then offering the red fruit to Tess, now in close-up, she looks down, looks up at Alec from under her country hat, attempts to dissuade him from feeding her, then accepts the strawberry into her pouting, red mouth. This close-up serves as index to the woman's penetrability: despite her hesitance, signified by her look down, the sequence proves she's seduceable. When Tess protests the roses' thorns, Alec pins blooms to her bodice; "beauty has its price," he avers as Polanski cuts to Alec's cutting bloody meat. Polanski's camera, however, also views Tess from Angel's idealizing point of view. As she talks of staring at the sky, losing her need for body and becoming spirit, the camera pans to Angel, reading; as he listens to Tess, he takes off his glasses, looks up from his book, leans forward, and looks toward the out-of-frame Tess. The camera follows the serving maid as she moves from Angel to Tess, relaying and "incarnating" both character's and spectator's look at the spiritual yet bodily woman.

Polanski's relay of looks, however, revises Hardy's and provides the woman a look of her own. After the camera pans across the group of May-dancing figures to the road from which Angel and his brothers approach, it singles out not Tess but the girl with whom Angel will dance. In close-up, Tess looks at Angel; he walks past her, and in shot-countershot Tess looks back at him and he at her, twice; the camera tracks to her face and, in an uncharacteristic moment of shallow focus, shows the spectator her longing. At Talbothays, too, visual metonymies stage the woman's desire. When Izz, Retty, and Marian watch "dear Mr. Clare" out their garret window, shot-countershot depicts Angel from the women's point of view. "I saw you; I saw you kissing his shadow," Retty accuses Izz. Polanski shoots as though through the window: the shadow of bars and frame fall on female faces; the bars cross the frame as deep focus singles out Angel's figure in the landscape. Polanski then cuts to the women's walk to church on a Sunday's flooded road. The maids enter the top of the frame as reflected images on water; the camera tilts up from inverted female images to feet and up to bodies, zooming out as it frames their figures. In shot-countershot, they watch Angel walk toward them, through a visual "tunnel"—light as hole in the background, arching trees as eagerly embracing walls. As Angel carries each girl through the water, shot-countershot of the girls' watching depicts their desire. When he carries Tess, the camera follows as Tess looks down, up, and in two-shot they look deeply at each other as the others watch them. Granting woman the look, shooting her look as desiring, Polanski insists on the look's structural reversibility, on the female glance Hardy hardly represents despite what he calls its "radian[ce]" (23.183).

Polanski nevertheless exposes this system of looks as governed by a logic of masculine desire. For although Tess too may look, the system summons a certain annihilation. After their "affair," Alec advises Tess to display her beauty, "before it fades"; after their wedding, Angel invites her to the mirror to "come and see" her beauty, enhanced by his "family jewels." In this scene, Polanski's complex tracking shots, pans, and shifting focuses invoke the danger inscribed in the look's reversibility. As Tess and Angel walk through the door toward the glass, Polanski shoots their images in the mirror, pans to the gilded frame, then to their embrace. As Angel confesses, Tess watches him; as she confesses, he watches her. As she talks, the camera pans to Angel; deep focus depicts his refusal to sympathize, as two pictures behind him portray women kneeling, their hands folded, presumably, in prayer or entreaty. Angel stirs the fire with a poker and, in the next scene, the camera pans the table at dawn, still set with uneaten food and unworn heirloom jewels. Polanski's visual metonymies for castration, his insistence on the watching character's move out of the visual field while a tale is told, reinforced by the iconography of the confessing or begging woman as picture, demonstrates that female desire, while double, can be framed. The look's reversibility may open a space for her desire, but the eroticized woman will necessarily be wounded. Polanski, then, represents female sexuality as tragic: the male hates to hurt her but nevertheless to see her in pain pleases and arouses him. That erotic wounding, that possibility of cutting, poking, and penetration, means the look "frames" the speaking woman even as it represents her desire.

The problematic of the gaze, which begins with questions of ego formation, ends with fascination with the image of woman. In Jacques Lacan's seminar, "Of the gaze as Object Petit a," questions of femininity, castration, and the "phallic ghost" join those of méconnaissance, identity, image, and subject formation: identified with the phallus, the gaze constitutes the woman as lacking and so penetrable. Yet for Freud and Lacan, sight of the female body constructs male sexuality while the seen image of the male child constructs the male subject. As Jacqueline Rose points out, this problem in psychoanalytic theory hinges on the relation of "splitting" to subject formation: the look functions to constitute the (male) self as coherent and misrecognized, the look at woman, the subject as certain of his (uncertain and sexual) identity. By a series of analogies, then, the image of woman seems to guarantee male subjectivity. But this supposition itself proves unstable when we look at Tess's image inserted in narrative.

Stories of Seduction

For Laura Mulvey and other feminist film theorists, narrative film encodes the pleasure of looking (at woman) into the "language of the dominant patriarchal order." In her groundbreaking essay, Mulvey analyzes such pleasures to "destroy" them and poses against the "plenitude" of "narrative fiction film"—Hollywood's "magic" and "aura"—an "alternative cinema" signifying a "new language of desire." Indeed, Mulvey identifies scopophilia and voyeurism, narcissistic (mis)recognition of and identification with the screen image as both pleasurable and fascinating for the spectator; only when narrative enters her narrative does Mulvey invoke the Master Narrative of patriarchy, the domination of (the image of) woman by (the) man (who is spectator). Combining "spectacle and narrative," mainstream film supports the male as active, the female as passive; this split implicates voyeurism with sadism and fetishism with scopophilia. In short, "sadism demands a story" (14–26). Raymond Bellour, too, maintains that mainstream American cinema assigns to woman a central place in which she is "figured, represented, inscribed in the fiction" by the "logic of masculine desire." This cinema posits an "Oedipal scenario" that naturalizes the paradigmatic position and desires of the male subject. This classic narrative trajectory fuses with the romance of psychoanalysis to figure the symbolic father as dead, to express desire for the mother and others who replace her (Bergstrom 93–99). For Bellour, then, as for Mulvey, the pleasure produced by narrative means the spectator (or spectator position) is necessarily masculine. Narrative thus solicits oedipal pleasures and provokes such critical metaphors for its structure as the "narrative striptease," the "orgiastic rhythm of tumescence and detumescence," and the sadistic wish for "what lies *beyond* the pleasure principle" (Barthes 10, Scholes 26, Brooks 50).[3]

In attempting to rescue narrative for feminist film theory, Teresa de Lauretis decides, reversing Mulvey, that "a story demands sadism." According to de Lauretis's structuralist poetics, the singular and male mythical subject crosses a feminine narrative space that serves only as obstacle or boundary (womb, cave, grave, house). Even when, for example, Freud attempts to posit female desire, to make a place for woman in culture and myth, to tell *her* story, it turns out to be his story after all. For in every retelling, however mythic, of the female's oedipal story, de Lauretis theorizes its "point": that "women *must either* consent *or* be seduced into consenting to femininity" (134). To "interrupt" this oedipal narrative teleology based on the erections and climaxes of masculine desire, de Lauretis locates woman as "narrative image" at the join of image and story (the figure of woman and woman as figure of narrative closure) (140). But this recuperation, too, equips the (female) subject with an "oedipal past" and "ancestry" that troubles the spectator's identification or makes "cinema work for Oedipus" (152–53). When film stages female desire as contradictory, de Lauretis decides, it necessarily resolves the problematic by destroying or colonizing woman. Theory, then, must work with and against narrative—must be "Oedipal with a vengeance"—to stress the "duplicity" of oedipal scenarios and the contradictions of the female subject in such narrative trajectories (156–57). The story must be told differently.

Hardy's telling and Polanski's retelling of Tess's story, I would argue, stage this oedipal problematic to stress its duplicity for the female subject. Both novelist and filmmaker represent Tess as seduced into *and* consenting to femininity. Hardy's story submits Tess to the "seduction plot," a narrative sequence in which female destiny, according to Nancy K. Miller's "feminist narratology," plays itself out in tropes of *Bildung* or fatality. Playing vice off against virtue, the seduction plot demands female innocence, vulnerability, and penetrability; the scene of "defloration" is central, regardless of whether it is narratively "seen" or figured by synecdoche. The logic of seduction then rewards or punishes the figural woman: the "kept woman," the resisting woman, the seduced and abandoned woman, all will be submitted to the signifying trajectory of death or education. She is troped as prey to the hunter, conquerable territory to the militarist, victim to the sadist, and sacrificial lamb to the sociality. The seduced woman's end therefore governs closure at multiple levels: it invokes as absent ideal both coupling and the machinery of the couple; as implied ideology, bourgeois happiness and the cliche of happily ever after; as moral necessity, the superintendence of female desire; as punishment, the sacrificial disposition of the female body through death. Female destiny thus proves, as Miller writes, "a crucial determinant in the readability of the text" (116).

Even as it emplots the logic of seduction and employs its normative tropes, however, Hardy's narrative calls these into question. In his "Preface to the Fifth Edition," the author describes *Tess* as a novel in which "the great campaign of the heroine begins after an event in her experience which has usually been treated as fatal to her part of protagonist, or at least as the virtual ending of her enterprises and hopes" (Orel 26). Declining to name the "event," Hardy censors his language as he bowdlerized the serial "Tess": replacing the defloration scene and consequential child with "sham marriage," the serialized story appeared alogical, "nonsensical" (Laird 150–51). In *Tess*, however, the scenes of seduction and child care, restored to the text, give, as Hardy says, "artistic form to a true sequence of things" (Orel 25). Although Hardy refuses to identify seduction as the "virtual ending" of his heroine's activities and initiatives, and although he marshalls military metaphors on her behalf, the logic of seduction nevertheless proves "fatal" to his "protagonist"; cross boundaries and map topographical space as she ironically does, she also links femininity with death's signifying trajectory.

Yet in Tess's narrative, fractured sequences combine the normative feminine endings, marriage or seduction, with a certain ironic multiplicity. (Unconsummated) marriage > (adulterous) "marriage" > (Alec's) death > (consummated) marriage > (Tess's) death > (Angel's implied re-)marriage. Moreover, the scene of "violation," as J. Hillis Miller calls it, deploys and contests the story's metaphors of seduction, suggesting competing interpretations of the "event" Hardy still refuses to name but as metaphor (*Repetition* 116–46). The defloration scene thus insists on Tess's bodily articulation with the sequential but multiple logic of seduction *and* with its tropes of fatality and doubleness. The structural shape of her journey—from maidenhood, through "consequence" and "pay[ment]," and to "fulfillment" —makes her mythical (female) subject because figuratively and teleologically she "falls," twice: although once "Maiden" she will ever thereafter be "Maiden No More," Tess chooses her second "seduction." And, having given up in 1891 on the good wishes of his "genteel reader," Hardy in

1895 reminds new readers that their profitable consumption of fiction owes "first place" to a story's organic construction. His exemplary tale, *Clarissa*, like *Tess*, enacts even as it interrogates the seduction plot's logic, figurative language, and mor(t)alities (Orel 26–29, 120).

Hardy also questions naturalized cultural myths about the machinery of the couple. At Talbothays, Hardy intricates Tess with nature's "recuperative power" and thus invokes Biblical tropes for narrative sexual emergence. In the "spectral" light of dawn, Tess and Angel feel "as if they were Adam and Eve"; at that "preternatural time," Tess is "visionary essence of woman": her flesh and soul produce "aura." Encountering Angel's "tender look," Tess gazes at him "as Eve at her second waking might have regarded Adam." The unwritten story of Eve's second waking, however, contaminates mythic origins with ends. Indeed, although Angel thinks, at daybreak, of the "Resurrection hour," the narrator knows that the "Magdalen might be at his side" (19.167, 27.218). And as Eve "seduced" Adam into acquiring (sexual) knowledge, Angel's auratic vision of Tess also invokes reversible figures for woman: Artemis and Demeter, Tess is both chaste Diana and mother; goddess of hunt, night, and moon as well as of corn, harvest, and fruitfulness.

Submitted to narrative's signifying trajectory, this oscillating figure of woman becomes double. Dominick LaCapra reads Sophocles's oedipal story as linking "narrative closure and the scapegoat mechanism." Because myth collapses "levels of intelligibility" by accounting for binary oppositions as played out in narrative events, it "fixates and 'totalizes' repetition" through story and seeks an "undivided origin" in a tale's opening event. Closure reduces repetitive processes to peripeteia between beginning and end and redeems original occurrence (24–25). Displaced onto a question of her ancestry and the "sins of the fathers," Tess's female oedipal story of seduction and violation destines her to repeat her family's legend, perhaps to redeem its masculine and violent rape of peasant women by the victimizing of an innocent female d'Urberville. Designated as seduceable, Tess declares herself victim; the narrative marks her as scapegoat; her figurative sacrifice secures narrative closure. Yet Tess's sacrifice fixes without repairing the social order. In arranging for Angel to "watch over," "train [and] teach," and marry 'Liza Lu—who possesses the "best" of Tess without her "bad"—Tess invokes a doubled narrative closure based on her desire to be "dead and buried"—to fulfill the scenario in which an unconscious, somnambulous Angel placed his bride in a sarcophogal coffin—and to vicariously enjoy the pleasures of marriage (503).[4] By replacing her with her double, Hardy's fantasy ending indulges even as it disallows the reader's desire for the marriage as happy ending, a recuperated Edenic sexuality, and the bourgeois ideology of the couple.[5]

Polanski's narrative film, hyperbolically idealizes scenarios of seduction. Whereas Alec's violation of the sleeping Tess occurs in Hardy's narrative gap, in Polanski's added scene, rape becomes Romance. Alec confesses to Tess in The Chase, his body bending contritely, "I've been in torment since you came; is there no hope for me?" "You're bleeding," she whispers as they embrace tenderly. Although Tess resists when seduction threatens to become sex, soft focus visualizes moonlit, misty aura and Polanski dissolves to Tess accepting Alec's gift—given in exchange, the spectator presumes, for her maidenhead. Montage then condenses their affair into romantic scenarios: Alec rows Tess on a pond as light or aura reflects off the water; swans surround the skiff as the music swells, guaranteeing the detemporalized moment's truth. Still, Polanski shoots Tess looking down under her parasol, an index, again, of her hesitance *and* her permeability. Does she resist her position as narrative image in a seduction story? Confined in Alec's house, dressed by the finery his ersatz wealth has purchased, Tess becomes kept woman as the tropes of seduction visually accumulate. Polanski, like Hardy, feels ambivalent about female sexual agency and gratifies masculine sexual persuasion even as he portrays its ironic consequence.

Polanski has said that he wanted to tell a "beautiful, tragic love story" in a "romantic, even sentimental" mode. His screenplay therefore redistributes the seduction plot's play of masculine vice and virtue. In Hardy's novel, the evangelist sign-painter works for the preaching Alec d'Urberville; in Polanski's film, Alec neither converts nor is retempted by Tess because he's no devil. From the moment he first appears, Hardy's Alec threatens: swarthy, smoking, bold-eyed, and sporting a curled mustache over his badly molded mouth, Alec emerges from the ornamental tent signifying "barbarism" and "singular force" (44). Polanski's Alec, however, looks elegant and, although dialogue emphasizes his reckless enjoyment of things "foolish," smilingly suave. The camera eschews to observe him from Tess's point of view; instead, his face often dominates the frame while hers, in two shots, fails to register emotional responses to his invitations. When Tess leaves Trantridge, Alec follows his beloved, hoping to provide for her needs and asking tenderly, "Why sneak away?" Polanski's Alec cares about Tess—in fact, loves her—and wants her back. Late in the film when Alec reappears, narrative pressure declares him the man she should have stayed with; he's still the good guy, still sympathetic, not Hardy's humiliated and mortified slave to sexual desire. "You put me even more in the wrong than I was," he tells Tess, hoping to rescue her from poverty. "Who is this husband of yours," he therefore demands, cooing, "I'm offering you my help; who else cares?" For not Alec but Angel is Polanski's villain, the husband who misreads his wife's violation and so abandons her. When the seduction plot becomes Romance, the seducer changes his stripes.

Polanski's logic of seduction-as-romance problematizes classical cinema's machinery of the couple. Although he shoots the one night of idyllic married bliss when Angel and Tess flee from the law, Polanski disallows marriage as narrative closure, as fixing the social order and totalizing the repetitions Tess has unwittingly put in play. 'Liza Lu, virtually effaced from Polanski's film, cannot redeem Tess's "fall" or sublate her sacrifice. Repetition of Tess with a difference, figure of peripeteia between beginning and end, 'Liza Lu, does not, by prophecy and implicature, join with Angel as the couple Tess could not complete. Polanski's romance, moreover, tropes not Eden but the Manson family, and so portrays his (personal) myth of modern victimage. Bearing the dedication, "To Sharon," Polanski's *Tess* suggests the violence done the woman who loved Hardy's novel and would have played the part of Tess: the dairy maids, the Manson family women, dominated by and obsessed with the filmicly flaccid Angel; Angel as villain, Manson; Alec, Polanski himself, seducer of female minors and the actress who did play Tess (Polanski 382; Glazer 42–44). Nevertheless, in *Tess* constables hunt down not the man who has "unlawful sexual intercourse" with an "innocent" girl, but the girl herself, who, having murdered the man who had violated her, then pays for her violation *and* her murder with her life.[6] Polanski's *Tess* mythologizes the woman as perfect sacrificeable victim, as inevitably violated through her enjoyment of sexual pleasure. Having attributed to woman the (desire to) look, Polanski consciously submits her to the victimizing seduction plot as her fate. Novel and film, despite their different representations of seduction—as defloration, as romance—ultimately converge in closure achieved by a woman's death.

Death at Work

Freud would call this mix of myth, closure, and scapegoat mechanisms "the death drive." Difficult to prove empirically, hypothetical and speculative as theory, the death drive may be verified or "seen," Freud acknowledges, only when "tinged" or "strongly alloyed with erotism" and thus defined as sadism or masochism (*Discontents*, 66–67). Directed inward and so producing masochism, or outward, and so sadism, the death drive articulates sexualities with clinical observation, with watching and investigation. Freud later links this visual register with narrative teleology when theorizing sadomasochism in *Beyond the Pleasure Principle*; while he begins with pleasure, then considers the necessity of displeasure, he ends, with a certain uncanny reversibility, by making the pleasure principle serve the death instincts after all. Whether a fable of a boy's dismay at, revenge for, and linguistic mastery of his mother's absence; whether a biological myth of bodily breaches and pain's ability to penetrate or permeate; whether a fiction of (im)mortality based on a "biology" that does not, it turns out, control the death instincts, Freud's formulation—"*the aim of all life is death*"—subsumes visualizable and pleasurable contradictions through narrative sequencing (97). Hardy's *Tess*, in contrast, narrates a theoretical eschatology. As analyst of history, Hardy opposes the "circumstantial will against enjoyment" to the individual "appetite for joy": Necessity battles pleasure on a signifying field, with the individual as site of contestation (365). Doubly bound in this philosophical battle, Tess is marked as masochist and so becomes victim of Hardy's figural sadists' aggressive drive for mastery of objects. For Tess, who desires pleasure, must die, her originator believes, despite his authorial love of her. Thus the pleasure principle, lodged in individual desire, ends up, with a certain uncanny reversibility, serving the death instincts.

Hardy therefore represents Tess as willing sacrifice. She submits to Angel's rebuke, allows him to place her in a coffin, and considers committing suicide to save his reputation; she reserves to him the "right of harming her," regards herself as "his absolute possession," and hopes he will "dispose" of her as he shall choose. "It is you, my ruined husband, who ought to strike the [death] blow," she whispers. "I will obey you like your perfect slave, even if it is to lie down and die," both Tesses tell the recalcitrant husband who scorns her "self sacrifice" (37.317, 306, 294). After striking Alec with her glove and drawing "scarlet ooze" from his lips, then, Tess weeps, "Now, punish me, . . . whip me, crush me"; "once victim, always victim; that's the law" (47.423). Her represented human agency thus signals the violent and volitional link between woman and the death drive; "I am ready," Tess says at Stonehenge. Masochistically claiming victimage as her narrative position, Tess participates in and assumes as her history the signifying trajectory of death, the sacrificial disposition of her body.

Hardy concludes by putting Tess's victimage on display. Just as the constables watch her on the Stone of Sacrifice, the "two speechless gazers" watch the black flag rise, and the narrator observes as Tess takes on her narrative image as "lesser creature" than woman (58.505). In both scenes of observation, the sun rises and day begins: identifiable only by touch during the night, Stonehenge becomes "visible for miles around" as the sun's rays thread its pillars; Wintoncester from the summit appears spread out below, "visible" and mapped as ancient town housing anomalous modern justice. As the reader looks with the focalizer, Angel, a "mere dot" on the horizon gradually becomes trained and marching figure, then speaking constable, his still figure silvered by the glowing light; as the reader walks with Angel and 'Liza-Lu into the hills outside Wintoncester and gazes down at the jail's tower, the black flag rises. The relay of gazes at Tess's image now signifies neither desire nor arousal but horror, for the reader, witness to Tess's sacrifice, watches her and so by implication complies with the "law" of victimage, participates in the law's superintendence of female desire. As readerly desire for Tess is submitted to the death drive's logic, the seduction plot marks out her narrative trajectory toward both primitive and modern retributive institutions. Desiring her happiness as wife in the seduction plot's signifying couple, desiring her death to fix the social order and to restore perepeteia between beginning and end, the reader experiences an uncanny mix of pleasure and pain: sadism, a pleasure in the suffering of this less-than-woman; rage, at willing witness of scapegoating; and aesthetic pleasure, as the reader, aroused by Tess's image and bearing the gaze, assents to her death yet also "suffer[s] with her," Donald Hall says (457). The death drive is thus "seen" or visualizable only when, as in these scenarios of watching, tinged or alloyed with a complex readerly erotism.

Hardy positions Tess beyond the pleasure principle. As Colin MacCabe reads Freud's *fort-da* fable, mastery of death—whether linguistic or from the look—is a fiction: "What lies beyond the pleasure principle is not a threatening and exterior reality but a reality whose virulence knows no cessation, the reality of those constitutive moments at which we experience ourselves in the very moment of separation; which moments we are compelled to repeat in that endless movement which can find satisfaction only in death" (67–68). The reversible look at the image of woman joins with narrative teleology, with the plot and logic of seduction, to remind us we, too—modern, psychologized individuals—take pleasure in consuming narratives of scapegoated woman, representations of constitutive moments that defer yet suggest death. *Tess* elicits from its observing reader, then, desire (produced by the system of looks at the female body), identification (a bourgeois psychological subjectivity invoked by the nineteenth-century novel; and in the film by the wide-angle panorama, the pan, and follow focus on the subject), horror (a cathartic emotive subjectivity invoked by superintending observation and rituals of scapegoating), and anger (a defensive emotion provoked by termination). The narrative image of woman in the novel produces a teleological fascination with the outcome of pleasure and its intrication with pain, as the pleasure principle ends up serving the death instincts after all.

For Polanski, this tale of sadism and masochism can only end in perverse pleasure for the narrative film's spectator. Adding gender to the question, Bellour theorizes that woman takes pleasure in viewing classical

American cinema only "from her own masochism" and from a "certain sadism that she can exercise in return on the masculine subject, within a system loaded with traps" (Bergstrom 97) Invoking Mulvey and de Lauretis on the narrative destruction of woman, however, Linda Williams believes that "sadism is *not* the whole story" of the spectator's pleasure—even for the viewer of sadomasochistic pornography. For Williams, masochism is a "ruse," a "masquerade," a "performance" of suffering *and* sexual pleasure for the subject and others. She argues, following Parveen Adams, that subject formation occurs through an oscillation between male and female subject positions "held simultaneously in a play of bisexuality at the level of both object choice and identification" (215–16). In reading Freud's tale of female oedipal scenarios, "A Child Is Being Beaten," Adams maintains that spectators, whether male or female, may identify with each figure in the analysand's three scenes: with the beating father; the beaten daughter or other (boy) child(ren); and the watching daughter (22–26). The spectator may thus experience the victim's pleasure *or* pain; and, although the beating father maintains final authority and power in the fantasy scenario, the violated daughter and her female spectator thus actively earn a share of pleasure. Sadomasochistic fantasy, therefore, according to Williams, represents for woman not only that she must negotiate her pleasures from a position of powerlessness, but "awareness" of "power in pleasure." I emphasize "awareness" because Williams contends that consciousness and consent redeem masochistic fantasy, aesthetics, and practice. While romance fiction heroines misrecognize their desires and so are "unconscious masochists," pornographic protagonists—consenting to rather than seduced into consenting to femininity—may subvert "fixed sexual identities" through the play of sadomasochistic pleasures (218–19).

Polanski's *Tess* puts in play just such sadomasochisms and, in addition, stages the spectator's consent. As Tess's end approaches, sadism and masochism rupture a hitherto verisimilar *mise-en-scène* as voyeurism produces excessive spectatorial pleasure. For when Mrs. Brooks looks through the keyhole, Polanski's camera and the spectator look with her. As the keyhole irises out, Mrs. Brooks, figure for the spectator, peeps at Tess's weeping figure from behind and watches the lovers' quarrel that eventually produces the blood she sees on the ceiling. When Tess catches the landlady spying, the keyhole no longer provides implicit frame: Mrs. Brooks runs away as we watch her from behind and the camera exploits the "behind" with straight-on backtracking shots. Yet the spectator, unlike the landlady, remains voyeur. The libidinal investment the film accords the look (the relay of gazes, the iconic close-up) now joins with the narrative position of woman (her intrication with romance/seduction plot, the making of the mythical subject, and termination) to produce voyeuristic perversity. Magically restored to his position as the villain he is in Hardy's novel, Polanski's Alec now snaps at his weeping "wife," threatens by implication to hurt her with the riding whip he brandishes, and accuses her of hysteria. In *Tess* the film, Polanski's appropriations and the cinematic apparatus identify spectatorship as necessarily—and consciously—perverse.

The play of dominance and submission in the visual register prepares the viewer-voyeur for such perversity. Tess's riding high on buggy or horse with Alec; her refusal to ride and proud insistence on walking, hat in hand; her knocking Alec from his horse and hurting him; her subsequent seduction by Alec, on top; her hitting him with her glove for maligning her husband as, in low-angle shot, Alec's hip-high whip crosses at mid-screen the image of her seated body. This spatial hierarchy articulates power with pleasure and narratively binds seduction with sadism: the whip as instrument of possible punishment identifies the woman as penetrable, marks each of these scenes as proleptic signs of perversity. Later, Tess's confession of violence and murder—"Since the day I hit his mouth with my glove; the blood in his mouth; I thought I might be killed; I've killed him"—produces the fetishized moment in which Angel removes her boot, then buries his head in her lap, as the camera zooms in on the two lovers for virtually the first time, and so inscribes their intimacy with a certain spectatorial disorientation, a proleptic awareness that the sacrificed, sexualized woman will be fetishized. Designating the spectator's activity as voyeuristic and so perverse, alerting the reader to his or her pleasure in watching images and scenarios of a woman in pain, making the spectator conscious of his or her binding in a narrative play of sadomasochisms, Polanski's "masquerade" unmasks cinema's perversity.

Rewriting the Script:
Spectacle and Spectatorship

Commentary on *Tess* praises or damns the film for loyalty to or betrayal of its original: Polanski, for example, "does violence to" and wrings "wanton changes" on Hardy's novel—a text nevertheless "unsuitable" for "film treatment" (Harris 122); because Polanski "share[s] Hardy's passion" for Tess, his film is "superb entertainment" (Waldman 435); and despite Polanski's fine screenwriting, casting, and shooting, film as medium fails to represent "figurative truths" as well as does writing (Costanzo 76). In a perverse inversion of original and copy, the publishing industry appropriates Polanski's *Tess* as advertisement or packaging for the Signet *Tess*, from the cover of which pouts Nastassia Kinski's iconic face: "amazing fidelity to the original," one blurb about the film reads; "faithful to the novel's outrage and deep conviction," avers another. Contaminated with erotic figuration, these naive arguments about the priority or superiority of one medium over another nevertheless thematize the problematic of film and literary intertextuality. Whether "violent," "wanton," or "faithful," rewriting or scripting participates in an exchange, a desiring although mediated economic in which pleasure and pain are always already at stake.

When he edited the narrative after three magazine editors had rejected it, Hardy himself reread and rewrote *Tess*. In the *Life*, Hardy calls this process a "dismemberment": with pieces "cut out," the "mutilated novel" appeared in the *Graphic*, a periodical dedicated to "household reading"; for the first edition, he restored its (implicitly fetishized) "trunk and limbs" (1:291, Orel 128, 25). According to N. N. Feltes, the *Graphic*'s readership (a "specialized clientele" constituted by the journal during the decades of the "new journalism") and its modes of production (personality-oriented news highlighted by advertisements and woodcuts) constitute the serial "Tess" as commodity-text, written to be consumed by readers themselves being constituted as subjects by the texts they read. The *Graphic*'s readers are the "alien observers" of Hardy's narrative; its editors, men who control the tale's ideological vantage point and so through their "superintendence" reduce Tess's conscious agency and sexual independence (64–75). For Mary Jacobus, Hardy's manuscript revisions and first edition bowdlerize the Ur-*Tess* and rob Tess of personal responsibility and sexual autonomy. The revised *Tess*'s blatant reliance on the sexual double standard forces a "character-assassination" of Alec and Angel: the first, not yet a nouveau-riche and "moustachioed seducer of Victorian melodrama" but rather a gentleman farmer; the second, less cold, more sexually aroused by Tess at Talbothays—and not himself the seducer of a city woman, for Hardy pasted the account of Angel's affair into the manuscript text (318–32). Hardy's rehabilitation of mistress and murderess into the "pure" woman of the novel's hastily written subtitle, according to Jacobus, distorts the story. Whether preserialized manuscript or Ur-*Tess*, however, both Feltes and Jacobus take a prior text as primary, seeking an ever-earlier justificatory moment of inscription immune from the pressures of the literary marketplace.

Polanski's film of *Tess* demonstrates that representation never extricates itself from the marketplace. For in the twentieth century, as Bellour says, film gratifies a "general demand for narrativity" that the modern and postmodern novel, refusing realistic diagesis, no longer satisfies; classic American cinema therefore "maxim[izes] narrativity" to market its film texts, just as, in the nineteenth-century, the serialized novel made literature "an industry" (Bergstrom 89). Hoping to be judged "faithful" to Tess, Polanski rewrites her story explicitly as an adaptation of the novel. Until the keyhole appears, he shoots a virtually seamless perspective on the profilmic material that serves to efface any particular point of view and to create as film presence the novel's paradoxical emotiveness and distantiation. Presenting its desire to narrate and to display the female body, Polanski's cinematic style here eschews the subjective camera of *Repulsion*, the point-of-view and short shots of *Rosemary's Baby*, and adopts instead long shots that efface the film's own marks of enunciation. "Ideally," Polanski says of the camera's relation to the spectator's "reality," "the lens should be at the same distance from the subject as the eye of the notional observer." Whereas in *Repulsion*, Polanski shot Carol's hallucinations "through the eye of the camera, augmenting their impact by using wide-angle lenses of progressively increasing scope," in *Tess* he represents the "rhythm of [Hardy's] epic" by panning to the crossing of roads that twist into the background, by follow focusing on figures who walk or ride them, by picturing, in short, an apparently stable, static, and panoramic landscape upon which change can be objectively seen as though simply happening. Whereas Polanski had built for *Repulsion* a set in which the walls moved and the visual space therefore "stretched" so as to make a narrow hall assume "nightmarish proportions," for *Tess*, he sought a French twentieth-century countryside equivalent to Hardy's nineteenth-century Dorset, the filming on which, from early spring through autumn and deep winter, would symbolize Tess's change of character, would portray nineteenth-century "sentiments and feelings" rather than the "realism and violence" twentieth-century film may now picture (Glazer 44, Polanski 405, 199, 254).

Polanski's naturalized visualization, however, is a lure. As film, it resembles what Ross Chambers calls a "duplicitous" (as opposed to "self-designating") and "readerly" text that "imitates" a "natural" narrative situation so as to "tell itself." Because narrative readability depends in part on a text's ability to situate itself as narrative, Chambers's paradigmatic nineteenth-century narratives trope their situations as seductive (26). No longer a text meant to transmit information but to pose questions, narrative must "seduce" its prospective reader; an "alienated" commodity produced by laboring writers for consumption by pleasure-seeking readers, the text must display its "desire to narrate" to arouse in its consumer a "desire" for narrative. While the writerly text, aware of its authority, makes its reader a "producer," the readerly acquires its authority through "the act of reading" and thus designates its reader a consumer. A "felicitous reading," Chambers says, must comprehend the duplicitous text's "doubleness," must respond to the "mimesis of 'natural' narrative and to the artistic assumptions of the narrative as a whole." However well its mechanisms are managed, duplicity does not function unless "seen through" (32).

Polanski's duplicitous narrative text desires to seduce moviegoers into becoming its spectators. Despite its having been shot in France, despite Polanski's being "on the lam" from criminal prosecution in the United States, *Tess* represents the filmmaker's attempt to out-Hollywood Hollywood, to recapture his audience and the recognition he'd achieved with *Rosemary's Baby* and *Chinatown*. Released five years after *Jaws* and three years after *Star Wars, Tess* entered the cinema marketplace when film producers had begun to bankroll and distributors and theater owners to exhibit the box-office "blockbuster." In the logic of ever-growing box-office receipts and profits, this continual escalation of representation produced a situation in which each hit outdid what came before and had to be outdone by what followed. Despite its resurgence in the 1970s, however, the "blockbuster" did not originate in that decade. After the 1940s, with replacement of the producer-unit system of production by the package-unit system, and the demise of the major studios, production companies used the excessive earnings of highly profitable films to diversify their holdings and so become—rather than be bought by—conglomerates; the profits from *Jaws* and *Star Wars* in the '70s allowed Twentieth Century-Fox and Universal to invest in, for example, a Coca-Cola bottling company (Bordwell, Staiger, and Thompson 368). Combining the package-unit system with a "classical" narrative property while, however, flouting the Hollywood star system, Polanski made with *Tess* a bid for success based on his name, his reputation as the director of art films *and* box-office hits. Knowing his film a commodity, aware of his laboring position as "alienated" —not only because of industry modes of production and spectatorial consumption but also because of his status in Hollywood as foreigner and "pervert"—Polanski needed his readerly text successfully to situate itself as narrative film, to desire its spectator, and so to be consumed. Competing with other film texts in a culture in which the cinematic apparatus cooperates with commodification to produce consumption as a primary goal and purpose of cinema, *Tess* solicited mass readings.[7]

Polanski needed, then, to produce not simply a seductive film text that manipulated and managed the mechanisms of duplicity but a spectacular one in which the signs of its own consumption and modes of production could be read out of the text. Doubly signifying "visualization" and "excessive or extravagant display," the spectacle originated in eighteenth-century public, monarchical rituals signifying lawful discipline and social order and, redesigned for public and transposed into private life, entered into nineteenth-century literature, theater, and culture as hyperbolic rhetoric or exaggerated represented event. Accustoming audiences to technological extravaganzas and making technology itself into "entertainment," the nineteenth-century spectacle produced the "figuration of a consuming subject" and a "democratic ideology for consumerism" (Richards 58;

Bordwell, Staiger, and Thompson 100). In this signifying system, 1970s cinematic duplicity and spectacle coincide to represent the spectator's felicitous individual choice to consume the latest blockbuster and the director's necessary duplicity as maker of fetishized images. When Polanski shoots the seduction story as Romance, with montage, music, and aura signifying the heroine's vulnerability and penetrability, he exposes even as he mimics the Hollywood aesthetic in which visualization creates the female "character" as seduceable. When in his autobiography, Polanski presents himself as successful seducer of school girls and reports his "affair" with Kinski during the filming of *Tess*, he perversely confirms the myth of the Hollywood "casting couch" (Polanski 311, 352–57, 377–83). "Dedicated to the consumption of female flesh," the spectacle that visualizes seduction allegorizes the culture of Hollywood as itself seductive, and the purveying of woman's image its unsavory consequence (Polanski 182).

As sign of its own consumption the film also invokes the spectator's act of having read the novel. Because Polanski edits out much of the judging, generalizing, and moralizing discourse that surrounds Tess's nineteenth-century novelistic figure, the spectator of the film must reconstruct figural motivations not visualized in the film's spectacle. Why, for example, did Mercy Chant discover Tess's shoes by the roadside? The spectator remembers, if she can, the novel's narratorial discourse surrounding Tess's long trek: her fear of her father-in-law; her hesitancy to reveal Angel's pitiless treatment of her; her shyness in the face of another woman's apparently confident religious understanding of an incomprehensible causality. Likewise, the spectator makes readerly sense despite gaps in the film's sequencing. Why did Tess's family so insistently need her to claim kin with the D'Urbervilles? The reader's memory (and the film's mention) of Prince's death provides the financial explanation that supports and sustains narrative causality. Watching the film, moreover, reminds the spectator that Polanski himself read *Tess* and knew it nearly by heart. Participating in the production of meanings that the readerly text solicits, the spectator becomes aware of his status as reader or spectator, his function as consumer: his seduceability. Entranced by the film and its romance, angry at the sadists who seduce, victimize, and fetishize Tess, the spectator, too, is led astray. Polanski's "faithful presentation" of Hardy's pure woman becomes, as Judith Mayne writes of other film adaptations, a "commentary on the narrative process itself" (6).

Yet Polanski demands that his film's spectator "see through" its duplicity, its apparently transparent picture of things as they were in a bygone time of innocence. When she joins Mrs. Brooks and looks through the keyhole, the spectator is positioned in relation to seeing and so becomes aware of having entered the realm of spectacle: Polanski shoots blood on the ceiling from Mrs. Brooks's point of view; Tess and Angel spied by and spying caretaker in long pan; Tess's body on the altar from Angel's, constables', and "objective" points of view as the camera pans up and tracks in from her skirt to her face. The play of hitherto unrepresented points of view tropes the spectator's position within a regime of specularity. Yet the film's expressive code, laced with dominance and submission and driving toward perversity, hardly makes the viewer "master." As Lacan argues, Hans Holbein's *The Ambassadors* portrays not simply two bourgeois masters symbolically defined by tropes for vanitas, but the spectating subject as constituted through the "imagined embodiment" of castration in the symbolic, language, and representation. For in looking away from the picture or leaving its field (MacCabe 65), the spectator, catching sight of the hitherto hidden symbolic death's head—"la tâche," the "blot"—sees his own nothingness reflected back to him. Called into the picture, the subject looks but never sees what he wishes. In Lacan's dialectic of gaze and eye, then, the picture is lure, a "trap for the gaze"; the spectator, the "captured subject." Made picture himself, gazed at by things around him, the subject is subjectified and his mastery mocked (88–89, 101, 106). And the spectator's look in *Tess* culminates in Lacan's "sidelong glance," the moment when he spies the death's head and knows he does not always know, when the look confers not mastery or domination but a sense (or scent) of mortality. Scarlet-clad and sexualized, Tess's represented body becomes Hardy's "scarlet blot" and Lacan's "tâche" or death's head; it accumulates the tropes for blood with which the narrative register associates her image as woman. This "blot" lures the spectator, traps and tames his or her gaze, captures the subject in the reversible structure of the look which, from the Other, makes him or her picture. The figure of Tess invokes the annihilated subject. Looking at her aslant, with sidelong glance, we—male and female—know our selves specular.

Polanski's "romantic, even sentimental" film thus can be read as commenting on the ideological work of narrative, on a modern commodity culture in which seductive products solicit seduceable consumers. Moreover, ironically "faithful" to what Feltes and Jacobus construe as Hardy's "authorial intent," Polanski's "reading" of *Tess*, like the Ur-*Tess*, represents its heroine as sexually independent, as seduced (and "kept") rather than nearly raped in the narrative gap produced by metaphors of nature and legend. Like the preserialized narrative, *Tess* the film interrogates even as it displays the ideological "superintendence" of female sexuality. And Polanski retells Hardy's storied sadomasochisms with a vengeance, perversely, to solicit a felicitous spectatorship. Polanski's seductive rereading of Hardy's heroine portrays scenarios of women victimized and in pain as Hollywood's most alluring subjects, its most spectacular commodity. In submitting Tess's look of desire to the voyeuristic, moreover, and her narrative position to cinematic perversion, Polanski demonstrates not only his own fascination with sadomasochistic violence, with classical cinema's images of woman, but the ways film inscribes these fascinations in its dominant teleologies of desire, through its cinematic apparatus and production technologies. For as Polanski's adaptation demonstrates, the culturally aware critic must read not in narratological or psychoanalytic terms alone but must likewise examine the material constraints under which texts are produced, the markets in which they are exchanged, and the personal claims of their creators.

NOTES

1. See Freeman for a moral interpretation of "ways of looking at Tess" that elides Hardy's narrator. Freeman describes the significance of Tess's "visibility," the ways Tess is "singled out" by the look, Hardy's implication of the reader in this activity of "intensity and risk," and Hardy's complicity with the "very immorality he has watched and deplored" (311–22). Kaja Silverman, on the contrary, pays careful attention to the narrator, although she refuses to believe Hardy complicit in Tess's violation; yet his "awareness," I will later argue, makes a significant difference.

2. While the inscription of Hardy's reader as spectator and Polanski's spectator as voyeur is encoded, as this paragraph implies, as male, women may occupy these subject positions, as I will argue later, in a bisexual play of identifications. I have nevertheless chosen throughout this essay to refer to the spectator as "he." For theorization of Tess's gendered reader, see Mitchell, in this volume.

3. For a feminist demystification of masculine metaphors for narrative structure— however flawed by unexamined grounding assumptions about the status of the female body and female "experience"—see Winnett.

4. Although, as Boumelha points out, this ending clearly contravenes moral law, since marriage to a sister-in-law remained illegal—and smacked of incest—until passage of the Deceased Wife's Sister Act in 1907 (125–26).

5. For theoretical discussion of woman and sacrifice, see Girard and Loraux.

6. Polanski called Tess the "story of innocence betrayed in a world where human behavior is governed by class barriers and social prejudice" (405).

7. For extended discussion of commodity culture and spectacle, see Debord 1–16 and Richards 54–71.

WORKS CITED

Adams, Parveen. "Per Os(cillation)." *Camera Obscura* no. 17 (1988): 7–29

Barthes, Roland. *The Pleasure of the Text.* Trans. Richard Miller. New York: Hill, 1975.

Bergstrom, Janet. "Alternation, Segmentation, Hypnosis: Interview with Raymond Bellour." *Camera Obscura* nos. 3–4 (Summer 1979): 71–103.

Bordwell, David, Janet Staiger, and Kristin Thompson. *The Classical Hollywood Cinema: Film Style and Mode of Production to 1960.* New York: Columbia University Press, 1985.

Boumelha, Penny. *Thomas Hardy and Women: Sexual Ideology and Narrative Form.* Sussex: Harvester, 1979.

Brooks, Peter. *Reading for the Plot: Design and Intention in Narrative.* New York: Random, 1984.

Chambers, Ross. *Story and Situation: Narrative Seduction and the Power of Fiction.* Minneapolis: University of Minnesota Press, 1984.

Costanzo, William V. "Polanski in Wessex: Filming *Tess of the d'Urbervilles.*" *Literature/Film Quarterly* 9:2 (1981): 71–78.

Debord, Guy. *Society of the Spectacle.* Detroit: Black, 1983.

De Lauretis, Teresa. *Alice Doesn't: Feminism, Semiotics, Cinema.* Bloomington: Indiana University Press, 1984.

Feltes, N. N. *Modes of Production of Victorian Novels.* Chicago: University of Chicago Press, 1986.

Freeman, Janet. "Ways of Looking at Tess." *Studies in Philology* 79:3 (Summer 1982): 311–23.

Freud, Sigmund. *Beyond the Pleasure Principle.* Trans. James Strachey. New York: Bantam, 1959.

————. *Civilization and Its Discontents.* Trans. James Strachey. New York: Norton, 1961.

Girard, René. *Violence and the Sacred.* Trans. Patrick Gregory. Baltimore: Johns Hopkins University Press, 1977.

Glazer, Mitchell. "On the Lam with Roman Polanski." *Rolling Stone* 2 April 1981: 40–45.

Hardy, Florence Emily. *The Early Life of Thomas Hardy, 1840–1891.* 2 vols. London: Macmillan, 1928.

Hardy, Thomas. *Tess of the D'Urbervilles: A Pure Woman.* Aftwd. Donald Hall. New York: Signet, 1964.

————. *Tess of the D'Urbervilles: A Pure Woman Faithfully Presented.* Wessex Edition. London: Macmillain, 1912.

Harris, Margaret. "Thomas Hardy's *Tess of the d'Urbervilles:* Faithfully presented by Roman Polanski?" *Sydney Studies in English* 7 (1981–82): 115–22.

Heath, Stephen. *Questions of Cinema.* Bloomington: Indiana University Press, 1981.

Jacobus, Mary. "Tess's Purity." *Essays in Criticism* 26 (Oct. 1976): 318–38.

LaCapra, Dominick. "History and Psychoanalysis." In *The Trial(s) of Psychoanalysis.* Ed. Francoise Meltzer. Chicago: University of Chicago Press, 1988.

Lacan, Jacques. *The Four Fundamental Concepts of Psycho-Analysis.* Ed. Jacques-Alain Miller. Trans. Alan Sheridan. New York: Norton, 1978.

Laird, J. T. *The Shaping of "Tess of the D'Urbervilles."* Oxford: Clarendon, 1975.

Little, Richard Purdy and Michael Millgate, eds. *The Collected Letters of Thomas Hardy.* 2 vols. Oxford: Clarendon, 1978.

Loraux, Nicole. *Tragic Ways of Killing a Woman.* Trans. Anthony Forster. Cambridge: Harvard University Press, 1987.

MacCabe, Colin. *Tracking the Signifier: Theoretical Essays: Film, Linguistics, Literature.* Minneapolis: University of Minnesota Press, 1985.

Mayne, Judith. *Private Novels, Public Films.* Athens: University of Georgia Press, 1988.

Miller, J. Hillis. *Fiction and Repetition: Seven English Novels.* Cambridge: Harvard University Press, 1982.

————. *Thomas Hardy: Distance and Desire.* Cambridge: Harvard University Press, 1970.

Miller, Nancy K. *The Heroine's Text: Readings in the French and English Novel, 1722–1782.* New York: Columbia University Press, 1980.

Mulvey, Laura. *Visual and Other Pleasures.* Bloomington: Indiana University Press, 1989.

Orel, Harold, ed. *Thomas Hardy's Personal Writings: Prefaces, Literary Opinions, Reminiscences.* Lawrence: University of Kansas Press, 1966.

Polanski, Roman. *Roman By Polanski.* New York: Ballantine, 1984.

Richards, Thomas. *The Commodity Culture of Victorian England: Advertising and Spectacle, 1851–1914.* Stanford: Stanford University Press, 1990.

Rose, Jacqueline. *Sexuality in the Field of Vision.* London: Verso, 1986.

Scholes, Robert. *Fabulation and Metafiction.* Urbana: University of Illinois Press, 1979.

Silverman, Kaja. "History, Figuration and Female Subjectivity in *Tess of the D'Urbervilles.*" *Novel* 18 (Fall 1989): 5–28.

Polanski, Roman (director). *Tess.* New York: Columbia Pictures, 1980.

Waldman, Nell Kozak. " 'All that she is': Hardy's Tess and Polanski's" *Queen's Quarterly* 88:3 (Autumn 1981): 429–36.

Williams, Linda. *Hard Core: Power, Pleasure, and the "Frenzy of the Visible."* Berkeley: University of California Press, 1989.

Winnett, Susan. "Coming Unstrung: Women, Men, Narrative, and Principles of Pleasure." *PMLA* 105:3 (May 1990): 505–18.

Hardy's Female Reader

Judith Mitchell

What counts is what the heroine provokes, or rather what she represents. She is the one, or rather the love or fear she inspires in the hero, or else the concern he feels for her, who makes him act the way he does. In herself the woman has not the slightest importance.

—Budd Boetticher, Hollywood director of B Westerns

The heroines of Hardy's early novels are presented primarily as objects of erotic interest not only for the narrators and for the male characters . . . but also for the implied reader/voyeur. . . . What they think or feel seems not to matter; the focus of attention is on the feelings they arouse in a variety of men.

—T. R. Wright, *Hardy and the Erotic*

How does a female reader—particularly a modern feminist reader—read Thomas Hardy? Does she applaud his feminism? Deplore his sexism? The question of Hardy's representation of women has perturbed literary critics since the turn of the century. Just as mainstream critics remain unsure about Hardy's formal virtuosity (citing him with equal conviction as both a great literary artist and a crass technical bungler), feminist critics seem undecided whether to accept Hardy with distaste or to reject him with reluctance. Like Hardy himself, many remain ambivalent; Katherine Rogers reaches the fairly typical conclusion that "These novels show the tenacity of sexist assumptions even in so humane and enlightened a man as Hardy."[1] He is noted both for his revolutionary protests against social conventions that restrict women's freedom—Sue's repugnance for being "licensed to be loved on the premises" comes to mind—and for the blatantly sexist remarks that are scattered throughout his oeuvre like some kind of sexist graffiti. Hardy's feminism (or lack of it) can be assessed partly in the approach his inscribed reader is invited to take toward his strong, interesting female protagonists, particularly as they are visualized. The question bears reexamination, especially in light of recent feminist film theory: how is Hardy's reader encouraged to "see" his heroines?

Such theory has far-reaching implications for the study of nineteenth-century novels and their female readership, simply because traditional realist film inherited the narrative conventions of traditional realist fiction. Annette Kuhn, describing classic Hollywood cinema, remarks that "All films are coded: it is simply that certain types of film are coded in such a way as actually to seem uncoded. . . . This of course is one of the pleasures of the classic realist cinema: an address which draws the spectator in to the representation by constructing a credible and coherent cinematic world, which at the same time situates her or him as a passive consumer of meanings which seem to be already there in the text."[2] The viewer of a Hollywood film and the reader of a Victorian novel, in other words, are in much the same viewing position, that of a "passive consumer" of the "obvious" meanings inherent in a seemingly uncoded fictional world.

Laura Mulvey's well-known article "Visual Pleasure and Narrative Cinema" subjects this viewing position to a searching analysis. Mulvey discerns "three different looks associated with the cinema: that of the camera as it records the profilmic event, that of the audience as it watches the final product, and that of each other within the screen illusion."[3] These positions have obvious parallels in those of the narrator, the reader and the characters of a novel. According to Mulvey, all three are constructed as male subjects, who together watch the woman, the sexual object. "Traditionally, the woman displayed has functioned on two levels: as erotic object for the characters within the screen story, and as erotic object for the spectator within the auditorium, with a shifting tension between the looks on both sides of the screen" (419). In addition, Mulvey locates in the female figure "a deeper problem" for the male viewer. "She also connotes something that the look continually circles around but disavows: her lack of a penis, implying a threat of castration and hence unpleasure" (421). According to Mulvey, the male viewer responds to this unconscious anxiety by means of two strategies, namely voyeurism and fetishism. Voyeurism, the devaluation and subjection of the woman via the gaze, is associated with sadism (of a controlling male protagonist, with whom the cinema audience pleasurably identifies) and with narrative ("Sadism demands a story"). On the other hand fetishism, the overvaluation of a feared object so that it becomes reassuring rather than dangerous, "can exist outside linear time as the erotic instinct is focused on the look alone" (422). This "fetishistic scopophilia" applies to moments of spectacle or iconicity in the film, moments in which the woman's visual presence draws attention to itself and "tends to work against the development of a story line, to freeze the flow of action in moments of erotic contemplation" (419). Such moments, termed "extradiegetic" by film critics because they seem to lie outside the movement of the narrative, occur during close-ups or musical numbers in films, and in passages of description and portraiture in novels.

Is there any place in this scenario for the female spectator? According to Mary Ann Doane, a female viewer confronted with the classical Hollywood text has basically "two modes of entry: a narcissistic identification with the female figure as spectacle and a 'transvestite' identification with the active male hero. . . . The female spectator is thus imaged by its text as . . . a hermaphrodite. It is precisely this oscillation which demonstrates the instability of the woman's position as spectator. . . . The female spectator identifies doubly—with the subject and the object of the gaze."[4] In her "Afterthoughts on 'Visual Pleasure and Narrative Cinema,' " Laura Mulvey speculates that the pleasure derived in this manner is an uneasy one: although the female spectator may secretly enjoy the "trans-sex identification" that has become second nature to her in Western culture, she also "may find herself so out of key with the pleasure on offer, with its 'masculinisation,' that the spell of fascination is broken."[5] This unstable, oscillating, bisexual subject position is also (interestingly) characteristic of the female novel-reader; Doane's and Mulvey's observations are strikingly reminiscent of Jonathan Culler's well-known account of "Reading as a Woman": "Reading as a woman is not necessarily what occurs when a woman reads: women can read, and have read, as men. . . . To ask a woman to read as a woman is in fact a double or divided request."[6]

The dynamics of looking and reading that these theorists describe apply particularly well to a novelist like Hardy because of what Judith Bryant Wittenberg refers to as his "spectatorial narrator."[7] Hardy is undoubtedly one of the most scopophilic novelists in the nineteenth century, and his vivid visualizations of figures as well as landscapes contribute to his reputation as a representative of high realism (a designation that remains unaltered by his mythological/romantic tendencies). The pleasure derived from reading a Hardy novel comes primarily from its air of solid "reality"; like the audience of a realist film, the reader of a Hardy novel is encouraged to "escape" into the narrative, suspending all disbelief and all critical sense in favor of an avid interest in the characters and their world. Feminist critics have noted, however, that this world seems real, is recognizable, partly because it parallels the patriarchal world we know, especially in its tacit assumptions about gender. As Elaine Showalter points out, citing Irving Howe's analysis of *The Mayor of Casterbridge*, traditional criticism uncritically posits both a male narrator and a male reader of Hardy's novels. Howe's praise of the opening scenes of *The Mayor* runs as follows: "To shake loose from one's wife; to discard that drooping rag of a woman, . . . through the public sale of her body, as horses are sold at a fair; and thus to wrest, through sheer amoral wilfulness, a second chance out of life—it is with this stroke, so insidiously attractive to male fantasy, that *The Mayor of Casterbridge* begins."[8] Such a statement no doubt reveals more about Howe's fantasies than it does about Hardy's; nevertheless, Hardy's narrator does seem to share a male perspective with his implied reader. The gaze shared by these two entities, in particular, is ineluctably gendered, as I shall show, and looking is their predominant activity. The "vision" Hardy shares in this way is intensely personal, undoubtedly a contributing factor in the plethora of criticism extolling the reader's sense of "knowing" Hardy through his novels.

What makes Hardy's vision so personal, I would submit, is the eroticism that informs it, so that the relation that constantly applies is a literary recapitulation of the dynamic that occurs in representational visual art between a male artist and his viewer. Art critic Sarah Kent describes this dynamic as "a complex interaction . . . focused on the nudity of the female model. Intimacy is created through sexual rivalry—perhaps a sublimated form of homosexuality—in which the model appears to be the subject of the conversation when she is, in fact, only a form of currency in a male centred exchange."[9] Hardy's females are not literally nude, but they are similarly exposed to the shared gaze of an overtly male narrator and a projected male reader. The look these entities share is compounded of curiosity, longing, affection, fear, contempt and adoration; in short, it is the look of desire of a defensively alienated, ambivalent male. Many theorists have held that the male gaze at women in Western culture is always of this type, sight being an erotic perceptual mode eminently suited to the somatophobic male psyche. With its automatic distancing of subject from object, looking provides a position from which it is possible to "possess" a woman without having to deal with her "in the flesh." The obsessive looking of pornography is an obvious instance of this, but all representations can be said to partake of such "safe" distancing between viewer and object. Helena Michie, in discussing Jocelyn Pierston's infatuation with women who are "copies" of each other in *The Well-Beloved* (an overt instance of such distancing), observes that "Eroticism lies in representation; a painting that stands for a woman, a woman that stands for another is a less direct and therefore a less terrifying confrontation of female sexuality."[10]

The gaze, then, is supremely important in Hardy's novels, which readily translate into film. They are "cinematic" in every sense, as critics have noted in dozens of books and articles on vision and perspective in Hardy's work. In Hardy's case the fictional "eye" could easily be a camera, and the questions of whose eye it is and what it sees are easily answered: the eye is Hardy's own (he himself observed that "A writer . . . looks upon the world with his personal eyes" [Orel 110]), and what it mainly sees is women. It is no accident that there is so much spying, particularly in the early novels

(Gabriel Oak's and the Reddleman's activities are obvious instances), or that the characters spied on are female. Gabriel spies on Bathsheba numerous times in the opening chapter of *Far from the Madding Crowd*, and while the erotic aspects of such looking are downplayed by touches of humor, the voyeuristic titillation these incidents afford is unmistakable: when Bathsheba looks in the mirror as Gabriel watches from behind the hedge, for instance, the narrator ingenuously remarks that "The change from the customary spot and necessary occasion of such an act—from the dressing hour in a bedroom to a time of travelling out of doors—lent to the idle deed a novelty it did not intrinsically possess" (1.5). "Novelty" here is obviously a Victorian euphemism for "eroticism," as the "dressing hour in a bedroom" suggests. This is not what Mulvey would term a "scopophilic" scene, a cinematic close-up, but rather an event, an action, in the midst of which the voyeur "catches" the woman. In such instances, according to Mulvey, "Pleasure lies in ascertaining guilt (immediately associated with castration), asserting control, and subjecting the guilty person through punishment or forgiveness" (422).

This is certainly the case in this instance, as the narrator casually makes the condemnatory remark that will cling to Bathsheba throughout the novel: "Woman's prescriptive infirmity had stalked into the sunlight" (1.5). It is the female character who is judged to be guilty (and guilty on the basis of her castrated sex—she is demonstrating *woman's* prescriptive infirmity), even though it is the male character who is conducting himself in a way that could be seen as morally questionable. This scene, and the others like it (such as Gabriel's spying on Bathsheba as she feeds the cows and as she does gymnastics on horseback), are characteristic examples of the viewing paradigm Mulvey describes, in which the male character, the male narrator and the male reader all engage in the activity of watching—and judging—a female character. Such looking is always erotic, and always implies power and control of the viewing subject over the viewed object. Nor is Hardy unaware of this dynamic; his narrator complacently observes that "Rays of male vision seem to have a tickling effect upon virgin faces in rural districts; she brushed hers with her hand, as if Gabriel had been irritating its pink surface by actual touch" (3.20). Gabriel does suffer some guilt—after he mentions her unconventional horseback riding to Bathsheba, he "withdraw[s] his . . . eyes from hers as suddenly as if he had been caught in a theft"—but the narrator makes it clear that it is his telling, rather than his looking, that is amiss ("His want of tact had deeply offended her—not by seeing what he could not help, but by letting her know that he had seen it" [3.21]). "What he could not help" is debatable, as Gabriel stations himself to watch for Bathsheba through the loophole in the wall of his hut rather than out in the open where she could have seen him; however, the important point is that the right of the male to observe and judge the female in this way is an unquestioned ideological "given" in Hardy's fictional ethos.

When the woman looks in Hardy's novels, on the other hand, she embodies no such power and control, nor does she participate in any such shared dynamic with the narrator and the reader. The male object of her gaze is not similarly objectified or eroticised, as he is in Charlotte Brontë's novels, for example (Jane Eyre confesses that "My eyes were drawn involuntarily to [Rochester's] face; ... I looked, and had an acute pleasure in looking—a precious yet poignant pleasure; pure gold, with a steely point of agony"),[11] because Hardy's women characters do not function as erotic subjects even when they exercise the power of the gaze. Instead of identifying with such a character and sharing her point of view (a potential mode of entry for a female reader of Hardy), the reader again is invited to share the perspective of the male narrator, and to "look at her looking." We watch Eustacia as she watches for Wildeve in *The Return of the Native*, for example, in the following way:

> Far away down the valley the faint shine from the window of the inn still lasted on; and a few additional moments proved that the window, or what was within it, had more to do with the woman's sigh than had either her own actions or the scene immediately around. She lifted her left hand, which held a closed telescope. This she rapidly extended. . . . The handkerchief which had hooded her head was now a little thrown back, her face being somewhat elevated. A profile was visible against the dull monochrome of cloud around her; and it was as though side shadows from the features of Sappho and Mrs. Siddons had converged upwards from the tomb to form an image like neither but suggesting both." (1.6.62)

Here we are given neither a description of the object of Eustacia's attention—the object, indeed, is "far away down the valley"—nor admittance to her perceptions; the scene is recounted, like so many scenes in Hardy's novels, from the viewpoint of an amorphous, anonymous narratorial "spectator." Eustacia herself, by a deft adjustment of narrative focus ("The handkerchief which had hooded her head was now a little thrown back. . . . A profile was visible") becomes the observed object, even though it is she who is doing the looking. Mary Ann Doane, in investigating the phenomenon of the woman's gaze in classical cinema, finds that such a scopic adjustment is a standard device in such scenes. The female gaze on the cinema screen, according to Doane, is typically "framed" in some way (by the use of mirrors, eyeglasses, etc) in order "to contain an aberrant and excessive female sexuality. For framing is the film's preferred strategy when it wishes to simultaneously state and negate.... The male gaze erases that of the woman."[12] Eustacia's telescope is just such a framing device, and it seems safe to conclude that Hardy's reasons for its use are similar to those of the filmmakers Doane describes.

The vision of Hardy's heroines thus constructed is at once intensely erotic and intensely personal, evoking a strong sense of "knowing" these women; but the character we really get to know in his novels, and to know very intimately, is Hardy. Tess, in particular, elicits this intimate response; there is no male spy as such in *Tess of the d'Urbervilles* simply because the voyeur in that novel is Hardy himself in the guise of the male narrator. "Voyeur," however, is not precisely the correct term, as in *Tess* the voyeuristic spying of the earlier novels is succeeded by Mulvey's "fetishistic scopophilia" in which "the powerful look of the male protagonist . . . is broken in favor of the image in direct erotic rapport with the spectator. The beauty of the woman as object and the screen space coalesce; she is no longer the bearer of guilt but a perfect product, whose body, stylized and fragmented by close-ups, is the content of the film" (423). The look of desire in such films, according to Mulvey (she is referring specifically to Josef von Sternberg's films starring Marlene Dietrich), is unmediated because "The male hero misunderstands and, above all, does not see" (424).

As Kaja Silverman points out in her excellent account of figuration and subjectivity in *Tess*, the male viewer in Hardy's penultimate novel is similarly elided because he, too, "does not see." Quoting the well-known passage describing Tess's lips ("To a young man with the least fire in him that little upward lift in the middle of her red top lip was distracting, infatuating, maddening. He had never seen a woman's lips and teeth which forced upon his mind with such insistent iteration the old Elizabethan simile of roses filled with snow"), Silverman points out that though it is ostensibly Angel's gaze that is turned upon Tess, the passage is less an account of Angel's perceptions than "an ironic admonition" to a young man who obviously does *not* have "the least fire in him." The admonition, of course, is given by the narrator himself, who is able to "see" Tess accurately and who is revealed to be "the speaking subject, the one whose desires structure our view of Tess."[13] This is confirmed by the next few sentences of the "lips" quotation: "Perfect, he, as a lover, might have called [Tess's lips] off-hand. But no—they were not perfect. And it was the touch of the imperfect upon the would-be perfect that gave the sweetness" (24.92). *Tess* is clearly one of the most erotic novels of the Victorian period; Tess herself, however, by virtue of such obsessive narratorial "looking," is a sexual object rather than a sexual subject, a sort of nineteenth-century Marilyn Monroe, so that a female reader can only identify with her by means of what Mary Ann Doane calls "a narcissistic identification with the female figure as spectacle." Nor can the female reader identify with the actively fantasizing narrator, other than by an extreme act of vicarious "transvestite" empathy. That female readers have managed this perceptual feat so successfully for so long is simply evidence of Jonathan Culler's assertion that "Women can read, and have read, as men."

To give him credit, Hardy did attempt to go beyond the scopophilic objectification of his female characters in his last novel, *Jude the Obscure*. As we might expect, Sue Bridehead commands a different sort of attention than Tess, both from the male characters in the novel and from the reader. More intellectual than Tess, she is an effective mouthpiece for much of Hardy's polemic; more importantly than this, her physical appearance, her status as an aesthetic and sexual object, is de-emphasized. Jude first notes that she is "so pretty," but then he reflects that "He had been so caught by her influence that he had taken no count of her general mould and build. He remembered now that she was not a large figure, that she was light and slight, of the type dubbed elegant. That was about all he had seen. There was nothing statuesque in her; all was nervous motion. She was mobile, living, yet a painter might not have called her handsome or beautiful" (2.2.104–5). This rather vague account (rendered, however, from the point of view of a "painter") is obviously very different from the sensual details of Tess's "mobile peony mouth," her "arm, cold and damp . . . as a new-gathered mushroom" or the "stop'd-diapason note which her voice acquired when her heart was in her speech." The concrete details we are given in connection with Sue tend to be "cute" (and safely diminutive) rather than voluptuous, such as her "little thumb stuck up by the stem of her sunshade," which reappears at intervals in the novel. It is clear that she does not function solely as a female object in *Jude*; and yet, curiously, the reader seems to have no readier access to Sue's consciousness than to that of Hardy's other female characters. The reason for this, I would submit, is that none of Hardy's heroines, including Sue, functions as a fictional subject.

This may seem like an absurd assertion, given the distinctive personalities of such characters as Bathsheba, Eustacia, Tess, and Sue; a close examination, however, reveals the subjectivity of these characters to be largely illusory, and the seeming absurdity to be a function of Hardy's persuasive realism. His female characters are seen almost exclusively from the outside, in terms of physical description, action and dialogue, a fact that has no doubt contributed to his reputation as a "balladeer" among novelists. Most of these characters, like Tess, are physically present in an immediate and very sensual way, which tends to obscure the fact that their point of view is explored only superficially. But Sue is also perceived from the outside rather than from the inside. We are never given access to her consciousness, so that she remains an enigma rather than a true subject. These elisions of female consciousness—which constitute another stumbling block to the female reader's appreciation of Hardy's novels— are at least partly a result of Hardy's consistent avoidance of the technical device of free indirect speech, a favored technique among nineteenth-century novelists and a key distinction between film and the novel. Even at crucial turns of the plot—points normally conducive to character revelation using this device—we are admitted only sketchily to the inner lives of his heroines. To illuminate the contrast between Hardy's handling of such moments and that of a more traditional Victorian novelist such as George Eliot, I would like to examine two passages of inner musing by two of their heroines who seem the most alike, Gwendolen Harleth and Eustacia Vye. In each passage the strong-willed heroine experiences a moment of disillusionment, Gwendolen when Herr Klesmer informs her of her lack of talent and Eustacia when she realizes that Clym is content to remain a furze cutter. After Herr Klesmer leaves, Eliot's narrator reports Gwendolen's state of mind in the following way:

> The "indignities" that she might be visited with had no very definite form for her, but the mere association of anything called "indignity" with herself, roused a resentful alarm. And along with the vaguer images which were raised by those biting words, came the more precise conception of disagreeables which her experience enabled her to imagine. How could she take her mamma and the four sisters to London, if it were not possible for her to earn money at once? And as for submitting to be a *protégée*, and asking her mamma to submit with her to the humiliation of being supported by Miss Arrowpoint—that was as bad as being a governess; nay, worse; for suppose the end of all her study to be as worthless as Klesmer clearly expected it to be, the sense of favours received and never repaid, would embitter the miseries of disappointment. Klesmer doubtless had magnificent ideas about helping artists; but how could he know the feelings of ladies in such matters? It was all over: she had entertained a mistaken hope; and there was an end of it.[14]

This rather unremarkable passage is an utterly typical instance of how Eliot (as well as most of her contemporaries) handles the thought processes of the important characters in her novels. Writing before the "discovery" of the stream-of-consciousness novel, authors of realist novels tended to rely heavily on a "blend" of voices—the character's and the narrator's—to convey their characters' inner musings. This blend (labeled free indirect speech by formal critics) basically consists of a reporting of the character's thoughts in the narrator's voice, marked linguistically by the idiom, semantics and emotive punctuation of direct speech. In the above passage, for example, Gwendolen's thoughts are reported in ordinary indirect speech up to the sentence beginning, "How could she take her mamma and the four sisters to London," after which point they are couched in free indirect speech, indicated by the questions ("how could he know the feelings of ladies?"), the vocabulary ("as bad as being a governess"; "Klesmer doubtless had magnificent ideas"), and the overall sense of despair evinced by the abrupt phraseology ("nay, worse"; "It was all over ... ; and there was an end of it"). In such passages we are made aware not only of what the character is thinking and feeling but also of the narrator's opinion of such musings; in the above passage, for instance, Eliot's narrator (as she so often does with Gwendolen) stands aside with a sort of ironic pity. Overall, such passages yield freer and more intimate access to a character's consciousness than either ordinary direct speech (" 'How can I take my mamma and four sisters to London?' thought Gwendolen") or ordinary indirect speech ("Gwendolen wondered how she could take her mother and four sisters to London").

Hardy tends to eschew this device in favor of precise and detailed descriptions of his female characters' physical qualities, an entirely different mode of "knowing" them. After Clym confesses to Eustacia that he intends to stay on Egdon Heath, for example, we are told that

> When he was gone she rested her head upon her hands and said to herself, "Two wasted lives—his and mine. And I am come to this! Will it drive me out of my mind?"
>
> She cast about for any possible course which offered the least improvement on the existing state of things, and could find none. She imagined how all those Budmouth ones who should learn what had become of her would say, "Look at the girl for whom nobody was good enough!" To Eustacia the situation seemed such a mockery of her hopes that death appeared the only door of relief if the satire of Heaven should go much further.
>
> Suddenly she aroused herself and exclaimed, "But I'll shake it off. Yes, I *will* shake it off! No one shall know my suffering. I'll be bitterly merry, and ironically gay, and I'll laugh in derision! And I'll begin by going to this dance on the green."
>
> She ascended to her bedroom and dressed herself with scrupulous care. To an onlooker her beauty would have made her feelings almost seem reasonable. ...
>
> It was five in the afternoon when she came out from the house ready

for her walk. There was material enough in the picture for twenty new conquests. (4.3.305)

The contrast in technique between this and Eliot's passage is obvious. Eustacia's thoughts and feelings are conveyed either directly ("Two wasted lives—his and mine . . . "; "But I'll shake it off,") or indirectly ("She cast about . . . "; "She imagined . . . "; "To Eustacia the situation seemed . . . "). Within the latter mode, there are no indications of Eustacia's emotions or vocabulary: "mockery of her hopes," "door of relief" and "satire of Heaven" (the most emotive of these indirect utterances) sound unequivocally like the dispassionate, observing narrator. And "observe" is exactly what this narrator does, inviting the reader to do the same. The sentence "To an onlooker her beauty would have made her feelings almost seem reasonable" encompasses a characteristic Hardyesque shift of perspective, from Eustacia's point of view to that of an unspecified, unobtrusive "onlooker." Such unobtrusive refocusing is a device that occurs with great regularity in Hardy's representations of women characters, reaching its culmination in _Tess of the d'Urbervilles,_ in which, as Kaja Silverman points out, the unspecified "onlooker" is invoked again and again. From this anonymous vantage point the narrator is free to distance himself from Eustacia and also to objectify her (her feelings "almost seem reasonable" from this purely external viewpoint, for example). When she emerges from the house, this viewpoint is still operational and her objectification is complete: Eustacia has become a "picture" which can only be interpreted from the outside. The sentences that follow simply elaborate on the details of this picture ("The rebellious sadness that was rather too apparent when she sat indoors . . . was cloaked and softened by her outdoor attire . . . ; so that her face looked from its environment as from a cloud, with no noticeable lines of demarcation between flesh and clothes" [305–6]).

The shift is subtle, but what has happened in this passage is a typical alteration of Hardy's narrative focus, from Eustacia's internal musing to her external appearance. The solid physical details of this appearance, so carefully and elaborately constructed and so freely interpreted by the observing narrator (the "rebellious sadness" is such an interpretation), produce the effect of "knowing" the character intimately, obscuring the fact that the consciousness being explored in such passages is not that of the female character at all, but that of the male observer. Ironically, this richness of detail in Hardy's descriptions of women has in fact helped to earn him the reputation of a novelist who portrays female characters with great sensitivity. Feminist critics, however, have noted that these portrayals are primarily physical; Rosalind Miles points out that "Hardy really is a lover of women in the fullest physical sense. E. M. Forster remarked that

Hardy conceived his novels from a great height, but his females are drawn from very close up; there is an almost myopic insistence upon the grain of their skin, and texture of hair. Sound, scent, mouth, cheeks, downy plumpness—no detail of their physical presence is allowed to escape our senses."[15] This detailed portraiture is myopic in more than just a physical sense, serving to distract the reader's attention from what would otherwise seem a glaring omission of female consciousness.

That male consciousness is not elided in this way is a telling comment on Hardy's patriarchal bias; Jude, for instance, muses at length during Sue's and Phillotson's wedding in the following way:

> By the time they were half way on with the service he wished from his heart that he had not undertaken the business of giving her away. How could Sue have had the temerity to ask him to do it—a cruelty possibly to herself as well as to him? Women were different from men in such matters. Was it that they were, instead of more sensitive, as reputed, more callous, and less romantic; or were they more heroic? Or was Sue simply so perverse that she wilfully gave herself and him pain for the odd and mournful luxury of practising long-suffering in her own person, and of being touched with tender pity for him at having made him practise it? He could perceive that her face was nervously set. (3.7.209)

Except for the first and last sentences, this passage consists entirely of Jude's free indirect speech—endorsed, in this case, by the male narrator. The perplexed questions, the mournful chagrin, are a skillful rendition of Jude's mental processes at this crucial turn of events. Sue's perceptions, by contrast, are hardly ever rendered in this mode, even when she is alone and pensive (as she is when she buys the statuary, for example). The reader, like Jude, is left to "interpret" her thoughts from her actions and her dialogue, a fact that undoubtedly has much to do with the mystery that has always surrounded her character in the copious amounts of criticism it has occasioned.

We can see, then, that Hardy seems at once peculiarly intimate with and peculiarly dissociated from his female characters, creating an authorial distance from them that seems too close physically and too remote in other ways. His unwillingness or inability to explore the consciousness of his heroines has led to much critical bafflement as readers try to deal with the enigmatic personalities Hardy thus presents them with. Tellingly, his creations include no Lucy Snowe, Maggie Tulliver, or Dorothea Brooke with whom the female reader can readily identify; as Rosalind Miles points out, "Hardy women seem different from one another—Bathsheba is mistress, Fanny is maid, Tess is rounded while Sue is slight—but on closer examination they all prove to originate from one prototype." And the prototype, in its visual aspects at least, tends to be invidiously sexist, a mysterious, unpredictable and alien entity called woman, a dangerous signifier admitting of endless scrutiny (Miles remarks that Hardy "saw women as dangerous simply in being, to themselves as well as to men").[16]

An analysis of the scopic elements of Hardy's novels on its own, in fact, points to the conventional patriarchal perspective of the rigidly differentiated, ambivalent male toward the castrated, castrating female other—which is why Laura Mulvey's analysis of the conventional (male) audience of the realist film fits Hardy so well. The angle of vision is from outside the female (hence we are not given her perspective) and obsessed with the female (hence we are given minutely detailed, fetishistic portraits of her). The look that is thus brought into play—the male look of desire, of curiosity, of control—is especially evident in the unobtrusive "shifts" of narrative focus I have described, which inevitably culminate in what Judith Bryant Wittenberg calls the "voyeuristic moment" ("the moment in which the seeing subject and the seen object intersect in a diegetic node that both explicitly and implicitly suggests the way in which the world is constituted in and through the scopic drive").[17]

Is there no answer, then, to my opening question? Can the enlightened female reader of the late twentieth century no longer read or enjoy Hardy's novels? And if she can enjoy them, what kinds of pleasure might they afford? Clearly the old pleasure of immersion in the realist text, the uncritical acceptance of a fictional precoded reality, is no longer possible for such a reader, just as it is no longer possible for the viewer of a realist film. Of her own analysis of the phallocentric viewing paradigm inherent in realist cinema, Laura Mulvey readily admits that "There is no doubt that this destroys the satisfaction, pleasure, and privilege of the 'invisible guest,' and highlights how film has depended on voyeuristic active/passive mechanisms. Women, whose image has continually been stolen and used for this end, cannot view the decline of the traditional film form with anything much more than sentimental regret" (428). This loss of pleasure, of course, comes as no surprise to the postmodern reader, who is abundantly aware that the ideological examination of realism—in any of the arts— inevitably entails such a close analysis of representational structures themselves. And the losses are more than offset by the gains of such a process, presumably, as the reader achieves a dispassionate critical distance from patriarchal novelistic forms. One possible pleasure Hardy's female reader can undoubtedly derive from his texts, then, is the sheerly intellectual satisfaction of unravelling the ideological ambiguities of her former somewhat blinkered enjoyment, an exercise that is particularly rewarding with an author like Hardy, whose novels can be seen as excellent examples of Myra Jehlen's point that "A work may be . . . quite wrong and even wrongheaded about life and politics and still an extremely successful rendering of its contrary vision."[18]

Also, we need to remember that Hardy's "scopic economy" is only one (albeit an important) aspect of his narrative achievement. If we examine his novels from the point of view of their "narrative grammar," for instance—a term Laura Mulvey uses in "Afterthoughts on 'Visual Pleasure and Narrative Cinema' "—they appear in a wholly different light. For although the gaze in Hardy's novels is relentlessly male, the narratives themselves invariably place a female character at the center of the action in precisely the same way that Mulvey describes in the "woman-orientated strand" of melodrama in classical cinema: "Introducing a woman as central to a story shifts its meanings, producing another kind of narrative discourse. . . . The landscape of action, although present, is not the dramatic core of the film's story, rather it is the interior drama of a girl caught between two conflicting desires. The conflicting desires . . . correspond closely with Freud's . . . oscillation between 'passive' femininity and regressive 'masculinity.' . . . Now the female presence as centre allows the story to be actually, *overtly* about sexuality. It is as though the narrational lens had zoomed in . . . to focus on the figure of the princess, waiting in the wings . . . , to ask 'what does she want?' "[19] These "two conflicting desires," according to Mulvey, are represented by the heroine's choice between the law-abiding "hero" (who represents her passive, feminine, socially acceptable self) and the exciting "villain" (who represents her active, masculine, regressive self). Ultimately, neither of these choices is adequate, because "although the male characters personify [her] dilemma, it is their terms that make and finally break her," and the heroine is "unable to settle or find a 'femininity' in which she and the male world can meet." In other words, there is no place for such a heroine either in the hero's masculine symbolic or in the villain's phallic, regressive rebellion against it. Hardy's novels, interestingly, can also be viewed in this way, as the "narrative grammar" of many of them follows exactly the pattern Mulvey describes, with a central heroine (Bathsheba, Eustacia, Tess, Sue) caught between two potential partners, neither of whom is entirely satisfactory. And, like Mulvey's melodramas, such texts can be viewed as implicit protests against the cultural marginalisation of the feminine, opening up an empathic narrative position with which the female reader/spectator can comfortably and pleasurably align herself.

Hardy's female reader, therefore, will undoubtedly continue both to applaud his feminism and to deplore his sexism, sensing simultaneously in his novels their "narrative grammar," which empathizes so deeply with the plight of the culturally marginalized female, and their "scopic economy," in which male consciousness is explored subjectively while female consciousness is quietly and systematically elided. The tension between these two aspects of Hardy's representation of women, in fact, makes his work one of the richest and most complex sources of feminist commentary in the realist novel. It is no wonder that Hardy's novels perplex and fascinate his female reader, yielding a peculiarly ambivalent kind of pleasure. In their representation of women, they function both as indignant condemnations of the ideological atrocities of patriarchy, and—ironically, paradoxically —as formidable examples of such atrocities themselves.

NOTES

1. Katherine Rogers, "Women in Thomas Hardy," *Centennial Review* 19 (1975): 257.

2. Annette Kuhn, "Real Women," in *Feminist Criticism and Social Change,* ed. Judith Newton and Deborah Rosenfelt (New York: Methuen, 1985), 268. In this paper I use "realism" in the same broad, general sense that Mulvey uses it, to refer simply to "the codes and conventions . . . that articulate a flowing, homogeneous, coherent fictional time, space and point of view" ("Changes: Thoughts on Myth, Narrative and Historical Experience," in *Visual and Other Pleasures,* ed. Laura Mulvey, Bloomington: Indiana University Press, 1989, 164, originally published in *Discourse* in 1985).

3. Laura Mulvey, "Visual Pleasure and Narrative Cinema," in *Women and the Cinema: A Critical Anthology,* ed. Karyn Kay and Gerald Peary (New York: E.P. Dutton, 1977), 427, originally published in *Screen* in 1975, hereafter cited in the text.

4. Mary Ann Doane, *The Desire to Desire: The Woman's Film of the 1940's* (Bloomington: Indiana University Press, 1987), 19, 117. See also Teresa de Lauretis, *Alice Doesn't: Feminism, Semiotics, Cinema* (Bloomington: Indiana University Press, 1984), 142.

5. Laura Mulvey, "Afterthoughts on 'Visual Pleasure and Narrative Cinema' inspired by King Vidor's *Duel in the Sun* (1946)," in *Visual and Other Pleasures,* 29, 33.

6. Jonathan Culler, *On Deconstruction: Theory and Criticism After Structuralism* (Ithaca: Cornell University Press, 1982), 49.

7. Judith Bryant Wittenberg, "Early Hardy Novels and the Fictional Eye," *Novel* 16 (Winter 1983): 152.

8. Elaine Showalter, "The Unmanning of the Mayor of Casterbridge," in *Critical Approaches to the Fiction of Thomas Hardy,* ed Dale Kramer (London: Macmillan, 1979), 102.

9. Sarah Kent, "Looking Back," in *Women's Images of Men,* ed. Sarah Kent and Jacqueline Morreau (New York: Writers, 1985), 59–60.

10. Helena Michie, *The Flesh Made Word: Female Figures and Women's Bodies* (Oxford: Oxford University Press, 1987), 112.

11. Charlotte Brontë, *Jane Eyre* (Harmondsworth: Penguin, 1966), 203.

12. Doane, *Desire to Desire,* 100.

13. Kaja Silverman, "History, Figuration and Female Subjectivity in *Tess of the d'Urbervilles*," *Novel* 18 (Fall 1984): 10–11.

14. George Eliot, *Daniel Deronda* (Oxford: Oxford University Press, 1988), 224. Subsequent references are to this edition.

15. Rosalind Miles, "The Women of Wessex," in *The Novels of Thomas Hardy*, ed. Anne Smith (London: Vision, 1979), 31.

16. Ibid., 28, 27.

17. Wittenberg, "Early Hardy Novels," 151.

18. Myra Jehlen, "Archimedes and the Paradox of Feminist Criticism," in *The "Signs" Reader: Women, Gender, and Scholarship*, ed. Elizabeth Abel and Emily Abel (Chicago: University of Chicago Press, 1983), 192.

19. Mulvey, "Afterthoughts," 35.

The Menace of Solitude:
The Politics and Aesthetics of Exclusion
in *The Woodlanders*

Robert Kiely

Thy glades forlorn confess the tyrant's power.
    —Oliver Goldsmith, *The Deserted Village*

Early in Hardy's *The Woodlanders*, a barber seeks out young Marty South, who is poor and unmarried, to buy her beautiful long hair. The description of Marty offers an image of solitude, caught by the barber through the half-open door of her cottage. At first, the soft light and framed concentration of the solitary woman at work suggests a serene painting of the Dutch school admired by George Eliot. But the narrowness of the barber's perspective mars this genre. Intent on his mercenary mission, Percomb has eyes only for the woman's hair, "while her face, shoulders, hands, and figure in general were a blurred mass of unimportant detail" (2.9). The nature of Marty South's seclusion, inseparable from her poverty and gender, leaves her vulnerable to a peculiarly violent form of subjective perception that obliterates everything that is not the desired commodity.

Because her father is ill, Marty is not spinning but cutting and sharpening spars; that is, she is doing "man's work." Even so, she is not permitted a viewpoint of her own. She does not see the barber staring at her, yet when she lays down the billhook and examines her right hand, we expect to be told what she is thinking. We are shown what she sees—a palm that was "red and blistering"—but her perception is overtaken by a generalizing, external narrative voice: "As with so many right hands born to manual labor, there was nothing in its fundamental shape to bear out the physiological conventionalism that gradations of birth show themselves primarily in the form of this member" (2.8).

Even though this narrative interruption reveals an egalitarian spirit and a sympathy for Marty, it repeats on a more abstract level the barber's reductive reification of the woman. Precisely when the text might have introduced the reader to Marty's own contemplation, it severs her hand from her gaze and reattaches the dismembered "member" to a narrative meditation on anatomy and class. The condition of Marty's isolation is curiously textual as well as political and social. She does not quite belong to the narrative; her place, not only in regard to the other characters, but with respect to the text itself, is anomalous. When the narrator draws a distinction between "fundamental shape" and "physiological conventionalism," he provides a metaphor for the discrepancy between the "true" but hidden and inaccessible character of Marty and the narratological convention to which she is condemned as if to an unmerited life of hard and, for the most part, unobserved manual labor.

Of all Hardy's novels, *The Woodlanders* most insistently calls attention to the political implications of solitude—its variability according to sex and class—as well as to formal difficulties in depicting it without giving in to sentimental and Romantic conventions. A century earlier, Goldsmith's deserted village was already a sad sight to the returning visitor because landlords had taken over more property, torn down cottages, turned forests into parks, and forced country people to seek work in the cities. Though Goldsmith undermines the idea of rural solitude as a natural and benign state, he also indulges in a form of melancholy self-regard that was to become a regular piece of equipment for poetic excursions into the countryside.

Between Goldsmith's and Hardy's lifetimes, solitude, especially for the poet who was male and financially independent, was a creative license. Wordsworth's "lonely wanderer," Byron's "Highland rover," and Arnold's "scholar gypsy" are figures of free movement quite different from evicted tenants or from the housebound solitaries of Emily Dickinson or Christina Rossetti. As long as it was primarily associated with a vaguely pleasing aesthetic mood, mobility, and the privileges of individuality, solitude remained difficult to connect with a potentially undesirable social condition and an unstable perspective.

The Woodlanders begins on a "forsaken coach-road" with the familiar and distinctively literary figure of the male rambler, who supposedly walks (and writes) without more purpose than to observe the changing scenery. Very quickly, however, the tone changes as the narrative insists on the peculiar loneliness of the place: "The physiognomy of a deserted highway expresses solitude to a degree that is not reached by mere dales or downs, and bespeaks a tomb-like stillness more emphatic than glades or pools. The contrast of what is with what might be, probably accounts for this. To step, for instance, at the place under notice, from the edge of the plantation into the adjoining thoroughfare, and pause amid its emptiness for a moment, was to exchange by the act of a single stride the simple absence of human companionship for an incubus of the forlorn" (1.1).

Solitude as described here, the first signal of a disturbing emphasis in the narrative, differs significantly from the pleasing sadness of the landscapes of Gray or Wordsworth. The road, a familiar analogue for narrative form, suggests public use, direction, and practical function. Yet emptied of people and signposts, it is like a useless copy of the original; the contours are the same, but life and a sense of purpose are gone. Isolation thus figured as an "incubus of the forlorn" seems less an individual or occasional state than a condition pertaining to social convenience and perhaps to the total environment. The road is there, but it does not accomodate the traveler. As a trace of intentionality once fashioned for human traffic, it is suddenly and distressingly recovered and reread as a vacant sign.

To make things worse, the reader's "guide"—the literary rambler—turns out to be an unpoetic barber (a hired tool utterly uninterested in landscape) who is lost and abandons us as soon as a van appears and takes him aboard. When the carriage and the "guide" drive off without us, the experience of forlorn disorientation is transferred to the reader. Though the vehicle is a public conveyance, the dialogue that occurs within it remains an indecipherable pantomime seen from outside. Receding from view, the rustic coach introduces a narrative journey in a radically different way from the coach in the beginning of *Tom Jones*, whose narrator-spectator settles comfortably inside and seems to know where he is going. Rambling through the roads and pages of *The Woodlanders* is not a pleasant pastime but an uncertain condition in which one moves on tracks that are sharply marked but, at odd times, vacant, unwelcoming, not meant for the comfort or even the use of readers or characters.[1]

Though they recede from the central action of the novel, Marty South and Barber Percomb establish the peculiar dominance and complexity of solitude as it pertains to action and contemplation. The forlorn coach-road and the half-open door of South's cottage represent a radical inadequacy of conventional form as a conveyor of the hidden intentions of the two isolated characters. The old-fashioned public path and the cosy domestic frame, as models of structure, are not simply too narrow or too wide; that is, they are not materials for the mock-heroic or comic irony. The old road is empty of life and direction; the snug cottage door defines the space through which Marty cannot reveal her true self, but instead is violated and deprived of a sign of her womanhood. One experience of isolation is to feel stranded in an undesirable place. Among the various sequestered concaves of *The Woodlanders*, generic convention (like stereotypes of gender and class) often seems to be such a place.

If characters are isolated as travelers and actors in the novel, they are no better off when they assume the narrative function and attempt to observe and comment on the behavior of others. Spectatorship also has its hazards.[2] Barber Percomb, even as a spy, is merely the instrument of someone else's will. In the few moments in which Marty South is allowed to speak her mind, her voice, like her hair, is cut off. First "framed," later "shorn" as if in a sacrificial ritual, she personifies the fate of a land, a class, and a gender, the abuse and neglect of which is imperfectly concealed by idealization and convention.

Hardy's refusal to sentimentalize Marty's misery or disguise the damage done to her sexuality is an early indication of deconstructive strategies to come. As the novel progresses, the text lays bare the intersection between the unstable structures of narrative conventions and the insecurity of the spaces occupied by the inhabitants of the woodlands. This interconnection among working, living, and textual space is most clearly seen when Giles Winterborne realizes that at the death of Marty's father, the cottage in which the Souths had lived and several nearby, including Giles's own, will revert to the estate currently owned by their wealthy neighbor, Mrs. Charmond: "Winterborne walked up and down his garden next day thinking of the contingency. The sense that the paths he was pacing . . . were all slipping away over his head and beneath his feet as if they were painted on a magic-lantern slide, was curious" (13.107).

Giles's sensation of displacement and disorientation, while he still paces familiar pathways, registers the beginning of his economic and social alienation. At the same time, he provides a paradigm for the other characters who are temporarily inhabiting roles and treading narratological (and geographical) paths that do not belong to them. What had seemed most familiar, permanent, and substantial begins to appear strange, temporary, and artificial.

In the bare outlines of its obvious structural symmetries (village and woodlands, hilltop and valley) and character pairings, the novel too has some of the qualities of predictability and rapid movement of a "magic-lantern" show or a highly stylized comedy of manners. Into this glossy and brittle structure, Hardy introduces not merely problems of plot but a larger and increasingly ominous unfitness, a deep malfunction in the social and narrative machine. For example, with each set of pairings, romantic or rivalrous, a third person is left out and alone. While female isolation is primarily connected to marriage, marriageability, and role in the family, male isolation is most frequently a matter of intellectual or physical inclinations and relations to a larger world. Grace Melbury's education alienates her from her family, her village, and her friend and lover, Giles Winterborne. Mrs. Charmond is isolated by wealth, her lack of family, and her reputation as a woman with a "foreign" and shady past. Fitzpiers stands apart as a relic of the aristocracy and a scientist with mysterious bookish interests. Giles's isolation is so much identified with the remoteness and silence of his work in the forest that it seems his "natural" condition. In short, though each character's loneliness may be associated with his or her being outside the equation of love, there appear to be other gendered and socioeconomic forms of isolation that none can avoid.

Traces of comic love and marriage plots are visible throughout the novel, but they increasingly appear to be empty ways through which characters wander alone getting nowhere. A path clearly articulated early in the book is one that Mr. Melbury has planned for his daughter Grace: that she should be educated, brought home, and married to Giles in compensation for a wrong Melbury had done to Giles's father. Melbury is not entirely happy with his plan, but that his daughter might find her own way does not occur to him. When Grace returns home, she is seen as oddly changed by her schooling, a puzzle that no longer fits into her family or her father's scheme.

Grace is said to be "difficult to describe," "a *reductio ad absurdum* of attempts to appraise a woman," "a conjectural creature," "a shape in the gloom" (5.41–42). Like so many characters in the novel, she is less clearly delineated than the narrative path that has been laid out for her. Yet Grace is not the only person in the book whose "imprint" and intended course precede and, in a sense, overtake her character. A grotesque counterpart of Grace's arranged betrothal and the sale of Marty's hair is the bargain struck between Fitzpiers and Grammer Oliver for the old woman's brain after her death. The scientist, like the barber and the merchant-father, sees the woman as a token of barter, part of a predetermined experiment, a severed member essential to a story yet to be realized in which her whole person is not only superfluous but a downright impediment to the denouement.

The story of Marty's hair and the grotesque tale of Grammer's brain are early and arresting versions of the ways in which narrative schemes seize on singular details and, while seemingly using them to represent a person, in fact, displace that person, estranging her from a structure that feeds on her but is antithetical to the autonomy and fullness of her character. As this pattern pertains to women, it parallels their role in a society, high and low, that assesses their worth according to a market system of exchange.

Once he realizes that his educated daughter is a more valuable property than he had reckoned before she left home, Melbury cannot keep from thinking of a marriage between Grace and Giles as a bad "bargain" for him. He tells Grace that she is a better investment than his "horses and wagons and corn" and will "yield a better return" (12.104). She objects to being thought of as "chattel," but he does not understand the word.

Although partly protected by her wealth, the widow Mrs. Charmond is also "read" by others according to a prefabricated plot. For most villagers, she is a "temptress" before she is seen or known. Metonymically, her damp, large, richly furnished house stands, in the minds of onlookers, for everything erotic and decadent about her. In fact, the threat she poses to the community has everything to do with economics and almost nothing to do with sex.

Hardy's male characters at first seem to enjoy the privileges of their gender, but they too are shown to be ill-suited to the stories told about them and poorly matched to the images with which they are identified. In Fitzpiers's case, the incongruity is primarily comic. Before the reader or Grace sees him, he is described as a Faustian figure, working late at night on scientific problems. At closer range, he proves to be bored, dilettantish, and lecherous; with his telescope, he pursues attractive women. When news circulates that he has met an accident, Suke Damson and Mrs. Charmond rush to the Melbury house in fear that their lover is dead and gather with his wife Grace around the empty bed, "staring . . . at his night-shirt lying on the pillow" (35.313). His character and fate are read in his absence by means of a sign that ludicrously represents and replaces him.

Giles Winterborne seems, on first consideration, different from all the other characters, more at home in his environment, both natural and narrative. Scenes of him among the trees—planting, pruning, harvesting fruit—identify him as simple, sturdy, and noble. Yet, like the others, he must submit to narratives and images not of his own making. Grace's equivocal feelings toward him—her old affection in conflict with her newfound class superiority—prompt her to create a picture of him and to weave a legend around him that suspend him and their relationship in a folkloric haze. After her marriage to Fitzpiers, through the window of her hotel room she catches sight of Giles filling bags with pommace, in a famous scene charged with sexual aura: "Fragments of apple-rind had alighted on the brim of his hat—probably bursting of a bag—while brown pips of the same fruit were sticking among the down upon his fine round arms, and in his beard" (25.209).

Grace sublimates her attraction, merging that disturbing impression into a larger rural scene of "horses, buckets, tubs, strainers," "codlins, costards, stubbards, ratherripes, and other well-known friends of her ravenous youth." The particular friend of her youth is no longer a privileged focal-point but simply another bucolic item lost among the cider-making paraphernalia and the apples. Later, Grace finds in his sunburnt face and corn-flower blue eyes "Autumn's very brother" (28.246), turning him into a god of vegetation.

Grace may appear to deny her sexual attraction to Giles, but she does in fact enjoy him sexually as a voyeur or as a reader whose indulgence in sexual fantasy is made possible not only by distance from the desirable object but also by inaction and isolation. Grace can let her gaze linger on Giles ramming pommace into horsehair bags and exercising his "fine round arms" because she is alone in her room, outside the scene, "unstained" by the physical work of making love or cider. For all her desire, she imagines Giles in terms that leave him outside her narrative track, alone. She glosses him through vaguely literary generalizations, as a "being, impersonating chivalrous and undiluted manliness" (28.247).

The connection between the labor of love and the labor of making a living is sustained metaphorically by repeated references to the "stains" and "smears" that adhere to Giles because of his work and which are unfailingly noticed by Grace in her ambivalent moments of sexual arousal and class consciousness. When she calls Giles from his work to her window, he responds: "'Why do you call me? . . . Is it not enough that you see me here moiling and muddling for my daily bread while you are sitting there in your success?'" (25.212)

The sharp class division between those who "moil and muddle" and those who sit in their rooms creating erotic and lyrical portraits of workers cuts across sexual and aesthetic lines.[3] It becomes clearer and clearer that Giles and Grace are alienated from one another not simply because of sexual inhibition or a trick of fate but because of a social and economic mechanism that affects all of the characters and leads to a gradual and relentless atomization of community.

Though men are subject, like women, to isolation and narrative misreadings, even the weakest and least articulate males have recourse to an important channel of potential bonding and self-definition: work. Fitzpiers may be a lazy cad, but there is little doubt that he belongs to a profession and can be a competent doctor if he chooses. Melbury is a shrewd, active and successful merchant. And Giles, of course, is most himself at work in the woods, either alone or as part of a team. By contrast, if Marty does "man's work," it isolates her from men and women by masking or eroding her conventional feminine identity without providing her with the means to define a new kind of womanhood. More typical of the middle and upper class, Grace and Mrs. Charmond have nothing to do but wait and watch by themselves.

Observing "nature," a "laborer" or a "lover" becomes a substitute for working in the field (woods, world) and making love. It is a parasitic, unproductive, isolating privilege, a sublimated and invisible form of domination through which superiority is achieved at the expense of participation. Even at best, the superiority of the spectator is fragile since the watcher can also be watched. The merchant's daughter, the aristocratic doctor, and the wealthy widow are not immune to the scrutiny of others. *The Woodlanders*, like all Hardy's novels, resembles Foucault's description of Jeremy Bentham's Panopticon, in which "each person, depending on his place, is watched by all or certain of the others. You have an apparatus of total and circulating mistrust, because there is no absolute point. The perfected form of surveillance consists in a summation of *malveillance*."[4] As is the case when Marty South is shown looking at her blistered palm, the narrative takes power away from the hand and gives it to the eye. Thus disembodied, power simulates focus but is in fact diffused. When it can no longer be located and stabilized in easily recognized shapes and ranks, it emerges momentarily in the stolen glances of the spy, the monitor, the intruder, the busybody, the rambler, the philosophical narrator, the reader. And it shifts position without warning whenever new figures occupy these roles.

The chameleon character whose status and behavior most closely reflect the shifting of power to the eye of the restless observer is Fitzpiers. He is poised between alienation and accomodation. An aristocrat without land or money, a doctor without ambition, he is on the constant lookout for diversion (sexual and intellectual), privilege (secret knowledge of others), and financial support through marriage. Insofar as potency of class, gender, or profession is associated with Fitzpiers, it is contingent on the superior level (his class, education and even his house on the hill) from which he looks down on others through his spy-glass. In the strange scene in which Grace comes upon him napping, he recovers ascendancy through his eyes. As Grace turns to leave the room, she is mortified but also captivated to see in the mirror the sleeping man open his eyes and stare at her.

Grace's spectatorship is less certain than that of Fitzpiers. When she observes him from her window in the dim light of early morning bidding farewell to Suke Damson in her nightdress, she seems too ready to accept Fitzpiers's invented explanation that Suke had come to him with a toothache. Grace takes refuge in a narrative convention, a compromise, which saves her from the humiliation (and clarity) of expressing her suspicion and jealousy. By accepting Fitzpiers's substitute narrative—his lie—Grace avoids making a judgment or betraying strong emotion; she remains a "conjectural," "two-sided" spectator even of her own life.

Surely the strangest, boldest instance of a character as isolated observer is that of Marty South's father who in his last illness stares out of his window obsessed by a great elm that had grown large in his own lifetime. The old man refers to the tree as his "enemy" and fears that it will be the death of him. When, by Fitzpiers's direction, Giles cuts it down, the old man gasps in horror at the blank space where it had been, and dies.

Even more important than old South's obsession is the way in which the text presents the cutting down of the tree as an act of violence that is a trauma for the narrative as well as for the old man. The associations with castration, patricide, and the destruction of the forest form a catastrophic network with an aesthetics of removal that has worked its way steadily through the novel. From the beginning when the van drives away leaving the reader with the blank pavement and presents the glory of Marty South's hair only to have it taken away, the narrative threatens the reader, as well as the characters, with abrupt and arbitrary abandonment and deprivation. There are hidden menaces in the text, like the man-traps in the woods, which threaten to bring things to a halt and withdraw from the scene the familiar signs of life.

It is characteristic of the aesthetics (and politics) of removal in this novel that the immediate act of destruction is performed by an intermediary rather than by one who can be identified as the source of power and authority. The menace to the reader—that the text will suddenly become null and void—like the menace to the characters—that the ground (and trees) will be taken from them—is increased by virtue of the fact that it is impossible to assign responsibility to a single rational source.

The distribution of power in the society depicted in *The Woodlanders* corresponds closely to Foucault's analysis of the nineteenth-century transition from hierarchical agrarianism to corporate industrialism. Even the metaphor of the "man-trap" has an echo in Foucault's words: "One doesn't have here a power which is wholly in the hands of one person. . . . It is a machine in which everyone is caught, those who exercise power just as much as those over whom it is exercised. . . . Everyone does not occupy the same position; certain positions preponderate. . . . This is so much the case that class domination can be exercised just to the extent that power is dissociated from individual might."[5]

The "death of the author" as a single controlling presence has its counterpart within the narrative in the "death" or absence of an originating figure of authority to whose doorstep can be traced the fate, especially the unhappy fate, of the characters. Readers of a book by an absent author are not much better off than the tenants of an absent landlord. What is eliminated or hidden, as in the case of man-traps set in the distant past, are direct lines of causation, predictable (and occasionally preventable) patterns of consequence, and a comprehensible personification of malice. But danger itself remains, especially the danger of seeing everything brought to nothing. The reader and Marty's father have in common their dependence on image: when the tree is felled, the view becomes void, and the viewer dies; when the text stops, the page becomes blank, and the reader ceases to exist as a reader. While some narratives seem to sublimate the connection between endings and death, *The Woodlanders* urges the connection on us. The absence of immediate authority and motivation in the felling of the elm exposes the helplessness of the old man (and reader) with terrifying clarity.

A major source of the isolation of each character—shared by the reader—is the recognition that power (the force to create and destroy) exists, but always exists elsewhere. The sexual power of Marty and Giles, her hair and his "fine round arms"; the money of Mrs. Charmond; the science of Fitzpiers; the education of Grace—all literally or metaphorically exist at a remove from the control and desires of those who seem to possess them. The text does not dismiss these emblems of power as illusory, but renders them in a strangely detached, almost autonomous state.

No episode brings this home more effectively than that of Giles's death from exposure while Grace occupies his cabin in the woods. Neither his strong arms nor her education can overcome the diffused power of social convention that dictates that a man and a woman not married to one another cannot spend the night together. Their actions are the negative imprint of stories others might tell about them. The reader must watch helplessly as several literary conventions play themselves out.

Determined not to stay with the unfaithful Fitzpiers, Grace runs into the forest where she knows Giles has been living since his cottage was torn down by Mrs. Charmond's agent. Giles insists and Grace reluctantly agrees that the legal and social forms be observed. He moves into a woodshed and Grace occupies the house and conducts her business with him through the window. What follows is not only a conflict of desires but a clash of genres and of gendered categories of isolation. While the woman is enclosed in a domestic frame, housebound and suffocated, the man languishes out of doors, romantically expiring from exposure to the elements. The woman's isolation is secure and selfish, the man's is risky, generous and heroic.

Like the entire book, the chapter is a masterpiece of frustration rather than of cathartic release. And the frustrations do not belong exclusively to the two characters and their inability to get together; they belong to a text composed, as if by more than one author, of heterogeneous generic conventions that continually collide and thwart one another's progress in a formal parody of the undirected interaction of socioeconomic forces. Grace's flight through the forest—"weird" and "spectral"—is narrated as in a fairy tale. When, like Snow White, she has wandered long and far, "that prescriptive comfort and relief to wanderers in the woods—a distant light" promises her rest (40.361).

When the fact that the house consists of one small room must be faced and dialogue with Giles becomes necessary ("This is awkward!"), a comic note associated with embarrassed lovers is sounded. Elaborate plans are made to prevent them from sleeping together. The door is locked, the shutters bolted, food left on a window-sill, all as in a broad and lewd farce, a Chaucerian fabliau or tale by Boccaccio, in which the lovers' ingenuity and lust are measured by the intricacy of the obstacles thrust in their path; as though a lascivious Giles would stop at nothing to break in at night.

When the scene shifts to Giles's "wretched little shelter," his inability to eat or sleep, his increasing fever, and the rain leaking through the thatch and soaking him, the genre abruptly switches to pre-Romantic sentimentality, thick with poetic diction—"damp obscurity" and "purity of affection" (41.367). Here, the dominant mode is pathos in that the scene and the perspective stem from impotence, feeling severed from action. As surely as Marty has been pressed by need to sacrifice her womanhood with her hair, Giles is coerced into giving up his manhood with the cabin. If farce depends on what might happen and probably will and pathos on what never can, they obviously make irreconcilable partners. The text therefore resorts to melodrama when Grace finally drags Giles's limp body indoors: "How Grace performed that labor she never could have exactly explained"; " 'O, my Giles,' she cried, 'what have I done to you!' " (42.378).

Grace's "labor," the physical power she exercises to move Giles's body, reminds us that her inactivity throughout the novel results not from inherent weakness but from a "privilege" of gender and class attained through money and education. To ask the unhearing Giles what she has done to him is to underline the only answer the text provides: she has done nothing. She is no more Giles's murderer or savior than she had been his lover. By virtue of her sex and station, Grace exerts a power over Giles, but it is not an engaged or transformative power. It is a form of *malveillance,* a cruel theater of watching and waiting. As Deleuze and Guattari would have it, "A whole theater [has been] put in place of production."[6]

There is little doubt, as Foucault observed, that power—including the power to do harm—is diffused in this society. Yet it is also true that class and gender differences remain and that some people are in more privileged (and safer) positions than others. The question, then, is who, if anyone, benefits from this system of dispersed power? Who are the survivors? Who best endures the harrowing of this theater of *malveillance* and the conflict of unorchestrated forces?

The obvious answer is, of course, Grace and Fitzpiers—the woman with two sides to her face and the two-faced husband. Both chameleon characters signal the triumph of ambivalence, the middle way, the middle class. The country-girl-as-leisured-lady and the aristocrat-as-physician are best equipped to adjust to new circumstances. Each can be plain or attractive; warm or cold; idealistic or practical. Neither is so attached to one person or place as to be incapable of transplantation. The secret of their survival is mobility and a reliance not on a lover's heart or laborer's hand but on the observer's eye always on the lookout for a new opportunity to assume the place of another.

When Grace moves into Giles's cottage in the woods, she apologizes, " 'What I regret is my enforced treatment of you—dislodging you, excluding you from your own house' " (41.370). The irony of these words reflects less on Grace's intentionality than on their pertinence to the entire social and narrative structure of the novel: a painful series of dislodgings of those who are most vulnerable, especially workers and women. The most vulnerable of all, of course, is one who is both.

The question of Marty South's survival or exclusion is a disturbing one. On one hand, she carries on Giles's work in the orchards and forests, and can therefore be said to go on to live a productive and independent life. On the other hand, she also inherits the sylvan mythology attached to Giles and seems more a disembodied spirit at the novel's end than a flesh-and-blood woman. The near completeness of Marty's exclusion from the narrative as an object of erotic or economic interest makes her reappearance at the end especially troubling. Like the other laborers in the woods, she has been, except in rare moments, background, or less than background, a silent absent solitary figure. Her solitude is not a romantic choice but a form of unintentional banishment from the plots of other lives. Her alienation from the narrative is itself a kind of neglect, a structural/aesthetic counterpart to her political and social status as an unacknowledged outcast.

Though Marty may seem more Lucy Gray than Madame LaFarge, one detail, a Hardyean coincidence, goes far in unsettling that benign image. The story of Mrs. Charmond's death from a shot fired by a disappointed lover unexpectedly involved Marty who had written to Fitzpiers about the true origin of the lady's beautiful hair. It is when Charmond reads the letter aloud to Mrs. Charmond that she runs out of the house and is accosted by her former lover. In an indirect but symbolically loaded way, Marty has had her revenge on the rich landowner who took her house and hair. As the text puts it, "Her bullet reached its billet at last" (43.395).

While *The Woodlanders* does not portray class struggle as open warfare, it includes the seeds of that struggle in the many contentions and displacements of the text, including the one that occurs indirectly between Marty and Grace. Since Grace's return to her birthplace is an event of social and economic significance for her and her family, her displacement of Marty as a possible partner for Giles is also more than merely personal and accidental. Because of Grace's newly attained polish, Giles begins to see his neighbors, including Marty, through her "superiority" and embarrassment: "In his mind's eye, before the event, they had been the mere background or padding of the scene; but somehow in the reality they were the most prominent personages there" (10.87–88).

Hardy's novel does not belong to these "prominent" though mostly neglected personages any more than it belongs to Marty. It is Grace's vehicle, as the country van had proved to be Barber Percomb's. Caught as she is between competing genres, affections and class interests, she nonetheless finds her "place." Her self-division comes to exemplify the site of the spectator, foreshadowed in the rented house Fitzpiers plans to occupy with Grace: "He described the place, and the surroundings, and the view from the windows; and Grace became much interested" (47.433). Grace is the spectator as survivor, but the price she pays for remaining outside the field of labor and passion is a permanent alienation from agency and authorship. If she is a beneficiary of a system of diffused power, her benefits are strictly and narrowly those of a nineteenth-century woman whose "liberation" from work and sexuality increases her distance from causation.

After Giles's death, Grace observes the results of his work: "The whole wood seemed to be a house of death, pervaded by loss to its uttermost length and breadth. Winterborne was gone, and the copses seemed to show the want of him." But because she has neither worked nor lived with Giles, her passive reading misses the messages sent out "at that very moment" by the roots that his "subtle hand" had directed (43.393–94).

By contrast, in a passage evocative of Ecclesiastes, the text unites Giles's and Marty's understanding of the forest with interpretation, labor, and conjuring. The artist and worker become one in a text that they help to create: "Giles and Marty . . . had been able to read its hieroglyphics as ordinary writing. . . . They had planted together, and together, they had with the run of the years, mentally collected those remoter signs and symbols which seen in few were of runic obscurity, but altogether made an alphabet. . . . The artifices of the seasons were seen by them from the conjuror's own point of view, *and not from that of the spectator*" (my emphasis, 44.399).

The fertile bonds between Marty and Giles, workers and woodlands, is what the narrative creates a reverence and longing for even as it relentlessly excludes them from its own ground and casts a haze over their alphabet.

The description of Marty in the churchyard at the end of the novel returns the reader to a concentrated figure of solitude that gathers to itself the strands of displacement and deprivation that have governed the entire narrative. If Grace maintains a semblance of feminine power by means of leisured detachment, Marty seems to have exchanged hers for a mystical, classless and sexless identity tested by unfulfilled love and unrecognized labor: "As this solitary and silent girl stood there in the moonlight, a straight slim figure, clothed in a plaitless gown, the contours of womanhood so undeveloped as to be scarcely perceptible in her, the marks of poverty and toil effaced by the misty hour, she touched sublimity at points, and looked almost like a being who had rejected with indifference the attributes of sex for the loftier quality of abstract humanism" (48.443).

The theatrical setting and the flowing rhetoric threaten to efface Marty as a worker and a woman, and to propose instead a myth of sublime nobility. One may blame the narrative for trying one last time to get away with this, but this same narrative has taught us to recognize the symptoms of effacement and to mistrust the process. Insofar as the text mythologizes Marty and Giles, separates them from the signs of their sex and labor, it cooperates with the socioeconomic trends that dislodge and isolate them, and place them outside the ordinary limits of human involvement and possible social reform. It is the fate of Marty and Giles to be beneath contempt or above criticism, debased or sublime. Either way, they are out of reach, inaccessible politically and sexually, impervious to moral or psychological analysis. By subjecting them to the literary conventions of noble sacrifice and the sublimity of solitude in nature, the narrative modulates outrage and frustration into pathos.

But this is not all. Through a relentless depiction of the radical unsuitability of inherited literary and social forms, and especially of their inability to contain or disguise injustice, the narrative also unsettles its own conservatism. The other face of the untouchable solitary object is an alienated and menacing subject.

NOTES

1. Solitary roads appear in many Hardy novels, including *Jude the Obscure*, but rarely with such metanarrative force.

2. A large body of Hardy scholarship deals with spectatorship and structures of narrative perception, for example, J. Hillis Miller, *Thomas Hardy: Distance and Desire* (Cambridge: Harvard University Press, 1970); David Lodge, "Thomas Hardy and Cinematographic Form," *Novel* 7 (1974); Tom Paulin, *Thomas Hardy: The Poetry of Perception* (Totowa, N.J.: Barnes, 1975); Judith Wittenberg, "Angles of Vision and Questions of Gender in *Far From the Madding Crowd*," *Centennial Review* 30 (1986): 25–40. Hardy conceives of the eye as possessing "epistemological, sexual and socio-moral" functions (Wittenberg 31).

3. Class relations, as John Goode notes, both incorporate and are traversed by sexual politics. John Goode, *Thomas Hardy, The Offensive Truth* (Oxford: Blackwell, 1988), 99, 101.

4. Michel Foucault, *Power/Knowledge: Selected Interviews and Other Writings, 1972–1977,* ed. Colin Gordon (New York: Pantheon, 1980), 158.

5. Ibid., 156.

6. Gilles Deleuze and Felix Guattari, *Anti-Oedipus* (Minneapolis: University of Minnesota Press, 1986), 305.

Club Laws: Chess and the Construction of Gender in A *Pair of Blue Eyes*

Mary Rimmer

Literary critics and theorists have increasingly coopted the terms of mathematical and psychoanalytical game theory: why should this be? Clearly the literature/game analogy reflects the general modern and postmodern interest in language as play and convention.[1] Yet game (generally seen by game theorists as a more structured activity than play) seems especially apposite as an analogy for narrative. Both narrative and game involve an interplay of convention and chance or, to use Gérard Genette's terms, of "expectation and surprise."[2] Readers approach any text with certain expectations, which the writer can variously satisfy or frustrate, but readers of narrative in particular usually seek specific information—the end of the story, the reasons for events—that the author may temporarily, partially, or completely withhold. Conventions, or expectations, make reading and writing possible just as they make games possible; still, even the most conventional of narratives can surprise, and we can never predict for certain the outcome of a game. In fact, suspense is itself one of the conventions, and a major source of pleasure, in narrative as in game.

Like an embedded narrative, then, an actual game embedded in a text can break through diegetic levels and pose metanarrative questions. By echoing the plot or structure of the larger text, an embedded game suggests the arbitrariness of narrative's attempts to contain the amorphous space of the unpredictable; it also suggests the way chance challenges and creates meaning in texts and in our lives. And a game such as chess with a strong narrative element creates still more complex possibilities; a chess game in a text is doubly embedded, for it superimposes the players' contest on the chess story, with its rival kings and queens.

Thomas Hardy's fascination with chance and his uneasiness with the tradition of realist narrative he inherited are well documented. Full-length studies such as those of Bert G. Hornback, Albert Pettigrew Elliott, and

Roy Morrell,[3] have dealt with chance, coincidence, and fate in Hardy, and commentators such as Albert Guerard and Irving Howe have seen Hardy's interest in chance as an aspect of his modernism. Guerard includes the grotesque coincidences that bothered Hardy's Victorian and post-Victorian commentators among "the demons of plot, irony and myth" that attract the twentieth-century reader.[4] On the other hand, Howe still seems uneasy with chance and coincidence in Hardy and seeks to explain them away as expressions of characters' hidden desires: "Hardy is trying to say through the workings of chance what later writers will try to say through the vocabulary of the unconscious."[5] *Pace* Guerard, a similar uneasiness is visible in much twentieth-century Hardy criticism, perhaps most strikingly so in Morrell's book, a sustained and intense argument against the centrality of chance in Hardy.[6]

By contrast, little attention has been given to Hardy's use of games to explore the arbitrary movements of chance; that is, to undo the links the realist tradition draws between act and consequence, "character" and fate.[7] The midnight dice game on the heath in *The Return of the Native*, for instance, twice rearranges the fates of the novel's characters through the actions of the dice, as Christian Cantle loses the Yeobright guineas to Damon Wildeve and Diggory Venn wins them back. Michael Henchard's ill-fated sports day in *The Mayor of Casterbridge*, designed to reassert his dominant position in the town, actually accelerates his downward slide when it falls victim to the vagaries of the weather; games need players if they are to be games at all, and Henchard loses his to Donald Farfrae's sheltered dancing pavilion. The uncertain and all-powerful workings of weather and dice mock individual attempts to control fate, and suggest that real power lies outside the individual character—in fate or, as readers of narrative know, with the omnipotent author.

Yet if both played and unplayed games in Hardy suggest the space of chance that opens between desire and event, they also suggest the power relations along class and/or gender lines that govern the players' relationships with each other. Henchard's increasing rivalry with Farfrae, whose "imported" methods and better education give him a competitive edge, sparks the mayor's desire to be the town gamesmaster. Significantly, Henchard provides traditional games such as hurdles, boxing, and greasy climbing poles, whereas Farfrae dispenses with games altogether in favor of the more genteel entertainment of dancing. In *The Return of the Native*, Wildeve's class-based dominance over Christian helps him persuade the gullible messenger into the game of dice in the first place. This game also contains an element of gender dominance, for when it continues between Wildeve and Venn, the battle for Thomasin Wildeve's guineas becomes a battle for Thomasin herself, fueled by Wildeve's desire to claim husband's rights over her property, and by Venn's determination to play knight-errant. Other games in Hardy similarly combine the ironies of chance with class- and gender-based power systems. Tess Durbeyfield, playing "lords and ladies" with flower buds while Angel Clare offers to teach her history, is rebuked by Angel and soon rebukes herself for her "childish" pursuit of the game and rejection of his offer, but Tess knows far better than Angel that history will not teach her " 'why the sun do shine on the just and the unjust alike' " (T18.162). Her endless, apparently pointless peeling of the flower buds to see which are "lords" and which "ladies," suggests her awareness of gender and erratic chance as the determining factors in her life; the kind of middle-class education Angel offers might disguise these factors, but could never eradicate them.

It may seem paradoxical to say that Hardy uses games to suggest the determining power of class and gender on the one hand, and the arbitrary nature of chance/fiction on the other. If the power relationships between players make ultimate loss and gain wearily predictable, does not chance become a mere tool of Hardy's macabre desire to stack the deck against the already disadvantaged—Christian, Tess, Henchard? Yet as commentators on game and play have often noted, the chance-necessity binarism is an illusion; necessity, in the words of Kostas Axelos, "activates chance";[8] we admit this by using "fate" to mean both fortuitous events and the posited power that causes them. Further, chance within a text indirectly expresses authorial power in any case: power over characters, plot, and the fulfil-ment or frustration of readers' expectations. In fact, the sense of this power may well be what readers actually resent when they object to Hardy's arbitrary manipulation of chance. To experience life as a pawn is to experience it as unpredictable chance but also to be at the mercy of power.

Hardy's use of the game motif is especially provocative in A *Pair of Blue Eyes*, where chess matches are the most resonant of the parallel events in Elfride Swancourt's two successive courtships. The two matches structure, develop, and symbolize the currents of social and sexual dominance that define Elfride's relations with her two suitors. Chess may be the privileged "game of games" in part because it so explicitly enacts the martial aggres-sion and social hierarchy that most games, and the social analogy of game theory, center on. In fact the hierarchical structure of the "royal game" has consistently invited social analogies, from medieval chess moralities such as Jacopo da Cessole's,[9] through political satires such as Thomas Middleton's A *Game at Chess* (1624), to the Freudian account of chess as an expression of sublimated patricidal and homosexual desires.[10] Moreover, since the medieval transformation of the Arab *firz* (counselor) into the queen piece,[11] the hierarchical ranking of the pieces has involved gender as well as class. Looking at the queen's power and mobility, a novice might even conclude that chess is a woman's game; indeed, when the "new chess" emerged at the end of the middle ages and gave the queen piece the wide range of moves it has today, it was often called *"eschés de la dame."*[12] A closer look suggests the limits of the queen's role, however: a lost queen does not necessarily mean a lost game in chess, and it is the tactically weak king that must be cornered to obtain a victory. Other nicknames applied to the "new chess" in the fifteenth century—*"eschés de la dame enragée"* and *"scachi ala rabiosa"* (mad chess)[13]—suggest that the powerful queen dovetailed neatly with the traditional idea that female power spends itself in fury and madness.

No less than its internal structure, the history of chess is bound up with forms of social power and hierarchy. Principally an aristocratic pastime in medieval Europe, by Hardy's time it was popular among the middle class, as the proliferation of chess clubs, chess columns in newspapers and chess handbooks in nineteenth-century England attests.[14] The game still however enjoyed considerable prestige, less from lingering aristocratic associations than from its status as an intellectual game, based on pure strategy rather than on chance.[15] And since it had little if any working-class following, no doubt in part because of the time it requires, chess remained a marker of class status in the nineteenth century.[16] With the development of the tournament circuit in the second half of the century top-level chess had become professional, but the idea of it as a recreational game for "gentlemanly" amateurs persisted.[17] Even Howard Staunton, a pioneer tournament organizer, insisted that chess was an amateur game, which "may to a great extent strengthen the mind of the professional man, but . . . must never become the object of his life."[18] Staunton's comment also reveals the tendency, especially prevalent among chess commentators of the eighteenth and nineteenth centuries, to emphasize the rational rather than the aggressive aspects of the game.[19] From such a perspective, chess banishes not only any vulnerability to chance but also any acknowledgement of its own military symbolism.[20] As "pure" intellectual activity, then, chess attracted middle-class players, like Elfride, who wished to be seen as intellectually inclined, and aspirants to middle-class status, like her first suitor Stephen Smith.[21]

Certainly Stephen, who has taught himself the game from a book, regards chess as one of his passports to middle-class status. He knows that his unorthodox handling of the chess pieces threatens to identify him as an interloper, just as his peculiar Latin pronunciation does. Similarly, Henry Knight's chess victories testify not only to a mind more disciplined than that of Elfride or Stephen but also to the power his class and gender give him over both. Knight, the mentor who has loaned Stephen the book on chess in the first place, inevitably plays better than his pupil; he also plays better than Elfride, who as a woman has had uncritical praise rather than challenge. Even Knight's name, in its connections with knighthood and with chess, emphasizes his position as an insider in a world that excludes Stephen, and that Elfride can enter only as the passive "lady" whom the knight defends against others and himself besieges for sexual favors.

We have already noted that the apparent validation of female power in chess does not extend very far, and certainly the half-humorous respect granted the power of the queen piece has never extended to respect for women as chess players. Stories about women players tend to be humorous anecdotes or episodes in love stories. In the Arab legend of Dilaram a shah's wife, offered by her husband as a stake at chess, saves the game for him by telling him what moves to make.[22] Like most good women players in literature, as John Graham has pointed out, Dilaram is seen as exceptional.[23] The losing shah talks to three wives as he tries to decide which one to give away; Dilaram alone has the initiative to ask to see the game. Further, women in literary chess matches often conceal their skill, out of love or pity for their adversaries, and deliberately throw games. Graham cites Elfride's match with Stephen as one example of this.[24] Love or compassion generally takes precedence over chess, as it does when Miranda in *The Tempest* happily condones Ferdinand's cheating.[25] Alternatively, though more rarely, the good woman chess player can appear as a "masculine" gorgon. In J. Maclaren-Ross's story "The Two Retired Chess Champions and the Girl Who Preferred to Play Draughts" a male chess champion drinks himself into a stupor before a match rather than face his opponent, "a woman doctor and a pretty tough specimen altogether."[26] To the subtle denigration of these literary accounts we may add many offhand comments by twentieth-century theorists of chess skill who have variously attributed the comparatively low ratings of women players to women's supposed lack of repressed aggression (patricidal or otherwise),[27] of physical strength,[28] or of spatial-perceptual skills.[29] Many chess organizations still segregate championships by gender, although the recent successes of the Polgar sisters of Hungary have challenged theories about gender and chess skill.

The rise of the tournament circuit and the professional player in the later nineteenth century made it increasingly difficult for a woman to join the ranks of male chess "masters."[30] Although her father and the narrator both call Elfride a good player, they assume that she cannot genuinely compete at chess, and that the limits on her skill derive from her womanhood. The narrator describes her playing as "above the average among women" (PBE 7.55), and her father tells Knight, " 'She plays very well for a lady' " (18.186); both comments imply that Knight will inevitably play as well as or better than she will. The dismissive tone of her father's comment stands out all the more because elsewhere the narrator notes that she has, until the match with Knight, "enjoyed the reputation throughout the globe of her father's brain . . . of being an excellent player" (18.188). Good enough to beat the men in her small provincial circle, Elfride is expected to lose to any male player (short of a beginner like Stephen) from the metropolis. She has been set up for a fall by what Ellen Moers calls "the admiration on which little girls are fed, in treacly spoonfuls, from their earliest years."[31] Praise has been lavished upon her in inverse proportion to the respect accorded her performance.

The chess matches, along with the courtships they echo and shape, bring Elfride into direct conflict with her oppressively gendered world for the first time. In the early chapters of the novel she has considerable autonomy and without consciously rebelling violates many of the decorums of femininity. She rides her horse bareheaded, unattended and recklessly through the countryside, and exploits her unladylike equestrian habits to elope with Stephen, the distinctly ineligible son of the local stonemason. She also asserts herself intellectually by writing better sermons than her clergyman father's, writing and publishing a romance, and arguing with a critic (Knight) who writes a negative review of it. Lack of money and a paucity of social equals or betters in the neighbourhood of his isolated parish encourage her widowed father to give Elfride her way. Further, the family history sets her the example of unorthodox behavior: her mother eloped with Mr. Swancourt in defiance of her family, and her grandmother's romantic elopement with a musician is a matter of local legend (26.285–86).

Patriarchal culture traditionally associates such unsanctioned female mobility as Elfride's with the feminine figures of chance and Nature, and the sexual betrayal of men.[32] As Peter J. Casagrande has pointed out, the "Nature" that tortures Knight in the famous cliff scene from A Pair of Blue Eyes operates according to "lawless caprice," shows "a feline fun in her tricks" (22.243), and unmistakeably echoes Elfride.[33] Like capricious Nature and the mobile, threatening queen in "new chess," Elfride subtly threatens to rage through or madden everything around her, bringing "lawless caprice" into Knight's celibate world and reintroducing chance into the ritualized, "pure" rationality of the chess game. Moreover, she disrupts the social order more seriously than her rebellious forebears; her mother's and grandmother's clandestine marriages allow them to be accepted back into their families, but Elfride's anomalous position after her abortive elopement resists conventional definition and leaves her without firm connections to either Stephen or her father. Although technically she has not "fallen," she resembles a fallen woman in her inability to be assimilated within orthodox (i.e., male-headed) family structures; she is neither married nor openly engaged, nor still unequivocally an inexperienced girl. Knight, when he discovers part of it, sees her history as a threat, and worries that it may enable her to ridicule him: "How childishly blind he must have seemed to this mere girl! How she must have laughed at him inwardly!" (30.348). Even her family, by the time she makes her marriage of convenience, has all but cast her out in disgust at her " 'tricks' " and " 'idiocies' " (35.388).[34]

Since courtship officially happens only once, Elfride's chess match with Knight is itself a "fickle" act, for in it she consciously repeats an episode from her earlier courtship: "The game began. Mr. Swancourt had forgotten a similar performance with Stephen Smith the year before. Elfride had not; but she had begun to take for her maxim the undoubted truth that the necessity of continuing faithful to Stephen, without suspicion, dictated a fickle behaviour almost as imperatively as fickleness itself; a fact, however, which would give a startling advantage to the latter quality should it ever appear" (18.186). By agreeing to marry Stephen, Elfride has used up the only measure of autonomy officially granted her in courtship, and yet she continues to act as a free agent. She may make her claim to autonomy uneasily and only half-consciously, but she nonetheless lives up to the impish subversion suggested by her nickname, "Elfie."[35]

Predictably, the order Elfride subverts not only overcomes her tentative attempts to unsettle it but also harshly punishes those attempts. Her autonomy decreases almost from the moment the novel opens; the chess matches chart its decline and foreshadow her movement, in the rest of the novel, from independent iconoclasm to the silence and stasis of death. We can see that movement beginning even in the first match, where Stephen's working-class origin and lack of chess experience seem to put him at a hopeless disadvantage. After deliberately losing two games out of pity for Stephen's inexperience, Elfride easily defeats him; immediately afterward though he regains the initiative by declaring his love. Before long he persuades her to become engaged, to elope, and to travel to London when he discovers that the marriage can only be performed there with the licence he has. He does give in to her last-minute insistence that they should break off the elopement, but apart from that he remains in control, and in his mind Elfride becomes a " 'prize' " which he has " 'won' " (20.216) for himself.

Knight's relationship with Elfride a year later steps up the pressure on her considerably, because his class and professional position as a reviewer, essayist, and arbiter of cultural worth enable him to dominate her much more thoroughly than Stephen can. As yet too uncertain of his membership in middle-class culture to have acquired the skills he would need even to give Elfride a good game, Stephen sees her as much " 'cleverer' " (7.55), or much better versed in those cultural skills, than he is. Knight's condescension, on the other hand, attracts Elfride because it connotes cultural power, and demonstrates that he is "a greater man" (27.288) than Stephen. As the narrator remarks, "By the side of the instructive and piquant snubbings she received from Knight, Stephen's general agreeableness seemed watery" (27.288).

Unsurprisingly then, Elfride goes through a much more intense struggle in the second chess match than in the first. Unlike Stephen, she has staked almost everything on the game. She wants to use victory over Knight to repair the wounds he has administered to her self-esteem in his review, in his refusal to withdraw his criticism when they meet in person, and most recently, in the schoolmasterly scolding he has given her for her daredevil walk around the parapet of the churchtower. For Elfride, the apparently neutral ground of chess is almost the only place where she can hope to make this claim; as John Goode has argued, the game "artificially encloses . . . conditions of equality . . . since theoretically it submits all players to the same rules."[36]

The idea that game offers an enclosed space, separate from the class- and gender-bound exigencies of "serious" life, appears in many analyses of game, notably Johan Huizinga's and Roger Caillois's.[37] Yet, as we have already seen, this separateness exists only "theoretically." Elfride does not step outside culture into a protected space when she challenges Knight; in fact, she enters a space that concentrates the limitations imposed on her by culture.[38] The "club laws" issue raised in her match with Knight suggests the way in which chess subdues her to "the rules of the game." In theory "club laws," the strict rules used by clubs and professional chess players, and under which a move ends once the player's fingers have left the piece, apply equally to any player, regardless of skill, class, or gender. The word "club" inevitably suggests exclusion though, and masculinist exclusion at that.[39] Certainly, chess at the club and professional levels was almost entirely male in 1873, when *A Pair of Blue Eyes* was published. A few clubs in England, such as the Brighton Chess Club, had "ladies' branches," but most excluded women until the first women's chess clubs opened in England and the United States in the 1890s.[40] The inexorable "justice" the club laws represent thus connotes the masculine domination of chess. For Elfride, playing chess at all, and certainly playing with such an obvious desire to win, implicitly challenges the conventional restrictions on "feminine" behavior just as her other self-assertions have. Knight plays by club laws at her request, and although she asks for them primarily to take advantage of a blunder he has made, her repetition of the first-person plural suggests that she also wants to present herself as someone who "belongs" to the inner circle of good chess players: " 'Club laws we'll have, won't we, Mr. Knight?' " (18.186). She reads chess columns and books, and refers to contemporary chess masters with studied familiarity. Her effort to identify herself with the masters parallels her earlier sense that publishing her romance marks her out from "ordinary young women who never [venture] into the fire of criticism at all" (16.168).

Elfride discovers, as the club laws are applied to her own moves, that singling herself out from "ordinary young women" makes her vulnerable to the rigid constraints of the clubs she aspires to join. Romance-writing may differentiate her from "ordinary" women, but it still places her within the limits of acceptable feminine behaviour, as long as she sees her work, in the words of her future husband Lord Luxellian, as " 'an elegant trifle' " (14.158). Competitive aggression however exposes her to a more searing "fire of criticism." Her somewhat petulant exclamation against " 'those cold-blooded ways of clubs and professional players' " (18.187), ignored by Knight, on the surface suggests that she is indeed the "conceited child" (20.212) he thinks her, wanting strict rules for others and indulgence for herself. Yet although the exclamation certainly reveals her inexperience, and consequent failure to allow for the risks of choosing to play by club laws, it also registers her ominous discovery that the codes of the sphere she has been trying to enter can be harsh and punitive. As Elfride plays and endures repeated losses, she learns the humiliating consequences that asking to be taken seriously may have for an outsider with low cultural status.

The high degree of prestige Elfride has invested in the games she plays with Knight affects her emotional and physical reactions to them. The final game, which she prepares for by staying up until five in the morning to study chess strategy, strains not only her mind but also her entire physical system to the utmost. Near the end of it her heart beats with an extreme and improbable violence that sets the flowers on the table "throbbing by its pulsations" (18.190), and after her defeat she falls into a feverish sleep in which her pulse is "twanging like a harp-string, at the rate of nearly a hundred and fifty a minute" (18.192); her condition seems so serious that Mrs. Swancourt sends for a doctor. Several observers within the novel interpret Elfride's reaction as the sort of "feminine" inability to cope with intellectual stress often cited in the nineteenth century as a reason to bar women from professional pursuits, from higher education and from chess tournaments.[41] Her stepmother, whom Mr. Swancourt has married partly to keep his daughter in line and to " 'introduce [Elfride] to the world a little' " (134), predictably considers Elfride too " 'excitable' " (18.189) to play chess safely in the evenings; she tells Knight that her stepdaughter's " 'tender brain won't bear cudgelling like [his] great head' "

(192).[42] The doctor appears to have similar ideas about the incompatibility of chess and young ladies, for he forbids Elfride to play in the future. The narrator too supports this view when he remarks that Elfride goes to her room after the first game, "her mind as distracted as if it would throb itself out of her head" (18.188), or when he refers to her flushes and tremblings in the last game.

The narrator's comment is itself part of a typically Hardyan narrative game, however, for he has already given us abundant grounds for disagreeing with his judgement of Elfride's nervous collapse. Here as elsewhere in the novel the gap between event and interpretation, or between conflicting interpretations, invites and even forces us into the role of interpreters. If the arbitrariness of chance in Hardy's novels make us into pawns, the narrator's often arbitrary judgments enlarge our role in the game by making us players as well as pieces. In this case, we may remember how Stephen experiences defeat, at least until he finds a way to "mate" Elfride away from the chess board. By the time they finish playing his heart throbs "even more excitedly than was hers, which itself had quickened when she seriously set to work on this last occasion" (7.55). His response to defeat differs from hers only in degree.[43] Moreover, neither Elfride's match with Stephen nor presumably the other matches she has played up to the time of Knight's arrival produce the symptoms of extreme strain in her that the games with Knight do. We may then use this remembered information to construct a different interpretation of Elfride's presumed inability to stand mental strain, one that emphasizes her awareness of the significance of losing. For Elfride as for Stephen, losing and winning matter; the insecurity that their gender and class respectively give to their positions makes them far more intensely aware of the game's stakes than Knight. On the other hand, Knight's "sportsmanlike" indifference to the outcome of his game with Elfride marks his status, indicating that he has no need to prove anything by the victory he wins so easily. The sporting code, and its premise that all players are equal, clearly works against those who have to overcome obstacles even to begin the game, let alone to win it. As Jacques Ehrmann has pointed out, play's "integrity, its gratuitousness are only apparent, since the very freedom of the expenditure made in it is part of a circuit which reaches beyond the spatial and temporal limits of play."[44]

Elfride's aggressive competitiveness, especially as revealed in her language, also elicits special criticism from the narrator during his account of her match with Knight. She talks of " 'armies of bishops and knights' " (18.189), quotes lines from *Richard II* in which the king is exhorted to fight Bullingbrook's forces to the death (18.190), and justifies her "vanity" in challenging Knight to a final game by referring to Nelson and pointing out that vanity can be a military virtue (18.190). In the reference to Nelson, as in her quote from *Richard II* (" ' "Fear and be slain? no worse can come to fight; / And fight and die, is death destroying death!" ' "), she assumes a militantly aggressive posture that will make her seem dangerous if she wins and foolishly vain if she loses; the narrator easily gives a mock-heroic edge to her desperation as he echoes her martial tone, calling the players "pitiless," "hard-pressed," "merciless," or "ignominiously overcome."[45] Again though, his commentary clashes with the sense of serious conflict the game evokes; the gap the contradictions create invites us to look more directly at the power relations that he glosses and glosses over. Ridiculing Elfride's appropriation of military language only emphasizes the threat associated with her: she has not only invaded another masculine sphere but also violated the decorums of game itself by drawing attention to the aggression they disguise. Her language ominously underlines the costs of losing and the game's implicit violence.[46]

It is at moments when Elfride seems a serious contender for power, threatening others with her open competitiveness and subversive mobility and risking a great deal herself, that the narrator's anxieties emerge in depreciatory commentary. Elfride as victim he can sympathize with, but Elfride as aggressor, as fickle "betrayer" or as rule-breaker unnerves him. He calls her "inconstant" nature "exquisite," but says that it will only seem so "to those who contemplate it from a standpoint beyond the influence of that inconstancy" (27.288). He responds to her unsettling influence by attempting to fix her in words, to "pack [her] into sentences like a workman" (18.193) as he says Knight does with women in his essays. Just as Knight apparently needs to write off the disturbing effect of Elfride's walk on the parapet by making notes on it and commenting " 'An innocent vanity is of course the origin of these displays' " (18.196), so the narrator needs to transform her self-assertion in the chess game into an easily dismissed example of immature petulance. When she first faces the prospect of losing a game the narrator describes her feelings as almost infantile: "She was on the brink of pouting, but was ashamed to show it; tears almost stood in her eyes. She had been trying so hard—so very hard—thinking and thinking till her brain was in a whirl; and it seemed so heartless of him to treat her so, after all" (18.187). Once reduced to a child's sulks, Elfride's desire to win no longer alarms or suggests the ruthless conqueror; her aggression can become a matter for amusement. (Later, as Knight tries to subdue the succubus-like spirit of love that has "entered into him" (20.211), he will remind himself that he has thought of her as a conceited child.) Yet since the narrator's strategic depreciations of Elfride are precisely what open the text up to us and lead us to a critical reappraisal of his interpretations, his defensive maneuvering paradoxically produces moments of textual energy. By projecting whatever anxieties he may have felt about female power onto such obviously fallible narrators, Hardy can distance those anxieties without actually disowning them, and turn them to account.[47]

The cultural loading that prevents chess in particular from being an innocent activity without consequences, is compounded in *A Pair of Blue Eyes* as in many other literary works by the role chess plays in the larger game of courtship. The courted woman playing chess has two conflicting roles to play: convention defines her desired end in courtship as the passive act of surrender, but chess requires her to compete in a mock battle. As we have seen, the literary resolution of this conflict often has the woman throw the game and play out her courtship role at the expense of the chess competition. But though Elfride falls in with this pattern in the match with Stephen, in the second match she chooses the more transgressive option and plays to win. True, the courtship pattern still constrains her, for she tries to play well in order to gain Knight's respect, but significantly she wants respect at this point rather than the admiration of a lover. Later she is chagrined when Knight declares his preference for hair and eyes of a different color from hers, but her reaction on that occasion has none of the intensity of her reactions to his review, to his criticism of her ideas or to his victories over her in chess.

The courtship ritual has an insidious hold on Elfride, however, for centering as it does on an act of female choice, it appears to enact a fantasy of female power, much as chess does. According to the narrator Elfride "rules" both her suitors (7.61; 20.212), and to Stephen she is even a "queen" (7.61; 22.249; 25.275; surely not a fortuitous choice of words). She enjoys playing "La belle dame sans merci" to Stephen (7.59), and once she has lost the chess games she tries to exercise a similar power over Knight by drawing his attention to her eyes and hair. Yet to exercise the power of this kind of queenship is also to lose it. Elfride's relationship with Knight, though it begins in an unorthodox fashion when she takes issue with his review, eventually reveals the weakness of her position and forces her into more conventional responses. Her resistance to his carelessly assumed dominance becomes attenuated and ever more defensive after the chess match; when she finally gives way to her love for him she is stripped of all power and volition until she feels that "To remain passive . . . encircled by his arms, [is] . . . a glorious crown to all the years of her life" (22.249).[48]

Rather than allow her to gain his respect and attention, the chess match with Knight ends in Elfride's speechless and mortified retreat. After her conversation with him about the review, she announces her intention never to write and publish another romance lest someone else " 'pen a condemnation and "nail't wi' Scripture" ' " (17.175), as he has just done in a pompous analogy between his review and the Pauline epistles.[49] After her walk on the churchtower parapet Knight forces her to obey his commands and to take his arm against her will so that she feels "like a colt in a halter for the first time" (18.185); after the chess game she cannot even give shape to her sense of defeat in her own mind. As her experience of Knight's courtship will ultimately teach her, she can only "win" him by losing to him, and by becoming completely dependent on him—in other words, by becoming the child he assumes her to be from the start. She has a role of a sort in the ritual of courtship, but the more prestigious cultural activities, which the masculine and quasi-military world of chess represents, offer her no place at all. Significantly, Knight has no thought of Elfride as a lover during the chess game; his sexual interest in her begins only afterwards, when all her attempts to meet him on his own ground have failed, and she has come to think of herself as " 'a poor nobody' " (19.201) in relation to him.

The writing-off of Elfride at the end of *A Pair of Blue Eyes* may seem excessive, as critics have sometimes complained.[50] Certainly her punishments are almost grotesquely out of proportion to her venial sexual transgressions: she is violently rejected by Knight and scorned by her family, listlessly accepts a marriage of convenience, quickly dies of a miscarriage, and disappears completely in the last chapters of the novel, while the three men who have possessed or tried to possess her variously mourn or squabble over her remains. Her relations with Knight and with Stephen, it seems, have progressively reduced her to the immobility suggested by the disembodied "pair of blue eyes" in the book's title, and like a captured queen in chess, she is put aside while the game she has seemed central to goes on without her. Yet the very completeness with which she is silenced and immobilized suggests the depth of her male observers' need to silence her and thus the seriousness of the questions her history raises about the games played in the novel. Like a woman accused of witchcraft, she is made the focus of fears about chance, "Nature," female sexuality and sexual betrayal, and is then ritually sacrificed, in part through the agency of the game whose club laws she violates—but Hardy's embedding of game in narrative exposes rather than reinforces the use of Elfride as scapegoat. The literal "manhandling" her opponents/suitors and the narrator subject her to, and the extreme physical consequences of her defeats, reveal the dynamics of power and violence within the ritual constructs of chess and courtship and within the narrator's traditional power to probe and comment authoritatively on a heroine's state of mind. She threatens and is silenced by Knight and the narrator for her role in that revelation, but Hardy's ambivalence leaves the novel open and invites us, as players in the narrative game, to explore the fears behind his narrator's attempts to close it.

NOTES

I am grateful for the kind assistance rendered by Dr. Melissa Hardie, of the Jamieson Library, Penzance, Cornwall, and Mr. Philip Jurgens, of the Chess Federation of Canada.

1. See for example Elizabeth Bruss, "The Game of Literature and Some Literary Games," *New Literary History* 9(1977): 153–72; Jacques Ehrmann, ed., *Game, Play, Literature*, spec. issue of *Yale French Studies* 41 (1968); Peter Hutchinson, *Games Authors Play* (London: Methuen, 1983), and Richard A. Lanham, *Tristram Shandy: The Games of Pleasure* (Berkeley: University of California Press, 1973).

2. Gérard Genette, *Figures of Literary Discourse*, trans. Alan Sheridan (New York: Columbia University Press, 1982), 17.

3. Bert G. Hornback, *The Metaphor of Chance: Vision and Technique in the Works of Thomas Hardy* (Athens: Ohio University Press, 1971); Albert Pettigrew Elliott, *Fatalism in the Works of Thomas Hardy* (New York: Russell, 1935); Roy Morrell, *Thomas Hardy: The Will and the Way* (Kuala Lumpur: University of Malaysia Press, 1965).

4. Albert Guerard, *Thomas Hardy* (1949; New York: New Directions, 1964), 6.

5. Irving Howe, *Thomas Hardy* (1966; New York: Macmillan, 1985), 66.

6. Richard C. Carpenter, for instance, in *Thomas Hardy* (New York: Twayne, 1964), 39–40, complains that the characters in *Desperate Remedies* "are puppets dancing to the demands of the plot." Norman Page, in *Thomas Hardy* (London: Routledge, 1977), 113, says that in *Two on a Tower* "the development of the story proceeds too exclusively through external events, which fall out with implausible obligingness," and F. B. Pinion's "Chance, Choice and Charity: Hardy and the Future of Civilization," in *Thomas Hardy and the Modern World*, ed. F. B. Pinion (Dorchester: Thomas Hardy Society, 1974), 71–89, expresses Pinion's uneasiness with "contrivance of Chance" in the plots of *The Return of the Native, Tess of the d'Urbervilles*, and *Jude the Obscure*.

7. John Goode, *Thomas Hardy: The Offensive Truth* (Oxford: Blackwell, 1988) 10–11, has recently discussed game (with particular reference to *A Pair of Blue Eyes*) as a Hardyan analogy for novel writing, but as I indicate below I do not share Goode's idea of game as a space where class and gender conflict may temporarily abate.

8. Kostas Axelos, "Planetary Interlude," Ehrmann, ed., 14.

9. Jacopo da Cessole, *Liber de moribus Hominum et officiis Nobilium ac Popularium super ludo* (Utrecht: 1473).

10. See for example Alexander Cockburn, *Idle Passion: Chess and the Dance of Death* (London: Weidenfield, 1974); Reuben Fine, *The Psychology of the Chess Player* (New York: Dover, 1967); Ernest Jones, "The Problem of Paul Morphy," *International Journal of Psychoanalysis* 12 (1931): 1–23, and Norman Reider, "Chess, Oedipus and the Mater Dolorosa," *International Journal of Psychoanalysis* 40 (1959): 320–33.

11. Richard Eales, *Chess: The History of a Game* (New York: Facts on File, 1985), 44–46.

12. Ibid., 72.

13. Ibid.

14. Ibid., 134–39.

15. Nevertheless Cockburn, *Idle Passion*, 66–67, points out that chance always remains a factor, and that in any case "the exclusion of chance, which appears to make chess more serious than other games, actually reduces the reality quotient of the game."

16. William Hartston and P. C. Wason, *The Psychology of Chess Skill* (New York: Facts on File, 1984), 118; Edward Lasker, *The Adventure of Chess* (Garden City, N.J.: Doubleday, 1949), 34.

17. Eales, *Chess*, 144–51.

18. Quoted in Eales, *Chess*, 144. Elfride refers to Staunton during her first game with Knight and, according to Ronald Blythe's note in the New Wessex edition of the novel (London: Macmillan, 1975), 413, consults Staunton's *Chess Praxis* (London: Bohn, 1860), when she is looking for a strategy to help her defeat Knight.

19. Eales, *Chess*, 102, 139.

20. Freudian chess theorists such as Fine and Cockburn argue that chess can effectively sublimate patricidal impulses because the element of violence in it is so thoroughly concealed by the game's aura of rationality and seriousness, and by the codes of chess behavior that channel aggression and prevent physical contact.

21. Eales, *Chess*, 139–40.

22. Recounted in Staunton's *Chess: Theory and Practice*, ed. Robert B. Wormald (London: Virtue, 1876), 12, as a humorous qualification of an Arab source's remark that "'to give any odds beyond the Rook can apply only to women, children and tyros.'" For a fuller version, see Jerome Salzman, comp., *The Chess Reader: The Royal Game in World Literature* (New York: Greenberg, 1949), 16–17.

23. John Graham, *Women in Chess: Players of the Modern Age* (Jefferson, N.C.: McFarland, 1987), 2.

24. Ibid., 1–2.

25. William Shakespeare, *The Tempest*, in *The Riverside Shakespeare*, ed. G. Blakemore Evans (Boston: Houghton, 1974), v.i.172–75.

26. J. Maclaren-Ross, "The Two Retired Chess Champions and the Girl Who Preferred to Play Draughts," *The Saturday Book* IV (1944), 210–15. The champion loses by default: after this opening episode, the story follows the friendship this man and another champion form with Lily, a destitute young woman whom they invite to share their flat. Lily, who cannot grasp the rules of chess and who refuses to take either the game or the men's assurances that they are champions seriously, does however beat them in game after game at draughts. Interestingly, although Lily's inability or unwillingness to understand chess contrasts sharply with the doctor's skill, the two women threaten the men in similar ways. The chess champions eventually decide to send Lily home because they cannot stand the repeated defeats, but they then discover that she has left of her own accord, and has sold their chess trophies to pay her train fare.

27. Cockburn, *Idle Passion*, 48.

28. Hartston and Wason, *Chess Skill*, 119.

29. Dennis H. Holding, *The Psychology of Chess Skill* (Hillsdale, N.J.: Erlbaum, 1985), 42.

30. Graham, *Women in Chess*, 6–8.

31. Ellen Moers, *Literary Women* (1963; London: Women's Press, 1978), 197.

32. Elliott argues that "Woman" is one of the "five forms" fate takes on in Hardy's works: "in Woman there exists a nature as direful as those of Coincidence and Time in bringing Man to destruction" (*Fatalism*, 57).

33. Peter J. Casagrande, *Unity in Thomas Hardy's Novels: Repetitive Symmetries* (Lawrence: Regents, 1982), 96–97.

34. Cf. Michelle Zimbalist Rosaldo, "Woman, Culture and Society: A Theoretical Overview," in *Woman, Culture and Society,* ed. Michelle Zimbalist Rosaldo and Louise Lamphere (Stanford: Stanford University Press, 1974), 32–4, on the tendency in many cultures to define any woman not attached to a husband or father as a dangerous anomaly.

35. Elfride's full name, another legacy from the rebellious female line of her family, suggests a still more threatening kind of subversion, and again a kind that echoes the chess game: the historical Queen Elfrida is supposed to have had her stepson, King Edward the Martyr, murdered in 978 so that her son Ethelred could succeed to the throne.

36. Goode, *Thomas Hardy*, 10.

37. Johan Huizinga, *Homo Ludens: A Study of the Play-Element in Culture* (1950; Boston: Beacon, 1955), 46, 26 and passim; Roger Caillois, *Man, Play and Games,* trans. Meyer Barash (New York: Free-Macmillan, 1961), 46, 44 and passim. See also Jacques Ehrmann's critique of Huizinga's and Caillois' concepts of game in "Homo Ludens Revisited," Ehrmann, ed., 31–57.

38. Cf. Cockburn's assertion that "play and games are certainly not leaves of absence from the sociohistorical and psychohistorical environments they inhabit" (*Idle Passion*, 213).

39. "Club" has remained a gendered word into the twentieth century, to judge by dictionary definitions. One of the meanings the OED gives for the word is "a knot of men associated together," and "clubbable" is there defined as "having such qualities as fit a man to be a member of a club." Webster's does not specify the gender of club members, but does give "a clubbable man" as an appropriate use of "clubbable."

40. Graham, *Women in Chess*, 6–7.

41. Ibid., 8.

42. Mrs. Swancourt has an equivocal influence in the novel; she does arrange for the publication of Elfride's romance, and take Knight to task for his ideas about testing young women's innocence. But she puts an end to Elfride's solitary riding, and approves of publishing the romance only " 'as a guarantee of mental respectability' " (14.136) to potential suitors.

43. In fact, male chess masters have often been known to show physical signs of nervous strain during matches, particularly when they are losing. Lasker, *Adventure of Chess*, 74, notes that in an 1858 match between Morphy (another master Elfride refers to as she plays) and Harrwitz, the loser Harrwitz "became extremely nervous . . . often shaking violently when he was about to move." Eales, *Chess Skill*, 144, notes that in the nineteenth century "physicians tended to have views about

nervous illness which led them to exaggerate greatly the strain caused by playing chess" in both men and women. And of course, any threat to nervous health would be seen as most serious for women, since nineteenth-century physiology regarded female health, especially mental and emotional health, as radically determined by the reproductive system.

44. Ehrmann, "Homo Ludens," 42–43.

45. Marlene Springer, in *Hardy's Use of Allusion* (Lawrence: University of Kansas Press, 1983), 50, suggests that Elfride's own quotations are also intended to undercut her, by poking fun at her "naive high seriousness," but I think that interpretation is conditioned by and grants too much authority to the narrator.

46. Elfride chooses especially ominous models in Richard II and Nelson; as Knight placidly points out, if Nelson's bravery lay in his vanity, so did his death (190).

47. Penny Boumelha, in *Thomas Hardy and Women: Sexual Ideology and Narrative Form* (Brighton, Eng.: Harvester, 1982), 32, has identified this "narrative ambivalence" as evidence of Hardy's tentative attempt, in his early novels, to "make the central female characters the subjects of their own experience, rather than the instruments of the man's." More recently, Rosemarie Morgan, in *Women and Sexuality in the Novels of Thomas Hardy* (London: Routledge, 1988), 1–29, argues that Hardy deliberately invented the voice of the sexist, moralizing commentator in *A Pair of Blue Eyes*. As Morgan sees it, this Grundyan "proprietary narrator" censures Elfride's transgressions, but in terms which palpably contradict the evidence of the rest of the text. In this way Hardy can at once present a self-assertive, sexually aware heroine, and conceal this radical project from the Grundyan forces among his critics and audience. Despite the suggestiveness of Morgan's approach, I think Hardy's allegiances were less clear-cut than she makes them. Although he clearly wants to unsettle any comfortable trust in received wisdom about women, he remains sympathetic to those who have that trust, and nostalgic for the authority which maxims such as Knight's and the narrator's lay claim to.

48. Elfride is almost stripped physically as well in the episode I am quoting from here, the cliff scene in which she rescues Knight with a rope made from her voluminous Victorian underclothes. Despite the heroism of her action, it literally and figuratively diminishes her. Immediately afterwards she becomes completely submissive to Knight, and seems "as small as an infant" (249).

49. The quotation is from Robert Burns' "Death and Doctor Hornbook" (1.6), *The Poems and Songs of Robert Burns*, ed. James Kinsley, vol. 1 (Oxford: Clarendon, 1968), 85. In its original context the quote refers to lies told by ministers and given spurious authority by biblical citation; Elfride's application of the quote to Knight subtly questions his authority as arbiter of literary and cultural worth. As Springer, *Hardy's Use of Allusion*, 47, has pointed out, Knight receives an "allusive trouncing" in *A Pair of Blue Eyes*. (Springer mentions Knight's Pauline pomposity but not, oddly, the Burns quotation.)

50. Guerard argues that Elfride turns too easily and completely into a victim,

until "she becomes a merely pathetic figure and virtually disappears from the plot" (71). J. I. M. Stewart, in *Thomas Hardy: A Critical Biography* (London: Longman, 1971), 64, notes that Elfride's "sustained bad luck" strains credibility.

Moral Authority in the Late Novels: The Gendering of Art

John Kucich

Discussions of Hardy's ethics usually focus on his struggle to break with Victorian moral standards. Most often, these discussions foreground his attacks on Victorian sexual codes, attempting to determine whether such attacks signal a more fluid ethical attitude, a systematic rejection of moral vision in general, or simply a disparate series of specific revisions.[1] In any case, what these debates often neglect are the ways in which Hardy rearticulates Victorian conditions for moral thought. Ethics is a system of symbolic distinctions upheld by various interrelated domains of cultural logic, rather than isolated sets of precepts. In such a system, change occurs in the form of extensive displacements and adjustments. If Hardy did disassemble certain features of Victorian ethics for his own ends, he was likely to have reassembled the discursive debris of that ethics in altered, but persistent forms. Ironically, by overlooking Hardy's fundamentally Victorian ethical commitments to focus on his sexual progressiveness, critics have overlooked one of the stronger sources of masculinist bias in his work. Hardy's commitment to Victorian standards of honesty—which are much more important to the Victorian ethical imagination than its more notorious sexual attitudes—may be seen as a central instance in which he transforms while preserving the basic symbolic structures of Victorian ethics, along with some of the misogynist genderings of virtue and vice that accompany them.

Buried in Hardy's high-profile challenges to sexual codes lies a basic Victorian concern for truth and honesty. In the general preface to the Wessex Edition of 1912, Hardy singled out his own artistic honesty as the strongest rebuke to those critics who found him to be without positive values: "It must be obvious that there is a higher characteristic of philosophy than pessimism, or than meliorism, or even than the optimism of these critics—which is truth" (T xii). Whenever Hardy defended his more controversial material, he always invoked the seemingly uncomplicated demands of truthfulness in writing. His "Candour in English Fiction" justifies the sexual explicitness of his novels as "sincere" and "conscientious:" "life being a physiological fact, its honest portrayal must be largely concerned with, for one thing, the relations of the sexes" (Orel 127). Even when repudiating didactic fiction, he did so in the name of a more urgent compulsion to honesty. In "The Profitable Reading of Fiction," he contended that "the novels which most conduce to moral profit are likely to be among those written without a moral purpose" because only they will achieve a "sincere presentation" (Orel 118).

Hardy's novels, however, would seem to belie such an unstudied confidence in honesty. There is a striking contrast between Hardy's apparently simple belief in his own authorial honesty and his radical skepticism about that of his characters. Squarely within the tradition of Victorian narrative, Hardy's plots pivot relentlessly around lies, or around nagging questions about his protagonists' honesty. But in Hardy's novels, the clear standards of truthtelling that always ultimately emerge in Victorian novels are constantly revealed to be inadequate. Most tellingly, the novels' plots explore the gray area between deliberate dishonesty and accidental deception, partially separating lying from intentionality. Throughout the novels, Hardy's characters seem to back into deceit inadvertently. Tess's famous confessional letter, which miscarries because it is slipped under Angel's carpet by mistake, is a classic example of this kind of inadvertent duplicity. But one need only recall the retrospective conditions of bad faith thrust by circumstances upon Stephen Smith, Michael Henchard, or Jude Fawley to recognize the systematic regularity of barriers to sincerity in Hardy's work. In general, Hardy's uncertainties about the unity or stability of the self, provoked by unanswerable questions about intentionality, seem to render the moral axis of honesty and dishonesty hopelessly problematic for his characters. Hardy's various well-known convictions about the genetic transmission of psychological flaws, the mediated nature of desire, and the interweaving of human destinies in overlapping, predetermined variations, all add to this ethical confusion by destabilizing subjectivity. Such perplexity about the self finally blocks ethical judgment.

Hardy's less troubled comments about his own authorial honesty, however, suggest that his novels' critique of honesty functions as a purgative assault on particular social and sexual categories, rather than as an indiscriminate moral despair. That is to say, Hardy sought to distinguish between various realms of moral possibility—in this first case, between art and life—in order to create scapegoats that might carry off moral confusion from the symbolic domains he wanted to protect. A more localized instance of this kind of segregation of domains involves Hardy's class-coding of moral possibilities. Specifically, Hardy's narrative critique of honesty is often meant to subvert the mid-Victorian novel's tendency to align honesty with middle-class standards of behavior. Hardy satirizes the persistence of this middle-class linkage of social merit and morality directly, for example, in Angel's appraisal of Tess's social deserts: "Distinction does not consist in the facile use of a contemptible set of conventions, but in being numbered among those who are true, and honest, and just, and pure, and lovely, and of good report—as you are, my Tess" (31.250). Angel's attitude, which cracks under the pressure of Tess's history, exemplifies middle-class moral justifications of social hierarchy that structure British novels from Richardson through George Eliot.[2] But through his skepticism about morally self-congratulating, "honorable" bourgeois men— like Angel, or like Mr. Knight in A Pair of Blue Eyes—Hardy rejects bourgeois class pride in its supposedly strict codes of honesty. Instead, however, Hardy often simply projects possibilities for honesty into more remote social sites. He was much more inclined to portray rural workers (Gabriel Oak, Dick Dewy) as uncomplicatedly honest, thereby relegating possibilities for honesty either to lower social classes, or to the superseded "traditional" past. Hardy's skeptical attacks on honesty are thus insepa- rable from his complex attempts to define his own relationship to class hierarchies. In general, Hardy's meditations on honesty are hardly uni- versalizing. Rather, they make use of moral ambivalence by differentiating the symbolic domains in which the very concept of honesty might be either affirmed or denied.

Hardy's own peculiar class pride comes to depend on claims to exem- plary honesty that are very similar to those of the middle-class figures he undermines, though they can survive only in a few carefully-protected symbolic domains. To help augment his own moral authority, Hardy ultimately aligns a resurgent form of honesty both with aesthetic conscious- ness and, more generally, with masculinity. From this point of view, Hardy's surprisingly virulent stereotypes of female dishonesty are more than just unusually pronounced instances of traditional sexism. They have a crucial role to play in defining the resurgent moral authority of the artist, distinguished by his superior ability to speak the truth. In the course of Hardy's localized destabilization of honesty in the novels, then, some of the basic procedures of Victorian moral thinking—including its reliance on honesty as a crucial element of class and sexual differentiations—are subtly reinvoked and redefined in order to uphold the cultural authority of men, and, more specifically, of an avant-garde aesthetic class that is gendered primarily as male.

The most important continuity between Hardy's ethical thought and that of his Victorian predecessors—and the symbolic equation that makes a masculinist semiotics of artistic honesty possible—is that, like the Victorians, Hardy cannot conceive sexual desire apart from concepts of moral transgression, and, in particular, from dishonesty. For Hardy, the condition of desire makes honesty impossible to define or achieve. It is crucial to understand how extensively symbolic, rather than simply logical, is the association Hardy makes between desire and dishonesty. Among Hardy's characters, dishonesty's affiliation with desire is overdetermined by a number of seemingly unrelated factors. In part, dishonesty is simply one of the desperate remedies of desire. Hardy's understanding of desire increasingly came to focus, in the later novels, on both the pathetic vulnerability to entrapment and the irresistible impulse to entrap others that desire generates.[3] But deceit in Hardy is also the inevitable product of desire's division of the subject. The tendency of desire toward inconstancy is one form this self-division takes. Another form is found in the familiar opposition of the flesh and the spirit that plagues so many of Hardy's characters, both male and female, and that forces them to betray their own efforts at sincerity. Moreover, deceitfulness often seems an integral aspect of the (feminine) object of desire itself. This notion may be travestied in Alec's accusations that Tess is a temptress, but it is made quite seriously in Jocelyn Pierston's sense that the second Avice is a "fictitious" (WB 2.6.90) copy, or even in Angel's befuddled rebuke to Tess that he had loved "another woman in your shape" (T 35.293). Finally, Hardy's systematic identification of deceit with desire resists any simple or univocal causal explanation. Hardy (the Victorian) seems determined to create a strangely absolute symbolic gap between honesty and desire, predicated on multiple and disparate sources. This confluence of apprehensions allowed Hardy to return obsessively in his plots to conjunctions of sexuality and dishonesty, and it compelled him to construct byzantine ethical dilemmas involving sex and deceit—like those of Smith or Henchard, or like Jocelyn Pierston's bizarre, comic struggle to love honestly. The middle chapters of *Tess*, in particular, are staged lopsidedly around accidents and competing pressures, as if to prove how unnatural it would be to expect that Tess's "conscientious wish for candour could hold out" (T 29.233) against desire. Even the "happy marriages" of Hardy's earlier fiction—like Fancy Day's, for example—involve the preservation of sexual secrets.

Through his maintenance of a basic symbolic linkage between desire and dishonesty, Hardy upholds a Victorian discursive system that the modern imagination has often struggled to overthrow—a system that upholds, in turn, polarizations of virtue based on sexual identity, and a gendering of art's relationship to desire. Hardy articulates the fundamental equation of desire and dishonesty most clearly in *The Well-Beloved*, especially in the 1897 version, and it is to that novel that I turn first. In revising the serial, Hardy drastically reshaped the plot by eliminating his protagonist's two marriages—the early marriage to Marcia Bencomb, and the marriage to the third Avice at the end of the novel. These changes freed the novel from the theme of mistaken marriage, and from attacks on the legal institution of marriage, which had preoccupied Hardy in many of the later works. Instead, the revised version of *The Well-Beloved* offers a relatively pure meditation on the nature of desire. What this meditation reveals is that desire must be regarded as morally problematic entirely for intrinsic reasons, rather than as a result of social injustice. This point of view was consistent with Hardy's thinking at the time: in 1896, denying that he was an advocate of "free love," he claimed that "seriously I don't see any possible scheme for the union of the sexes that [would] be satisfactory."[4] To delineate the ethical component of its apparently metaphysical meditation on the nature of desire, I look first at this final novel of Hardy's. Then, by relocating Hardy's ethical ideas about desire in *Tess of the d'Urbervilles* and *Jude the Obscure,* I can better demonstrate his social and sexual codification of honesty. In the process, I will isolate the ethical oppositions Hardy constructs in the symbolic domains of sexual desire, authorship, class, and—finally—gender, to show how the linked ethical dynamics within these various domains contributed to Hardy's masculinizing of the artist's moral authority.

The basic pretext of *The Well Beloved,* of course, is the notion of an ideal object of desire that takes up temporary residence in a sequence of individual women. For Jocelyn Pierston, there is no such thing as a first or a true love, since all the women he loves are ephemeral incarnations of an object of desire radically distinct from human selfhood. In this way, inconstancy comes to seem the basic condition of desire, the more so because Pierston cannot control the shifting of his "migratory" (3.2.158) ideal beloved. Hardy may very well have been ambivalent about Pierston's quasi-Platonic theories—similar theories are invoked cynically by Fitzpiers in *The Woodlanders.*[5] It would be an oversimplification, however, to see in *The Well-Beloved* only "contrived whimsy" or a "mock fable," as some critics have done.[6] Hardy was at pains to generalize his character's condition in the novel's preface of 1912, claiming that Pierston gives "objective continuity and a name to a delicate dream which in a vaguer form is more or less common to all men" (vii). And in the *Life,* he wrote of the novel that "there is, of course, underlying the fantasy followed by the visionary artist the truth that all men are pursuing a shadow, the Unattainable, and I venture to hope that this may redeem the tragi-comedy from the charge of frivolity" (304). In 1926, he also claimed, proudly enough, that "the theory" of the novel was a precursor of Proust's ideas about desire (466).

Pierston's sense that desire migrates away from the human shapes it pursues is also strongly reflected in other late novels. Tess, for instance, recognizes love's essential impermanence when she tells Angel frankly at the end of the novel that he will outgrow his "present feeling" (58.498) for her, and when she asks him to marry 'Liza-Lu. More importantly, as Kathleen Blake has shown, certain idealizing, de-individualizing properties of desire are more valued by Hardy in Tess than critics often recognize, since the attention of readers usually focuses only on Angel's oppressive distortions. These abstracting properties of desire underlie Tess's experience of souls leaving bodies, as well as various mystifying effects of nature, inebriation, or sexuality, which tend to blur human identity in "marginless" emotional states.[7] In Jude, Sue recognizes the unstable, impersonal aspect of desire when she admits the "insatiable" character of her "love of being loved" (4.1.245), and when she complains of expectations for constancy in the marriage vow. Arabella is blunter, answering the charge that she is "always wanting another man than [her] own" by retorting: "Well, and what woman don't I should like to know?" (5.5.354). From this point of view, we can see it as a representative condition, and not an aberrant one, that Hardy's characters always find themselves trapped between competing romantic commitments.[8] In The Well-Beloved, though, Hardy creates a plot that for the first time makes inconstancy not the partial result of accident or circumstance, but entirely the consequence of the nature of desire itself.

The theory of inconstant, idealizing desire that Pierston articulates need not logically link desire with dishonesty. Yet The Well-Beloved systematically enforces this link. The association between desire and dishonesty is even increased in Hardy's 1897 revision, which gives Pierston several significant lies not found in the serial version, and expands a narrative string of fatal broken promises (the third Avice causes her mother's death by eloping with Levarre on the eve of her wedding to Pierston). But the plots of both versions of The Well-Beloved are rampant with deceit and evasion. Pierston often comes in contact with conspiracies that remain opaque to him: he overhears the second Avice quarreling with her secret husband, but is prevented from recognizing her voice, ironically, by the marital tone of the argument; he lends a stranger a cane, not knowing that the stranger is about to elope with his bride; he watches the islanders stare at a boat in the distance, unaware that it carries the third Avice and her lover. The atmosphere of secrecy and constraint underscores the symbolic importance of the novel's numerous lies, broken promises, or manipulations: Pierston's betrayal of his promise to marry the first Avice; his lie to Marcia that legal technicalities prevent their marriage; Marcia's startling "forgetfulness" (1.8.42) of her pledge to a former lover;

the secret marriage of the second Avice; Pierston's concealment of his relationship to the second Avice's mother; the second Avice's "contrivance" (3.4.170) in engaging Pierston to her daughter; Pierston's deceptions about his age during his courtship of the third Avice. This list could be lengthened with innumerable secondary deceptions, all of them revolving around various stages of sexual desire. The well-beloved herself, the very site of sexual desire, is imagined by Pierston primarily as a duplicitous force: she is referred to as a "jade" (3.3.169) or as "capricious" (2.5.88), and she is accused of playing a "trick" (2.1.58) on Pierston or "masquerading" (1.2.11). This link between dishonesty and a feminine emblem of desire is borne out elsewhere in the novels with telling regularity, as we will see later in more detail.

Perhaps the most disturbing linkage between desire and dishonesty—given Hardy's championing of art's candor—is forged by the narrative's reflections about art itself. *The Well-Beloved* hints—like no other Hardy novel—at how tenuous the canon of artistic honesty is. In the first place, Pierston's art is conceived as the direct manifestation of inconstant or infinite desire. We are often told that the energy of Pierston's art comes from his ability to channel his idealistic, but morally dangerous, passion into sculptured form: "Jocelyn threw into plastic creations that ever-bubbling spring of emotion which, without some conduit into space, will surge upwards and ruin all but the greatest men" (1.9.49). Pierston further confesses, at one point in the serial, to have raided his love letters in order to write lyric poetry. The resulting moral ambiguity of art is everywhere acknowledged, though often ironically: "It was in his weaknesses as a citizen and a national-unit that his strength lay as an artist" (2.7.101). The essential congruity between art and inconstant desire is made absolutely clear at the end, when Pierston's loss of migratory erotic desire coincides with his loss of interest and capability in art. One must respect the seriousness of this conjunction: though Hardy may have drawn Pierston satirically from the example of Rossetti—who quite literally painted one face in many shapes—his biographers have made it clear that Hardy also crafted his own art out of his erotic experience, including his sense of sexual guilt.[9] The peculiar power of Pierston's art is also identified wholly with its nature as artifice. Pierston constantly views art as misrepresentation, as a deceptive attempt to shadow forth the original, inaccessible well-beloved. Besides the latent dishonesty of his relationship to his public—for he captures "a public taste he had never deliberately aimed at, and mostly despised" (1.9.51)—his work itself is only a series of hypocritical "failures" (2.1.64), in which he "insulted" (3.8.213) the ideal. Allegorically, this connection is strengthened at the end by Marcia's abandonment of the "artifices" (211) of beauty. Her rejection of the cosmetic means of cultivating desire, which parallels Pierston's rejection of aesthetic representations of desire, prompts her to claim that at last she has become "passably honest" (212).

Moreover, *The Well-Beloved* self-consciously lays bare the artistic devices and ruses underlying all of Hardy's own work.[10] Besides the mechanical plot twists and the stylized ironies, Hardy's highly artificial repetition of the same story in three different versions suggests his fiction's tendency to "migrate" from a single truth, to pursue overlapping but divergent plots and themes. Like Pierston's funnelling of eroticism into aesthetic form, writing for Hardy is often dangerously inconstant, or inconsistent. Although Hardy was meticulous about the realistic accuracy of his novels, he also had a persistent half-acknowledged awareness about the "falseness" of fiction. "Hence, one may say, Art is the secret of how to produce by a false thing the effect of a true," he wrote on the subject of a Royal Academy exhibition (*Life,* 226). Such remarks are more than just the concessions of a realistic novelist to late nineteenth-century aestheticism. Many of the stylistic quirks of Hardy's novels, in particular their willful evasiveness, must be understood as forms of cultivated narrative deceit intimately related to the relationship between desire and dishonesty. Hardy's prose constantly tantalizes the reader with what the narrative knows but will not tell, or what it knowingly misrepresents or evades. When Alec first leaves Tess, for example, we are told ambiguously that "he emitted a laboured breath, as if the scene were getting rather oppressive to his heart, or to his conscience, or to his gentility" (12.99). Earlier, just after Alec has called Tess "artful" (8.66), the narrator uses a coy simile to describe her walking beside Alec "thoughtfully, as if wondering whether it would be wiser to return home" (67). Hardy's style always flaunts its equivocations in this manner. The novels also pointedly exclude key scenes, like Tess's rape/seduction and her later confession, or the wording of Henchard's "carefully framed" (12.92) letter breaking his engagement to Lucetta. Any writer who planned for years to pass off his own autobiography as the work of his wife had to have a somewhat developed consciousness of the duplicities of writing.

This disturbing contamination of art with deceit, though distanced by irony in *The Well-Beloved,* and though never directly formulated by Hardy himself, suggests, nevertheless, the urgency of Hardy's strategies for ordering moral ambivalence. It expresses, again, the dilemmas of ethical contradiction to which Hardy's thinking about honesty often led him. It also suggests, as I have been arguing, that if Hardy were ever to clarify his own practice and to convince himself of his own authorial honesty, he might need to project dishonesty rather strenuously onto various scapegoats— Pierston being one. Hardy's irony about the integrity of art is, in this sense, a negative form of candor: an affirmation of the artist's ability to be honest about art's own complicity with dishonesty. Yet such irony is obviously very volatile, and needs to be stabilized. The catastrophe of any full concession of art's duplicity might ultimately be forestalled by enforcing linked ethical oppositions—between art and life, between asceticism and sexuality, between one class and another, or between men and women—in order to scapegoat one set of these terms in tandem to the advantage of the other. Even if each of these oppositions, taken in itself, might prove to be precarious, a parallel alignment of them all serves to bolster Hardy's implicit convictions about artistic moral authority.

One such linkage of ethical oppositions is Hardy's sense that desire is inextricable from social, as well as moral transgression. That is to say, a second lingering Victorianism in Hardy's work is his tacitly expressed conviction that social aspiration always has affinities with dishonesty and, by implication, with sexual desire. Characters like Alec, who is deceit incarnate and whose father is rumored to have made his fortune through usury, or Arabella, whose steady climb toward respectability depends on various ruses ("Don't you ask questions, and you won't hear lies" [JO 3.8.216], she tells one of her tavern customers), or the second Avice, who admits that she would have married Pierston for his social advantages if not for her secret marriage—all repeat in almost caricatural ways Victorian tendencies to merge moral and sexual concerns with anxieties about social mobility. The fact that these figures repeatedly prey on the exemplary trustfulness, as well as the social naiveté, of Tess, Jude, and Pierston further underscores the characteristic duplicity of individuals motivated by social ambition.[11] Hardy regularly embodies the force of desire in the symbolic domains of both social and sexual transgression, commonly linked through dishonesty.

The dishonesty of social ambition is complexly intertwined in all of Hardy's sexual relationships; it is not just a flaw of his more vulgar characters. In *Tess*, for example, Tess's "gross deceit" (37.323), as Angel terms it, is magnified not just by gender difference but also by the social disparity between the two lovers. The subdued rivalry between Tess and the other three aspirants to Angel's hand—Izz, Retty, and Marian, all of whom recognize with anguish their social unworthiness—stresses the social dimension of Tess's inadvertent dishonesty. This social dimension is also emphasized by Tess's disturbingly ambiguous desires to rise above her fellow workers. Her "triumph" (10.84) at escaping the "whole crew" of workers that she had "majestically" called "a whorage," when she leaps onto Alec's horse, and her refusal earlier that evening to dance with company she considered low and disreputable, are reflected by her consistent preference for values and behavior that are symbolically coded to class distinctions. While Tess may consciously "wish for no better" name than her own (5.48), nevertheless her desires are very much mediated by her awareness of class difference. After meeting Angel at the May Dance, she spurns her other partners because "they did not speak so nicely as the strange young man had done" (3.18). After her seduction, "at moments, in spite of thought, she would reply to their inquiries with a manner of superiority, as if recognizing that her experiences in the field of courtship had, indeed, been slightly enviable" (13.106). Such moments are less an indictment of Tess than a testament to the ineradicability of socially mediated desire. Hardy has created neither a social saint nor a fool in Tess but rather a woman trapped in bad faith through the inexorable intersections of social and sexual desire.

Angel's love for Tess rests, in turn, on slightly more ephemeral signs of her social superiority. Though Angel despises "the material distinctions of rank and wealth" (18.150), he is attracted to Tess for less material signs of such distinction. He relishes the fact that Tess "though but a milkmaid had that touch of rarity about her which might make her the envied of her housemates" (19.160). In reflecting on the difference between "the political value and the imaginative value" (49.436) of her genealogy, Angel "thought now that he could see therein a flash of the dignity which must have graced her grand-dames." As Angel dwells on her superiority to other women, his terms identify character traits with class hierarchies (e.g., her "dignity"). The narrative itself constantly draws our attention to culturally coded signs of Tess's superiority, speaking of "the soberer richer note of Tess among those of the other work-people" (10.82), or of her greater "eloquence" (2.12).

Similarly, Jude's love for Sue is continually mediated by his awareness of symbolic social hierarchies, by the parallels between Sue's "pureness" and the ideals embodied in social stations above his own. Hardy reinforces these parallels between a certain kind of sexual desirability and class ideals in various ways. He stresses Jude's perception of Sue as "elegant" (2.2.105), "elevating," and "refined" (6.3.414), not "gross" and "earthly" (4.5.294)—terms Jude uses to describe himself. He also makes it clear that Jude's aspirations in general depend on the mediation of social hierarchies: "Yet he sometimes felt that by caring for books he was not escaping commonplace nor gaining rare ideas, every working-man being of that taste now" (1.10.76). Jude's outburst in the Christminster tavern reveals a kind of class contempt that conditions all of his desires: "See what I have brought myself to—the crew I have come among" (2.7.145), he complains bitterly, locating his intellectual failure in class terms. In contrast to Jude's own wish for a clean opposition between intellectual promotion and sexual desire, the entanglement of the two is dramatized by frequent comparisons of Christminster to a woman: "like a young lover alluding to his mistress, he felt bashful at mentioning its name again" (1.3.22). Just as he imagines that Sue, that "disembodied creature" (4.5.294), will elevate him above the earthly, so, too, he fantasizes that once inside Christminster's hallowed buildings, "he might some day look down on the world through their panes" (2.2.100–101).

In general, Hardy insisted that, whatever his characters' attempts to transcend concerns of social class, the social axis is an inextricable part of their desire. His characters' blindness to this intersection only leads to various kinds of misrepresentation, including self-deception. It is not simply that Hardy seeks to dramatize the realities of class conflict by foregrounding the social barriers his lovers must overcome; rather, he stigmatizes all desire by invoking the inevitable duplicities of social mobility that it generates. The betrayal of one lover for another, for example, and therefore the violation of pledges of constancy, most often takes place upward along a social gradient. In *The Well-Beloved*, Pierston's one and only betrayal—of the first Avice—is committed for the sake of a woman who, at the time, presents an advantageous match for him. In *Jude,* Sue's eventual marriage to Phillotson is mediated by her conventional sense of her social obligations. Her final commitment to Phillotson, which betrays Jude's "love of truth" (6.10.484)—even Arabella knows that any of Sue's self-justifications "won't be true" (6.11.494)—is compromised in its honesty not just by her own divided affections, but by the general return to middle-class respectability that she has chosen.

Hardy entangles dishonesty between lovers in the inequities of class partly, of course, to express his sense of the alienating effects of nineteenth-century social transformations. He frequently dramatized the growing gulf between self-awareness and class in his characters' sense of inner exile from their social identities.[12] This gulf, however, becomes simply another division within subjectivity that further disrupts the conditions necessary for honesty. Even those characters like Angel, Pierston, or Sue, who try to flaunt their downward mobility as evidence of the purity of their love, covertly undermine their claims to social disinterest by invoking signs of social distinction or aspiration. Some use the contrast of stations itself, the self-conscious inversion of social aspiration, to stress the superior refinement of their love—thereby entangling themselves in even greater contradictions. For Pierston, the disparity between his social station and the vulgarity of the second Avice only confirms for him that his desire is directed toward an ideal, a goddess that transcends all social classification. Yet the relationship of commodification between Pierston's ideal beloved and the artistic works that have elevated him socially makes it quite impossible to separate his desire from social mobility, and thus from the stigma of dishonesty always attached to such mobility.

Hardy was himself both plagued and fascinated by the guilt he associated with social desire. He insisted, defensively, on the complete lack of commercial ambition in his father and grandfather (as well as in himself), and his refusal to cultivate social connections in London was a constant source of tension with Emma.[13] Yet Hardy's gestures of social disinterest are fully consistent both with secret pleasure in his own dramatic rise, and with an awareness that it was made possible by the "falseness" of fiction—a situation he satirized self-consciously in *The Hand of Ethelberta,* as well as in *The Well-Beloved.* Partly because of his struggles with vocational choice—literature or architecture, poetry or fiction—Hardy was preoccupied with what he saw as the fundamental incompatibility of noble or lofty ideas and social success: "It is, in a worldly sense, a matter for regret that a child who has to win a living should be born of a noble nature. Social greatness requires littleness to inflate & float it, & a high soul may bring a man to the workhouse."[14] Trite as such convictions may be, one crucial corollary for Hardy is that sexual desire, too, becomes incompatible with the loftiness of disinterest, and is hopelessly entangled with ambition, in ways that make coming clean about one's desire a contradiction in terms. Hardy always imagines sexual desire as both morally and socially transgressive, the expression of a general, "natural" dishonesty. As a consequence of this linkage, his efforts to fortify distinctions between honesty and dishonesty necessarily come to depend heavily on oppositions constructed around gender. In fact, gender distinctions prove crucial to Hardy's attempts to establish a domain of ethical purity that he identifies, ultimately, with artistic perception.

Although Hardy systematically banishes honesty from the domain of desire, his moral commitment to honesty is by no means weakened as a result. Gestures of fidelity or honesty in the novels are a constant counterweight to Hardy's association of desire with dishonesty. The novels often feature unambiguous moments of honesty and in some cases give such honesty heroic proportions: Jude's gratuitous confession to Phillotson of the exact state of his relations to Sue; Izz Huett's admission of Tess's devotion to Angel. One of the fascinating complications of *The Well-Beloved,* in fact, is its elaborate celebration of moral earnestness. In terms of fidelity, for example, Pierston's desire may be inherently inconstant to individual women, but he argues strenuously with Somers that he never deviates from fidelity to the ideal itself. The narrator confirms the point: "To his Well-Beloved he had always been faithful" (1.2.10). Although it may not be clear exactly what this means, Pierston seems to claim that he never allows personal or selfish desires—what he calls "wanton" impulse (1.7.38)—to divert him from his idealism. In this sense, even Pierston's initial betrayal of Avice can be understood, as a form of fidelity. For in leaving Avice for Marcia, Pierston resists a wayward impulse that had nothing to do with the well-beloved, since his ideal never inhabits the first Avice, but does reside in Marcia. Whatever the ambiguities here, Pierston eventually does become strictly faithful to a single image of the beloved repeated in three generations of women, which gives the notion of fidelity some tenuous physical substance. The plot is also arranged so that Pierston never technically jilts anyone, despite his dangerous desires. The women who incarnate the well-beloved always leave him, or are taken from him: "Not a woman in the world had been wrecked by him, though he had been impassioned by so many" (3.7.202). It would be easier to regard such claims as ironic if they came from Pierston himself, rather than from the narrator. The mixture of fidelity and infidelity in Pierston's treatment of the first Avice, or any of his other women, is flagrantly contradictory, in ways that suggest an irresolvable dynamic between two distinct aspects of Pierston's character. The contradictions appear in numerous elliptical contrasts: in the course of his betrayal of the first Avice, for instance, what Pierston experiences emotionally is actually his scrupulous fidelity to Marcia: "He felt bound in honor to remain . . . as long as there was the slightest chance of Marcia's reappearance" (1.8.46). The apparent inconsistencies of Pierston's character are constructed around a dynamic doubleness, in which constancy and inconstancy, as well as honesty and dishonesty, are in perpetual tension, but without ever disrupting each other—inconsistencies that seem to parallel the latent, inconsistent relationship of Hardyan art itself to both honesty and dishonesty.

In Pierston's case, a number of important features prevent this doubleness from being simply an incoherence. Through the linked oppositions I have been tracing, Hardy's performatively "candid" exploration of the moral ambiguities threatened by Pierston is firmly anchored in Victorian ideology. To begin with, what is striking about the odd emphasis on fidelity in The Well-Beloved (in the last chapter, Pierston and Marcia smugly compel the third Avice to return to her husband) is that it is routinely externalized from desire itself, and made to express forces of character peripheral to desire, if not the sign of its triumphal suppression, or its complete exhaustion. Pierston's final vow of fidelity to Marcia depends precisely on the loss of his own capacity for desire: "I have no love to give," he says, "But such friendship as I am capable of is yours till the end" (3.8.216). The couple's mutual honesty about aging puts them both beyond desire, in a companionate marriage more extremely chaste even than Victorian domestic ideals. Because of this possibility of a victory over desire, The Well-Beloved—alone among the later works—is able to end "happily."

In other novels, Hardy suggests possibilities of a kind of fidelity beyond desire, but is unable to represent the condition of desirelessness quite so thoroughly. When Angel overcomes his prejudices and returns to Tess, for example, the quality of his love is altered, made milder—it becomes a kind of "fondness" (49.434), which contrasts sharply with Alec's reawakened "passion" (46.403) for Tess. The possibility that Angel might fulfill his vow to marry 'Liza-Lu also leaves us with the prospect of a desexualized marriage—'Liza-Lu is "a spiritualized image of Tess" (59.506). In *The Woodlanders*, the serene faithfulness of Giles Winter-bourne and Marty South depends on their radical freedom from sexual desire. Marty, in particular, "touched sublimity at points, and looked almost like a being who had rejected with indifference the attribute of sex for the loftier quality of abstract humanism" (48.443). Even the occasional happy endings of the earlier novels, as in *Far From the Madding Crowd*, feature marriages of people who, as J. Hillis Miller puts it, "have outlived the time when they might have sought the bliss of full union with another person."[15] Honesty and fidelity are so imperilled by the encroachments of desire in Hardy's work—both social and sexual desire—that he can reimagine them only as a stringent distantiation from it.

A second, crucial component of Hardy's resuscitation of honesty is his projection of dishonesty systematically onto women. Readers have often commented on Hardy's negative stereotypes of women, but his attack on feminine dishonesty in particular is worth reexamining, both because of the chain of symbolic connections on which it depends and because of its dialectical creation of a precious space of male honesty. Though the assertion must be qualified in important ways, Hardy's women are regularly aligned with emotionalism, as opposed to the customary rationality of his men. Everything Sue does "seemed to have its source in feeling" (2.4.120), and Tess is "a vessel of emotions rather than reasons" (47.421). Many readers have noted that Hardy's women are further identified with sexual emotion. While the crisis in Hardy's novels for men is often intellectual, for women it is always sexual in nature.[16] As we have seen, the nature of Hardyan sexuality is inherently inconstant and duplicitous, the enemy of sincerity. Hardy's narrator persistently generalizes about women's linked affinity with the emotions and with dishonesty. In *Jude*, commenting on one of Sue's incomplete confessions, he observes that "a contrite woman always keeps back a little" (6.9.479). In *The Return of the Native*, we hear of "the fact of the indirectness of a woman's movement towards her desire" (4.2.293). As a result of this conjunction, women are more consistently associated with the pattern of sexual entrapment in Hardy than are men.[17] Instances of entrapment by men are often made to appear aberrant, or are qualified by greater male capacities for self-consciousness and self-renunciation.

Hardy's men, by virtue of their greater distance from emotion and from desire, acquire an aura of truthfulness by contrast. The novels consistently feature men who, however passionate, transcend the temptations of passion and resist the contaminating influence of their desire—as we will see more clearly when we consider the issue of male observation of women. Hardy could not, of course, draw an absolute distinction between the sexes in their capacities for moral transgression. His sense of the link between dishonesty and desire was far too strict for that. The novels do, of course, feature male characters who are also identified with emotion and with deceit—Wildeve, Fitzpiers, or Sergeant Troy, among others. Yet it is crucial to note that such men are often diagnosed as the source of great social and sexual disturbance, and that the deviance they represent is often almost ritualistically purged from the novels, either through their deaths or through other persistent signs of fatality (as in Grace Melbury's ominous reunion with Fitzpiers). Many of these men are also explicitly feminized—in physical description and in terms of a certain impulsiveness that Hardy often uses to align the feminine with inconstant behavior. Most important, fundamentally dishonest men are always closely paired and contrasted with almost preternaturally honest male characters—Winterbourne, Diggory Venn, Gabriel Oak—as a way to objectify their deviance. Moreover, Hardy permits even his more morally tortured male protagonists greater opportunities than his women to overcome, finally, their own weaknesses for desire and the dishonesty it entails. Consider the compulsive, morally compromised acts of Tess and Sue at the conclusions of their narratives, in contrast to the long trajectory toward philosophical clarity and detachment that marks the moral progress of Angel and Jude. All these strategies help to project onto women the ethically problematic qualities of desire. What often results is simply a more negative interpretation of the inflexibility of female dishonesty in desire or an excessively stark delineation of feminine dishonesty. The second Avice, for example, who shares more than anyone else Pierston's addiction to inconstancy, is derogated as "common" (2.7.102), as a "very wicked woman" (2.12.134), or even as an "elf" and a "witch" (3.2.155). In opposition, the symbolic terrain of the masculine—rather than all of Hardy's male characters individually—becomes a theater of charged moral ambivalence that can lead to resurgent moral purity, either through self-resistance or through resistance to the deviant examples of other villified men or of unregenerate women. In these ways, masculinity comes to partake of the same dynamic ethical ambivalence—as well as possibilities for purity through the strenuous expulsion of that moral confusion—that conditions Hardy's sense of authorship itself. In general, by regularizing female deceit, and by positing male ambivalence as an arena of dynamic resistance to dishonesty, Hardy creates ethical standards in severely gendered terms.

One inevitable correlative of this sexual stigmatization of women is their greater identification with social ambition. Early heroines like Fancy Day, Elfride Swancourt, and, of course, Ethelberta Petherwin, give dishonesty in service of social mobility a distinctly feminine stamp. In the later novels, Arabella and the second Avice are the most glaring instances of this equation, but even Tess's evasions are linked to her social gain. Sue's dishonesty about the nature of her desire, as we have noted, takes the form of a grasping for respectability as well. While Jude's sexual desires, like Angel's, may also be associated with social hierarchies through the mediation of symbolic forms, they are never graphed in terms of achieved economic or class gains. In these ways, women are more consistently and more overtly tied to the practices of class, and thus more compromised in their cultural and erotic idealism than men. In *Under the Greenwood Tree,* Fancy Day's letter of confession to Maybold makes the association clear: "It is my nature—perhaps all women's—to love refinement of mind and manners; but even more than this, to be ever fascinated with the idea of surroundings more elegant and pleasing than those which have been customary. . . . Ambition and vanity they would be called; perhaps they are so" (4.7.189). We might very well wonder that this stigmatization of female ambition is so routinely echoed, by Hardy and by his biographers, in the projection of social aspiration onto the women in his life, particularly his mother and Emma.[18]

Hardy's division of gender along an axis of sexual and social desire overlaps with the most important opposition in his rearticulation of honesty: his attempt to attribute honesty to artistic observation, that is, to the vantage that art holds over life. In Hardy, the desirelessness achievable within artistic perception always depends on confining desire to the (feminine) object of observation. While the detached, spectatorlike posture of Hardy's narrators seems to correspond simply to Hardy's own faith in the documentary qualities of fiction, the honesty that accrues to artistic consciousness finds its foundation primarily in Hardy's sexually coded representation of the act of observation itself.

Observation in Hardy is always represented as distinctly double. Much has been said recently of the appropriative gaze of desire in Hardy, and its primary affinity with male desire.[19] Self-consciously, the novels consistently feature scenes of male observation of women that suggest the projective, inaccurate perspective of observers who are contaminated by desire. But Hardy doubles the trope of a misrepresenting male gaze by postulating as well certain male observers who have escaped their desire and have presumably achieved truthful perception as a consequence. The novels repeatedly dramatize privileged moments of honest and accurate observation in which men successfully oppose themselves to the sexuality they survey in women. Jude's sudden, sympathetic recognition of Arabella at the end of their life together, for instance, takes shape as a moment in which he observes her hysteria without desire: "Jude was exasperated, and went out to drag her in by main force. Then he suddenly lost his heat. Illuminated with the sense that all was over between them and that it mattered not what she did, or he, her husband stood still, regarding her. Their lives were ruined, he thought" (1.11.80). Later, Jude watches her with "the eye of a dazed philosopher" (3.8.216) when he encounters her unexpectedly in a Christminster tavern and finds her flirting with a customer. In a related fashion, when Phillotson spies on Sue's meeting with Jude, he is freed of his own desire for her, and gains an honest appreciation of the two cousins' love for each other that convinces him, disinterestedly, to dissolve his own marriage to Sue.

Throughout the novels, male characters occasionally attain this plane of accurate observation, on condition that they free themselves of desire for the sexually-active women they observe. Gabriel Oak spies protectively on Bathsheba's trysts, motivated by his constancy. Diggory Venn, who has put himself outside social and romantic relations entirely, is an accurate, clandestine, almost choral observer of both Eustacia and Thomasin. Never do women observe men in Hardy with the same transcendence of desire at stake. Hardy's narrators implicitly try to echo this sexually coded objectivity, in a form of detachment that Miller has described as outside of desire, or, indeed, "outside of life."[20] Hardy's characteristically tragic or pessimistic view itself must be understood in both moral and sexual terms, as a perspective of honest (male) recognition of sexual fatality, which may be focused on the impossible contradictions of dishonest (female) desire, thereby gendering the relation of art to life.

The real moral hero of the late novels is aesthetic perception. And for Hardy, the honesty of art—which must be achieved through an act of energetic resistance, given the potentials for aesthetic duplicity that we have seen—is constructed mainly through a series of linked negations that depend on detached observation: negations of femininity, of sexual desire, of lived experience, of social ambition, and even, in a form of ironic doubling, of art itself. The production of artistic honor through negation is most visible in the moral progress of Pierston, in which sustained aesthetic concentration leads finally even to the rejection of art as a career. Significantly, all Hardy's late protagonists are affiliated with aesthetic sensibility—but not with artistic vocations—through their pointedly peripheral forms of artistry: Angel's harp-playing and his study of musical scores;

Jude's stonework, his urban model design, his interest in music, and his creative pastry. More important, all exhibit a kind of immaterial aesthetic perception through their self-negating visionary tendencies. And all aspire ultimately, like Pierston, to be beyond both sexual and social desire, even if there is always a shortfall between their persistent worldly involvements and the narrator's implicitly perfect removal.

Aesthetic consciousness, once defined as impassive distance—rather than as the production of artistic works themselves—acquires moral authority in Hardy not simply through a naked appropriation of middle-class standards of honesty but also by making honesty a negative condition. In Hardy honesty is available only to those who, like artists, are in some sense able to negate the pressures of their desire. Moral authority, then, is representable only as an act of refusal that must oppose and judge the desires of others. The will-to-honesty lies outside any reconciliation between self and others, which is one reason Hardyan honesty relies so much on acts of exclusion. Aesthetic consciousness also surrounds the detached observer in a specific aura of classlessness, by opposing his observation to the worldly involvement he reports in others. In effect, while Hardy's radical destabilization of honesty makes it possible to subvert the moral authority of middle-class ideals, it allows him to exalt instead the moral authority of those whose class position appears to be unresolvable, as a sign of distance from desire. The fantasy of social indifference this distance involves is played out in Pierston's utter disdain for advantageous matches, as well as in his contempt for commercial success, which parallels Hardy's publicly staged disdain for social standards about art. But all the late protagonists range themselves against the sordidness of social ambition, and aspire to escape social classification completely. All aspire as well to the perfect distance from themselves that Hardy claimed to have acquired, as an enabling condition of his autobiography: he once told Sydney Cockerell that he could "think with almost complete detachment" about his youthful self (*Life*, xi).

Art's special relationship to honesty, as we have seen, is dynamically, dangerously entwined with the moral ambivalence Hardy identifies with every form of human aspiration. Yet through a process of self-reflexiveness, in which the dishonesty of desire is objectified through clear self-perception, such dishonesty can be distanced or expelled. The resulting contradictoriness about art's ethical status, it should be noted, typifies much modernist irony, not just Hardy's. While Hardy appropriates bourgeois ethics, as a crucial device of his cultural authority, he refuses to subscribe to it simplistically, in the name of a more sophisticated consciousness of the transgressiveness of all desire. This transgressiveness forms a limit to bourgeois capabilities for honesty; that is, aesthetic honesty recognizes the impossibility of any worldly honesty. Yet it allows the artist honestly and objectively to represent, from the vantage of an aesthetic distance, the ethical failures of all human activity, even, in a restricted sense, of art itself. Hardy's favored characters sometimes achieve a similarly honest perception of the dishonesty of their own desire, and it is this internal moral dynamism through self-observation that often defines their social singularity. The paradox is frequently made explicit in these characters' thoughts about sexual fidelity. The nonmarriage of Jude and Sue, what they refer to as "our dream" (5.4.345), has as its presupposition the notion that fidelity depends on an honest admission that desire is inconstant, a paradox that only Jude, ultimately, seems able to endure. But it is partly this impossible double consciousness that makes them a "more exceptional couple" (5.5.357). In their honest perceptions about the inevitability of dishonesty, Hardy's protagonists are represented as exceptional to characters who never struggle with such ambivalence, or who never recognize its centrality in ethical experience.

For Hardy, the social distinction of aesthetic consciousness is grounded ultimately in the dynamic, performatively "candid" apprehension of both desire and morality, dishonesty and honesty, worldliness and detachment, as well as in the possibilities for the distantiation of dishonesty that this candid apprehension makes available. Unfortunately, such distantiation depends fundamentally on a kind of symbolic scapegoating that uses gender as a springboard for ethical purification. Hardy's ethical imagination may be complex and contradictory, but it is hardly confused. Its chief innovation is the grafting of a middle-class Victorian moral discourse onto the separate cultural authority of aesthetic observation, and the subtle transformation of nineteenth-century standards of honesty—which Victorian culture also identified primarily with men—by focusing them on the detached recognition of their opposite, that is, on the inherent transgressiveness of desire. From a middle-class perspective, this shift, then, ought to have seemed scandalous, not Hardy's sexually explicit material itself. From a critical perspective, this shift underlies the moral authority of modernist distantiations of both subjectivity and desire, as well as the underlying masculinist current that such aesthetic detachment often sustains.

NOTES

1. For an example of the first line of argument, see John Holloway's famous essay in *The Victorian Sage: Studies in Argument* (London: Macmillan, 1953), 244–89. An influential claim for Hardy's moral nihilism is Robert C. Schweik, "Moral Perspective in *Tess of the d'Urbervilles,*" *College English* 24 (1962): 14–18.

2. Michael McKeon has summarized the principles, if not the extended develop-

ment, of the merit/morality connection in *The Origins of the English Novel, 1600–1740* (Baltimore: Johns Hopkins University Press, 1987), 212–70.

3. As Alexander Fischler points out, in "Gins and Spirits: The Letter's Edge in Hardy's *Jude the Obscure*," *SNNTS* 16 (1984): 1–19, Hardy's growing sense of the fatal link between entrapment and desire eliminates any of the lightness of seduction present in the early novels.

4. Richard Little Purdy and Michael Millgate, eds., *The Collected Letters of Thomas Hardy* (Oxford: Clarendon Press, 1978–88), 7 vols., 1 June 1896, 2: 122.

5. This is a point made by Michael Millgate, *Thomas Hardy: A Biography* (London: Oxford University Press, 1982), 330.

6. George Wing, "Theme and Fancy in Hardy's *The Well-Beloved*," *Dalhousie Review*, 56 (1977): 633; Michael Ryan, "One Name of Many Shapes: *The Well-Beloved*," *Critical Approaches to the Fiction of Thomas Hardy*, ed. Dale Kramer (London: Macmillan, 1979), 176.

7. Kathleen Blake, "Pure Tess: Hardy on Knowing a Woman," *SEL* 22 (1982): 689–705.

8. J. Hillis Miller, *Thomas Hardy: Distance and Desire* (Cambridge: Harvard University Press, 1970), 115–16, points out that we are always introduced to Hardy's characters at the moment of a displacement in their affections.

9. For the connection with Rossetti, see J. B. Bullen, *The Expressive Eye: Fiction and Perception in the Work of Thomas Hardy* (London: Oxford University Press, 1986), 236.

10. See the comments of J. Hillis Miller, "Introduction," *The Well-Beloved* (London: Macmillan, 1975), 14.

11. Patricia Alden, *Social Mobility in the English Bildungsroman: Gissing, Hardy, Bennett, and Lawrence* (Ann Arbor: University Microfilms International, 1986), 42, has described the "typical" Hardy protagonist as a figure who finds that his mixed social and psychological "attempt to enlarge himself involves him in some deception, secrecy, or betrayal."

12. See George Wotton, *Thomas Hardy: Towards a Materialist Criticism* (Totowa, N.J.: Barnes, 1985), 52.

13. See also Millgate, *Thomas Hardy*, 9; *Life*, 9; or Alden, *Social Mobility*, 44.

14. Richard H. Taylor, ed., *The Personal Notebooks of Thomas Hardy*, (London: Macmillan, 1978), 6.

15. Miller, *Thomas Hardy*, 54.

16. See Penny Boumelha, *Thomas Hardy and Women: Sexual Ideology and Narrative Form* (Sussex: Harvester, 1982), 48; or Patricia Stubbs, *Women and Fiction: Feminism and the Novel, 1880–1920* (Sussex: Harvester, 1979), 58–87.

17. See Fischler, "Gins and Spirits," 2.

18. Millgate, *Thomas Hardy*, 21, follows Hardy in identifying his mother as the source of the family's social ambition. Emma's disappointed social-climbing is a persistent theme of the Millgate biography. See also Robert Gittings, *Young Thomas Hardy* (London: Heinemann, 1975), 136.

19. Perhaps the best account is Kaja Silverman, "History, Figuration and Female Subjectivity in *Tess of the d'Urbervilles*," *Novel* 18 (1984): 5–28. See also Boumelha, *Thomas Hardy and Women*, 32–36; 120–22.

20. Miller, *Thomas Hardy,* 7. Mary Jacobus, "Hardy's Magian Retrospect," *Essays in Criticism* 32 (1982): 258–79, describes Hardy's narrative posture of seeing and speaking as if from beyond the grave.

"A Complicated Position for a Woman": The Hand of Ethelberta

Penny Boumelha

The Hand of Ethelberta has never been among the most popular of Hardy's novels, though its contemporary readers seem to have felt more kindly toward it than many modern critics; Irving Howe's descriptions of it as "execrable" and "trash" only put intemperately what has commonly been a more discreetly worded verdict.[1] *The Hand of Ethelberta* fits only uneasily into that long-dominant characterisation of the novels as pessimistic, doom-ridden chronicles of rural decline, leavened with the occasional charmingly nostalgic pastoral. It is a comedy, for one thing; contemporary critics remarked upon its "delicate satire" and its "tender irony," which Havelock Ellis considered even to be "the most characteristic outcome of his genius."[2] Then too, it has an urban setting and aristocratic characters, even though Emma Hardy allegedly objected to the book on the grounds that "it had 'too much about servants in it,'"[3] and it has a purposeful heroine who takes things quite successfully into her own hands. But looked at now in the light of feminist criticism, it appears as a fascinatingly experimental work which never allows us to lose sight of the fact that its socially mobile, writing, active protagonist is a woman, nor that this provokes far-reaching changes in the plot paradigms (a "hero's plot" of ambition and a "heroine's plot" of romance) on which it draws and their ideological implications. Of course, even the most realist of plots do not simply reflect the real options and conditions of women in the world. Nevertheless, in the representation of what we might, following Rachel Blau DuPlessis, call "woman as a narrated group"[4] there is a metaphorical relation to those real options, and to their social and ideological conditions of possibility. In Ethelberta Chickerel's ascent from below stairs to Enckworth Court, we do not, certainly, discover much about the route or frequency of class transition for Victorian women. But the novel's manipulation of the plots of social mobility and marriage demonstrates how the ideas of ambition, success, family responsibility and self-fulfilment which must be negotiated in the process of such class transition are specifically inflected through ideologies of gender, in ways which in fact permeated the lives of Victorian women. And in the figure of Ethelberta as producer of language (writer, storyteller, coiner of aphorisms for the edification of her sister), there is in turn some interrogation of the status of those plots of mobility and stability in their relation to gender.

Ethelberta on the Rise

Franco Moretti has commented on the "peculiarly 'innocent' way of seeing and presenting itself typical of the English middle class. Whereas in France, or in Dostoevsky, this class identifies itself with *mobility*, even to the point of transgression or crime, in England it is the champion of the opposite values: security, stability, transparency."[5] Such "innocence" in the service of the status quo underpins the self-image of the Victorian bourgeoisie as heirs and guardians of a meritocratic society, in which poetic justice has become merely prosaic and in which success in the world and individual moral qualities will guarantee one another. Strikingly often, it appears that one does not *become* a success at all; the plots of finding one's place that abound in Victorian fiction commonly depict, not the transgressive mobility that Moretti detects elsewhere, but the confirmation of a preexisting class position—a confirmation often mediated by tropes of the reclamation of inheritance or the rediscovery of family. The dynamic basis of the idea of meritocracy reveals itself to be, at bottom, an illusion, and what is at stake is rather the preservation of stability. Nonetheless, the ideology of class position as the recognition of individual merit, is a powerful one, and one which shapes many of the "hero's plots" of Victorian fiction to some degree.

The great literary vehicle for the meritocratic myth in this period is of course the *Bildungsroman* and it is in *Jude the Obscure* that Hardy most directly confronts this form and its ideological underpinnings. The novel begins as if it should fit into the biographical-meritocratic mould of the English *Bildungsroman;* certainly, Jude appears to have the very qualities (ambition, dedication) that might, in another novel, have led him toward some moderate worldly success, some degree of satisfaction of personal aspiration. But here they notably fail to do so, and he ends as he begins: obscure. Among the reasons for this is the way in which Hardy takes at its word, so to speak, the individualistic nature of this ideology and makes his hero so truly a lone individual; Jude has no immediate family, no workmates, and, for the greater part of the book, no society in which he has known place. As he comes into contact with those who control the means to success—employers, teachers, heads of educational institutions, and so on—he finds in them neither the long-lost relatives nor the intercepted inheritances so beloved of the nineteenth-century novel. There is, rather, a continual confrontation with what lies, precisely, beyond the control of his individual qualities of will and desire.

Jude diverges from the more orthodox hero of such a novel, of course, in that he is not middle class, and once the ground of the meritocratic myth is shifted beyond the dominant class whose interests it serves, it comes to seem much more obviously myth. For Jude Fawley to become successful, in the social-material terms that the myth posits, would require a class transition more radical than anything that happens to the impoverished or endangered bourgeois hero of the *Bildungsroman*. When he attempts to break through the barriers of class privilege by entering a Christminster college, he draws from the Master of Biblioll a response in which two of the great Victorian social ideologies are thrown directly into conflict. The letter runs:

> SIR,—I have read your letter with interest; and, judging from your description of yourself as a working-man, I venture to think that you will have a much better chance of success in life by remaining in your own sphere and sticking to your trade than by adopting any other course. That, therefore, is what I advise you to do. Yours faithfully,
> T. TETUPHENAY (JO 2.6.143)

Stressed by their insolent juxtaposition, the incompatibility of these two desiderata—a "chance of success in life," "remaining in your own sphere"— becomes only too blatant. What Jude, and what the reader, encounters here is the blank refusal of his society to yield what his individual qualities might seem to deserve. The mutual mirroring of inner life and social plot is fractured, and, by one of those inversions of the classic English *Bildungsroman* in which the novel abounds, Jude's very sincerity serves to guarantee his unsuccess.

But if *Jude the Obscure* constitutes Hardy's most searching interrogation of the plot of male social mobility through education and vocation, then in *The Hand of Ethelberta* he takes on in a similarly self-conscious fashion what was unquestionably, throughout the nineteenth century, the predominant mode of social mobility for the heroine: the marriage plot. In much of Hardy's work, issues of class expectations and allegiances and issues of gender determination converge upon the act of apparent erotic free will that is the choice of a marriage partner. But the essentially comic structure of the romance plot becomes increasingly problematic in the course of his writing. His more comic mode is closely connected with the extent to which his female protagonist is able to exercise the power of choice, and in this he is at one with George Meredith. Meredith's "Essay: On the Idea of Comedy and the Uses of the Comic Spirit," published in the year following *The Hand of Ethelberta*, specifically relates comedy to the social status and the linguistic freedom of women: "Now, Comedy is the fountain of sound sense: not the less perfectly sound on account of the sparkle: and Comedy lifts women to a station offering them free play for their wit, as they usually show it, when they have it, on the side of sound sense."[6] Indeed, Meredith goes so far as to propose that "there never will be civilization where Comedy is not possible; and that comes of some degree of social equality of the sexes"(31).

Hardy is nowhere more Meredithian than in the social satire of *The Hand of Ethelberta*, and he nowhere gives us a more *active* female protagonist than here; that perfectly ambiguous title draws attention to the way in which the passive female plot of the nineteenth-century heroine (as we might say: her hand is sought) is here transformed into something rather different. The "Hand" that controls Ethelberta's marital destiny belongs, not to fate, but to the heroine herself,[7] and her sister too is prepared to cast her in the role of "an eternal Providence" (*Sequel*, 459). In the course of the novel, indeed, Hardy takes up, repeats, inverts and modifies this "heroine's plot" through a range of different characters and allusions. In the figure of Picotee, we find it restated in the more or less orthodox form: single-hearted, tender, Picotee loves her man at once but waits until she is sought. But it is evident that, just as the character of Picotee is only a pale shadow of the "vigorous shape" (4.39) of her sister, "what the moon is to the sun, a star to the moon" (45.420), so is her story only a faded version of the straightforward marital plot. It is not only in the marriage register that the writing of Ethelberta seems to make the writing of Picotee dwindle into virtual insignificance: "[Ethelberta's] strokes were firm, and comparatively thick for a woman's. . . . In the space for witness's names appeared in trembling lines as fine as silk the autograph of Picotee" (45.410–11).

What is most unconventional about the marriage plot of Ethelberta Chickerel, though, is not the question of *whom* she will marry: fairy-tale plots in the Cinderella mould have accustomed us to such spectacular ascents through the class system. It is, rather, the degree of consciousness with which the marriage is brought about that surprises the reader, and this point becomes clear if Hardy's protagonist is compared with another comic heroine, Austen's Elizabeth Bennet.

Elizabeth is by no means the most passive of heroines, of course, and in particular she is allowed a striking degree of linguistic activity. She speaks her feelings to an extent unusual in a female character of the period and all the more so in that her love for Darcy is stressed at a point when she cannot be sure that it is reciprocated: "She was humbled, she was grieved; she repented, though she hardly knew of what. She became jealous of his esteem when she could no longer hope to be benefited by it. She wanted to hear of him, when there seemed the least chance of gaining intelligence. She was convinced that she could have been happy with him; when it was no longer likely they should meet."[8] Nevertheless, in *Pride and Prejudice* marriage is to be achieved only by a combination of luck and the display of attractions and accomplishments which become devalued as soon as their marketability comes to seem in any way calculated or acknowledged. That, after all, is the reason why Miss Bingley is satirized, and the reason why her pursuit of Darcy is doomed (or at least, the *other* reason: the first is that convention of plot by which we expect the heroine herself to make the most successful marriage). Her obvious and fulsome praise of his handwriting, and her parading about the drawing-room to show her figure to its best advantage, are simply too transparent as a scheme, and the condemnation of them is generalized from individual to generic woman by Darcy: " 'Undoubtedly . . . there is meanness in *all* the arts which ladies sometimes condescend to employ for captivation. Whatever bears affinity to cunning is despicable' " (34).

It is also so with the mothers of marriageable daughters: Mrs. Bennet's concern with getting her daughters well married is shown to be culpable, not so much in its degree as in its *style*. She is simply too obvious. This emerges at the very beginning of the novel, when Mr. Bennet questions whether Bingley's removal to Netherfield is motivated by the search for a bride:

> "My dear Mr. Bennet," replied his wife, "how can you be so tiresome! You must know that I am thinking of his marrying one of them."
> "Is that his design in settling here?"
> "Design! Nonsense, how can you talk so! But it is very likely that he *may* fall in love with one of them, and therefore you must visit him as soon as he comes."
> "I see no occasion for that."(2)

This exchange brings out rather vividly the double bind by which the achieving of marriage, for themselves or for their daughters, is to be the primary concern of women's lives, and yet it is to be brought about apparently without intention, without consciousness. Here, Mrs. Bennet is reminded that an appearance of simple good fortune must be retained, yet she is obliged to persist in her own "design" of dispatching her husband to establish acquaintance at the first opportunity. Correspondingly, although

Mr. Bennet in this conversation remarks that " 'I see no occasion for that,' " he, too, clearly recognizes the need for the visit; in the next chapter it emerges that "Mr. Bennet was among the earliest of those who waited on Mr. Bingley. He had always intended to visit him, though to the last always assuring his wife that he should not go" (4). His reticence on the subject is a teasing rebuke to his wife's obviousness of intention, while his visit is a tacit recognition of the need for its existence. It is part of the unacknowledged ideological dimension of the novel that Elizabeth's refusal of any such intention turns out, in the end, to guarantee her receiving what it might most have sought to bring about: the best of both worlds. Elizabeth will be rewarded at once with the richest man in the book and his magnificent estate, and with the happiest of the novel's unusually wide display of marriages.

Ethelberta Chickerel is a different case altogether. In her trajectory from what the novel terms "romance as an object" to "a vow to marry for the good of her family" (36.321), she takes on a determination and an ambition more commonly found (and endorsed) in the male hero. In other words, Ethelberta takes the pursuit of marriage—not just any marriage, but one both acceptable and advantageous—quite literally as her career. And there is no such condemnation from the narrative voice here as Darcy voices in *Pride and Prejudice;* her musings over Neigh's prospects are reported in a strikingly dispassionate fashion:

> Well, she had not accepted him yet . . . and then recurred the perpetual question, would the advantage that might accrue to her people by her marriage be worth the sacrifice? One palliative feature must be remembered when we survey the matrimonial ponderings of the poetess and romancer. What she contemplated was not meanly to ensnare a husband just to provide incomes for her and her family, but to find some man she might respect, who would maintain her in such a stage of comfort as should, by setting her mind free from temporal anxiety, enable her to further organize her talent, and provide incomes for them herself. Plenty of saleable originality was left in her as yet, but it was getting crushed under the rubbish of her necessities. (28.224)

In that one word "saleable," there is an inexplicit recognition of the parallel to be drawn between marriage and prostitution—a polemical comparison made by feminists at least since Mary Wollstonecraft, and very widespread in the last decades of the nineteenth century. It colors Ethelberta's perceptions of herself and her chosen path, when she remarks, for instance, that " 'a proposal of marriage is only removed from being a proposal of a very different kind by an accident' " (36.316); and it colors the narrative account of her relative freedom, granted by her society "only to women of three sorts—the famous, the ministering, and the improper" (31.262). Yet this implicit comparison nowhere draws from the narrative voice any rebuke or condemnation. Interestingly, it is also made clear that to follow a career of any sort, to enter in any way into the public sphere, lays her open to precisely the same charge: "'a woman who attempts a public career must expect to be treated as public property,'" she informs her aunt (35.300). In other words, the conscious exercise of either the "private" vocation of marriage or the "public" vocation of career makes a woman tantamount to a prostitute. In such circumstances, Ethelberta's marital careerism appears less perverse than rational, and it is entirely consonant that she should consult Bentham rather than that much-vaunted organ of the heroine, the heart, as to her best course of action.

The contrast I have drawn between Ethelberta Chickerel and Elizabeth Bennet is shown to be particularly appropriate, I think, by that moment in *The Hand of Ethelberta* when the heroine, like the heroine of a Jane Austen novel, visits the estate of a potential suitor. In *Pride and Prejudice*, we are invited to make a more or less cynical interpretation of Elizabeth's marriage, by drawing on her half-serious avowal that her love for Darcy could be dated back to her having seen his estate; yet that very avowal serves to disarm any such view. Ethelberta, however, makes what is quite unequivocally a research trip to Neigh's property:

> The exact size and value of the estate would, she mused, be curious, interesting, and almost necessary information to her who must become mistress of it were she to allow him to carry out his singularly cool and crude, if tender, intention. Moreover, its importance would afford a very good random sample of his worldly substance throughout, from which alone, after all, could the true spirit and worth and seriousness of his words be apprehended. Impecuniosity may revel in unqualified vows and brim over with confessions as blithely as a bird of May, but such careless pleasures are not for the solvent, whose very dreams are negotiable. (25.196)

The trip serves in the end to discredit each in the eyes of the other: Neigh by virtue of his association with the knacker's yard, and Ethelberta because her calculations compromise her in the eyes of the estate owner. Neigh as *arriviste* and Ethelberta on the rise are, in fact, "too nearly cattle of one colour" (25.201) for a marriage between them to serve her turn.

Ethelberta's clear-sightedness about her own needs and desires recalls once more some comments from Meredith's "Essay on Comedy": "The heroines of Comedy are like women of the world, not necessarily heartless from being clear-sighted: they seem so to the sentimentally reared, only for the reason that they use their wits, and are not wandering vessels crying for a captain or a pilot. Comedy is an exhibition of their battle with men, and that of men with them: and as the two, however divergent, both look on one object, namely, Life, the gradual similarity of their impressions must bring them to some resemblance" (15). And indeed, it is notable that, in *The Hand of Ethelberta*, the heroine's likeness to her suitors is stressed again and again: Christopher Julian's status as struggling artist clearly parallels her own, Neigh is ruled out as potential partner because of the similarity of their social situation, and her attempt to escape her marriage to Lord Mountclere resolves itself into an " 'armed neutrality' " after their mutual recognition as strategists (47.447). In this stress upon likeness we are to discern, I think, not a heroine "masculine" in her character, as has sometimes been suggested,[9] but rather a tacit recognition of the way in which the traditionally womanly vocation of marriage is being modulated in the direction of the equally traditionally gender-specific structure of career.

But if Ethelberta gets precisely what she wants, that is not to say that the novel serves to support the meritocratic self-image of Victorian society. It is true, as one contemporary critic astutely remarked, that "If *The Hand of Ethelberta* could be taken seriously, it would be the most vigorous disclaimer of social disabilities ever embodied in fiction."[10] Here, though, the fable of success is brought about so much through the medium of an occasionally disconcerting blend of farce and fairy-tale that its ideological power is dissolved. In any case, the heroine's success is thrown into question by a certain ambiguity about the terms, whether they are seen as moral or political, of her dilemma. After all, the upper classes are vitiated by satire, even if Ethelberta's desire to join them is treated more or less sympathetically, and certainly their principal representative in the novel, Lord Mountclere, is made to seem both grotesque and corrupt as the object of Ethelberta's ambition/desire, with that chilling description of his mouth twitching with the "telegraph-needles of a hundred little erotic messages" (40.360). The central romance plot is not only foreshadowed but also undercut in the hostler's comment that " 'Pouncing upon young flesh like a carrion crow—'tis a vile thing in a old man' " (1.3). Then too, the Chickerels are the main vehicles of a substantial doubt about the value and the human implications of class transition. There is, for example, her father's admonition that " 'Much lies in minding this, that your best plan for lightness of heart is to raise yourself a little higher than your old mates, but not so high as to be quite out of their reach. . . . getting on *a little* has this good in it, you still keep in your old class where your feelings are, and are thoughtfully treated by this class: while by getting on *too much* you are sneered at by your new acquaintance, who don't know the skill of your rise, and you are parted from and forgot by the old ones who do' " (7.64).

Again, Ethelberta's continual invocation of her sense of duty to her family as the motive force behind her ambition—an explanation that threatens to recuperate such ambition for femininity by masking it in the guise of self-sacrifice—is similarly undermined by her father's insistence that he is happy to stay in service, in his " 'honourable calling' " (28.230); and the equally feminizing suggestion that her " 'brilliant match' " involves the suppression of her real desires is put in a different light by Faith Julian: " 'Ethelberta, fortified by her sapphires and gold cups and wax candles, will not mind facts which look like spectres to us outside. A title will turn trouble into romances, and she will shine an interesting viscountess in spite of them' " (40.362). We are, then, debarred from taking the tragic route of the Tess Durbeyfield plot with which this novel has otherwise so much in common; Ethelberta's ambition must be accepted for what it is, not as disguised self-sacrifice, but simply as ambition. And we are forced to contend with both the desire for " 'doing well,' " as Clym Yeobright calls it (RN 3.2.208), and the ambivalence it arouses, on the same terms as we might in the case of a male protagonist. Clym Yeobright, who "wished to raise the class at the expense of individuals rather than individuals at the expense of the class" (3.2.203), and Jude Fawley, who attempts a course of individual social and intellectual self-improvement, are both figures of more or less tragic failure, the one marginalized by his society as eccentric and the other rejected and embittered. But the fact that Ethelberta's social ambition is fulfilled should not obscure the way in which precisely these same questions about " 'doing well' " (unanswered here as they are unanswered for many of us who have experienced class transitions of a probably less spectacular kind) surround her success. For Sol, she is a class traitor—" 'a deserter of your own lot,' " as he puts it (HE 46.424)—and for her father, some such starting point as Clym Yeobright's would have been a more acceptable one: " 'What she should have done was glorify herself by glorifying her own line of life, not by forsaking that line of life for another' " (45.418). Certainly, the fact that the newly aristocratic Ethelberta is " 'occasionally too severe with the servants' " and does not see her family very often " 'because of her lofty position, which has its juties' " (*Sequel*, 456) serves to highlight the contradiction by which her trajectory of personal success removes her definitively from those whom she might most wish to assist by the power that results from it. In such contradictions, and in the commentaries of her brother Sol in particular, there is, as John Goode has pointed out, a powerful if oblique reminder of "a different way of overcoming class oppression," albeit "a politics which the comedy is designed to exclude."[11] In the figure of Ethelberta the marital career woman, Hardy is confronting the question of how ambition, success, and allegiance might be figured for the nineteenth-century heroine; and it is part of the interest of the novel that he does so without recourse to the ideological structures of self-unknowingness that commonly shelter the heroine of the marriage plot from the brutal complexities of class position and transition.

Telling Stories

There has long been another name for the marital career woman: the adventuress. As one contemporary critic pointed out of *The Hand of Ethelberta:* "A less able author with this conception in his brain would scarcely have avoided imitation of a great model: he would have drawn an adventuress of the Becky Sharpe type."[12] This alternative version of the novel's heroine is, indeed, voiced within it; when Lord Mountclere's brother seeks to tell the story of the marriage plot, he sees it simply as a case (*another* case) of " 'an old booby and a damned scheming young widow' " (44.394). But in a novel as overtly concerned with the *manner* of telling stories as this—in which the quality of Ethelberta's stage performances depends, we are told, "not upon the intrinsic merits of her story as a piece of construction, but upon her method of telling it" (16.120)—the continual reference to writing and plots serves to mark an explicit recognition of the possibility of telling the "same" story in a different mode. The novel's stress upon the facticity, the un-"naturalness" of narration is at one with its stress upon the exploration of the possibilities of writing the stories of woman.

To begin with, Ethelberta is in a sense a survivor of the central plot paradigms of the nineteenth-century heroine: ex-virgin, ex-governess, ex-wife, she seems to live beyond the orthodox array of endings for the narrated woman of Victorian fiction. This, together with the, as it were, over-supply of plot paradigms mobilized in her (she is all at once a woman who works, an artist, a widow, a daughter, a marriageable young woman) means that the novel's protagonist exists in what we might call a state of narrative suspension. And correspondingly, she is liberated into a whole range of plots, literal, symbolic, allusive, or adumbrated. There is, for example, that symbolic chase early in the book, in which Ethelberta witnesses the contest of the duck and the duck-hawk. "The chase" has, of course, long been a metaphor with erotic possibilities, and in this "struggle for a life so small and unheard of" (1.7) it is surely possible to see an allegory of the plot of sexual choice. It would be easy enough to cast such an allegory in gender terms, along the lines of those in the hostler's version: " 'pouncing upon young flesh like a carrion crow—'tis a vile thing in a old man' " (1.3). Here, the chase does not end in the expected, perfectly predictable fashion: the duck at last overcomes the superior strength of the duck-hawk by drawing on its wits and its experience. Very well, then: it might be tempting to see here some exemplum such as how male strength can be evaded by the quick-wittedness of the female. But Ethelberta's active role in her own story forbids us such easy recourse to notions of predation and victimage, and we need in particular to remember that it is Ethelberta rather than her male suitors who displays superior strength. So, Christopher Julian reflects that "she was immeasurably the stronger" of the two (17.127); she drags Mountclere up the two hundred and five steps of the cathedral spire, only to point out ambiguously to the breathless and aged man that " 'there is no prospect for you, after all, Lord Mountclere' " (34.295); and, thwarted in her attempt to escape her marriage with (as she thinks) Sol, she contemplates pushing Mountclere into the ditch: " 'We are one to one, and I am the stronger!' she at last exclaimed triumphantly, and lifted her hand for a thrust" (47.444). In this last instance, one might almost conclude that it is the male who escapes by the use of his wits, for Mountclere has taken the precaution of arranging for his employees to back him up; although the episode might equally be seen as a case in which the man has access to authority and status to support his own physical resources, while the woman has been deserted even by her family in the name of the marital possession of the woman. (" 'You have married your man, and your duty is towards him,' " says Sol [46.434].) In either case, what we have here is the invocation of a plot paradigm consigning the female to the role of victimage and passivity, which is then seemingly inverted, and its very terms interrogated.

Similar narrative tactics of allusion and interrogation pervade the novel. They can be seen again, for instance, in the use of biblical quotation. To portray Ethelberta as the rejuvenating Abishag to the corrupt aristocrat's David is perhaps conventional enough; more unexpected are the adumbrations of an alternative plot in the quotation from Hosea: "She shall follow after her lovers, but she shall not overtake them; and she shall seek them, but shall not find them; then shall she say, I will go and return to my first" (35.302). The plot that Ethelberta appears to foreshadow for herself here (one in which she will eventually marry her "first," Christopher Julian) is in essence one that Hardy uses elsewhere: in Bathsheba Everdene's chastened return to Gabriel Oak, for instance, or, in a residual form, in the missed opportunity of the early near-encounter of Tess Durbeyfield and Angel Clare. It is a plot that lends itself all too easily both to tragic ironies and to those forms of comedy which culminate in what is as nearly as possible the restitution of the status quo. According to Franco Moretti, this "constant of the English plot" is one of the structures by which the English *Bildungsroman* seeks to eliminate the necessity for or meaningfulness of change, and he characterizes it in this way: "[There is] another constant of the English plot: the notion that the hero [sic] . . . would do well not to bind himself to those whom fate throws in his path during his youth. This lesson is most explicit in the theme of the erotic 'double choice.' . . . In each case the 'right' partner is always met first; then, as the plot gradually develops, the hero meets the wrong one, to whom he, or she, risks being tied for life."[13] For this plot to work itself out in *The Hand of Ethelberta* would require the equalizing power of either a renunciation of ambition on the heroine's part or one of those mysterious acquisitions of a fortune by the hero. But here again, the novel swerves away from the "constant" by first invoking it and then refusing to fulfill those expectations. Rather as Tess Durbeyfield will bequeath her husband to a desexualized and attenuated version of herself, so, here, there is a displaced culmination of the Hosea plot in Christopher Julian's eventual marriage to the timorous and loving Picotee. In neither case does the presence of the "right" man solve the problem of the axiomatic status of the romance plot for the nineteenth-century heroine, and the combination of repetition and displacement of the marital resolution serves to throw that status into relief and thus to challenge its ideological power.

The Hand of Ethelberta holds, then, a number of stories: stories about her, but also stories told by her. Whether as narrators or as objects of narration, women are shown to stand in a particularly problematic relation to the telling of stories: what it is possible to say about them, and also for whom it is possible to say it. I do not forget here, of course, that Ethelberta is herself the textual creation of a male writer; rather, I want to draw attention to the way in which the novel shows a productive awareness of its own status in this regard. Rather as the question Chaucer's Wife of Bath poses in the prologue ("Who peyntede the leon, tel me who?")[14] casts a sceptical light over the nature of the text in which she appears, so in *The Hand of Ethelberta* Hardy at once writes a woman and draws attention to the fact that he cannot but write within the constraints of a history of gendered representation. In the course of the novel's allusive and multiple plotting, a set of related questions is raised again and again: What is the connection between what a woman feels and what she says? What is the relation between her inner life and the social plots available to chart it? What becomes for the heroine, we might say, of that "sincerity" so valued in the aspiring English hero?

Ethelberta's greatest success as a writer and as a teller of stories comes when the feelings and lives she recounts are not her own. And in each case, they are accompanied by a perfectly evident association with masculine models of literary form. Her book of poems, *Metres by E.*, for example, is described as a collection of *vers de société* aiming "to justify the ways of girls to men" (2.19); the allusion to Milton, together with the choice of the word "girls" as opposed to, say, "women," serves of course to put her literary ambitions in an awesomely overwhelming framework. Similarly, we are informed that her storytelling is based on the model of Defoe; and one of the only specific instances of such storytelling that we see here is in fact the story of a "'masquerading madam'" (13.99), a cross-dressed woman on the verge of being exposed for what (in terms of biological sex) she actually is. Even the retiring Picotee finds her letters from Italy compared to those of Walpole. Now it would be possible to suggest that the function of such allusions is satirical, that Hardy aims here to demonstrate the limitations of these women's talents, or to make it clear that marriage is after all a much better career option. But it seems to me that in Ethelberta in particular we have, rather, a case in which a woman, in order to become an artist at all, must herself become a kind of "'masquerading madam'"; whenever we encounter Ethelberta as writer/teller, we also encounter the obtrusive presence of the male literary canon, or the enabling adoption of a masculine voice. This is the framework within which it is possible for the woman to write in the first place, and the stories of women are always already to hand.

Women in literary texts have seemed often to represent a space of secrecy: enigma, puzzle, question. In Hardy, the central woman character comes repeatedly to be identified with a secret. Most commonly it is, in a broad sense at least, a sexual secret, as it is for Fancy Day, for Elfride Swancourt or for Tess Durbeyfield. Sometimes it is a secret about writing— again in the broad sense, about authorship—as it is in the short stories for Ella Marchmill, for Edith Harnham and for her maid Anna. In what is still one of the few articles (to quote its own title) "In Defense of Ethelberta," Clarice Short contends that Ethelberta is most sharply differentiated from Hardy's other heroines by her honesty: "The concealment of past or motive, a course which causes such misery to Tess, to Eustacia, to Lucetta, and others of Hardy's heroines, Ethelberta scorns."[15] Yet matters are surely not as simple as that. To begin with, Ethelberta goes to some lengths to conceal her family and class origin, although it is true that she marries Mountclere only when he knows the facts. And then, as some of Short's own examples would suggest, it is less the secret than the revelation that causes most of the "misery." When confession ensues, it commonly brings disaster upon the woman, while Fancy's "secret she would never tell" (UGT 211), by contrast, accompanies what is probably the most straightforwardly comic ending to be found in Hardy. It would seem, then, that the confessional mode brings its risks.

Verses by E. occasions a great deal of speculation in the novel concerning its relation to the writer's life; and when Christopher Julian chances upon Ethelberta recounting her transvestite adventure story to her family, he at once takes it to be an account of her own life: " 'For Heaven's sake, Ethelberta,' he exclaimed with great excitement, 'where did you meet with such a terrible experience as that?' " (13.99). The story that Ethelberta has to tell about herself is never in fact told by her; she destroys the letter to Julian in which she broaches it, for example. When she seeks to employ her usual storytelling format as a way of representing the truth about herself, she causes consternation and embarrassment: "The guests began to look perplexed, and one or two exchanged whispers. This was not at all the kind of story that they had expected" (38.333). Seeing the response of her audience, she finds herself reduced to silence: "her voice trembled, she moved her lips but uttered nothing" (38.334).

In Ethelberta's narratorial predicament here—stories on the model of Defoe and other male recounters of the feminine " 'run off her tongue like cotton from a reel' " (5.46), while the truth of her own story falters and dies on her lips—there is a specifically focused version of something that figures in a more general sense throughout the novel: an alienation from their own language that breaks up, in the case of women, the continuum of inner life and social plot. Ethelberta repeatedly advises Picotee on the necessity, for women, of some strategem for dissevering language and truth: " 'never tell him what you feel' " (6.49), or " 'more often than not "No" is said to a man's importunities because it is traditionally the correct modest reply' " (22.164), or, most explicitly and aphoristically of all: " 'Don't you go believing in sayings, Picotee: they are all made by men, for their own advantages. Women who use public proverbs as a guide through events are those who have not ingenuity enough to make private ones as each event occurs' " (20.151). It is of course a long-established patriarchal commonplace that a woman's "No" means "yes," that women never mean what they say or say what they mean, and this is a view that finds its place within the novel. Ladywell defends the apparent outspokenness of Ethelberta's poetry on the grounds that " 'I don't think that she has written a word more than what every woman would deny feeling in a society where no woman says what she means or does what she says' " (7.57). But even this tired satiric cliché serves to generalize what I think emerges from Ethelberta's sisterly admonitions: that some form of linguistic self-alienation is the condition of social survival for a woman. Although it has very commonly been assumed, both in and out of *The Hand of Ethelberta*, that a woman's writings are, as Christopher Julian puts it, " 'natural outpourings' " (8.66), the novel shows a radical discontinuity between the private life of its heroine and the "public proverbs" of what it is possible for her to say. Speaking aloud in a strikingly domestic setting what her audiences take to be the truth because they have heard it before, she exemplifies that proposition: as story-teller, she *performs* "truth and naturalness" (16.120) of the sort that her first readers assume inheres in her writing. Her success on what is, after all, a stage comes from the skill with which she is able to mimic the "public proverbs" of femininity. Or, if we restore its more literal sense to his linguistic metaphor, Havelock Ellis puts the point succinctly: "She has succeeded in adapting herself to the maxims of the society into which she has been translated" (Cox 117).

Given such a situation, it seems entirely appropriate that Ethelberta's only serious poem—the one which, it is implied, comes closest to expressing her actual feelings—should be entitled "Cancelled Words"; and even this is, we are told, "somewhat in the tone of many of Sir Thomas Wyatt's poems" (2.19). The idea of cancellation as self-censorship recurs, too, in an episode which perhaps owes something to that celebrated moment in Charlotte Brontë's *Villette* when the heroine of the novel, Lucy Snowe, writes two letters and buries the one which expresses her strongest feelings. Here, Ethelberta sets out to write the truth about her situation to Christopher Julian, but burns that letter in favor of a polished yet conventional second, a letter which concludes most ironically with a testimony to its own frankness: " 'Some women might have written distantly, and wept at the repression of their real feeling; but it is better to be more frank, and keep a dry eye' " (9.82). In the cases both of Lucy Snowe and of Ethelberta, the intended recipient of the canceled and the second letter is a man, and in neither case does he exercise any form of direct or intentional censorship over their contents. What is at stake, nevertheless, is a self-protective internalization of the rules of the patriarchal societies in which these heroines must live, rules that govern what can be said without incurring a potentially damning judgment. In *Villette,* this fate is displaced from the heroine on to the actress Vashti, who is judged by criteria less aesthetic than moral. But here, it is in the responses to *Metres by E.* as they are cataloged early in the novel that we see how the writing woman is continually assessed as woman rather than as writer. Faith Julian supposes that " 'of course poets have morals and manners of their own' " but, nonetheless, implies a criticism of Ethelberta's femininity when she remarks that " 'I would not have sent [such a book] to a man for the world' " (2.21). Similarly, the dinner-party guests at Lady Doncastle's house debate whether the brilliance of the verses betrays a " 'rather warm . . . assumed character' " or the " 'actual coldness' " of the writer (7.56); and Lady Petherwin sees the volume as an example of " 'how improper some, even virtuous, ladies become when they get into print' " (10.84). In this last case, Ethelberta refuses the course of self-censorship—" 'suppress the poems instantly' " (10.86) —counseled by her mother-in-law. Nonetheless, the point is made clearly enough: language and writing pose very considerable threats to women.

But accompanying this question of what it is possible for the woman to say without risk, there is also the question of what may be said about her. This would-be narrator is always in danger of being turned into an object of narration, as the novel's mobilization of the structures of gossip, speculation and reportage makes clear. It is noticeable that, when Ethelberta appears as character in the stories told by men, a kind of narrative victimization is often involved. She is thus the object of ridicule for the " 'boozy men' " who form the audience of Neigh's story: " 'it was about some lady who thought Mr. Neigh was in love with her, and, to find whether he was worth accepting or not, she went with her maid at night to see his estate, and wandered about and got lost, and was frightened, and I don't know what besides. Then Mr. Neigh laughed too, and said he liked such common sense in a woman' " (29.246). And Lord Mountclere reduces her to "unnatural . . . hysterical . . . fearful" laughter (47.446) by usurping her role as storyteller and making her the victim of his narrative practical joke:

> "I will tell you a story, to pass the time away. I have learnt the art from you—your mantle has fallen upon me, and all your inspiration with it. . . .
>
> ....
>
> "Lord Mountclere ordered a brougham to be at the west lodge, as fixed by Lady Mountclere's note. Probably Lady Mountclere's friend ordered a brougham to be at the north gate, as fixed by my note, written in imitation of Lady Mountclere's hand. Lady Mountclere came to the spot she had mentioned, and like a good wife rushed into the arms of her husband—hoo-hoo-hoo-hoo-hoo!" (47.445–46)

In this episode, Ethelberta's predicament is precisely imaged: she tells her own feelings, she makes her own plot, she writes it out; but at each stage it is overheard, interrupted, forged by the husband, the personification of a marital closure which even this self-writing heroine cannot evade, it appears. Mountclere's victory in the contest for control in the telling of her story transforms her into "Lady Mountclere" and also marks the textual silencing of Ethelberta. " 'Women, attend to Lady Mountclere,' " commands the husband (47.447), and as she accedes to the " 'armed neutrality' " of marriage (47.447), she also passes into the domain of silence. Or so it may seem; but at the end of the novel, Picotee informs us that her sister " 'is writing an epic poem' " (*Sequel*, 456), and in the inevitable recall of the earlier Miltonic allusion, there is some sign here that she begins over again, living once more beyond the heroine's ending.

Insofar as Ethelberta Chickerel—a woman, and working class—is an artist and a speaker, she is engaged in a double struggle: for the right to tell her own story, and for the right not always to be telling her own story. Such double binds are characteristic of those figures, crucial to his work, whom Hardy places at the meeting point of class and gender oppression. For the most part, they are brought to tragic endings by such multiple determinations of victimage. *The Hand of Ethelberta* is remarkable in that it brings its issues to a comic outcome, after its fashion a happy ending, and yet it does not finally resolve itself into a comforting fable of individual transcendence. Now, Nancy K. Miller has identified in women's writing what she calls the "italicization" of plots: a certain way of "marking what has always already been said, of making a common text one's own."[16] Perhaps it will be thought illicit to take from Miller a term that she clearly intends to have a gender-specific application, but this notion of "italicization," of self-consciously marked quotation, seems to me to be also a useful description of the ironically knowing representation of mobility and transcendence in Hardy's comic resolution of issues of gender and class. There is here, effectively, a replication at the level of plot of the linguistic self-alienation that allows Ethelberta's social survival. *The Hand of Ethelberta* takes up, certainly, the plot of "making good" which seems to posit self-determination; and its central trope of the story-telling heroine appears to figure a concomitant linguistic empowerment. But I would like to suggest that these paradigms are, in Miller's term, "italicized": even as it restates those "common texts" of class and gender, the novel hollows them out from within, putting their ideological force into question by preserving, however obliquely, all the sharpness of its sense of class and gender as systems of power.

NOTES

1. Irving Howe, *Thomas Hardy* (London: Weidenfeld and Nicolson, 1968), 38, 69.

2. The phrase "delicate satire" is from W. P. Trent, "The Novels of Thomas Hardy," *Sewanee Review*, 1 (Nov. 1882), partially rptd in *Thomas Hardy: The Critical Heritage*, ed. R. G. Cox (London: Routledge, 1970), 221–37; 226. Havelock Ellis, "Thomas Hardy's Novels," *Westminster Review*, 63 (1883): 334–64, rptd in *The Critical Heritage*, ed. Cox, 103–32, speaks of "tender irony" (127) and of "the most characteristic outcome of his genius" (132).

3. Michael Millgate, *Thomas Hardy: A Biography* (New York: Random, 1982), 327. The allegation seems to have originated with Rebekah Owen.

4. Rachel Blau DuPlessis, *Writing Beyond the Ending: Narrative Strategies of Twentieth-Century Women Writers* (Bloomington: Indiana University Press, 1985), 3.

5. Franco Moretti, *The Way of the World: The 'Bildungsroman' in European Culture* (London: Verso, 1987), 200.

6. George Meredith, "Essay: On the Idea of Comedy and the Uses of the Comic Spirit," in *Essays*, vol. 23 of *The Works of George Meredith*, Memorial Edition (London: Constable, 1910), 14.

7. Cf. Patricia Ingham, *Thomas Hardy* (Hemel Hempstead: Harvester, 1989), 34.

8. Jane Austen, *Pride and Prejudice*, ed. Frank W. Bradbrook (1813; London: Oxford University Press, 1970), 275.

9. Some examples spanning four decades: Albert J. Guerard, *Thomas Hardy: The Novels and Stories* (London: Oxford University Press, 1949) speaks of "the masculinity of Ethelberta" (109); Richard Carpenter, *Thomas Hardy* (New York: St. Martin's, 1964) suggests that "she is a woman of strong purpose, masculine command, and a powerful ambition" (54–55); and Richard H. Taylor, *The Neglected Hardy: Thomas Hardy's Lesser Novels* (London: Macmillan, 1982), finds her "both a vamp and a symbol of purposive masculinity" (65).

10. Survey, *New Quarterly Magazine*, 2 (1879): 412–31, partially rptd in *The Critical Heritage*, ed. Cox, 60–70; 67.

11. John Goode, *Thomas Hardy: The Offensive Truth* (Oxford: Blackwell, 1988), 36. Goode's contention that "the novel . . . makes it clear that life is not a comedy, that in the last resort, the only loser is Ethelberta herself" (34) seems to me, however, to be a psychological sentimentalism, and I would argue that it is important to the gender dimension of the novel that she is precisely *not* victimized or martyred by the achievement of her own ambitions.

12. Survey, *British Quarterly Review* 73 (1881): 342–60, rptd in *The Critical Heritage*, ed. Cox, 78–94; 89.

13. Moretti, *The Way of the World*, 248–49n. 33.

14. Geoffrey Chaucer, "The Wife of Bath's Prologue," l.692.

15. Clarice Short, "In Defense of *Ethelberta*," *Nineteenth-Century Fiction* 13 (1958): 48–57; 52.

16. Nancy K. Miller, *Subject to Change: Reading Feminist Writing* (New York: Columbia University Press, 1988), 29.

Notes on Contributors

PENNY BOUMELHA, who holds the Jury Chair in English at the University of Adelaide, made her mark on Hardy studies with *Thomas Hardy and Women: Sexual Ideology and Narrative Form*. She is editor of the Macmillan casebook on *Jude the Obscure*.

KRISTIN BRADY, associate professor at the University of Western Toronto, has written *The Short Stories of Thomas Hardy* and articles on Hardy, Eliot, Hawthorne, and feminist theory. Her volume on *George Eliot* will appear in the Macmillan Women Writers Series.

ELISABETH BRONFEN, associate professor of English at the University of Munich, has published a book on theories of narrative space, *Der literarische Raum*, and numerous essays on the representation of femininity and death. Her second book, *Over Her Dead Body*, traces the configuration of death, femininity, and the aesthetic.

MARGARET R. HIGONNET, professor of English at the University of Connecticut, has coedited *The Representation of Women in Fiction* and *Behind the Lines: Gender and the Two World Wars*. She has published a book on Jean Paul Richter and essays in feminist criticism, Romantic theory, and children's literature.

ROBERT KIELY, professor of English at Harvard University, has published *The Romantic Novel in England*, *Beyond Egotism: The Fiction of James Joyce, Virginia Woolf, and D. H. Lawrence*, *Modernism Reconsidered*, and *Reverse Tradition*, a book on postmodernism and its effects on the way we read nineteenth-century novels.

JAMES R. KINCAID, professor of English at the University of Southern California, has published *Dickens and the Rhetoric of Laughter*, *Tennyson's Major Poems: The Comic and Ironic Patterns*, and *The Novels of Anthony Trollope*.

U. C. KNOEPFLMACHER, Paton Foundation Professor at Princeton University, has written four books on the Victorian novel and coedited volumes on Mary Shelley, George Eliot, and nature and the Victorian imagination. He also writes on nineteenth-century literature for children.

JOHN KUCICH, professor of English at the University of Michigan, has received Guggenheim and NEH fellowships for his work on Victorian and contemporary fiction. Author of *Excess and Restraint in the Novels of Charles Dickens* and *Repression in Victorian Fiction*, as well as numerous essays, he is working on a study of the social and sexual encoding of Victorian ethics.

ELIZABETH LANGLAND, professor of English at the University of Florida, is the author of *Society in the Novel* and *Anne Brontë: The Other One*. She has coedited three collections: *The Voyage In: Fictions of Female Development*, *A Feminist Perspective in the Academy: The Difference It Makes*, and *Out of Bounds: Male Writers and Gender(ed) Criticism*. She is working on a study of domestic ideology and middle-class women in the Victorian novel.

JUDITH MITCHELL, who teaches at the University of Victoria, British Columbia, has published articles on the Victorian novel in *English Literature in Transition, English Studies, The Victorian Newsletter, English Studies in Canada, The Dalhousie Review, Cahiers Victoriens et Edouardiens*, and *Modern Language Studies*. She is completing a book on feminist counter-readings of sexual ideology in Victorian authors.

MARY RIMMER, assistant professor of English at Concordia University (Montreal), is preparing a book on Hardy's narrators.

DIANNE FALLON SADOFF, professor of English at Colby College, has published *Monsters of Affection: Dickens, Brontë and Eliot on Fatherhood* as well as articles on nineteenth-century fiction, psychoanalysis, and feminism in journals such as *PMLA, Signs, Genre*, and *The Massachusetts Review*. Recipient of a Guggenheim Fellowship, she is at work on a book about the emergence of psychoanalysis from nineteenth-century medical, cultural, and scientific discourses.

LINDA SHIRES, associate professor of English at Syracuse University, has published books, essays, and reviews on narrative and poetic technique, feminism, and nineteenth- and twentieth-century British literature. She edited *Theory, History, and the Politics of Gender: Rewriting the Victorians* and is researching studies on masculinity and authorship in Hardy and Tennyson and on Victorian movements of dissent.

Index